CHINESE CIVIL LAW

Statutes, Cases, and Materials

Gao Lingyun

Chinese Business Law Textbook Series

復旦大學出版社

序

本书是复旦大学法学院"中国商法"硕士项目的"中国民法"课程的全英文教材，主要分为七大部分：第一章是中国民事法律制度概览，第二章是民法典总则编，第三章到第七章分别介绍物权法、合同法、侵权法、家庭法和继承法。本书的内容根据法学院国际留学生的具体情况进行组织和剪裁，既包含《民法典》以及其他相关法律的英文介绍，又包含四十多个近年来的国内民事案例译述，语言准确，内容丰富，资料权威。除可以作为法学院国际学生的专业教材外，还可以作为对涉外法律感兴趣的法学院学生以及外国语学院的法律英语专业学生的高阶教材，同时也可以作为涉外律师的参考资料。

复旦大学法学院的"中国商法"硕士项目是国内第一个面向国际学生开设的有关中国商法的全英文法学硕士项目，如今已经培养了十多届国际学生。我有幸见证了这个项目从无到有的发展进程，亲自参与了该项目的筹建、总体教学方案设计、师资建设、招生宣传、学生录取与管理、教务和评估工作，以及最初几年每门课程的设置。该项目的发展得到了复旦大学和法学院的大力支持，也得到法学院同事的鼎力协助。我虽然后来不再负责该项目的工作，但仍然担任项目课程的教学工作。

最初该项目的任课教师选用自编讲义，向国际学生讲授中国商法的各门课程。经过十多年的教学经验积累，法学院计划出版该项目的全英文教材，鼓励任课教师将讲义修订为教材，因此才有了这本书的完成。

自2010年"中国商法"硕士项目开办以来，我就一直给国际学生讲授"中国民法"课（作为该项目的前置必修课程），并编写了全英文讲义。其间不断补充、完善。2020年5月，《民法典》正式颁布，我又根据新的法典对讲义进行了全面修订。修订工作持续了将近三年。

全英文教材，尤其是民法这样典型的国内法的全英文教材的撰写，其难度不言而喻。一方面需要对法典内容全面把握，另一方面需要提供案例分析，同时还对语言有较高要求，需要用准确而地道的英语来表达我们的民法概念。为此，除了对民法体系进行系统介绍外，我还选取并翻译了四十多个近年来有关民事案件的案例放在书中，供学生学习。

至于法典本身的英译，这里要感谢全国人民代表大会常务委员会法制工作委员会，他们于2020年组织专家翻译《民法典》，我有幸参与其中，并负责最后的统稿工作。《民法典》的英译本已在法律出版社出版，在人大官网上也有免费下载，这为"中国民法"这门课程的教学提供了非常大的帮助。在编写本教材时，我也不需要另行准备法典的英译本，可以将官方译本作为课程的参考资料供学生阅读。同时，本教材中所引用的法典英译大部分以官方译本为准。

还要感谢复旦大学法学院提供的良好的研究条件与政策，以及复旦大学出版社的支持，这本书才得以出版。

因时间和能力所限，书中肯定有很多不完善之处，敬请读者指教。

高凌云

Preface

This book is originally designed for the international students enrolled in the LL. M. Program in Chinese Business Law of Fudan University School of Law to study Chinese civil law, and is composed of seven chapters. The first chapter is an overview of the Chinese civil law system, while the other chapters introduce the general part of the Civil Code, the real rights law, the contract law, the tort law, the family law, and the succession law respectively. In addition to the Civil Code and the other related laws, the book also discusses over 40 civil cases decided by the Chinese courts in recent years. It features accurate language, rich resources, and authoritative materials. It may be used as a law textbook for the international students, a reference book for international lawyers, as well as upper-class teaching materials for local law students and the students majoring in legal English.

The LL. M. Program in Chinese Business Law of Fudan is the first LL. M. program in Chinese mainland focusing on the introduction of Chinese business laws open to international students, which has been launched for over 10 years. Fortunately, I have witnessed the program growing out of nothing, and personally participated in its preparation, designing of the overall curriculum, enrollment, admission, and management of the students, and evaluation of the program. The program has been greatly supported by Fudan University and Fudan Law School, as well as the law faculty. Although I no longer work for the program, I am still teaching there.

The faculty members of the program have been using their own teaching materials to teach the various courses relating to Chinese business laws. With over ten years' experience, the Law School determines that it is the right time to publish the teaching materials and encourages the faculty members to do so, without which this book would probably never have been accomplished.

Since 2010 when the LL. M. Program in Chinese Business Law was launched, I have been teaching Chinese Civil Law to the LL. M. students as a mandatory prerequisite course, and prepared handouts for the students. Since the Civil Code has been formally enacted in 2020, I have spent nearly three years to comprehensively review and revise the handouts.

Civil law is a typical domestic law, and it is difficult to write a Chinese civil law book in English. It requires a thorough understanding of the Civil Code and an accurate expression of the Chinese legal concepts in English. Although China is not a case law country, the students still expect to read cases. Considering all of these demands, I have selected and included in this book over 40 civil cases decided by the Chinese courts in recent years and translated them into English.

Regarding the English version of the Civil Code, I would thank the Legislative Affairs Commission of the Standing Committee of the National People's Congress (NPC) who organized the translation of the Code in 2020. I was invited to participate in the translation and be the final "unified reviewer." The translation has been published by the Law Press China, and could also be downloaded from the official website of the NPC, which provides huge help to my teaching of this course. With it, when finalizing this book, I did not have to prepare an English translation of the Code, and the students can use the official translation as one of the reference books. Most of the articles of the Civil Code cited in this book are from the official English version.

I am grateful to Fudan Law School for the excellent research conditions and policies it provides to the faculty members, and would thank Fudan University Press for its support, without which this book would never have been published.

These being said, owing to the limited time and ability, the book is not flawless, and all deficiencies are mine. Any comments, suggestions, and advices are welcome.

Gao Lingyun

Table of Contents

Chapter 1　Overview of Chinese Civil Law System ·············· 001
　§1:1　General Comments ·············· 001
　§1:2　Codification of Chinese Civil Law ·············· 006
　　　§1:2:1　Codification before 1949: Penal Law Codification ········ 006
　　　§1:2:2　Codification after 1949: Civil Law Codification ····· 007
　　　§1:2:3　The Latest Achievement: The Civil Code ············ 009
　§1:3　Legal Framework of Chinese Civil Law ·············· 011
　§1:4　General Principles of Chinese Civil Law ·············· 014
　　　§1:4:1　Principle of Protection of Lawful Rights and
　　　　　　　Interests ·············· 015
　　　§1:4:2　Principle of Equality ·············· 015
　　　§1:4:3　Principle of Voluntariness ·············· 017
　　　§1:4:4　Principle of Fairness ·············· 018
　　　§1:4:5　Principle of Honesty and Good Faith ·············· 020
　　　§1:4:6　Principle of Compliance with Law and Public
　　　　　　　Order ·············· 021
　　　§1:4:7　Principle of Environmental Protection ·············· 021
　　　§1:4:8　Principle of Application of Local Customs ············ 022
　　　Case 1 ·············· 023
　§1:5　Protection of Civil Law Rights in China ·············· 024
　　　§1:5:1　Public Remedies ·············· 024
　　　Case 2 ·············· 033
　　　Case 3 ·············· 045
　　　§1:5:2　Private Remedies ·············· 049

Chapter 2　General Part of the Civil Code ·············· 051
　§2:1　Civil Juristic Relationships ·············· 052

§ 2:1:1 Subjects of Civil Juristic Relationship: Persons of
the Civil Law ·· 053
§ 2:1:2 Objects of Civil Juristic Relationship ···················· 053
§ 2:1:3 Civil Law Rights and Obligations ························ 054
Case 4 ·· 055
§ 2:2 Persons of the Civil Law ·· 056
§ 2:2:1 Natural Persons ··· 056
Case 5 ·· 064
§ 2:2:2 Legal Persons ·· 071
Case 6 ·· 080
§ 2:2:3 Unincorporated Organizations ···························· 081
§ 2:3 Civil Law Rights ··· 081
§ 2:3:1 Categorization of Civil Law Rights ······················ 082
§ 2:3:2 The Rights of Personality ·································· 087
Case 7 ·· 090
Case 8 ·· 093
Case 9 ·· 097
Case 10 ·· 100
Case 11 ·· 103
Case 12 ·· 106
§ 2:4 Juristic Acts ··· 109
§ 2:4:1 Juridically Significant Facts ······························· 109
§ 2:4:2 Juristic Acts ·· 110
Case 13 ·· 116
Case 14 ·· 119
§ 2:5 Agency Relationship ·· 122
§ 2:5:1 Agency Relationship in General ·························· 122
§ 2:5:2 Categorization of Agency ·································· 124
§ 2:5:3 Creation and Termination of an Agency
Relationship ·· 126
§ 2:5:4 Duties of Agent ··· 129
§ 2:5:5 Specific Issues on Agency Relationship ················ 131
Case 15 ·· 134
§ 2:6 Limitation Periods ··· 136

	§2:6:1	Overview	136
	§2:6:2	Specific Limitation Periods	138
	§2:6:3	Commencement of Limitation Periods	139
	§2:6:4	Suspension, Interruption, and Extension of the Limitation Period	140
		Case Review	141
§2:7		Counting of the Periods of Time	142
§2:8		Civil Liability and Defenses	143
	§2:8:1	Civil Liability	143
		Case 16	146
	§2:8:2	Defenses	151
		Case 17	153

Chapter 3 Real Rights Law 156

§3:1 General Introduction 156
   §3:1:1 Principles of the Real Rights Law 156
   §3:1:2 Thing/Property 159
   §3:1:3 Real Rights 161
   §3:1:4 Acquisition of Real Rights 162
      Case 18 168
   §3:1:5 Change to Real Rights 170
   §3:1:6 Public Notice of Real Rights 172
§3:2 Ownership Rights 180
   §3:2:1 Ownership of the State, Collectives, and Private Individuals 180
   §3:2:2 Ownership of a Building's Units 187
      Case 19 192
   §3:2:3 Contiguous Relationship 194
      Case 20 195
   §3:2:4 Co-Ownership 196
      Case 21 201
§3:3 Rights to Usufruct 204
   §3:3:1 The Rights to Use Land for Construction Purposes 205

§ 3:3:2　The Rights to Use Rural Land ········· 209
§ 3:3:3　The Rights to Use House Site ········· 214
§ 3:3:4　The Rights of Habitation ········· 215
§ 3:3:5　The Rights to Servitudes ········· 216
§ 3:4　Security Interests ········· 218
§ 3:4:1　The Security System in General ········· 218
§ 3:4:2　Mortgage ········· 220
§ 3:4:3　Pledge ········· 230
§ 3:4:4　Lien ········· 236
　　　　Case 22 ········· 237
　　　　Case 23 ········· 241
§ 3:5　Legal Remedies ········· 243

Chapter 4　Contract Law ········· 245
§ 4:1　General Introduction ········· 245
§ 4:1:1　Historical Development and the Sources of Chinese Contract Law ········· 245
§ 4:1:2　General Rules ········· 248
§ 4:1:3　Types of Contract ········· 249
§ 4:2　Concluding a Contract ········· 252
§ 4:2:1　Offer ········· 253
§ 4:2:2　Acceptance ········· 256
§ 4:2:3　Formation of Contract ········· 259
　　　　Case 24 ········· 261
§ 4:3　Effectiveness of Contract ········· 265
§ 4:3:1　Limitations on Effectiveness of Contract ········· 265
§ 4:3:2　Basic Elements for Effectiveness of Contract ········· 267
§ 4:3:3　Status of Contracts ········· 271
　　　　Case 25 ········· 277
§ 4:3:4　Legal Effect of a Revoked or Voided Contract ········· 279
　　　　Case 26 ········· 280
§ 4:4　Performance ········· 283
§ 4:4:1　The Principles of Performance ········· 283
§ 4:4:2　Defenses to Non-Performance ········· 285

§ 4:4:3　Securing Contractual Debts ········· 287
§ 4:4:4　Third Parties Involved ········· 290
　　　Case 27 ········· 292
§ 4:5　Modification of Contract ········· 296
§ 4:5:1　Change of Contract Terms ········· 297
§ 4:5:2　Change of Parties ········· 298
§ 4:6　Termination of Contract ········· 302
§ 4:6:1　Grounds for Termination ········· 303
§ 4:6:2　Consequences of Termination ········· 309
§ 4:7　Legal Liability ········· 310
§ 4:7:1　Default ········· 311
　　　Case 28 ········· 315
§ 4:7:2　Remedies ········· 316
　　　Case 29 ········· 321
§ 4:8　Quasi-Contracts ········· 323
§ 4:8:1　Negotiorum Gestio ········· 323
§ 4:8:2　Unjust Enrichment ········· 324

Chapter 5　Tort Law ········· 326
§ 5:1　General Introduction ········· 326
§ 5:1:1　Basis for Finding Tort Liability ········· 327
§ 5:1:2　Joint Liability ········· 329
§ 5:2　Legal Elements ········· 331
　　　Case 30 ········· 332
§ 5:3　Categorization of Torts ········· 335
§ 5:3:1　General Torts ········· 336
　　　Case 31 ········· 343
　　　Case 32 ········· 346
　　　Case 33 ········· 350
§ 5:3:2　Vicarious Liability Torts ········· 358
　　　Case 34 ········· 364
　　　Case 35 ········· 365
§ 5:3:3　Special Torts ········· 369
§ 5:3:4　Non-Fault Liability Torts ········· 378

	Case 36	384
§ 5.4	Remedies and Defenses	386
§ 5.4.1	Overview of Remedies	386
§ 5.4.2	Forms of Remedies	389
§ 5.4.3	Defenses	396
	Case 37	399

Chapter 6 Family Law 402

§ 6.1 General Introduction 402
　　§ 6.1.1 Historical Development of Chinese Marriage Law 402
　　§ 6.1.2 Principles of Chinese Family Law 405
　　§ 6.1.3 Kinship 413
§ 6.2 Entering into Marriage 418
　　§ 6.2.1 Marriage in General 418
　　§ 6.2.2 Legal Requirements for Entering into Marriage 418
　　§ 6.2.3 Marriage Agreement 420
　　§ 6.2.4 Procedure for Entering into Marriage 421
　　§ 6.2.5 Invalid Marriages 423
§ 6.3 Spousal Relationship 425
　　§ 6.3.1 The Personal Relationship between Spouses 425
　　§ 6.3.2 The Proprietary Relationship between Spouses 427
　　Case 38 430
§ 6.4 Relationship between Parents and Children 434
　　§ 6.4.1 Parent-Child Relationship in General 434
　　§ 6.4.2 Children Born out of Wedlock 438
　　§ 6.4.3 Stepchildren 439
　　Case 39 441
　　Case 40 442
　　§ 6.4.4 Adoption 442
§ 6.5 Divorce 452
　　§ 6.5.1 Termination of Marriage in General 452
　　§ 6.5.2 Legal Requirements and Procedure for Divorce 454
　　§ 6.5.3 Legal Consequences of Divorce 458

§ 6:6   Foreign-Related Marriages ··· 463
         § 6:6:1   Entering into Marriage ································ 464
         § 6:6:2   Divorce ··· 465

Chapter 7   Succession Law ·· 468
   § 7:1   General Introduction ··· 468
            § 7:1:1   Basic Principles of Chinese Succession Law ············ 469
            § 7:1:2   Heirs v. Donees-by-Will ·· 471
            § 7:1:3   Rights to Inheritance ·· 472
   § 7:2   Intestate Succession ·· 473
            § 7:2:1   In General ·· 473
            § 7:2:2   Inheritance by Representation and Re-Inheritance ······ 476
                      Case 41 ·· 478
   § 7:3   Testate Succession ·· 480
            § 7:3:1   In General ·· 480
            § 7:3:2   Ways of Making a Will ·· 482
            § 7:3:3   Content of a Will ·· 484
            § 7:3:4   Administrator and Executor ····································· 485
            § 7:3:5   Testamentary Gift and Agreement on Testamentary
                      Gift for *Inter Vivos* Support ······································ 486
   § 7:4   Disposal of Estate ··· 487
            § 7:4:1   General Principles ··· 487
            § 7:4:2   Distribution of Estate ·· 489
            § 7:4:3   Disposal of Estate without an Heir or Donee ············ 491
   § 7:5   Foreign-Related Succession ·· 492

Conclusive Remarks ·· 494

Index of Cases ·· 496

Chapter 1
Overview of Chinese Civil Law System

§ 1:1 General Comments

With the globalization of economic development, business transactions are done frequently in a transnational manner all over the world, and China in recent decades has become an increasingly important market for foreign investors. There are many legal literatures about Chinese law written in English or in a language other than Chinese, and most of them are about Chinese economic law or business law. Many people think that civil law is of a domestic nature and has nothing to do with foreign individuals or companies; but it has been quickly discovered to be wrong. Using a hypothetical example to illustrate:

> West Co., a company registered in New York, U.S., plans to sell a special kind of electronic dictionary — E-Books to East Co., a company registered in Shanghai, China. West Co. and East Co. are negotiating a contract for sale of the E-Books. Who will be the qualified representative of each company responsible for negotiating the contract? Will the contract signed by such individual persons bind the two companies? If a Chinese consumer is somehow injured by an E-Book owing to explosion of its battery, who will be liable, which law is to be applied, and what will be the remedies? Suppose West Co. has decided to establish a joint venture (JV) in China and Mr. White is to be one of the JV's directors who will be relocated to China, may Mr. White purchase an apartment in Shanghai? May he invest

his income in the Chinese stock market or remit the money back home? May he marry a Chinese girl? May he adopt a Chinese baby? If he later on divorces his Chinese wife, what will be his support obligations? May he inherit his Chinese mother-in-law's estate?

The answers to all of these questions are to be found in the Chinese civil law, specifically, e.g., agency law, contract law, tort law, real rights law, family law, succession law, and the like. It is obvious that Chinese civil law is not only important for foreign legal researchers and scholars, but also important for foreign investors and even visitors.

On March 10, 2011, Mr. Bangguo Wu, the then head of the Chinese legislature — the National People's Congress (NPC)[1], announced in the Fourth Plenary Session of the Eleventh NPC that "a socialist legal system with Chinese characteristics" had formally been established in China.[2] This legal system is centered on the Chinese Constitution and is composed of multi-levels of regulations, i.e., statutes, administrative regulations, and local legislations. Wu further commented that this was an exciting moment for China because establishing a comprehensive socialist legal system with Chinese characteristics had been one of the most significant achievements that China had accomplished in three decades after the economic reform was initiated.[3] It means that ever since, there have been laws regulating all of the economic, political, cultural, social, and ecological areas in the nation. Considering the situation in China prior to the end of the 1970s when there were only a few laws on paper, it has been no doubt a great improvement and achievement.

Within the Chinese legal system, civil law is in a very important position.

---

[1] The National People's Congress (hereinafter referred to as "NPC") is the legislature of the People's Republic of China (hereinafter referred to as "PRC" or "China") and responsible for promulgating statutes which are effective nationwide.

[2] See the cover page of GUANG MING DAILY, March 11, 2011.

[3] Until the end of February 2011, there had been 239 national laws (including the Constitution), more than 690 administrative regulations, and almost 8,600 local legislations effective in China. These numbers have been changed to 277 national laws, 610 administrative regulations, and more than 10,000 local legislations up to October 2020. The data are from the official website of the NPC: http://www.npc.gov.cn/npc/c30834/202101/170eaa5d4a994214aaf88e5dfac97665.shtml, the official website of the Department of Justice: http://xzfg.moj.gov.cn/search2.html, and Xinhua Net: http://www.xinhuanet.com/2020-10/10/c_1126590517.htm (visited on June 7, 2021).

Civil law in China includes both the traditional civil law and commercial law, because China adopts a broader view in this regard and civil law is believed to be capable of regulating both civil and commercial relationships.① In this sense, the civil law provides the default rules for all business transactions. This book, however, will mainly focus on the traditional civil law.

Generally, the term "civil law" may refer to a civil code which systematically codifies the various fundamental civil law systems; it may also refer to all of the laws and regulations regulating civil juristic relationships, which may include a civil code, civil laws, and other regulations on civil juristic relationships. "Civil law" is generally defined in China as the laws regulating personal and proprietary relationships between and among "the persons of the civil law" who are equal in their legal status, and such persons of the civil law include natural persons, legal persons, and unincorporated organizations.② Before the Civil Code of the People's Republic of China (the Civil Code) was finally enacted in 2020, the General Provisions of the Civil Law③(GPCL) had been the basic law in China regulating civil juristic relations, except for the short while when the General Part of the Civil Code④ (CCGP) had been effective. Most of the CCGP provisions have been integrated into the Civil Code unchanged. Discussions and analyses in this book are mainly based on the Civil Code (including the CCGP), along with comparisons with the GPCL,

---

① See WANG, Liming, et al., THE CIVIL LAW (2D ED.) 11 (Law Press China 2008).
② See article 2 of the Civil Code of the People's Republic of China (hereinafter referred to as the "Civil Code"), which was promulgated by the Thirteenth National People's Congress (NPC) on May 28, 2020 and has taken effect on January 1, 2021. The Civil Code cited through this book is based on CIVIL CODE OF THE PEOPLE'S REPUBLIC OF CHINA (ENGLISH VERSION), translated by the Legislative Affairs Commission of the Standing Committee of the National People's Congress of the People's Republic of China (posted on the official website of the NPC, available at: http://www.npc.gov.cn/englishnpc/c23934/202103/c487476d061844beb093bc3f22e729ae/files/4aaa35619b4c446dbc704f4376bfccd6.pdf (last visited on June 7, 2021), and published by Law Press China in July 2021).
③ The General Provisions of the Civil Law of the People's Republic of China (GPCL) was promulgated by the Sixth NPC on April 12, 1986, became effective on January 1, 1987, and has been repealed since January 1, 2021 when the Civil Code took effect. The provisions of the GPCL cited through this book, unless otherwise indicated, are translated by the author.
④ The Civil Code of the People's Republic of China — General Part (CCGP) was promulgated by the Twelfth NPC on March 15, 2017, became effective on October 1, 2017, and has been repealed since January 1, 2021 when the Civil Code took effect. The CCGP cited through this book is based on CIVIL CODE OF THE PEOPLE'S REPUBLIC OF CHINA — GENERAL PART, translated by Lingyun Gao (published by Fudan University Press 2017).

when necessary, to illustrate the development.

The purposes of the Civil Code are stated in its Article 1:

> This Code is formulated in accordance with the Constitution of the People's Republic of China for the purposes of protecting the lawful rights and interests of the persons of the civil law, regulating civil-law relations, maintaining social and economic order, meeting the needs for developing socialism with Chinese characteristics, and carrying forward the core socialist values.

Compared with the purposes stated in the GPCL, there is no significant change in the Civil Code, except that "Chinese characteristics" and "the socialist core values" are added. ①

Chinese civil law governs the personal and proprietary relationships between and among the persons of the civil law that are "equal in status,"② and equally protects all of the persons of the civil law. ③ The "equality" herein not only means that the persons of the civil law are equal and none of them are in a superior position to the others, but also means that the civil law and regulations equally apply to all persons of the civil law and none of them have superior rights.

The two relationships particularly protected by the civil law are "the personal relationship and proprietary relationship" between and among the persons of the civil law that are equal in status. A proprietary relationship is a relationship with economic factors which has been created in the process of production, distribution, exchange, and consumption of commodities. For instance, when West Co. and East Co. sign a contract for sale of the E-Books, there forms a proprietary relationship between the two companies involving the payment of the purchase price and the delivery of the dictionaries. This relationship is protected by the civil law and specifically, the contract law. To the contrary, a personal relationship protected by civil law is a social

---

① Article 1 of the GPCL provides that the law is formulated "to protect the civil-law rights and interests of citizens and legal persons and properly regulate the civil juristic relations so as to meet the needs of developing socialist modernization."
② Article 2 of the Civil Code.
③ Article 4 of the Civil Code.

relationship which is non-proprietary but personal in nature. The interests protected hereby are closely related to and not detachable from the persons of the civil law, such as the right to life and the right to health. The value of the rights and interests in person cannot be represented by money; instead, they reflect a kind of spiritual or ethical interest. However, certain personal relationships may be transformed into proprietary interests. When such interests are infringed upon, the aggrieved party may receive monetary compensation. For example, if a consumer is injured owing to explosion of the battery of an E-Book sold by West Co., his right to corporeal integrity and right to health may have been harmed and these rights are personal in nature; although these interests cannot be represented by money, the consumer may claim against the West Co. for monetary compensation.

Chinese civil law applies to civil activities conducted within the territory of China, disregarding the nationality of the actors, which means that non-Chinese citizens and foreign legal persons residing or duly established in China will also be protected and regulated by Chinese civil law. ①

This book serves as an overview of the Chinese civil law system. The first chapter introduces the general civil law system in China, the codification process of the civil law, the important civil law principles, as well as the system guarantee for the civil law rights. The second chapter focuses on the General Part of the Civil Code, introducing some important civil law concepts and discussing about the specific rules protecting and regulating the persons of the civil law. The third chapter is about the real rights law, with emphasis on the ownership, rights to usufruct, and secured interests. The fourth chapter analyzes the main issues of contract law, from formation to termination of a contract, also including the legal liability for breach of contract. It is to be noted that this chapter only discusses about the general provisions of the contract law, and the specific types of named contracts listed in the Civil Code will be a subject of another textbook. The fifth chapter of this Book touches base of the tort law, including the general torts and special torts as well as the liabilities of the tortfeasors. The sixth chapter involves marriage law and adoption law, as well as other aspects of the family law, and the seventh

---

① Article 12 of the Civil Code.

chapter is about the succession law. These chapters largely cover all of the Books of the Civil Code, except that the introduction to the rights of personality is placed in chapter one, and the liabilities for infringing upon these rights are discussed in chapter five. Since there is no binding case law in China, the cases discussed in this book are mainly from the Supreme People's Court (SPC) Gazettes or the Guiding Cases regularly published by the SPC. Although they are not legally binding, they do have persuasive authority and may serve as guidance for the courts to try cases in the future. Obviously, most of these cases were decided not based on the Civil Code, but based on the GPCL and the other civil laws since the Civil Code has become effective only since January 1, 2021, but most of them would still have merits because the general principles of the Chinese civil law have not been significantly changed.

The statutes and regulations cited through this book are translated by the author, except that the Civil Code articles are cited from the Civil Code of the People's Republic of China (English Version), translated by the Legislative Affairs Commission of the Standing Committee of the National People's Congress of the People's Republic of China and published by Law Press China in July 2021. While some articles of the statutes are reprinted in the main text of the book, the numbers of articles of the statutes cited through the book are listed in the footnotes so that the relevant article will be easily located. The last thing to be noted is that third person singular male pronouns used through this book should be construed to include the corresponding female and neuter pronouns except where the context clearly requires otherwise.

§ 1:2　Codification of Chinese Civil Law

Codification of laws has always been regarded as important in China. A brief history of the Chinese codification process is introduced in the following sub-sections.

§ 1:2:1　Codification before 1949: Penal Law Codification

The first code of the Chinese law is believed to be the Qin Code initiated by Qin Shi Huang, the first emperor of the Qin Dynasty which was the first universal Chinese empire established in 221 BCE. After Qin was overthrown and replaced by Han, Han Gaozu immediately ordered codification of Han Code after taking the title of emperor of the Han Dynasty. When China was reunited in the Tang Dynasty, the emperor ordered another codification of law, and the Tang Code enacted in 653 was largely modeled by the Ming Code, created later during the 1300s in the Ming Dynasty. ① It seems to be a pattern for the first emperor of every Chinese dynasty to codify the penal law.

During the Qing Dynasty, the drafting of a civil code was proposed in 1911 but upon completion of the draft in the same year, the dynasty collapsed. Although each Chinese dynasty tried to codify its laws, their focuses were largely on penal code, and civil law had long been ignored.

§1:2:2 Codification after 1949: Civil Law Codification

After the People's Republic of China② was founded in 1949, the Chinese legislature, *i.e.*, the National People's Congress (NPC) had put the legislation of civil law on top of its agenda. However, the codification of Chinese civil law has been zigzagged in the past seven decades since 1949. A comprehensive civil code was expected in the beginning of the 1950s. The NPC formed a task force in 1954 and 1962, respectively, to draft a civil code, but both efforts failed owing to the then political movements. Then from 1979, the legislation of civil law was re-considered and four drafts had been completed in 1982; however, none of them were ever passed into law. ③

The fourth codification movement started in 1983 but ended with the legislature's decision to adopt a different legislative approach: instead of making a civil code, the Chinese legislature decided to make separate laws regulating different aspects of civil juristic relations. As a result, the first basic civil law in China — the General Provisions of Civil Law (GPCL) — was enacted by the Sixth NPC in 1986. ④ Although the GPCL was not a civil code, it contained the fundamental principles of Chinese civil law as well as the

---

① See John W. Head, *Codes, Cultures, Chaos, and Champions: Common Features of Legal Codification Experiences in China, Europe, and North America*, 13 DUKE J. COMP. & INT'L L. 1, 12-32 (2003).
② "The People's Republic of China" in this book is also referred to as "PRC" or "China."
③ Liming Wang, *et al.*, THE CIVIL LAW (2D ED.) 30-31 (Law Press China 2008).
④ The last version of the GPCL was revised at the Tenth Session of the Standing Committee of the Eleventh NPC on Aug. 27, 2009, which has now been repealed by the Civil Code.

important rules governing contracts, torts, ownership and other real rights, intellectual property rights, and civil liabilities; therefore it was praised as a "mini civil code" and regarded as a milestone in the Chinese civil law legislation history. ①

However, China's efforts for codification has never ended. In 1998, the NPC initiated another movement for civil law codification. This time the legislature planned to make more specific civil laws so that these new laws, along with the GPCL and the other civil laws already enacted, could cover almost all aspects of civil juristic relations, based on which the general part of a civil code would then be drafted. The ultimate plan was to complete a comprehensive civil code by 2010. ②

The first step went quite well. Some important civil laws had been enacted or revised in the subsequent years, including, *inter alia*, a unified contract law and the revised marriage law. However, the process was accelerated partly because of the commitment made by the Chinese government upon accession to the World Trade Organization (WTO). Therefore, a draft of civil code was completed in a haste in 2002. ③

This draft had at least two distinctive features: First, it consisted of nine parts and 1209 articles, which made it the draft of a law with the most articles④ and covering the most contents in the Chinese legal history. Second, six scholars⑤ each was delegated to draft one or more titles of the code. In addition, many other non-delegated legal scholars also voluntarily participated in the process by submitting their own proposals on the civil code. During the

---

① Tao Du, *Codification of the Civil Law and the Major Contents of the General Part of the Civil Code of the People's Republic of China*, COMPARISON OF ARTICLES OF THE GENERAL PART OF THE CIVIL CODE AND THE GENERAL PROVISIONS OF THE CIVIL LAW 1 (People's Court Press 2017).

② For more information, see Lihong Zhang, *The Latest Developments in the Codification of Chinese Civil Law*, 83 TUL. L. REV. 999, 1003 (2009).

③ See Guodong Xu, *Structures of Three Major Civil Code Projects in Today's China*, 19 TUL. EUR. & CIVIL. L. F. 37, 40 (2004).

④ The Civil Code finally enacted in 2020 consists of 1260 articles.

⑤ The six scholars are: Professors Ping Jiang (China University of Political Science and Law), Huixing Liang (China Academy of Social Sciences), Liming Wang (Renmin University), Jiafu Wang (Tsinghua University), Changzhen Wu (Renmin University), Baoshu Wang (Tsinghua University), and Zhenying Wei (Peking University). There is a very interesting comment on the composition of the drafting team, showing that many other scholars in China would like to participate in the drafting process, see Guodong Xu, *Structures of Three Major Civil Code Projects in Today's China*, 19 TUL. EUR. & CIVIL. L. F. 37, 38 (2004).

drafting process, there had been lots of debates, discussions, and disagreements on the structure of the code. This draft was also said to be strongly influenced by common law.①

The 2002 Civil Code Draft was not passed into law for reasons including a "technical" barrier: it consisted of too many legal concepts and terminologies with which many members of the congress were not familiar; therefore, the deliberation did not go through well. Nevertheless, the civil law legislation did not stop. Soon the NPC enacted three important civil laws: the Real Rights Law,② the Tort Liability Law,③ and the Law on Application of Laws to Civil Juristic Relations with Foreign Elements.④ It was not surprising that Wu, the then head of the NPC, announced that "a socialist legal system with Chinese characteristics ha[d] formally been established in China."⑤

§1:2:3　The Latest Achievement: The Civil Code

Codification of Chinese civil law was again put on agenda in 2015 after most of the important civil laws (including, *inter alia*, the GPCL, the Contract Law⑥, the Tort Liability Law, the Real Rights Law, the Marriage Law,⑦ the Adoption Law,⑧ and the Succession Law⑨) had been made, and

---

① Lihong Zhang, *The Latest Developments in the Codification of Chinese Civil Law*, 83 TUL. L. REV. 999, 1010-11 (2009).
② The title of this law has been translated in many different ways, such as "The Real Law," "The Real Rights Law," "The Law of the Thing," or "The Real Rights Law." This law was promulgated at the Fifth Session of the Tenth NPC on March 16, 2007, effective since Oct. 1, 2007, which has now been repealed by the Civil Code.
③ The title of this law could be literally translated as "The Law on Tort Liabilities," which was promulgated at the Twelfth Session of the Standing Committee of the Eleventh NPC on Dec. 26, 2009, effective since July 1, 2010, and now repealed and replaced by the Civil Code.
④ This law was promulgated at the Seventeenth Session of the Standing Committee of the Eleventh NPC on Oct. 28, 2010, effective since April 1, 2011.
⑤ *See* the cover page of GUANG MING DAILY, March 11, 2011.
⑥ The Contract Law was promulgated at the Second Session of the Ninth NPC on March 15, 1999, effective since October 1, 1999, and now repealed and replaced by the Civil Code.
⑦ The Marriage Law was promulgated at the Third Session of the Fifth NPC on September 10, 1980, effective since January 1, 1981, revised by the Twenty-first Session of the Standing Committee of the Ninth NPC on April 28, 2001, and now repealed and replaced by the Civil Code.
⑧ The Adoption Law was promulgated at the Twenty-third Session of the Standing Committee of the Seventh NPC on December 29, 1991, revised at the Fifth Session of the Standing Committee of the Ninth NPC on November 4, 1998, and now repealed and replaced by the Civil Code.
⑨ The Succession Law was promulgated at the Third Session of the Sixth NPC on April 10, 1985, effective since October 1, 1985, and now repealed and replaced by the Civil Code.

the time was ripe for Chinese legislature to integrate all of them into one civil code.

The Legislative Affairs Commission of the NPC Standing Committee took a lead and organized a task force involving experts and scholars from the Supreme People's Court, the Supreme People's Procuratorate, Legal Affairs Office of the State Council, China Academy of Social Sciences, and China Law Society. ① There was a general consensus that the drafters of the civil code would not make a brand-new civil law, nor simply compile the enacted civil laws into one code. Instead, they would examine the then current laws, remove repetitive prescriptions, revise conflicting regulations, repeal out-of-date provisions, and make new rules in responding to the new issues. ②

This codification process had been divided into two steps: as the first step, the General Part of the Civil Code was expected to become law in 2017, and then the other parts (Books) were expected to be submitted to the NPC for discussion in the first half of 2018, and anticipated to be enacted into law in March 2020. ③

The draft of the General Part was completed in February 2016, revised for several times based on public comments, submitted in June 2016 for legislative discussion, and finally passed into law on March 15, 2017. ④ Then the other Books of the Civil Code were completed in early 2020. Owing to the COVID-19, the third Session of the Thirteenth NPC was postponed for two months so that the Civil Code was finally approved and promulgated on May 28, 2020, and has taken effect since January 1, 2021. It is indeed a remarkable

---

① Shishi Li, *Explanations on the CCGP (Draft)* (June 27, 2016), reprinted in Bixin Jiang & Dongning He, COMPARISON AND APPLICATION OF THE ARTICLES OF THE GENERAL PART OF THE CIVIL CODE AND THE GENERAL PROVISIONS OF THE CIVIL LAW 217 (China Law Press 2017).

② Shishi Li, *Explanations on the CCGP (Draft)* (June 27, 2016), reprinted in Bixin Jiang & Dongning He, COMPARISON AND APPLICATION OF THE ARTICLES OF THE GENERAL PART OF THE CIVIL CODE AND THE GENERAL PROVISIONS OF THE CIVIL LAW 214 (China Law Press 2017).

③ Shishi Li, *Explanations on the CCGP (Draft)* (June 27, 2016), reprinted in Bixin Jiang & Dongning He, COMPARISON AND APPLICATION OF THE ARTICLES OF THE GENERAL PART OF THE CIVIL CODE AND THE GENERAL PROVISIONS OF THE CIVIL LAW 216 (China Law Press 2017).

④ See Report on Review of the General Part of the Civil Code of the People's Republic of China (Draft) by the Legal Committee of the 12th national People's Congress (March 12, 2017), reprinted in Tao Du, COMPARISON OF ARTICLES OF THE GENERAL PART OF THE CIVIL CODE AND THE GENERAL PROVISIONS OF THE CIVIL LAW 135 (People's Court Press 2017).

achievement considering the decades-long efforts for codification of the Chinese civil law.

§ 1:3 Legal Framework of Chinese Civil Law

Chinese legal system more resembles European continental legal system which features written statutes instead of cases with precedential value. Chinese civil laws and regulations take various forms and are expressed in different regulatory documents made by the legislature and State agencies within their delegated authority. The sources of Chinese civil law mainly include the Constitution, statutes, administrative regulations and departmental rules, judicial interpretations, local legislations and local administrative rules, international treaties and conventions, and civil customs recognized by the State.

The Constitution① is the fundamental law of China made by the NPC and has the supreme legal power in the nation. No statute or regulation may contradict with the provisions of the Constitution. Within the legal framework of Chinese civil law, the Constitution is at the top and provides the basic guidance for regulating civil juristic relations. Throughout the Constitution, there are many provisions relating to civil juristic relations, especially in its Chapter 2, which sets out the fundamental rights and duties that Chinese citizens are entitled to exercise or obligated to perform. These provisions form a legal basis for the legislation of the other civil laws and regulations to protect and regulate these constitutional rights and duties, whereas the various statutes enacted under the spirits of the Constitution would provide legal basis for courts to try specific cases.

The statutes act as the second important legal source of Chinese civil law, which refer to the "laws" or "national laws" that are promulgated by the NPC or its Standing Committee and effective nationwide. The statutes regulating civil juristic relations are the main forms of Chinese civil law. Before the enactment of the Civil Code, the GPCL was at the center of the civil law

---

① The Constitution of the PRC was promulgated by the NPC on Dec. 4, 1982 and amended in 1988, 1993, 1999, 2004, and most recently on March 11, 2018 at the First Session of the Thirteenth NPC.

system, whereas the Contract Law, Tort Liability Law, Real Rights Law, family laws, and the relevant provisions of the other laws served as supplements. Since 2021, the Civil Code has integrated and replaced these laws to become the most comprehensive civil law statute in China. In addition, the Civil Procedure Law[①] and the Law on Application of Laws on Civil Juristic Relations with Foreign Elements[②] are also part of the civil law system because they provide special rules for the protection of the civil law rights. The Civil Code and the other statutes must be in compliance with the Constitution, and are applicable all over the nation.

In addition to the Constitution and the statutes regulating civil juristic relations, the administrative regulations enacted by the State Council regulating civil juristic relations also are part of the legal framework of Chinese civil law. The State Council is the Central Government of China with the power of enacting the administrative regulations, directives, and orders regulating the civil juristic relationships between and among the persons of the civil law equal in legal status. These administrative regulations are very important because they specify the civil law statutes and provide specific implementation rules. The administrative regulations must be in compliance with the Constitution and the statutes, and are also applicable all over the nation.

Furthermore, the ministries, committees of the State Council, the People's Bank of China, the Audit Commission, and the other institutions under the State Council which have administrative functions may make departmental rules within their delegated authority. In addition, local legislations and local regulations regulating civil juristic relations made by local people's congresses and local people's governments within the power and authority delegated by the Constitution and statutes also form the sources of civil law in China as long as they do not contradict with the Constitution, national laws, or administrative regulations. However, they are only applicable within the local region and not effective nationwide.

---

① The Civil Procedure Law was promulgated by the Seventh NPC in 1991 and last amended at the Thirty-Two Session of the Standing Committee of the Thirteenth NPC on December 24, 2021.
② The Law on Application of Laws on Civil Juristic Relations with Foreign Elements was promulgated at the Seventeenth Session of the Standing Committee of the Eleventh NPC on October 28, 2010, effective since April 1, 2011.

Since China generally adopts the civil law① tradition which features statutory law, there is no case law in China and the cases previously decided are not binding to the courts when dealing with future cases. However, the Supreme People's Court of China (SPC) regularly issues judicial interpretations based on its trial practice which may either interpret a statute, or guide the lower courts when applying a provision of law in specific cases. Judicial interpretations may also be made by the Standing Committee of the NPC, the State Council, and the Supreme People's Procuratorate (SPP). These judicial interpretations are however binding, and thus are one of the sources of Chinese civil law. In addition, local customs that are recognized by the State may also be part of the Chinese civil law. ②

International treaties or conventions regulating civil juristic relations are binding in China if China has become a party or acceded to it, except for the provisions that China has declared preservation thereon. Therefore, when applying Chinese civil law, the international treaties or conventions that China has signed or acceded to must be abide by if they have provisions different from those of the other Chinese civil laws, unless there is a declaration of preservation on a specific provision thereof.

The applicability of the various civil laws of China is different. All of the laws promulgated by the NPC and its Standing Committee and the regulations and rules that have been enacted by the State Council and its agencies are applicable to the civil activities done within the territory of China and any other regions that are regarded, according to international law and international practices and customs, as part of the Chinese territory, including the embassy of China located in a foreign country and the Chinese ships or aircrafts traveling or anchored outside the territory of China. If the legislations, regulations, or rules are made by local people's congresses, local governments, or local administrative bureaus, they are only effective locally.

---

① Here "civil law" is opposed to "common law."
② Article 10 of the Civil Code.

§ 1:4 General Principles of Chinese Civil Law

There are a series of basic principles that run through the whole civil law system in China which guide the civil law legislation and provide important legal basis for Chinese courts to apply the civil law and the other regulations when dealing with civil cases. These principles are very important because Chinese courts may apply these general principles to deal with various civil disputes where there is no law otherwise specifically governs them. These general principles include the principle of protection of lawful rights and interests, principle of equality, principle of voluntariness, principle of fairness, principle of honesty and good faith, and principle of compliance with law and public order.① The newly enacted Civil Code has added two more principles: principle of environmental protection and principle of application of customs.②

Read the following case facts and then analyze what principle(s) may be applied to the case after reading the principles introduced in the following subsections.

> On November 24, 2009, Liu applied for a pre-paid cell phone SIM card with a number of 159XXXXXXXX from China Mobile Xuzhou Branch. He paid 50 yuan, and participated in the "Pay 50, Get 50 More" promotion. On July 5, 2010, Liu recharged 50 yuan through China Mobile's online website. However, when he tried to use this number on November 7, 2010, he found that this number was disconnected. He went to the branch and was told that the number was disconnected because the pre-paid fee expired on October 23, 2010, and there were still 11.7 yuan left in his account. The agreement signed between Liu and China Mobile included clauses on both parties' rights and obligations, but nothing was said about the expiration day of the pre-paid fee. Liu sued in court claiming that China Mobile breached the contract by having unilaterally terminated its services.③

---

① Articles 3-8 of the Civil Code.
② Articles 9-10 of the Civil Code.
③ See Liu v. China Mobile, (2011) Quan Shang Chu Zi No. 240, reprinted in the SPC's Guiding Cases No. 64. Unless otherwise indicated, the cases introduced through this Book are all summarized and translated by the author.

§1:4:1 Principle of Protection of Lawful Rights and Interests

> **Article 3**
>
> The personal rights, proprietary rights, and other lawful rights and interests of the persons of the civil law are protected by law and free from infringement by any organization or individual.

The first principle the Civil Code sets out is the principle of protection of lawful rights and interests of the persons of the civil law. Owing to historical reasons, some people may have a misunderstanding that Chinese law does not protect the private rights, which is not correct. Actually, the PRC Constitution has conferred various rights to citizens, and many of these rights, *i.e.*, the personal rights, proprietary rights, and the other lawful rights and interests, are specifically protected by the civil law and no one may infringe upon such rights or interests. The right-holders are the persons of the civil law, including the natural persons, legal persons, and unincorporated organizations. As a matter of fact, this principle had been integrated into the GPCL in 1986,[①] except that the GPCL focused more on the Chinese citizens but the Civil Code has expanded its coverage to protect all of the natural persons' rights and interests.

§1:4:2 Principle of Equality

> **Article 4**
>
> All persons of the civil law are equal in legal status when conducting civil activities.

Since civil law regulates the proprietary and personal relationships between and among the persons of the civil law that are equal in legal status, the

---

① Article 5 of the GPCL.

principle of equality is of paramount importance in China, featuring the fundamental characteristics of the social relationship regulated by the civil law, and forming the basis of the whole civil law system. By providing that all persons of the civil law are equal in legal status when conducting civil activities, this principle firstly implies that the parties to a civil juristic relationship are in an equal position and any party who infringes upon the other party's rights will bear liability. It also means that the same law applies to all of the persons of the civil law and each person of the civil law has equal status before the law, even if one of the parties is the State, as long as the State acts as a person of the civil law.

In China, the State, as the representative of the whole people, is both the right-holder of the State political rights and the owner of the State-owned property. Thus, the State may perform its administrative function based on its political power, in which case it is the subject of administrative law; meanwhile, the State may also be a person of the civil law to participate in civil activities, such as signing contracts or conducting other civil activities in the name of the State treasurer. While conducting civil activities, the State uses its own name, and exercises an obligee's rights and assumes an obligor's obligations by itself. The scope and conditions of the civil activities that the State may engage in is regulated by law.

The Civil Code does not clearly state that the State is a special person of the civil law; however, it does provide that the State is the owner of the state property,[1] and the lost thing, drifting thing, the thing found from underground, or the hidden thing that the owner is unclear should belong to the State.[2] Anyone who infringes upon the State property should bear civil liability. In addition, a person may write a will to leave his estate with the State.[3] Therefore, the State in these situations is a special person of the civil law.

As a person of the civil law, the State has a very special and exclusive capacity to engage in certain civil activities, and such capacity should be limited

---

[1] Article 246 of the Civil Code.
[2] Articles 318 and 319 of the Civil Code.
[3] Article 1133 of the Civil Code.

by its special policy purpose. For example, only the State has the capacity to issue government bonds. Generally, the State may only participate in civil activities with a view to regulating and controlling the market and cannot actually enter into various competitive industries and compete against the other persons of the civil law. When engaging in civil activities, the State needs to do it through the government agencies with legal person status. In this case, it is important to distinguish the activities of the government agencies and the activities of the State as a special person of the civil law.

The principle of equality requires the persons of the civil law to equally consult with each other when creating, altering, or terminating any civil juristic relationship, and none of the parties may impose their own will upon others. Furthermore, all of the natural persons and legal persons are equally protected, no matter how different they are. No one will get more protection than the others, and private property and public property are both equally protected by Chinese civil law.

§ 1:4:3 Principle of Voluntariness

Article 5

> When conducting a civil activity, a person of the civil law shall, in compliance with the principle of voluntariness, create, alter, or terminate a civil juristic relationship according to his own will.

The principle of voluntariness, also known as the principle of free will, is the basic principle of private law under which the parties are free to form and express their opinions. Specifically, when a person of the civil law conducts a civil activity intending to create, alter, or terminate a civil juristic relationship, he must act according to his own will under the principle of voluntariness. In other words, a person of the civil law is free to acquire a civil-law right according to law and by his own will, and is also free to transfer or waive the right according to the legal procedures, as long as the interests of the State or the public are not harmed when he acts. For instance, West Co.

and East Co. may voluntarily decide whether or not to sign a contract for sale of the E-Books, and they are also free to determine the price and quantity of the dictionaries they want to sell and buy, as well as the method of payment for the sale, as long as no mandatory provisions of law are violated.

However, the "free will" is not limitless. A person of the civil law must act within the limits of law. For instance, a male person may not marry before he reaches 22 because it is the legal age for marriage provided by the Civil Code. ① Also, a person may not create a new type of real right other than the ownership, right to usufruct, or secured interest because the Chinese law adopts the principle of *numerus clauses*. ②

§ 1:4:4 Principle of Fairness

Article 6

> When conducting a civil activity, a person of the civil law shall, in compliance with the principle of fairness, reasonably establish the rights and obligations of each party.

The principle of fairness requires that a person of the civil law must be fair when conducting civil activities, and the rights and obligations of each party must be reasonably established and allocated. If a commercial seller provides to a consumer a form contract under which there is a boilerplate clause printed in fine lines exempting or alleviating the seller's liability, unless the consumer has been warned and actually agreed to this clause, the court mostly would hold that such a contract violates the principle of fairness because it unfairly reduces the seller's liabilities. For instance, if West Co. inserts a clause in the contract with East Co. exempting its liability arising from any personal injury or property damage caused by the defect of the E-Books it has sold to East Co., such a clause would most probably be held invalid as against the principle of fairness.

---

① See Article 1047 of the Civil Code.
② See Article 116 of the Civil Code.

Fairness may be achieved through balancing the values and interests of the parties while allocating rights and obligations between or among them. In a contractual relationship, for example, the principle of fairness requires the parties to the contract to exchange in equal value by paying consideration. In a case over an agreement on testamentary gift for *inter vivos* support①, a senior person would like to give his house to his niece in return for his niece's promise of taking care of him and another person for life. However, when they went to notarize this agreement, the local notary public officer issued a notarized document of "Letter of Gift," changing the nature of the agreement from a conditional agreement to a gifting contract. The court held that the principle of fairness was violated.②

Sometimes, a person who is not at fault may also be held liable if the law so provides,③ such as in a product liability case where strict liability or non-fault liability is imposed. Article 1186 of the Civil Code goes even further to provide that a court may order the parties to share liability even when none of them are at fault. Such provisions have been criticized as not fair and not just at all; however, it is believed that they properly reflect the spirit of the principle of fairness.④ In a 2002 case, a couple took their 8-year-old son to dine in a restaurant. One of the customers at another table brought a bottle of alcohol from home which was given to him by someone else. The bottle, which was actually a disguised explosive, exploded and injured the couple and killed their son. In a suit brought by the couple against the restaurant, the court reasoned that neither the couple nor the restaurant was at fault so the restaurant was not liable for their losses. However, considering that the couple's losses involved the right to life and the right to health which were more severe than the damage suffered by the restaurant, and that the couple and their son went to the restaurant for the benefit of the latter, the court held

---

① For the definition and legal provision on an agreement on testamentary gift for *inter vivos* support, see § 7:3:5 of this Book.
② See Mao & Long v. Mei, (1998) Qian Min Zai Zi No. 25, reprinted in the SPC Gazette, Issue 5, 2000. More about this case is discussed in § 1:6 (Case 3) of this Book.
③ Article 1166 of the Civil Code.
④ In this context, it is probably more accurate to be called as the "principle of balancing" because the court is actually balancing the financial situations and the other situations of the parties when making a decision.

that the restaurant should pay certain amount of money to the couple according to the principle of fairness. ①

§1:4:5 Principle of Honesty and Good Faith

Article 7

When conducting a civil activity, a person of the civil law shall, in compliance with the principle of good faith, uphold honesty and honor commitments.

Chinese civil law requires all civil activities be conducted under the principle of honesty and good faith. This principle fills in the gap when neither the law nor the contract between the parties has clearly provided solutions to an issue, and it provides a standard of interpretation for the courts to make decisions. It requires the persons of the civil law to be honest, keep promises, and duly exercise their rights and perform their duties when participating in civil activities. The parties should exercise their rights in good faith and fully respect the interests of the other party and the public when obtaining benefits, and may not abuse such rights. The parties must perform their duties in good faith even if the law or contract does not expressly so require, or if the law or contract is unclear in the situation.

Therefore, this principle is very significant for the courts to deal with civil disputes when there is no strong legal basis, and the court may resolve the disputes based on the purpose of the civil law and according to the principle of honesty and good faith. To this end, this principle is the basic rule for market participation and an important legal principle to coordinate and balance the interests between and among the parties, and between the parties and the society. It is said that this principle reflects the rules of both morality and law.

---

① See Li & Gong v. May Flower Co., reprinted in the SPC Gazette, Issue 2, 2002. The case is further discussed in §1:5:6 (Case 12).

§1:4:6 Principle of Compliance with Law and Public Order

Article 8

When conducting a civil activity, no person of the civil law may violate the law, or offend public order or good morals.

The principle of compliance with law and public order has been integrated into the Civil Code. Basically, it requires a person of the civil law not to violate law or offend public order and good morals when conducting civil activities. This principle applies not only to the proprietary relationships, but also to the personal relationships. In the context of a contractual relationship, for example, the parties must observe the law and administrative regulations, respect social ethics, and may not disturb the social economic order or harm the social public interest when executing or enforcing a contract. For another example, if a married person uses community property to buy an apartment and registers it in the name of his mistress, this act is apparently against the principle of compliance with law and public order and thus is invalid.

§1:4:7 Principle of Environmental Protection

Article 9

When conducting a civil activity, a person of the civil law shall act in a manner that facilitates conservation of resources and protection of the ecosystem.

A "green principle" has been added to the Civil Code which specifically provides that the persons of the civil law must act in a manner that conserves resources and protects the ecosystem. This principle is added to reflect the fact that environmental protection has become an important State policy in China. It also provides a legal basis for imposing liability on the persons of the civil law who violate environmental protection laws.

§1:4:8 Principle of Application of Local Customs

Article 10

Civil disputes shall be resolved in accordance with law. Where the law does not specify, custom may be applied, provided that public order and good morals may not be offended.

Another new principle added to the Civil Code is the principle of application of local customs. It provides that civil disputes shall be resolved in accordance with custom if the law is silent. However, the application of the custom may not offend public order and good morals. In other words, a "good" custom may be applied when resolving a dispute if the law is absent. The significance of this principle may be seen when compared with the provision of the GPCL which provided that "the civil activities must be conducted in accordance with law; where the law does not specify, the State policy shall be complied with."[1] By replacing the State policy with local customs, the Chinese legislature has gone one step further toward the rule of law.

* * *

Now let's review the case stated in the beginning of this Section and see whether the defendant — China Mobile violated any principle of civil law by unilaterally disconnecting its services, and if so, what principle(s).

When reading the cases restated in this Book, please keep in mind that China is not a case law country; therefore, there is no *stare decisis* doctrine nor a systematically arranged case reporting system. The SPC regularly publishes some typical cases in its Gazettes or as Guiding Cases, while other cases may be found on the websites of local courts or scattered here and there. The cases are not binding to courts but may have certain persuasive value. Please also keep in

---

[1] Article 6 of the GPCL.

mind that most of the cases discussed in this Book were decided before the Civil Code was promulgated, therefore the legal rules cited therein were based on the GPCL and the other civil laws and regulations. These rules have largely been integrated into the Civil Code, and the regulations or interpretations on the GPCL or other civil laws will most probably remain unchanged unless there is a clear change of the law, under which circumstance the change will be pointed out. Lastly, the cases restated in this Book were not reprinted word by word but summarized and translated by the author.

Case 1

Case 1: Liu v. China Mobile[①]

On November 24, 2009, Liu applied for a pre-paid cell phone SIM card with a number of 159XXXXXXXX from China Mobile Xuzhou Branch. He paid 50 yuan, and participated in the "Pay 50, Get 50 More" promotion. On July 5, 2010, Liu recharged 50 yuan through China Mobile's online website. However, when he tried to use this number on November 7, 2010, he found that this number was disconnected. He went to the branch and was told that the number was disconnected because the pre-paid fee expired on October 23, 2010, and there were still 11.7 yuan left in his account. The agreement signed between Liu and China Mobile included clauses on both parties' rights and obligations, but nothing was said about the expiration day of the pre-paid fee. Liu sued in court claiming that China Mobile breached the contract by having unilaterally terminated its services.

The court reasons that a user of telecommunication services has a right to information and the service provider must explain to the user the coverage of the services, including the functions, the ways of fee collection, the time of payment, *etc*. In this case, China Mobile provided a form contract providing the rights and obligations of both parties.

---

① See (2011) Quan Shang Chu Zi No. 240, reprinted in the SPC's Guiding Cases No. 64. Unless otherwise indicated, the cases introduced through this Book are all summarized and translated by the author.

However, nowhere in this contract provided that the contract would be suspended, rescinded, or terminated under any circumstance. If the pre-paid fee had an expiration date, it would directly affect the user's normal use of the cell phone number, so China Mobile had a duty to expressly and honestly notify the user before they signed the contract. Even if it notified the user at the time when the user paid the fee, it already deprived of the user's right not to choose its services. China Mobile's act was against the principle of fairness and the principle of honesty and good faith.

The court holds that China Mobile breaches the contract and orders it to remove the restriction and continue to perform the contract with the plaintiff.

§ 1:5　Protection of Civil Law Rights in China

Chinese Constitution provides that the people's civil-law rights are protected by law.① Chinese civil law protects the civil-law rights of the persons of the civil law by requiring the State to grant protection to them, and also allows the persons of the civil law to adopt self-help measures to protect their own civil-law rights. The former is called public remedies or remedies by public force, whereas the latter called private remedies.

§1:5:1　Public Remedies

§1:5:1:1　Overview

Public remedies are mainly granted through litigation. A person may request a court to clarify a right, to enforce an obligation, or alter a civil juristic relationship.

In a litigation for clarification of a right, a person may request the court to declare whether a certain right exists. For example, a plaintiff may request the court to declare the priority order and coverage of his right over specific property, to determine the validity of a contract, or to determine the existence

---

① Article 51 of the Constitution.

of a relation-based right. Generally, the rights to be clarified in this type of litigation are absolute rights, including real rights, intellectual property rights, and personal rights. The rights protected are mainly the rights to control and domination.① In a litigation for enforcement of an obligation, a person may request the court to order another person to make payment, deliver the property, or pay the agreed penalties and compensation, *etc*. The rights protected therein are mainly the rights to claim. Still, in a litigation for alteration of a civil juristic relationship, a person may request the court to rectify an existing civil-law right or obligation, or create a new civil-law right and obligation through making a judgment. For example, a person may request the court to partition jointly-owned property, terminate a contractual relationship, dissolve an adoption relationship, or to declare a person as legally dead. The rights protected here mainly are the rights to affect a juristic relationship by a unilateral action.

Since many provisions of the civil law and the relevant regulations are discretionary in nature, a right-holder may freely decide whether or not to bring a lawsuit when his rights are infringed upon. However, if the State interests or public interest is infringed upon, the State government may intervene according to the legal procedures. To protect the substantive civil-law rights of the persons of the civil law, procedures are very important. Although this book focuses on the substantive civil law, a very brief introduction to the civil procedure in the beginning of the book will be helpful for the readers to better understand the Chinese civil law system. Therefore, the following sub-sections will briefly introduce Chinese trial system, civil procedure, and their functions in protecting people's civil-law rights.

§ 1:5:1:2 Trial System
General Principles for Civil Adjudication

Chinese courts are granted judicial power of adjudicating civil cases.② When dealing with civil cases, a Chinese court must follow a series of principles: The most fundamental principles are the principle of independency

---

① The civil-law rights mentioned in this section will be explained and discussed in Chapter 2.
② Article 6 of the Civil Procedure Law.

and the principle of equality. The principle of independency requires that all courts try civil cases independently in accordance with law and are free from interference by any administrative agency, social organization, or individual. Each case must be adjudicated based on facts and in accordance with law. ① The principle of equality ensures that all parties have an equal right to litigation, and the law is equally applied to everyone; ② even foreign citizens, persons without nationality, foreign enterprises, or foreign organizations who sue or are sued in a Chinese court have the equal rights and obligations as Chinese citizens, legal persons, and other organizations on the basis of reciprocity. ③

In addition to the above general principles, a court must follow the principle of mediation and conduct mediations, whenever possible, between the parties on a voluntary basis, and should make a timely judgment or ruling if the mediation fails. ④ A court should also ensure that the parties may use their own ethnic minority language during the court hearing, ⑤ considering that there are over fifty different ethnic minority groups in China and many of them have their own language. A court must provide a translator or interpreter for any participant in a proceeding who is not familiar with the spoken or written language commonly used by the local ethnic minority group. ⑥

The parties to a litigation are entitled to represent themselves and argue against each other during the court hearing, ⑦ and a defendant is entitled to defend himself. This principle ensures that each party will be heard so that justice will be achieved. The parties to a litigation are also free to deal with their own civil-law rights and litigation rights the way they prefer within the scope provided by law. ⑧ Specifically, a party may waive one or more claims through withdrawal of the complaint or through reaching a mediation agreement with the other party. This principle is applied through the whole civil proceeding. For example, when a person's rights have been infringed

---

① Articles 6 and 7 of the Civil Procedure Law.
② Article 8 of the Civil Procedure Law.
③ Article 5 of the Civil Procedure Law.
④ Article 9 of the Civil Procedure Law.
⑤ Article 11 of the Civil Procedure Law.
⑥ Article 11 of the Civil Procedure Law.
⑦ Article 12 of the Civil Procedure Law.
⑧ Article 13 of the Civil Procedure Law.

upon, or, when a dispute arises, the person may decide whether or not to initiate a lawsuit with the court. After the proceeding commences, the plaintiff may waive or change his claims, whereas the defendant may admit or deny the plaintiff's claims or raise counter-claims, if any. Moreover, the parties may, on their own initiative, reconcile with each other or request a mediation. After the trial is completed, the party with the right to appeal may freely decide whether or not to appeal against the judgment. The proceeding to enforce a judgment will also depend on the party's request. In other words, after a judgment, ruling, or mediation agreement becomes effective, if one party fails to perform it, the other party may freely decide whether or not to request the court to enforce it. However, such a right is not absolute and must be exercised within the scope provided by law.

Whenever an act has infringed upon the civil-law rights and interests of the State, a collective organization, or an individual, a State agency, a public organization, an enterprise, or an institution may support the injured person to bring an action in court.① However, such person may not sue in their own name because they are not the parties to the litigation.

Lastly the principle of supervision by the people's procuratorate over the adjudication procedure is one of the features of the Chinese legal system, under which the people's procuratorates have the right to supervise over the civil proceedings conducted by the courts.② If they find any irregularities occurred in an adjudication proceeding conducted by a court at the same level, they may submit recommendations against the judgment or ruling with the court at the same level, or request the procuratorate at the immediate superior level to file a protest against the judgment or ruling with the court that makes the judgment or ruling.③ Where the Supreme People's Procuratorate (SPP) determines that a judgment or ruling made by a court at any level is in violation of law, or where a people's procurator determines that a judgment or ruling made by a court at the lower level is in violation of law, they may file a protest against the judgment or ruling.④ The case discussed in the end of this sub-section, which

---

① Article 15 of the Civil Procedure Law.
② Article 215 of the Civil Procedure Law.
③ Article 215 of the Civil Procedure Law.
④ Article 215 of the Civil Procedure Law.

involves re-opening of a case upon the procuratorate's protest, illustrates how such supervision may help protect a person's rights and interests.

Basic Rules of Adjudication of Civil Cases

The Civil Procedure Law of the People's Republic of China establishes various rules for all courts to follow when adjudicating civil cases, including, among others, the rule of hearing a case by a collegial-panel, the rule of recusation, the rule of public trial, and the rule that the second instance judgment is final.①

The rule of collegial-panel hearing requires each court to form a collegial panel to try a civil case in the first instance proceeding② unless the case warrants a summary proceeding③, in which case only one judge presides over the trial. The panel is composed of at least three members, including three judges, or one judge and two or more judicial assessors.④ There must be an odd number of persons on the panel. Likewise, a court that tries a civil case in the second instance proceeding (appeal) must also form a collegial panel of at least three judges, but people's assessors are not allowed upon appeal. During deliberation, the collegial panel must follow the rule of majority voting, and the dissenting opinions must be truthfully recorded in the transcript.

The rule of recusation requires that certain people recuse themselves in order to ensure the justice of the trial. Specifically, it requires that a judge or people's assessor, clerk, interpreter, expert witness, or inspection personnel who is a party, a close relative of a party or his attorney at *litem*, or who has an interest or other relationship with a party to the case recuses himself if the aforementioned interest or relationship may affect the impartiality of the trial. If the aforementioned persons fail to recuse themselves, any party to the litigation may, orally or in a written form, request the court to have such a

---

① Article 10 of the Civil Procedure Law.
② Article 40 of the Civil Procedure Law.
③ A summary proceeding may be adopted by a district people's court when trying simple civil cases in which the facts are evident, the rights and obligations clear, and the disputes trivial in character. See Articles 160-170 of the Civil Procedure Law.
④ Judicial assessors are also called people's assessors, who generally are the persons with special expertise which may be needed in trying certain cases involving special knowledge. People's assessors may help collect and examine the evidence, correctly determine the facts, and properly handle the case. They have the same rights and obligations as that of a judge during the trial. See *generally*, The Law on People's Assessors, enacted by the Standing Committee of the Thirteenth NPC on May 27, 2018.

person recused. The court will make a decision approving or disapproving the request for recusation within three days after the request is made. ①

Under the Chinese law, the whole civil proceeding, other than the deliberation of the panel judges and assessors, is required to be open to the public. Under this system, a court should, before the trial date, publicize the names of the parties, the cause of action, the time and location of the hearing so that the public may access the information and come to the court to hear it if interested. Generally, the whole trial proceeding will be open to the public; people are allowed to observe, and journalists are allowed to watch and report the proceeding. However, this rule is not absolute and all trial proceedings are not open to the public. For example, if a case involves State secrets, personal privacies, or other situations as provided by law, the case should not be tried publicly. If a case involves divorces or trade secrets, and one party requests a non-public hearing, the case should not be tried publicly either. ② Nevertheless, the judgment of these cases still must be announced to the public. ③

Another rule for civil adjudication is that each case may only be tried twice and the decision made by a second instance court is final and not appealable. ④ This system makes sense considering the large geographical area of the nation, unevenly scattered population, and the inconvenience of transportation. It may help alleviate the burden upon the parties, relieve the courts from heavy caseloads, and ease the difficulties in a court's supervision over a trial conducted by a lower court. It is to be noted that the second instance trial in China is both a trial of the facts and the review of legal issues. In addition, China has also established a procedure for trial supervision under which the mistakes, if any, in the final decision made by the second instance court may be corrected through the retrial proceeding. ⑤ Details will be discussed below in § 1:5:1:3 of this chapter.

---

① Articles 47 and 50 of the Civil Procedure Law.
② Article 137 of the Civil Procedure Law.
③ Article 151 of the Civil Procedure Law.
④ Article 182 of the Civil Procedure Law.
⑤ Articles 205-220 of Civil Procedure Law. The "retrial proceeding" is a proceeding for supervision over adjudication in which a case against which a final judgment has been made is re-opened and re-adjudicated according to law. This proceeding is called "retrial," "re-adjudication," or "re-opening of a case" in this book.

Jurisdiction of Courts

China has four levels of courts: the Supreme People's Court (SPC) at the national level, the High People's Courts at the provincial level, the Intermediate People's Courts at the city/county level, and the District People's Courts at the district/town level. In addition to the four levels of courts, there are also several specialized courts, such as the military courts, railroad courts, and maritime courts. While the SPC is the highest court in the nation, all of the other courts have at least one higher-level court superior to them. In other words, a first instance judgment made by any court other than the SPC may be appealed to a court at a higher level.

The jurisdiction of a court is clearly provided by law. A district court has general first instance jurisdiction over the civil cases; therefore, it may try any first instance civil case unless otherwise provided by law.① An intermediate people's court has first instance jurisdiction over the significant cases involving foreign affairs or foreign nationals, the cases that have significant regional impact, and the cases that the SPC assigns to the intermediate people's court.② When determining whether a case concerning foreign affairs is significant, the court will consider the factors such as the value of the disputed subject matter, the complexity of the case, or the number of parties who are residing in foreign countries. To determine whether a case has a significant regional impact, the court will consider the complexity of the case, the number of people involved, the value of the disputed subject matter, and whether the possible impact of the case may exceed the region within the court's jurisdiction. The impact to be considered includes both economic impact and political impact. The cases that the SPC may assign to an intermediate people's court include the cases such as the maritime cases, patent cases, economic cases involving residents or enterprises and organizations of Hong Kong, Macau, and Taiwan, and the cases involving disputed subject matters with a huge value.

A high people's court has first instance jurisdiction over civil cases that have a significant regional impact,③ and the SPC has jurisdiction over the cases

---

① Article 18 of the Civil Procedure Law.
② Article 19 of the Civil Procedure Law.
③ Article 20 of the Civil Procedure Law.

that have a significant national impact and the cases that the SPC decides to try by itself.[①] The SPC is the highest judicial body in China; its main task is to guide and supervise the trial work conducted by the lower courts and the specialized courts, to issue judicial interpretations on how to specifically apply the laws and regulations according to the needs for trial, and to try the cases appealed from the high people's courts. Through trying the first instance and second instance cases, the SPC is actually providing guidance to the lower courts and the specialized courts; meanwhile, it may prevent the local protectionism and the disturbance coming from the various parties to the local courts, so as to ensure the quality of the trials and maintain the dignity of law. Therefore, the SPC only tries a very limited number of first instance cases, and its decisions on these cases are final and non-appealable.

If a party objects to the jurisdiction of a court after the court has already entertained the case, the party must raise an objection within the legally provided period for the defendant to submit the answer. If the court finds, after examination, that the objection is valid, the court will make a ruling and remove the case to the court with jurisdiction; otherwise the objection will be overruled.[②]

Venue for Trial

The venue for a trial is determined according to the administrative division of China. Administratively, China is composed of provinces, municipalities/cities directly administered under the State Council, autonomous regions, and special administrative regions. All of them are at the provincial level. Under each of them, there are various cities, counties, towns, districts, and villages which are at the city/county or town/village level.

The venue for trial is provided by law. The general rule is that the venue is the court of the place where the defendant has his domicile. If a defendant's domicile is different from his residence, then the venue should be the court of the place where the defendant's residence is located. If the domiciles or residences of multiple defendants are located in different administrative

---

① Article 21 of the Civil Procedure Law.
② Article 36 of the Civil Procedure Law.

districts, the courts at these districts all have concurrent jurisdiction over the case.① Under this circumstance, the plaintiff may file with any of such courts. If the plaintiff files simultaneously with two or more courts with jurisdiction, the court in which the case was firstly accepted has the jurisdiction.②

Exceptions exist to the general rule. The venue for trial of a litigation should be the court in the place where the plaintiff's domicile is located if the litigation concerns the identity of a person who is not residing in China, if the litigation concerns the identity of a person who cannot be located or who is declared by a court to be missing, or if the litigation is against a person who is under rehabilitation in prison. Likewise, if the domicile of a plaintiff is different from his residence, then the venue should be the court in the place where the plaintiff's residence is located.③

In addition, Chinese law also provides some special rules. For example, the parties to a contract may agree on the venue in a written contract, and may stipulate that the venue for trial is the court of the place where the defendant's domicile is located, where the contract is to be performed, where the contract is signed, where the plaintiff's domicile is located, or where the subject matter of the contract is located, unless it is against the mandatory provisions of law.④ If the parties have not agreed upon the venue in their contract, then the litigation arising from a contractual dispute should be under the jurisdiction of the court in the place where the defendant's domicile is located or where the contract is to be performed.⑤ The Civil Procedure Law has several articles specifically dealing with the venue for the trial of cases involving insurance contracts, negotiable instruments, corporate disputes, transport contracts, torts, *etc.* considering the special nature and different situations of these cases.⑥

However, the venue for the trial of some special cases is provided by law and may not be changed by the parties. For instance, if a litigation involves a

---

① Article 22 of the Civil Procedure Law.
② Article 36 of the Civil Procedure Law.
③ Article 23 of the Civil Procedure Law.
④ Article 35 of the Civil Procedure Law.
⑤ Article 24 of the Civil Procedure Law.
⑥ Articles 24 and 33 of the Civil Procedure Law.

dispute on real estate, then the court of the place where the real estate is located has exclusive jurisdiction over the case; if a litigation involves a dispute arising from harbor operations, the court of the place where the harbor is located has exclusive jurisdiction over it; if a litigation involves estate succession, then the court of the place where the deceased resided upon death or where the main estate is located has exclusive jurisdiction over it. ①

The following case explains the function of the proceeding of adjudicating a re-opened case and the requirements to be satisfied in order to apply for such a re-opening.

Case 2

Case 2: Wang v. Lu②

This is a retrial case. In the first instance trial, the Intermediate People's Court of Yinchuan City, Ningxia Hui Autonomous Region held that Lu should repay Wang 7,080,000 yuan's loan principal plus interests and dismissed the other claims of Wang, and Wang did not appeal against this judgment, so he was deemed to have accepted the result of the first instance trial.

However, Lu was not satisfied with the first instance judgment and appealed, alleging that the Construction Engineering Group (CEG) induced Wang to provide loans to Lu through defrauding means, and that Wang provided the loan because of CEG's commitment; therefore, CEG should assume the surety liability. Wang defended against Lu's claim by saying that the first instance trial had correctly found the facts and sufficient evidences, and properly applied the law; therefore, it should be affirmed. Accordingly, the High People's Court only examined Lu's claims on appeal and made a corresponding judgment.

This is in compliance with Article 323 of the SPC's Interpretation on the Application of the Civil Procedure Law, which provides that the second instance court shall try the case based on the claims raised by the

---

① Article 34 of the Civil Procedure Law.
② See (2017) Zui Gao Fa Min Shen No. 2483, reprinted in the SPC Gazette, Issue 7, 2018.

parties on appeal, and may not consider an issue not mentioned by the parties, unless the first instance judgment has violated mandatory prohibitions of law, harmed the State interests, the social public interest, or other's lawful rights and interests.

After the second instance court made the decision, Wang applied for a retrial, alleging that the first and second instance trials omitted some facts and harmed his lawful rights and interests. Wang's claim apparently is not in compliance with his act of not appealing after the first instance judgment was made, also against his act of requesting the second instance court to affirm the first instance judgment. In addition, on appeal, the High People's Court dismissed Lu's claims and affirmed the first instance judgment, and did not change the judgment on Wang's rights. Therefore, Wang has no interests in initiating a retrial.

Article 164 of the Civil Procedure Law provides that a party not satisfied with the first instance judgment may appeal to a higher-level court within 15 days after the judgment is served. Article 168 provides that the second instance court shall examine the relevant facts and the application of law regarding the claims alleged on appeal.

According to these provisions, the second instance proceeding is the final proceeding. If a party believes that the first instance court made a mistake, he should have appealed and exercised his right to adjudication through the second instance proceeding. In other words, a party should firstly choose the ordinary proceedings to seek remedies for his rights through the first and second instance proceedings. The retrial proceeding is a special proceeding provided to a party the final judgment against whom may have a significant error. If a party, who has exhausted the ordinary proceedings, still believes that the final judgment is mistaken, he may apply to the court for a retrial. Where a party has not appealed against the party who won or partially won the case in the first instance trial, if the second instance court affirmed the lower court's decision and the party in the second instance proceeding expressed that the first instance trial was correct and should be affirmed, his later-on request for a retrial should not be upheld because the party no longer has any interest in the retrial. Otherwise, it may encourage a dishonest or bad faith party to abuse the retrial proceeding, and make the special proceeding to become an ordinary proceeding. This is an abuse of the right to adjudication and a waste of judicial resources, and is also against the fundamental principle that a second instance judgment is final.

For these reasons, the SPC dismisses Wang's application for a retrial.

§ 1:5:1:3   Trial Proceedings
In General

To initiate a civil law suit in China, a plaintiff needs to file a complaint with a court having jurisdiction. Generally, a plaintiff must be a person of the civil law who has a direct interest in the case, and must have a specific cause of action and claim against a specific or identifiable defendant supported by sufficient facts. In addition, the case must be actionable under the Civil Procedure Law.① The complaint must state the basic information of the parties, *e.g.*, the parties' name, gender, age, nationality, occupation, employer, domicile, contact information, *etc.*, the cause of action, claims, the alleged facts, the evidences and their sources, and the name and address of the witnesses.②

After receiving a complaint, a court must, within seven days, decide whether or not to try the case. If the court decides not to try the case, the plaintiff may appeal on such a ruling.③ If the court decides to try the case, it should serve the defendant within five days after the decision is made, and the defendant will have fifteen days' time to file an answer, starting from the date when he receives the complaint. The court will then send a copy of the answer to the plaintiff within five days after receiving it. Failure of the defendant to file an answer within the specified period of time will not affect the proceeding.④

The parties will be notified within three days after the collegial panel for the hearing of the case is determined.⑤ Then the panel members must carefully

---

① Article 122 of the Civil Procedure Law.
② Article 124 of the Civil Procedure Law.
③ Article 126 of the Civil Procedure Law.
④ Article 128 of the Civil Procedure Law.
⑤ Article 131 of the Civil Procedure Law.

examine and verify the litigation materials, and investigate and collect the necessary evidences. ① When necessary, a court may entrust a court in another locality to help investigate the case. ② The court should notify the person who is an indispensable party to participate in the trial if he fails to join. ③ The court should also notify the parties and the other participants in the proceeding three days before the opening of the court session. ④

On the trial date, a court clerk should firstly determine whether the parties and the other participants in the proceeding are present, and then announce the rules of order of the court. Upon opening of a trial, the presiding judge will verify the identity of the parties, announce the cause of action and the name of the collegial panel members and the court clerks, and inform the parties their relevant rights and obligations. The presiding judge will then ask the parties whether they wish to request recusation of any court personnel. ⑤

If a plaintiff who has been served with a summons somehow does not appear in court on the trial date without just cause, or if he withdraws during a court session without permission of the court, the case will be considered as withdrawn; if a defendant has filed a counterclaim against the plaintiff, the court may make a default judgment against the plaintiff. ⑥ After a trial starts, the plaintiff may apply for withdrawal of the case before the judgment is announced, but it will be subject to the judges' approval. If it is not approved, and if the plaintiff does not appear in court without just cause, the court may still make a default judgment against the plaintiff. ⑦ On the other hand, if a defendant who has been served with a summons refuses to appear in court without just cause, or if he withdraws during a court session without permission of the court, the court may make a default judgment against the defendant. ⑧

A trial will be conducted in three phases: investigation, argumentation, and announcement of the judgment.

---

① Article 132 of the Civil Procedure Law.
② Article 134 of the Civil Procedure Law.
③ Article 135 of the Civil Procedure Law.
④ Article 139 of the Civil Procedure Law.
⑤ Article 140 of the Civil Procedure Law.
⑥ Article 146 of the Civil Procedure Law.
⑦ Article 148 of the Civil Procedure Law.
⑧ Article 147 of the Civil Procedure Law.

During the investigation phase, the parties each may make their statements, and then the witnesses will be called to the stand to testify. The court will inform the witnesses their rights and obligations before they testify. After that, the written statements (affidavits) of the absent witnesses, documentary evidences, physical evidences, video and audio evidences, and other electronic data will be presented, and the expert opinions and inspection records will be read to the court. ① The parties may present new evidences and question the witnesses, expert witnesses, and inspectors during this phase. ②

In the argumentation phase, the plaintiff and his attorney will speak first, followed by the defendant and his attorney. Then it is the turn for any third person to speak. After that, the parties will argue against each other. Upon completion of the argumentation phase, the presiding judge may allow the plaintiff, the defendant, and the third party to present their final statement in this sequence. ③

When the argumentation phase is ended, it is the time for the court to make a judgment. A mediation may be conducted, if it is possible to reach an agreement, before the judgment is made; otherwise the court shall make a judgment in a timely manner. ④ When the judgment is announced, the parties must be informed of their right to appeal, the time limit of the appeal, and the court that the petition for the appeal should be filed with. If divorce is granted by the judgment, the parties must be informed that they may not enter into a new marriage before the judgment becomes effective. ⑤ A judgment should be signed by all members of the collegial panel and the court clerk, with the official seal of the court affixed to it, which should clearly set forth the following: (1) the cause of action, the claims, the alleged facts and causes of the dispute; (2) the facts and causes as found by the court and the basis of the application of law; (3) the outcome of adjudication and the costs to be borne

---

① Article 141 of the Civil Procedure Law.
② Article 142 of the Civil Procedure Law.
③ Article 144 of the Civil Procedure Law.
④ Article 145 of the Civil Procedure Law.
⑤ Article 151 of the Civil Procedure Law.

by each party; and (4) the time limit for filing an appeal. ① The judgment should be announced publicly no matter the case is tried publicly or not. ② Generally, a court is required to conclude a civil case within six months after the case has been filed with the court. When an extension of the period is necessary under a special circumstance, a six-month extension may be allowed subject to approval of the president of the court. Further extension, if needed, shall be reported to the court at a higher level for approval. ③

A court may make a ruling instead of a judgment where: (1) a refusal to accept a case is made; (2) the jurisdiction of the court is challenged; (3) a complaint is dismissed; (4) an asset preservation order or prejudgment enforcement is granted; (5) a withdrawal of the litigation is approved or disapproved; (6) the legal proceeding is suspended or terminated; (7) a clerical error in the judgment is to be corrected; (8) enforcement is suspended or terminated; (9) an arbitral award is revoked or a petition for its enforcement is denied; or (10) a petition for enforcement of a notarized document affirming the rights of a creditor is denied. The party receiving a ruling involving the first three matters may appeal against it, while a ruling involving the other matters is non-appealable. ④ All judgments and rulings made by the SPC are final, and the judgments and rulings made by the other courts that are non-appealable according to law or have not been appealed within the prescribed time limit are final and effective. ⑤

The above is a brief introduction to the ordinary proceeding for a first instance trial. Sometimes a district court and its circuit tribunals may adopt a summary proceeding to try a case where the facts of the case are evident, the rights and obligations of the parties are clear, and the disputes are trivial in character. The parties to the litigation may also stipulate that a summary proceeding is adopted to resolve the dispute between them. ⑥ In a summary proceeding, a plaintiff may orally complain to the court. Such a case may be tried by a single judge alone and should be concluded within three months after

---

① Article 155 of the Civil Procedure Law.
② Article 151 of the Civil Procedure Law.
③ Article 152 of the Civil Procedure Law.
④ Article 157 of the Civil Procedure Law.
⑤ Article 158 of the Civil Procedure Law.
⑥ Article 160 if the Civil Procedure Law.

the case is filed. ①

For a civil case which may be tried through a summary proceeding, if it involves a simple payment of money, and the disputed amount is less than 50% of the average annual income of the employed persons in the local province, autonomous region, or municipality directly under the State Council, a small claims proceeding may be adopted. The judgment made through such a proceeding is non-appealable. ② However, the small claims proceeding may not be adopted to try the following cases: (1) a case involving determination of a personal relationship or a proprietary right; (2) a case involving foreign elements; (3) a case involving evaluation or appraisal of an asset, or involving a dispute over the pre-litigation evaluation or appraisal; (4) a case in which a party's whereabouts is unknown; (5) a case involving a counter-claim raised by a party; or (6) any other case that a small claims proceeding is regarded as not appropriate therefor. ③ The court is generally required to conclude a small claims proceeding within two months, and, under special circumstances, the time limit may be extended for one more month subject to approval of the president of the court. ④

No matter a case is tried in a summary proceeding or a small claims proceeding, if, during the trial, the court finds that the summary proceeding or small claims proceeding is not suitable for trying the case, or if a party successfully makes a challenge, the court should adopt the ordinary proceeding or the summary proceeding, as applicable, to try the case. ⑤

In addition to the ordinary proceeding, the summary proceeding, and the small claims proceeding, Chinese law also provides some special proceedings to deal with special kinds of cases, such as the voter's qualification cases, the cases about declaration of a person as missing or dead, declaration of a person to be with no or limited capacity for performing civil juristic acts, and the cases relating to declaration of a property as ownerless. ⑥

---

① Articles 161-164 of the Civil Procedure Law.
② Article 165 of the Civil Procedure Law.
③ Article 166 of the Civil Procedure Law.
④ Article 168 of the Civil Procedure Law.
⑤ Articles 169 and 170 of the Civil Procedure Law.
⑥ See Articles 184-204 of the Civil Procedure Law.

Appeal

A party who is not satisfied with the judgment made by a court of first instance has the right to file an appeal within fifteen days after the date on which the written judgment has been served, or within ten days after the date on which the written ruling has been served.①

The appellant should prepare a petition and submit it to the original court that tried the case in the first instance proceeding. If a party directly submits a petition to a court at a higher level, the latter should within five days transfer it to the original court.② The petition should include the name of the parties, the name of the court for the first instance, the file number assigned by and the cause of action submitted to the trial court, and the claims or the grounds for the appeal.③ After the first instance court receives the appellant's petition, it should within five days serve it to the respondent, who must submit an answer within fifteen days after receipt of the appellant's petition. The court will serve the answer to the appellant within five days. Failure of the respondent to timely submit an answer will not affect the proceeding of the case. After receiving both the petition and answer, a court should within five days transfer the petition along with all of the case files and exhibits to the appellate court.④

An appellate court should review the relevant facts found and the law applied by the lower court,⑤ and will try the case again on appeal. When trying a case in the second instance proceeding, an appellate court may hold a hearing in the place where the appellate court is located, or in the place where the case occurs or where the first instance court is located. An appellate court should review the records, investigate the case through questioning the parties and witnesses, and clarify the facts of the case before making a judgment. They may also directly make a judgment without having a hearing if there are no new facts, evidences, or causes presented, or otherwise they believe it is not

---

① Article 171 of the Civil Procedure Law.
② Articles 171-173 of the Civil Procedure Law.
③ Article 172 of the Civil Procedure Law.
④ Article 174 of the Civil Procedure Law.
⑤ Article 175 of the Civil Procedure Law.

necessary to do so. ①

After trying a case in the second instance proceeding, an appellate court may make one of the following decisions: (1) if the appellate court determines that the lower court has correctly found the facts and properly applied the law, it will make a judgment or ruling dismissing the appeal and affirming the original judgment; (2) if the appellate court determines that the lower court wrongfully found the facts or applied the law, it will reverse, vacate, or modify the original judgment in accordance with law through making a new judgment or ruling; (3) if the appellate court determines that the facts found by the first instance court are not clearly ascertained, it may either make a ruling to set aside the judgment and remand it to the original court for a retrial, or make a new judgment after investigating and examining the facts by itself; (4) if the appellate court determines that the original judgment was made not incompliance with the legal procedure, in a situation such as a party is omitted or a default judgment was made in violation of law, which might have affected the just adjudication of the case, it will make a ruling to set aside the original judgment and remand it to the original court for a retrial. ② If a case has been remanded and retried by the original court and the losing party appeals again, the second instance court may not remand the case to the original court again. ③ It is to be noted that the appellate court, on appeal, may also conduct mediation. Once a mediation agreement is made and served to the parties, the original judgment is deemed to be vacated. ④

For an appeal against a judgment, the appellate court must conclude the case within three months; for an appeal against a ruling, the appellate court must conclude the case within thirty days. The decision made by an appellate court is final. ⑤

After a judgment becomes final, the following step would be enforcement or execution of the judgment. The difficulties in enforcing a judgment have been a big problem in many countries including China. The

---

① Article 176 of the Civil Procedure Law.
② Article 177 of the Civil Procedure Law.
③ Article 177 of the Civil Procedure Law.
④ Article 179 of the Civil Procedure Law.
⑤ Articles 182 and 183 of the Civil Procedure Law.

Chinese civil procedure law provides a proceeding for enforcement under which the first instance court, through its enforcement tribunal, is responsible for enforcing an effective judgment or ruling upon request by a judgment creditor. A final judgment or ruling may also be enforced by a court, which is at the same level with the first instance court, in the place where the executed assets are located. Sometimes a court also may initiate an enforcement proceeding by itself. ①

Supervision of Adjudication

Although each case may only be tried twice under the system that the second instance judgment is final (except for a retrial upon remand ordered on appeal) under the Chinese civil procedure law, there is still a trial supervision system making it possible for a case which has already been tried twice to be reconsidered if certain requirements are satisfied. This proceeding may be initiated by a court, by the parties themselves, or by a procuratorate.

The president of a court who finds a clear error in any final and effective judgment or ruling made by the court itself and determines that the case should be retried should refer it to the judicial committee of the court for reconsideration. Similarly, the SPC or any other court that finds a clear error in any final and effective judgment or ruling made by a lower court and determines that the case should be retried should direct the lower court to retry the case, or bring the case up for retrial by itself. ②

The second way to invoke the supervisory proceeding is that the parties may submit such a request to the court. Specifically, a party who believes that the final and effective judgment or ruling made by a court is wrong may apply to a court at the immediate superior level for a retrial; however, this application, before approved, will not suspend the enforcement of the judgment or ruling. ③ Article 207 of the Civil Procedure Law lists the situations in which a court should retry a case upon application of a party:

---

① Articles 231 and 242 of the Civil Procedure Law.
② Article 205 of the Civil Procedure Law.
③ Article 206 of the Civil Procedure Law.

(1) there is new evidence sufficient to reverse the original judgment or ruling;

(2) the basic facts found by the lower court in making the judgment or ruling are not supported by sufficient evidence;

(3) the main evidence supporting the finding of the facts found in the judgment or ruling is forged;

(4) the main evidence supporting the finding of the facts found in the judgment or ruling has not been cross-examined;

(5) owing to some objective reasons beyond a party's control, the evidence needed for trial cannot be collected by such party who has therefore applied in writing to the court for assistance, but the court fails to investigate and collect the evidence;

(6) the application of law contained in the original judgment or ruling is clearly wrong;

(7) the composition of the trial panel is illegal, or a panel member who is required by law to recuse himself fails to do so;

(8) a party who is a person without capacity for performing civil juristic acts is not represented by his legal representative in the proceeding, or a party who should have participated in the proceeding fails to do so for a reason other than his own fault or the fault of his or her attorney;

(9) a party's right to argument in the proceeding is deprived of in violation of law;

(10) a default judgment is made against a party upon whom a summons is not properly served;

(11) the original judgment or ruling has omitted one or more of the claims or exceeded the scope of the claims;

(12) a legal document based on which the original judgment or ruling is made has been revoked or revised; or

(13) one or more judges have committed embezzlement, accepted bribes, done malpractice for personal benefits, or perverted the law in adjudicating a case. ①

---

① Article 207 of the Civil Procedure Law.

However, if a party applies for a retrial against a final and effective judgment dissolving a marriage relationship, such an application will not be approved.①

If a party intends to apply for a retrial, an application must be submitted within six months after the judgment or ruling has become final and effective, except that where the cause for retrial is items (1), (3), (12), or (13) as listed above, the limitations period will be six months since the petitioner knows or should have known about the cause for retrial.②

The supervisory proceeding may also be invoked by a procuratorate's protest to the court. If the Supreme People's Procuratorate (SPP) finds a final and effective judgment or ruling made by a lower court involves any of the situations listed in Article 207 of the Civil Procedure Law (as listed above), or if a people's procuratorate at a higher level finds a final and effective judgment or ruling made by a lower level court involves any situation as listed above, the procuratorate should protest against the judgment or ruling. If a local procuratorate finds a final and effective judgment or ruling made by a court at the same level involves any of the situations listed above, it may request the procuratorate at a higher level to protest against the judgment or ruling.③ A party who believes that his right to a retrial has been wrongfully rejected by a court may request the procuratorate to protest against the court's judgment or ruling. In this case, the procuratorate should review the request and decide whether or not to make protest within three months.④ Once a protest is made, the court should make a ruling approving or disapproving the retrial application within thirty days after receiving such a protest.⑤

If a court decides to reopen a case, it should form a new collegial panel to retry it. If the retrial is against a judgment or ruling made by a first instance court, then the case will be retried according to the first instance trial procedure, and the party who is not satisfied with the judgment or ruling made

---

① Article 209 of the Civil Procedure Law.
② Article 212 of the Civil Procedure Law. The old version of the law actually allowed a two-year statute of limitations.
③ Article 215 of the Civil Procedure Law.
④ Article 216 of the Civil Procedure Law.
⑤ Article 218 of the Civil Procedure Law.

by the retrial court may appeal against it; if the retrial is against a judgment or ruling made by a second instance court, then the case will be retried according to the appellate procedure, and the judgment or ruling made by the retrial court is final and non-appealable. If the case is retried by a court at a higher level, then the judgment or ruling is also final. ①

The case summarized below involves multiple protests made by a procuratorate for a retrial proceeding. Please be advised that this case was decided according to the Civil Procedure Law before its new amendment was made in December 2021.

Case 3

Case 3: Mao & Long v. Mei②

On February 17, 1987, Mao and Long, who were monks, asked three persons to write a will on their behalf in the presence of two other witnesses. The main content of the will was as follows:

> Mao and Long were master and disciple, and they did not have work ability owing to their senior age, therefore they decided to deliver their 3-bedroom house to Mao's niece Mei for the latter to inherit the house, on the condition that Mei would be responsible for taking care of them until they die. Since the date of execution of this will, the said house would belong to Mei and nobody may infringe upon or interfere with it.

On March 6 the same year, Mao and Long, together with Mei, went to the local notary public office to notarize the document. The notary public office issued a notarized document entitled "Letter of Gift," and the main content of which was that Mao and Long were donors, Mei was a donee, and the donors decided to gift their house located at 299 Jiefangdong Road of Chengguan Town, Hezhang County, with 60 square meters and a value of 11,000 yuan to Mei on the condition that Mei would be responsible for taking care of Mao and Long's life until they died.

---

① Article 214 of the Civil Procedure Law.
② See (1998) Qian Min Zai Zi No. 25, reprinted in the SPC Gazette, Issue 5, 2000.

Since the effective date of the Letter of Gift, the title of the house would belong to Mei. It also stated that the reason was that they were old and sick, and did not have other relatives, so they made this decision in order to alleviate the burden on the State and the society.

The notary public personnel talked to Mei and recorded the conversation before they issued the notarized document. Mei said that as long as the two elders were alive, she would be responsible for their food and clothes; and upon their death, she would be responsible for their funerals; and that if she did not perform these duties, the elders had the right to take back the property. The notary public issued a notarized document on April 16, 1987.

After the agreement was signed, Mao and Long delivered the house and other property to Mei, and Mei provided food, vegetables, *etc.* to them in return. In the same year, upon consent of the two elders, Mei demolished the old house and reconstructed the house and expanded it to 120 square meters, which costed 15,000 yuan. When the house was demolished, Mao and Long loaned a place from the local residents' committee to live. After the house was rebuilt, Mei did not take them back, but used the house to do her own business. She operated hotel rooms on the second floor and opened a restaurant downstairs.

In 1990, Lei, a nun, was recommended by others to live with Mao and Long, and work to support herself. Mei was not satisfied and there had been confrontations. Meanwhile, some of Mao's religious texts were forfeited by the local police and Mao suspected that it was reported by Mei, the relationship between Mao and Mei was thus deteriorated. Finally, Mei stopped supporting Mao and Long. Mao and Long loaned land from others to grow crops, and maintain their lives by rag-picking and accepting financial help from other people. Mao and Long reported to the local residents' committee and the notary public office for several times about the fact that Mei failed to perform her duty to support them. The notary public and the local residents' committee organized three mediations. In a mediation organized by the local residents' committee in May 1991, Mei admitted that she had not performed her duty for several years and said that she felt sorry for them. However, since Mei did not have the good faith in supporting Mao and Long, the mediations all failed.

Supported by the residents' committee and the other people, Mao and Long sued in June 1991 claiming that the gifting of the house to Mei was based on the condition that Mei would support them. Since Mei failed to do so, they requested that the gifting be revoked and the house and other property be returned.

The county court held that the agreement on testamentary gift for *inter vivos* support was valid, but Mei failed to perform her duty so that their relationship deteriorated and the agreement was nonperformable. Mei should return the property received. The price difference between the reconstructed house and the old house should be appropriately compensated by Mao and Long. The court made a judgment on November 5, 1991 holding that the gifting contract was revoked since the date the judgment became effective, and that Mei should return the house and the other relevant property to Mao and Long, and Mao and Long should pay to Mei 15,000 yuan within two months after the judgment became effective.

Mei appealed to the Intermediate People's Court of Bijie District.

On appeal, the court reasoned that after the agreement on testamentary gift for *inter vivos* support was signed, Mei had exercised certain duties. The reason why their relationship became bad was because Lei came to live with Mao, and that Mao suspected that Mei reported to the police so that Mao's religious texts were forfeited. Mei reconstructed the house upon consent of Mao and Long, now the old house did not exist, and Mei's old house had also been sold and she did not have a place to live. Therefore, the court did not support Mao's claim of returning the house, but requested Mei to compensate Mao and Long for their old house. The court made a judgment in May 1992 holding that the reconstructed house belonged to Mei, and Mei should compensate Mao and Long 15,000 yuan.

Mao and Long petitioned to the procuratorate for a retrial on June 21, 1992. In July 1992, Long died and his burial was handled by the local people.

The People's Procuratorate of Guizhou Province determined that the agreement on testamentary gift for *inter vivos* support was a conditional juristic act, and the support obligor would have the right to accept the gifted property only after she had fully and actually performed the duties under the agreement. Mei refused to exercise her duty to Mao and Long. The second instance court held that she should keep the house, which incorrectly applied the law. Upon investigation, the procuratorate discovered that Mei had another residence to live. In August 1993, the procuratorate petitioned to the High People's Court of Guizhou Province for a retrial.

On September 3, 1993, the High People's Court ruled that the intermediate people's court of Bijie district should form another collegial panel to retry this case. The retrial court held that the house should be dealt with according to the first instance court's decision. Mei appealed to the High People's Court again.

In November 1995, the High People's Court retried this case and held that the agreement between the parties was not an agreement on testamentary gift for *inter vivos* support or a conditional juristic act, but a gifting agreement. This agreement had been notarized so it was lawful and valid. From the performance of the gifting contract, now the ownership right over the house and the other property had been transferred to Mei, and Mao and Long had also accepted Mei's support. Now Mao and Long's claim for the return of the house and the other property was without any legal basis. It held that the house belonged to Mei, the other property is owned by Mei but may be used by Mao, and that Mei should pay 5,000 yuan to Mao as the life support fee since Feb. 1991 until the date the judgment was made, and that starting from the date the judgment became effective, Mei should pay 200 yuan each month to Mao as his life support until he died. Mei should also be responsible for Mao's medical and funeral expenses.

After the judgment was served, Mei paid 5,000 yuan to Mao but Mao refused to accept it, so the money was deposited with the local court. On May 3, 1995, Mao wrote a will saying that after he died, his right would be passed on to the local residents' committee. He died on Jan. 9, 1996, and Mei took care of his funeral and spent 13,717.38 yuan for it.

The Procuratorate of Guizhou Province determined that the retrial decision made by the High People's Court of Guizhou Province was again wrong, and petitioned to the Supreme People's Procuratorate (SPP) for a retrial. The residents' committee of Chengguan Town Hezhang County, as Mao's successor, also petitioned to the SPP.

After reviewing the case, the SPP protested to the SPC for a retrial. The SPC instructed the High People's Court of Guizhou Province to retry the case on March 10, 1998.

On April 26, 1998, Guizhou High People's Court retried the case for the second time, and held that the parties intended to sign an agreement on testamentary gift for *inter vivos* support; however, the notary public made the notarized document as a "Letter of Gift," which changed the legal relationship from a conditional gifting to an absolute gifting relationship and violated the principle of fairness and compensation for equal value, also against the true expression of intent made by Mao and Long. As a result, this Letter of Gift was invalid. Since Mei did not perform her duty to take care of Mao and Long until they died, which had made adverse effect in the local society, she did not have the right to enjoy the gifted property. The judgment of the first retrial wrongfully held that the letter of gift was valid and the agreement between the two parties was a conditional gifting contract, and should be reversed.

After deliberation of the Judicial Committee of the High People's Court of Guizhou Province, according to Article 21 of the Succession Law and Article 184 of the Civil Procedure Law, the High People's Court held that the disputed house and the relevant property belonged to the residents' committee, and the residents' committee should pay to Mei 15,000 yuan for the reconstruction of the house, and 13,717.38 yuan for Mao's funeral, 28,717.38 yuan in total. The 5,000 yuan deposited by Mei in the local court should be returned to Mei, and the litigation costs for the original first and second instance trials of 1,200 yuan should be paid by Mei.

§1:5:2 Private Remedies

Private remedies are self-help measures adopted by the persons of the civil law to protect their own civil-law rights. In other words, a right-holder may adopt various lawful measures to protect his own rights free from infringement. In addition to justifiable defenses and necessities in an emergency to be discussed later, there are other self-help measures that a person of the civil law may take to protect his civil-law rights. For example, a right-holder may hold in custody the obligor's property in order to protect his own right to claim against the obligor in an emergent situation when he could not ask for the State institution for help. For instance, a hotel may withhold the luggage of their guest if the latter refuses to pay. These self-help measures must be used for protecting the obligee's own civil-law rights other than the civil-law rights of others or the social public interest. The purpose of these self-help measures is also to ensure one's right to claim, and it should not exceed the necessary extent for that purpose.

Chapter 2
General Part of the Civil Code

The General Provisions of Civil Law (GPCL) was the first civil law and had been the basic civil law regulating civil juristic relations in China since its enactment on April 12, 1986 until January 1, 2021 when it was repealed and replaced by the Civil Code. The GPCL had nine chapters and 156 articles. Among the nine chapters, the first chapter was about the general provisions and the last chapter was supplementary provisions. The other seven chapters regulated the natural persons, legal persons, civil juristic acts and agency relationship, civil-law rights, civil liability, limitation periods, and the application of civil laws to civil juristic relations with foreign elements.

In 2017, the Civil Code — General Part (CCGP) was enacted and intended to replace the GPCL, and it now has been integrated into the Civil Code barely without any change. The General Part (Book One) of the Civil Code is composed of ten chapters and 204 articles, with each chapter dealing with one of the following matters: general provisions, natural persons, legal persons, unincorporated organizations, civil-law rights, civil juristic acts, agency, civil liability, limitation of action, and the counting of periods of time. The structure of the General Part has been adjusted and the most significant change is that the section on the application of civil laws to civil juristic relations with foreign elements has not been integrated into the Civil Code and this part of the law had been enacted as a separate law in 2011. [1]

---

[1] The Law on Application of Laws to Civil Juristic Relations with Foreign Elements was adopted at the Seventeenth Session of the Standing Committee of the Eleventh NPC on Oct. 28, 2010 and has become effective since April 1, 2011.

Chinese civil law adopts some unique concepts and terminologies, and some of them have been introduced into China from European continental law or the former Soviet Union law with modifications. These concepts and terminologies are sometimes quite abstract or even hard to understand by common law lawyers, it is nevertheless helpful to know them before learning the Chinese civil law. This Chapter will introduce some of these important concepts, including civil juristic relationships, civil juristic acts, agency relationship, civil liability, limitation of action, and counting of time periods which are provided in Book One of the Civil Code, and will focus on the provisions on the persons of the civil law and their civil-law rights.

§ 2:1 Civil Juristic Relationships

Civil juristic relationships are the social relationships recognized, regulated, and protected by civil law. The essence of a civil juristic relationship is about rights and obligations. A civil juristic relationship, which has characteristics different from the other legal relationships, is a relationship between and among persons, not one between persons and property or one between persons and the natural world, although it may sometimes involve a property or thing. The nature of a civil juristic relationship is its equality represented by the principle of equality as discussed earlier. The parties are equal in legal status, and their rights and obligations are equal and corresponding to each other. A contractual relationship is a typical civil juristic relationship. In a contractual relationship, one party's right is the other party's obligation and *vice versa*. Under the contract for sale of E-Books, for instance, West Co. is obligated to deliver the dictionaries and entitled to the payment, whereas East Co. is entitled to receive the dictionaries and obligated to make payment. This relationship between West Co. and East Co. is a civil juristic relationship under Chinese Civil Law.

A civil juristic relationship may be created by the parties through their own will and the parties may alter or terminate the relationship through consultation and agreement. The parties may also freely determine their rights and obligations through consultation, as long as it does not violate any mandatory provision of law or against social ethics or public interest. A civil juristic relationship is composed of three elements: subjects, objects, and the content, *i.e.*, the rights and obligations of the parties to the relationship.

§2:1:1 Subjects of Civil Juristic Relationship: Persons of the Civil Law

In the context of Chinese civil law, the "subjects" of a civil juristic relationship refer to the parties to such a relationship who are entitled to exercise civil-law rights and/or obligated to perform civil-law duties or obligations. In a typical civil juristic relationship, a party is both a subject of right and a subject of duty/obligation. For the same example, under the sales contract signed by West Co. and East Co., West Co. has an obligation to deliver the dictionaries according to the contract, and East Co. has a right to receive the dictionaries. To this extent, West Co. is a subject of obligation, and East Co. is a subject of right. On the other hand, East Co. has an obligation to make payment of the purchase price to West Co., and West Co. has a right to receive the payment made by East Co., now East Co. is a subject of obligation, and West Co. is a subject of right.

However, in some special situations, one party only has rights while the other party only has duties or obligations. For example, if Eastern Bank signs a surety contract with West Co. promising to pay West Co. on behalf of East Co. if East Co. fails to pay, then in this juristic relationship, Eastern Bank is a subject of obligation, while West Co. is a subject of right.

A subject of a civil juristic relationship can be a natural person, legal person, or unincorporated organization; sometimes the State may also be a special type of subject. They are collectively called "the persons of the civil law." Any person or organization who intends to be a subject of a civil juristic relationship must be qualified in accordance with law. The regulations and protections on the persons of the civil law are further discussed in §2:2.

§2:1:2 Objects of Civil Juristic Relationship

An object of a civil juristic relationship is the object of the civil-law rights and civil-law obligations. The object may vary depending on the nature of the civil juristic relationship; it may be a thing or property, an act, an intellectual product, or a personal interest. For example, in a lease contract scenario, the object of the lease relationship is the leased apartment, which exists independently from the parties, but is controlled by and may satisfy the needs of the parties. In a debtor-creditor relationship, on the other hand, the object may be an act which is to be conducted by a party, such as making payment, and the other party has a right to ask the first party to make payment in accordance with the contract. Likewise, an intellectual product is the object of an intellectual property relationship while a personal right, such as the right to life, health, or honor, is the object of a civil juristic relationship of dignitary rights.

§ 2:1:3 Civil Law Rights and Obligations

Each civil juristic relationship is composed of subjects, objects, and civil law rights and obligations. A civil law right is a right that a person of the civil law may legally exercise, and a civil law obligation is an obligation that a person of the civil law is legally obligated to perform.

§ 2:1:3:1 Civil Law Rights

Civil law rights are the benefits and interests held by a person of the civil law in a certain civil juristic relationship and are protected by law. The exercise of Civil law rights must be in compliance with the Constitution and the other national laws, and may not be against social public interest. A right-holder[①] may not abuse his rights and cause harm to others. Article 51 of the Constitution provides the fundamental basis for the right-holders to enjoy their rights; however, the exercise of the civil law rights is not limitless. The persons of the civil law, when exercising their rights, may not infringe upon the interests of the State, society, or collective, or the lawful rights of any other person. The principle of honesty and good faith is the basic principle for the persons of the civil law to exercise their civil law rights. The specific civil-law rights protected by the Civil Code are further discussed in § 2:3 of this Chapter.

§ 2:1:3:2 Civil Law Obligations

Civil law obligations are the legal duties imposed upon an obligor to do or

---

① In this Book, the "right-holder" sometimes is referred to as the "obligee" and the party with an obligation to perform an act is sometimes called the "obligor."

not to do a certain act in order to satisfy an obligee's request. Apparently, Civil law rights and civil-law obligations are independent from each other, but they are also mutually connected to each other to a certain extent. In a normal situation, people cannot talk about obligations without firstly talking about the rights because the two are actually consistent with and corresponding to each other. The content of a right should be reflected in a corresponding obligation, and *vice versa*. When one party has a right, the other party under the same legal relationship must have a corresponding obligation. In addition, the rights and obligations usually are created, altered, and terminated at the same time.

The following case illustrates the consequence when a person infringes upon other's civil-law rights.

Case 4

Case 4: Ran v. Xie[①]

Ran and Xie were both students of Chongqing Three Gorges Vocational College and Xie co-rented an apartment with Chen in Wanzhou District. On August 21, 2020 at about 11 pm, when Xie returned to the apartment, he could not unlock the apartment door so he entered into the apartment through a window, and found that Ran and Chen were sleeping on bed. Xie took pictures and recorded videos and sent some of them to Chen's girlfriend Zhang, as a result, some of the pictures and videos were spread.

Ran sued Xie for infringement of her right to reputation and privacy and requested 10,000 yuan for her mental distress (pains and suffering).

The court reasons that a natural person enjoys a right to privacy and no individual or organization may infringe upon such right through prying into, intruding, disclosing, or publishing private matters of the person. Unless otherwise provided by law or explicitly consented to by the person, no one may enter into, taking pictures of, or peeping into his residence, hotel room, or other private space of him, or taking photos of or peeping

---

① See (2021) Yu 0101 Min Chu No. 2425.

into his private body parts. In this case, Xie entered into Ran's private space without her authorization to take pictures and videos of her private body parts and spread them to others, which act infringed upon Ran's personality rights and made Ran's social evaluation degraded and her reputation harmed. Therefore, Ran's requesting Xie to delete the pictures and videos and extend apology is held reasonable.

After consideration, the court holds that Xie should immediately delete the pictures and videos he took and stored concerned Ran, extend an apology to Ran within 10 days after the judgement becomes final, and publish a statement of apology to Ran in his WeChat Moments every day for at least 15 days. The court also requests Xie to pay 1,000 yuan for Ran's pains and suffering, as well as 2,500 yuan's attorney's fees. The litigation cost of 200 yuan should also be paid by Xie.

§ 2:2　Persons of the Civil Law

The persons of the Civil Law may exercise civil-law rights and perform civil-law obligations under Chinese Civil Law. There are three types of persons of the civil law: natural persons, legal persons, and unincorporated organizations.

§ 2:2:1　Natural Persons

A natural person is generally regarded as a naturally born human being. Chapter 2 of the GPCL was titled "Citizens (Natural Persons)" but the Civil Code has expanded the coverage of the civil law by naming its Chapter II as "Natural Persons," which means that non-citizen natural persons are also protected by the Civil Code. A Chinese citizen who has reached 16 may apply for an identity certificate as the legal proof of his natural person's status in China, and each citizen would be assigned a sole number as his identification number through his whole life.[1]

---

[1] See the Law on the Residents' Identity Certificate which was promulgated by the NPC on June 28, 2003.

§ 2:2:1:1 A Natural Person's Capacity for Enjoying Civil-law Rights

All natural persons have equal capacity for enjoying civil-law rights,① and such capacity cannot be deprived of by anyone or abandoned by the natural person himself. The capacity for enjoying civil-law rights starts from the date when a natural person is born and ends on the date when the natural person dies,② no matter the person dies naturally or is declared to be dead by a court.③ Article 15 of the Civil Code provides the ways to determine the time of birth and time of death of a natural person. The Civil Code also provides an exception for an unborn fetus who is deemed to have such capacity in estate succession, acceptance of gift, and other situations where the fetus' interests need to be protected, unless the fetus is later on stillborn.④

Such capacity cannot be detached from the person or transferred to anyone else. A natural person's capacity for enjoying civil-law rights makes the natural person qualified to be a "person of the civil law" in a civil juristic relationship. Generally, such capacity has nothing to do with the natural person's age or health situation; however, a natural person who has not reached a certain age may not be able to enjoy some special civil-law rights. For instance, a male person may not marry until he has reached 22 and a female person may not marry until 20.⑤

§ 2:2:1:2 A Natural Person's Capacity for Performing Civil Juristic Acts

A natural person needs to have the capacity for performing civil juristic acts in order to perform their civil-law duties or obligations. A person with such capacity is able to exercise civil-law rights and perform civil-law obligations through his own act and is able to bear civil liability for the illegal acts he has done. In this sense, the capacity for performing civil juristic acts is the ability of a natural person to independently conduct civil activities and assume liabilities. While a natural person's capacity for enjoying civil-law

---

① See Articles 13 and 14 of the Civil Code.
② See Article 13 of the Civil Code.
③ See Article 46 of the Civil Code, which provides the situation in which a natural person may be declared as dead by a court.
④ Article 16 of the Civil Code.
⑤ See Article 1047 of the Civil Code.

rights cannot be restricted or deprived of, his capacity for performing civil juristic acts may be restricted according to the provisions and the procedure provided by law. Under Chinese law, a person may have full capacity, limited capacity, or no capacity for performing civil juristic acts. The purposes of the law on natural persons' capacity for performing civil juristic acts are to protect the rights and interests of the persons with limited or no capacity and to maintain the security and order of transactions.

Full Capacity for Performing Civil Juristic Acts

A natural person with full capacity for performing civil juristic acts may independently exercise civil-law rights and perform civil-law obligations through his own acts. In China, 18 is the majority age and a natural person who has reached 18 is regarded as an adult. ① Such a person has full capacity for performing civil juristic acts and may independently conduct civil activities unless his mental status makes him only have limited or no capacity. ② In addition, the Constitution of the PRC grants the voting rights to the Chinese citizens over 18 years of age. A natural person who has reached 16 but below 18 may also have full capacity if his main living resources come from his own labor. ③ When we say that a person has full capacity for performing civil juristic acts, it does not mean that the act conducted by such a person is a valid act because an act must meet the other legal requirements to be effective.

Limited Capacity for Performing Civil Juristic Acts

A natural person with limited capacity for performing civil juristic acts may independently perform civil juristic acts only within a limited scope, *i.e.*, only if upon consent or ratification of his legal representative, if the act is solely beneficial to him, or if it is appropriate considering his age and intelligence. ④ Generally, the guardian of such a person is the legal representative of the person. ⑤

---

① See Article 17 of the Civil Code.
② See Article 18 of the Civil Code.
③ See Article 18 of the Civil Code.
④ See Article 19 of the Civil Code.
⑤ Article 23 of the Civil Code.

According to the Civil Code, two types of natural persons have limited capacity for performing civil juristic acts. First, those who are above 8 but below 18 have only limited capacity because they are still minors and cannot fully comprehend and judge their own conducts or the consequences of their conducts, although they do have the ability to perceive and make judgment on it to a limited extent. However, such a minor may engage in an act which will only bring to him benefits.

Secondly, those who have mental problems and thus neither can perceive their conducts or have independent judgment when facing complicated situations, nor can fully comprehend the consequences of their activities, have only limited capacity. The declaration of a mentally disabled person to be one with limited capacity for performing civil juristic acts must be made by a court through a special proceeding initiated by any interested person of the said person or a relevant organization. ① The "interested person" may include those who have a special relationship with the person, such as the spouse, parents, adult children, or other relatives of the person. The "relevant organization" may be a residents' committee (i.e., a neighborhood committee in the urban areas), a villagers' committee, a school, a medical institution, the women's federation, the disabled person's federation, a legally established organization for senior people, or the local civil affairs department. An adult with limited capacity may also perform a civil juristic act through or upon consent or ratification of his legal representative, except that he may independently perform a civil juristic act that is solely beneficial to him or that is considered to be appropriate to his intelligence and mental status.

A "solely beneficial" act is one that will only bring benefits to the person, such as an act rendering bonuses, gifts, remunerations, etc., and the other people cannot claim that such act is invalid solely because the actor does not have full capacity for performing civil juristic acts. The law is actually providing protections to the persons with limited capacity for performing civil juristic acts through this rule. ②

---

① Article 24 of the Civil Code.
② See Article 19 of the Civil Code.

No Capacity for Performing Civil Juristic Acts

A natural person with no capacity for performing civil juristic acts may not independently conduct civil acts. Minors below 8 years of age and mentally disabled persons who cannot comprehend or judge their own conducts do not have the capacity for performing civil juristic acts.① Similarly, a declaration of a mentally disabled person to have no capacity for performing civil juristic acts must also be made by the court through a special proceeding initiated by an interested person of the mentally disabled person.② The Civil Code provides that a civil juristic act performed by a natural person without the capacity for performing civil juristic acts is void,③ but a civil juristic act performed by a natural person with limited capacity for performing civil juristic acts could be valid if his legal representative has given consent or ratification to the act.④

* * *

A natural person's capacity for performing civil juristic acts may be gained, suspended, resumed, or lost. A minor may gain the capacity for performing civil juristic acts upon reaching the majority age. A person's capacity for performing civil juristic acts may be suspended when he is declared by the court to be a person with no such capacity owing to his health situation. In this case, the person's capacity may be resumed upon his recovery from the health deficiency. The court may, upon request of the person, an interested person of him, or a relevant organization, and based on the recovery of his intelligence and mental health, declare that he has fully or partially resumed his capacity.⑤ A person's capacity for performing civil juristic acts is lost upon his death.

§2:2:1:3 Guardianship

Guardianship is a system by which the civil law provides protection to and supervision over the persons with no or limited capacity for performing civil juristic acts regarding their personal, proprietary, and other lawful rights and

---

① Articles 20 and 21 of the Civil Code.
② Article 24 of the Civil Code.
③ See Article 144 of the Civil Code.
④ See Article 145 of the Civil Code.
⑤ Article 24 of the Civil Code.

interests by covering the deficiency in their capacity and preventing them from conducting illegal acts which may cause damage to other people and the society. The person performing the duty of supervision and protection is the guardian, and the person to be supervised and protected is the ward.

A guardian represents the ward to perform civil juristic acts and protects the personal, proprietary, and other lawful rights and interests of the ward, and will bear legal liability for failing to perform such duties. When a guardian is temporarily unable to perform his duties owing to an emergency, the residents' committee, the villagers' committee, or the local civil affairs department in the place where the ward's domicile is located is responsible for arranging temporary measures to protect the ward from an unattended situation. ①

A guardian may be designated by law, by court, or in a person's will. The parents are the legal guardians of their minor children. ② A parent's right to be a guardian of his minor child cannot be deprived of or limited until the parent dies, except that this right may be deprived of by a court through a legal proceeding. However, if a minor child has been adopted by another person, the adoptive person becomes the legal guardian of the child, and the natural parents are no longer guardians of the minor. Upon divorce of the parents, the parent living with the child is the guardian of the minor child; meanwhile, the other parent also has the right and duty to support and educate the child. If the parent-guardian fails to exercise the duties of guardian, the other parent may request the court to change the guardianship and allow the child to live with him as the parent-guardian. The parent-guardian may designate a succeeding guardian for his child in his will. ③

If both parents of a minor die, like in the case cited below, or neither of them is competent to be a guardian, the child's grandparents who are competent will be his guardians, or, if the child's grandparents are deceased or incompetent, his elder brothers and sisters will be his guardians. Where such a minor child does not have any elder siblings or none of his elder siblings are competent, then any other person, including an organization, who is willing to

---

① See Article 34 of the Civil Code.
② See Article 27 of the Civil Code.
③ See Article 29 of the Civil Code.

act as his guardian may be appointed as his guardian, as long as consent is obtained from the residents' committee, the villagers' committee, or the local civil affairs department in the place where the minor's domicile is located.① The appointment must be made in the best interests of the minor child and must be from among the legally qualified persons. If anyone is not satisfied with the determination of the guardianship and brings a lawsuit, the court may appoint a guardian through ruling on it. The parties may also directly request the court to appoint a guardian for the minor child. ② The ward should be consulted with and his true will must be respected when a guardian is designated or appointed so that his interests will be protected. ③ In the following case (Case 5), the residents' committee decided to nominate the minor's uncle to be his guardian; however, the ward was not satisfied and the court finally changed the guardianship and nominated his grandparents as his guardians.

In addition to minor children, a person with limited or no capacity for performing civil juristic acts owing to a mental problem should also have a guardian. Article 28 of the Civil Code provides the scope of persons among whom a guardian may be appointed for a mentally deficient person. These persons include his spouse, parents, children, any close relatives, or any other individual or organization that is willing to assume the guardianship responsibility, as long as consent is obtained from the residents' committee, villagers' committee, or the local civil affairs department in the place where the adult person's domicile is located. ④ There is a priority order among these groups of persons, i.e., the person(s) in the subsequent group may be considered only when the persons in the preceding group all decease or are incompetent.

A guardian may also be determined upon agreement among the legally qualified persons, except that the ward's will should be respected when doing so. ⑤ If there is no legally qualified person to be a guardian, the local civil affairs department should act as the guardian, and the local residents' committee or villagers' committee may also act as the guardian if they are

---

① Article 27 of the Civil Code.
② Article 31 of the Civil Code.
③ Article 31 of the Civil Code.
④ Article 28 of the Civil Code.
⑤ See Article 30 of the Civil Code.

competent in performing the duties of guardian. ①

A guardian of a person with limited or no capacity for performing civil juristic acts is the legal representative of the person② and is responsible for conducting civil activities on behalf of the ward; therefore, a guardian must have full capacity for performing civil juristic acts. A guardian has the duties to protect the ward's person, property, and other lawful rights and interests, to manage the property of the ward, and to take care of, supervise, educate, and discipline the ward. When performing the duties of guardian, a guardian is protected by law and the guardianship is free from interference by any individual or organization. However, if a guardian ill-treats or deserts the ward, the guardian may be criminally liable where the situation is serious. If the property of the ward has been lost owing to the guardian's failure to perform or appropriately perform the duties of guardian, the guardian should compensate for the loss. Upon request of a relevant person or organization, a court may disqualify a guardian who fails to perform his duty, and designate another person as the guardian. ③

A guardian once appointed may not be replaced without authorization; otherwise his responsibility as a guardian is not discharged. ④

A new type of guardian — a guardian for an adult with full capacity for performing civil juristic acts in anticipation of his incapacity in the future — has been provided by the Civil Code. Such an adult may designate a guardian for himself from his close relatives or other individuals or organizations who are willing to be his guardian, and the guardian, thus appointed will only perform the duties of guardian when the adult loses all or part of his capacity for performing civil juristic acts in the future. Such a designation must be made in writing. ⑤

Regardless of the different types of guardianship, a guardian must perform his duties in the best interests of the ward, and may not dispose of the ward's property unless it is for protecting the interests of the ward. Whenever

---

① See Article 32 of the Civil Code.
② Article 23 of the Civil Code.
③ Article 36 of the Civil Code.
④ See Article 31 of the Civil Code.
⑤ See Article 33 of the Civil Code.

possible, the ward's true will should be respected based on the ward's age and intelligence, especially when the ward is an adult.① A guardian may be disqualified by a court if he engages in any act which severely harms the physical or mental health of the ward, is indolent in performing the duties of guardian, or unable to perform such duties but refuses to delegate all or part of the duties to others, and thus places the ward in a desperate situation, or engages in any other act which severely infringes upon the lawful rights and interests of the ward.② However, the disqualification of a parent, child, or spouse as a guardian made by a court does not affect such persons' duty to perform his support obligations.③ Once being disqualified, a person, other than the ward's parent or child, will never be appointed as the guardian of the ward again, but such a guardian who is the ward's parent or child may be reinstated as a guardian if he is disqualified for a reason other than having committed an intentional crime against the ward, and now he has truly repented and mended his ways. Upon application by such a person, the court may consider the actual situation and the ward's true will before making the decision.

A guardianship may be terminated if the ward has gained or regained full capacity for performing civil juristic acts, *i.e.*, a minor has reached the majority age or a mentally disabled person has been cured. A guardianship may also be terminated if the guardian has lost capacity for performing civil juristic acts, or has been disqualified by a court as a guardian. A guardianship is also terminated where either the guardian or the ward deceases.④

Case 5

Case 5: Jiang & Meng v. Uncle Qiao⑤

Qiao was born in May 2002. His mother died in September 2010 and

---

① See Article 35 of the Civil Code.
② See Article 36 of the Civil Code.
③ See Article 37 of the Civil Code.
④ See Article 39 of the Civil Code.
⑤ The cases introduced in this book are simplified and translated based on either actual cases or hypothetical cases. This case is compiled by the Case Study Institute of the SPC in Typical Cases Involving Protection of Rights and Interests of Minors and Innovation of Juvenile Judicial System.

his father died in July 2012, leaving 300,000 yuan with Qiao. After consulting with his relatives, the local residents' committee appointed Qiao's uncle Uncle Qiao as his guardian, who was also responsible for keeping the 300,000 yuan left by Qiao's parents for Qiao. Qiao had been living with Uncle Qiao since October 2012 until July 2016 during which period Qiao and his uncle had not been getting along well. Afterwards, Qiao moved out and lived with his maternal grandparents Jiang & Meng.

Jiang & Meng sued in court requesting a change of Qiao's guardian from Uncle Qiao to themselves. During the trial, Qiao also expressed his intention to live with his maternal grandparents.

After hearing the case, the court concludes that Uncle Qiao, who was appointed by the residents' committee as Qiao's guardian, had performed his duties of guardian. However, Qiao and his uncle had some confrontations when they lived together, and now Qiao would like to have his maternal grandparents to be his guardians. Since the petitioners and respondent had reached agreement and the process was in compliance with law, it should be permitted.

Regarding the money left by Qiao's parents, Uncle Qiao requested that it be kept by a third person trusted by both the petitioners and the respondent in order to protect Qiao's lawful rights and interests. The court holds that such request is reasonable since Qiao is still a minor, and his grandparents are both almost 70 years old and without substantial education background. Both parties agree that Uncle Qiao should deliver the 300,000 yuan under his custody to Han, who is a third person trusted by both parties, in order to protect the lawful rights and interests of Qiao. Han also agrees to keep the money under his custody for Qiao's benefit.

The court reasons that a guardian has a duty to manage and protect the ward's property. However, where a guardian is unable to reasonably and efficiently manage the minor's property or might harm the minor's proprietary interests, or where a guardian is not competent owing to his own inability of managing the property, the guardian may voluntarily deliver the minor's property to a third person custodian in order to prevent a conflict of proprietary interests between the guardian and his ward. Where a custodian of a minor's property infringes upon the minor's property, the minor or his guardian may request the custodian to assume legal liability.

Finally, the court holds that Qiao's guardian has since changed from Uncle Qiao to his maternal grandparents Jiang & Meng. Uncle Qiao is ordered to deliver 300,000 yuan to Han as the custodian of Qiao's property until Qiao reaches 18.

§ 2:2:1:4 A Natural Person's Domicile

The domicile of a natural person is the place where the person is residing. According to the Chinese law, each natural person may only have one domicile. A person with limited or no capacity for performing civil juristic acts normally lives with his guardian, and the guardian's domicile is the domicile of the person. The proof of a natural person's domicile in China is the household registration certificate.① If a person has been habitually residing in a place other than his domicile, then the habitual residence is deemed as his domicile.

If a person left his domicile and has lived in a place, other than a hospital for treatment purpose, continuously for more than one year, that place would be deemed to be his domicile; if a person has moved out of the place which is recorded as his domicile in the household registration certificate, but has not moved into a new place and has not yet established a domicile, his domicile is still the place recorded on his original household registration certificate.② It is important to determine the domicile of a natural person because a person's domicile will help determine the status of the natural person as a person of the civil law, decide the place of repayment of his debts, determine the place where a marriage should be registered, or determine the applicable law if foreign elements are involved in a civil juristic relationship.

§ 2:2:1:5 A Natural Person's Missing by Law

Where a natural person has left his residence and cannot be located afterwards, his property will be left unattended and his obligations unperformed. Both his rights and interests, as well as the rights and interests of

---

① See Article 25 of the Civil Code.
② Article 9 of the Opinions on the GPCL.

the interested persons of his, are exposed as unprotected. In order to protect the interests of the missing person and the other interested persons and maintain the stability of social economic order, the Chinese civil law establishes a system by which a court may, upon request of an interested person of the person who cannot be located, declare the latter person as a missing person. Specifically, where a natural person has left his residence for a period exceeding two years, upon request of any interested person of his, a court may declare that the person has been missing if all legal requirements are satisfied. ①

In order to initiate such a proceeding, an interested person of the person who cannot be located must firstly prove that the person has actually been missing for two years, *i.e.*, the person's whereabouts are unknown after he has left his last known residence and the situation has continued on for over two years. If during wartime, the two-year period is to be counted from the day the war ends, or from the day as determined by the relevant authority. ② The interested persons may include his spouse, parents, children, siblings, grandparents, grandchildren, and other persons who have a civil juristic relationship with the person. After receiving the request, the court will post a public notice to look for the person for a certain period of time. If the person has not been found upon expiration of this period, the court will declare that the person is missing.

Once a person is declared missing, the court will designate a person to be the custodian of the missing person's property to help manage it. If the missing person has limited or no capacity for performing civil juristic acts, his guardian will be the custodian of his property. Otherwise, the custodian may be appointed from the spouse, parents, adult children, or other relatives or friends who have a close relationship with the missing person. ③ The relatives with a close relationship may include the siblings, grandparents, and grandchildren of the person. Such a custodian is obligated to manage the missing person's property and safeguard his proprietary interests, and will

---

① Articles 40 and 41 of the Civil Code.
② See Article 41 of the Civil Code.
③ See Articles 42 of the Civil Code.

claim the rights and clear off the debts for the missing person. For example, a custodian has a right to pay tax and repay other debts or support obligations out of the missing person's assets. The custodian also has an obligation to claim against the missing person's debtor and receive repayment therefrom on behalf of the missing person. A custodian has no right to conduct any activities out of this scope. If a custodian fails to perform the duties of custodian, infringes upon the proprietary rights or interests of the missing person, or if a custodian becomes incompetent to be a custodian, any interested person of the missing person may request the court to replace the custodian.① If any damage is caused to the property of the missing person owing to the custodian's intentional or grossly negligent act, the custodian is liable for compensation.②

If a person who has been declared missing reappears or is found, upon request of the missing person or any interested person of his, a court should revoke the declaration of his being missing.③ Upon revocation, the custodianship ends and the custodian should deliver the property back to the person declared missing and report to him the management and disposal of the property during the period of custody. The person who has been declared missing has no right to ask the custodian to return any expenses incurred during the period of custody as long as the custodian did not do it in bad faith.

§ 2:2:1:6 A Natural Person's Death by Law

A person may be declared dead if he cannot be located for four years, or for two years since the occurrence of an accidental event. If a person cannot be located as a result of an accidental event, and if a relevant authority certifies that it is impossible for such natural person to survive, the two-year requirement does not apply and the person may be declared dead right after the accident occurs.④ A person may be declared dead only by a court. The rationale behind the system of declaration of death of a natural person is similar to the rationale of the system of declaration of missing, but the legal requirements are different.

---

① See Article 44 of the Civil Code.
② See Article 43 of the Civil Code.
③ Article 45 of the Civil Code.
④ See Article 46 of the Civil Code.

The declaration of death of a person may only be made upon request of an interested person. The scope of the interested persons is the same as to those who may request a court to declare a person missing, including (a) his spouse; (b) his parents and children; (c) his siblings, grandparents, and grandchildren; and (d) any other person having a civil-law right and obligation relationship with the person.

After receiving the request, a court must, under the Civil Procedure Law, post a public notice in accordance with the special procedure to locate the person whose whereabouts are unknown for the legally specified period. Upon expiration of the notice period, if there is no information is heard about the person, the court may announce the declaration of his death. The date when the court makes a judgment declaring the death of a person is deemed as the date of death of the person. If a person is declared dead as a result of an accident, then the date of his death is the date when the accident occurs. ①

A declaration of death and a declaration of missing of a person are closely related because most times the person is firstly declared missing, and then declared dead. However, declaration of missing of a person is not the first step of declaration of death of the same person. No matter whether the person has already been declared missing, a qualified interested person may directly request the court to declare the person dead as long as the legal requirements for declaration of death are satisfied. Sometimes the interested persons disagree with each other regarding whether to request a court to declare the person missing or dead. If one such interested person requests the court to declare a person dead, whereas another interested person requests the court to declare the person missing, the court will declare the person dead if the conditions for declaration of death are satisfied. ②

Once a person is declared dead, the consequence will be as if the person had died naturally; therefore, the proprietary and personal relationships of the person with the others will be changed, *i.e.*, the person's estate will be inherited by his heirs and the person's creditors may ask the heirs to repay the debts. The purpose of the declaration of death is not to absolutely deprive the

---

① See Article 48 of the Civil Code.
② See Article 47 of the Civil Code.

person of his capacity as a person of the civil law; instead, it is to terminate the civil juristic relationship centered on the original domicile of the person who has been declared dead. Therefore, a person with full capacity for performing civil juristic acts, even if declared dead, can still independently conduct various civil activities.① However, if a person conceals the true information about the whereabouts of another person and causes the latter to be declared dead so as to obtain the latter's property, the former person not only needs to return the wrongfully obtained property, but also should make compensation for any loss thus caused.②

A declaration of death may be revoked if the person declared dead reappears or has been located. The court may revoke the declaration of death upon request of the person who has been declared dead, or any interested person of him.③ The sole condition for revocation of a declaration of death is that the person is still alive, and such a revocation can only be made by a court. If a declaration of death is revoked, the proprietary relationship must be resumed to its original status, *i.e.*, the property received through succession, gift, or through other ways must be returned to the person who was wrongfully declared dead. If the original property does not exist anymore, compensation should be paid instead, considering the value of the property received by the person, his ability of returning it, as well as the benefits thus received.④

However, a personal relationship, *e.g.*, a marital relationship, may not be automatically resumed after a declaration of death is revoked. If the spouse of a person declared dead is not remarried, the marriage relationship may automatically be resumed unless the spouse states in writing to the marriage registration authority that he or she decides not to resume the marriage. If the person's spouse has remarried, even if he or she has later on divorced after the remarriage or if the new spouse died after the remarriage, the original marital relationship between the person who has been declared dead and his original spouse cannot be automatically resumed after the declaration of death of the

---

① See Article 49 of the Civil Code.
② See Article 53 of the Civil Code.
③ See Article 50 of the Civil Code.
④ See Article 53 of the Civil Code.

person is revoked.① However, a parent-child relationship will be resumed unless the child of the person declared dead has been legally adopted by another person or persons during the period when the declaration of death is effective,② in which case the adoption relationship may not be dissolved unilaterally.

§ 2:2:2 Legal Persons

Legal person, also called "artificial person," "juridical person," or "juristic person," is one type of the persons of the civil law under the Civil Code, and is defined as an organization which has the capacity for enjoying civil-law rights and the capacity for performing civil juristic acts, and may independently bear civil liability according to law.③ The Civil Code categorizes legal persons into three types: for-profit legal persons, non-profit legal persons, and special legal persons. They are subject to various qualification requirements. East Co., for instance, is a typical for-profit legal person.

§ 2:2:2:1 Qualification of Legal Persons

A legal person must be duly established in accordance with law, must have its own entity name, organization, and domicile, and must have assets or funds which are necessary for them to be able to independently assuming liabilities.④

A Chinese legal person must be established according to Chinese law in order to be protected and must comply with the procedure and requirements provided by law for the establishment of a legal person. For example, the Corporation Law provides special procedures for establishing a corporation. If an entity intending to be a corporation fails to comply with these procedures, it will not be recognized or protected by law as a corporation. If a law requires a legal person to register or to be approved, an entity that fails to be so registered or so approved will not be protected by law as such a legal person.⑤ If, during

---

① See Article 51 of the Civil Code.
② See Article 52 of the Civil Code.
③ See Articles 57 and 59 of the Civil Code.
④ Articles 58 and 60 of the Civil Code.
⑤ See Article 58 of the Civil Code.

the term of existence of a legal person, there is any change in a registered matter of the legal person, it shall go through a registration for modification. ①

A legal person must have an entity name which would distinguish it from other legal persons. Upon establishment, a legal person is required to register its entity name. A legal person has a right to entity name and may sue or be sued in court in its own entity name.

A legal person must have an organization structure to enforce governance of the legal person. It controls the internal affairs of the legal person and deals with the external parties on behalf of the legal person. The different types of legal persons are required to have different organizational structures. For example, a joint-stock corporation limited by shares is required to establish a board of directors, whereas a small sized limited liability company is only required to have an executive director.

A legal person must have its domicile. The domicile of a legal person is the place where its principal business office is located. ② Having its own domicile will facilitate the legal person to perform its obligations and may also enable the State to supervise it. A legal person is required to open a bank account at its domicile. A legal person's domicile will be considered as the basis for determining a legal person's performance of debts, the jurisdiction of litigation involving the legal person, the place of liquidation of the legal person, or the place where legal documents and other legal pleadings against the legal person may be served. A legal person may also have one or more premises. A legal person's premise is different from its domicile in that a premise may be the domicile of the legal person, and may also be any other place where the legal person conducts production and operation.

A legal person must have assets or funds which are necessary for it to operate the business and assume liabilities. Having assets or funds enables a legal person to have the ability to exercise its civil-law rights and perform its civil-law duties, and is also a guarantee that a legal person may independently bear civil liability. A legal person must have independent assets, *i.e.*, assets which are independent from the assets of its investors and the other members of

---

① See Article 64 of the Civil Code.
② Article 63 of the Civil Code.

the organization. In this sense, the investors of a legal person are not liable for the legal person's debts beyond their capital contribution. The Chinese law imposes different capital requirements on different types of legal persons. For several decades, all enterprise-legal persons had been required to meet certain minimum capital requirements, which requirements were recently removed by the new corporate law. However, some business enterprises, such as banks or security firms, are still required to meet the requirement of a minimum amount of registered capital considering the nature of their business. The State agencies and many institutions or social organizations are not required to have minimum registered capital upon establishment because their assets and funds mainly come from financial budget or through donations from the public, or from the investment of its members.

A legal person must be able to independently bear civil liability. Civil liability is the adverse consequence that a person of the civil law may be held for owing to its violation or breach of its civil-law obligations. The investors or members of a legal person are not required to assume the full liability of the legal person; instead, the legal person bears unlimited liability to the extent of its own independent assets, whereas the investors or members of the legal person are only liable to the extent of their capital contribution.

§ 2:2:2:2 Categories of Legal Persons

Legal persons were categorized by the GPCL based on whether they were enterprises or not, since an enterprise legal person might conduct a wider range of business operations for making profits. The Civil Code has changed the way of categorization and distinguishes the legal persons based on whether they operate for profits. By the new standard, a legal person may be a for-profit legal person, a non-profit legal person, or a special legal person.

A for-profit legal person is actually an enterprise legal person established for the purpose of making profits and distributing the profits to its shareholders or capital contributors. A for-profit legal person must be registered upon establishment and may be a limited liability company, a joint stock company limited by shares, or an enterprise otherwise having the legal person status.① A

---

① See Article 76 – 78 of the Civil Code.

for-profit legal person engages in operational activities and must comply with laws and administrative regulations, observe commercial ethics, maintain the security of transactions, subject itself to the supervision of the government and the public, and assume social responsibilities. ①

A non-profit legal person is an organization established for public welfare or other non-profit purposes. A non-profit legal person may not conduct profitable activities or distribute any profit to its capital contributors, incorporators, or members. Non-profit legal persons include public institutions, social organizations, foundations, social service institutions, and the other organizations similar in nature.② Among the non-profit legal persons, public institutions are the legal persons engaging in nonprofit social public welfare activities,③ such as the legal persons engaging in press, publication, broadcasting, television, movie, education, or arts. Social organizations are the various organizations voluntarily organized by their members to engage in social public welfare, literature and arts, or academic research, such as a trade union or the women's union.④ Donation-funded foundations, social service institutions, or other institutions established with donated property for the purpose of public welfare also are non-profit legal persons. In addition, a religious site established in accordance with law to hold religious activities, e.g., a church, may also be registered as a non-profit donation-funded legal person as long as the legal requirements are met.⑤

The Civil Code also regulates some special types of legal persons that are neither for-profit nor non-profit in nature, which include State-organs, rural economic collectives, urban and rural cooperative economic organizations, and primary-level self-governing organizations.⑥ The State-organ legal persons were categorized as non-enterprise legal persons under the GPCL, but now has been re-categorized in the Civil Code as one type of special legal persons. Government agencies, including the various State government departments at

---

① See Article 86 of the Civil Code.
② See Article 87 of the Civil Code.
③ See Article 88 of the Civil Code.
④ See Article 90 of the Civil Code.
⑤ See Article 92 of the Civil Code.
⑥ See Article 96 of the Civil Code.

different levels with independent budgets are State-organ legal persons under the Civil Code.① They are organized according to law or administrative ordinances, with delegated power and are authorized to engage in the State administrative activities. A rural economic collective, an urban or rural economic cooperative, an urban residents' committee or a villagers' committee may also attain the status of a legal person if legal requirements are all met. The latter two committees are primary-level self-governing organizations.②

A legal person, just like a natural person, has the capacity for enjoying civil-law rights, and also has the capacity for performing civil juristic acts to perform its civil-law duties and obligations, and independently bears civil liability.③ However, a legal person's capacity for enjoying civil-law rights is different from that of a natural person in that a legal person may not enjoy those dignitary rights that cannot be detached from a natural person, such as the right to life and the right to health. A legal person's capacity for performing civil juristic acts is also restricted by laws and administrative regulations, as well as its charter and purpose. It starts upon establishment of the legal person and ends when the legal person is terminated.④

The law imposes different restrictions on different types of legal persons. For example, a for-profit legal person must have a complete organizational structure including a decision-making body, executive body, and supervisory board. However, a non-profit legal person is not required to have such a strict structure.

§ 2:2:2:3 Establishment and Operation of Legal Persons
Registration and Approval

A legal person is required to register with the registration authority upon establishment, alteration, and termination. Establishment of a legal person starts when the incorporators agree to establish it and register it with the government if the law so requires. The incorporators must formulate a charter, also called "articles of incorporation" or "articles of association," which is to

---

① See Article 97 of the Civil Code.
② See Articles 99-101 of the Civil Code.
③ See Article 57 of the Civil Code.
④ See Article 59 of the Civil Code.

be submitted for the registration of the legal person.① A charter is a written document providing the scope of activities, governance structure, and the rights and obligations of the members of the legal person. Generally, a for-profit legal person only needs to comply with the legal requirements for registration and file with the administrative department of industry and commerce, and does not need to be specially approved by any administrative agency. After a legal person is established, if there is any change to the recorded matters, a registration for alteration must be filed. Upon termination, the legal person needs to de-register it with the registration authority.②

A non-profit legal person may be established according to the Civil Code or a special law, and may or may not need to register upon establishment; and if registration is required, the registration authority is a department other than the administrative department of industry and commerce. A public institution legal person or a social organization legal person should register with the government unless the law does not so require. However, a State-organ legal person does not need to be registered.③ A non-profit legal person will mostly need governmental approval in order to be established.

Governing Structure

A for-profit legal person is required to establish a governing body, an executive body, and a supervisory body. The governing body has the authority to revise the articles of association, elect or replace members of the executive or supervisory body, and perform other responsibilities stipulated in the articles of association. The executive body has the authority to convene meetings of the governing body, decide on business and investment plans, establish internal management structure, and perform other responsibilities stipulated in the articles of association. The supervisory body has the authority to inspect the financial matters of the legal person, supervise the performance of duty by the members of the executive body and the senior management officers, and

---

① See Articles 77, 79 & 91 of the Civil Code.
② See Article 58 of the Civil Code.
③ See Article 58 of the Civil Code.

perform other responsibilities stipulated in the articles of association. ①

A legal person must have a legal representative who is a natural person designated by law or by its charter to be in charge of the legal person. A legal representative has the right to engage in civil activities on behalf of the legal person and is responsible for representing the legal person to conduct civil activities and sue or be sued in court on behalf of the legal person. A legal person is bound by the acts conducted by its legal representative in such capacity. ② The legal representative could be the chairman of the board of directors, the executive director, or the manager, as stipulated in its charter. ③ The legal representative of a for-profit legal person should be registered with the administration of industry and commerce for records.

A legal representative has duties to have the legal person be in strict compliance with the laws and regulations, and to protect the lawful operation of the legal person. A legal representative may be held liable for failing to perform such duties. If a legal representative causes damage to others while performing his responsibilities, the civil liability thus incurred shall be assumed by the legal person, except that the legal person has a right to indemnification against the legal representative who is at fault. ④

A non-profit legal person should also establish a decision-making body, an executive body, and a supervisory body, as well as a legal representative, and formulate a charter upon establishment. ⑤

Rights and Obligations of Capital Contributors

The capital contributors, also known as the investors or shareholders, of a for-profit legal person are shielded from unlimited liability, which means that they would assume the liability of the legal person only to the extent of their capital contribution. Therefore, the law imposes strict restrictions on the rights of the capital contributors. A capital contributor of a for-profit legal person

---

① See Articles 80 – 82 of the Civil Code.
② See Article 61 of the Civil Code.
③ Article 13 of the Corporation Law, which was promulgated by the NPC in 1993 and significantly revised on October 26, 2018. Also see Article 81 of the Civil Code.
④ See Article 62 of the Civil Code.
⑤ See Articles 91 and 93 of the Civil Code.

may not abuse his rights to harm the interests of the legal person or any other capital contributor; otherwise he is liable for compensating the loss caused by his abusive act to the legal person or the other capital contributor(s). Neither a capital contributor may misuse the legal person's independent status and his own limited liability status to harm the interests of the legal person's creditors to evade repayment of debts; otherwise the corporate veil will be pierced and the capital contributor is jointly and severally liable for the legal person's obligations.① The controlling capital contributors, actual controllers, directors, supervisors, and senior management officers of a for-profit legal person owe a duty of loyalty to the legal person and may not harm the legal person's interests by taking advantage of any affiliated relations, and shall compensate for any loss thus caused to the legal person.②

On the other hand, the law also grants the capital contributors of for-profit legal persons certain investor's rights. For instance, a capital contributor may request the court to revoke a resolution which is made at a meeting of the governing body or executive body of the legal person if the procedure for convening the meeting or the voting method adopted in the meeting is in violation of the laws, administrative regulations, or the legal person's articles of association, or, if the content of the resolution violates the articles of association. When doing so, the civil juristic relationship already formed between the legal person and a *bona fide* counterparty based on such a resolution may not be affected.③ Likewise, the donors of donation-funded legal persons have the similar rights.④

§ 2:2:2:4 Termination of Legal Persons

A legal person may be terminated if it is dissolved, declared bankrupt, or so required by law.⑤

A legal person may be dissolved if its governing body makes a resolution to dissolve it, the term stipulated in its articles of association expires, there exists

---

① See Article 83 of the Civil Code.
② See Article 84 of the Civil Code.
③ See Article 85 of the Civil Code.
④ See Article 94 of the Civil Code.
⑤ See Article 68 of the Civil Code.

any other cause for dissolution as is stipulated in its charter, or if it has been merged with another legal person or split into two or more legal persons. A legal person may also be dissolved if its business license or registration certificate is legally revoked, or the legal person has received an order of closure. ① Sometimes a legal person can be dissolved according to a special law. For instance, the shareholders holding 10% or more of the voting shares of a corporation may request the court to dissolve the legal person if there is a severe difficulty for the corporation to operate and the shareholders' interests will suffer huge loss if the corporation is not dissolved, and if there is no other alternative to solve the problem. The court may dissolve the corporation if there is sufficient evidence to support the shareholders' allegations. ② It is to be noted that the "severe difficulty for the corporation" does not necessarily mean that the corporation is facing financial difficulty, but may refer to the situation in which the shareholders or the management cannot reach consensus regarding the operation of the business.

A State-organ legal person is terminated when the State organ is closed, and its civil-law rights and obligations are both succeeded by the succeeding State-organ legal person; in the absence of a succeeding State organ, the said rights and obligations shall be succeeded by the State-organ legal person that has made the decision to close it. ③

Before its termination, a legal person must liquidate, inventory its assets, and clear up its debts, and cannot conduct any business activities during the liquidation period. Upon termination, a legal person must go to the registration authority to de-register the legal person and post a public notice. ④

The common law rule of "*cy pres*" has been adopted by the Chinese civil law when dealing with the termination of a non-profit legal person. Specifically, upon termination, a non-profit legal person established for the purpose of public welfare is not allowed to distribute the residual assets among its capital contributors, incorporators, or members. Instead, the residual assets should continue to be used for the purpose of public welfare, as is stipulated in

---

① See Article 69 of the Civil Code.
② See Articles 180 & 182 of the Corporation Law.
③ See Article 98 of the Civil Code.
④ See Article 68 – 73 of the Civil Code.

its charger or the resolution made by the governing body; where it is not possible to dispose of such residual assets in accordance with its charter or the resolution, the competent authority will direct the assets to be transferred to another legal person with the same or similar purposes and then make a public notice. ①

Case 6

Case 6: Contractual Disputes on Transfer of Land-Use Rights②

In 1993, A Co. signed a contract with B Co. regarding development of a lot of land. A Co. paid the land development fee according to the contract, but B Co. did not transfer the land-use right to A Co. as agreed. Later on, A Co. discovered that B Co. did not have authority to sign this contract and that the contract was invalid for violating mandatory provisions of law. In 2005, A Co. sued in court requesting the court to declare the above contract invalid and order B Co. to return the land development fee it received from A Co. along with the interests.

During the hearing, the defendant challenged A Co.'s standing to sue since A Co.'s business license had been revoked in 2003 owing to its failure of submission for annual inspection. However, A Co. had never formed a liquidation committee to liquidate the business. The court cited Article 36 of the GPCL which provided that a legal person's capacity for enjoying civil-law rights and capacity for performing civil juristic acts started upon establishment of the legal person, and ceased upon termination of it. Article 38 of the Administrative Rules on Registration of Corporations provides that a corporation is terminated upon approval by and de-registration with the registration authority. Since A Co. neither went through liquidation nor de-registered itself, it is not terminated, and therefore still has the capacity for enjoying civil-law rights and capacity for performing civil juristic acts. The court holds that A Co. has the standing to sue.

---

① See Article 95 of the Civil Code.
② See (2005) Min 1 Zhong Zi No. 104.

§2:2:3 Unincorporated Organizations

Unincorporated organizations are the third type of the persons of the civil law under the Chinese Civil Code.① An unincorporated organization is an organization which does not have the legal person status but may engage in civil activities in its own name in accordance with law. An unincorporated organization may be a sole proprietorship, a partnership, a professional service institution, or a similar organization that does not have the legal person status.② Unincorporated organizations must be registered, and must be approved by the relevant authority if so required by law.③ An unincorporated organization may designate one or more of its members to represent it to engage in civil activities, and all of its capital contributors would assume unlimited liability for its debts with exceptions provided by law.④

An unincorporated organization is dissolved if its term stipulated in its charter expires or any other cause for dissolution as stipulated in the charter occurs, the capital contributors or founders decide to dissolve it, or dissolution is required by law.⑤ An unincorporated organization must be liquidated upon dissolution.⑥

§2:3 Civil Law Rights

A civil-law right may be acquired by a person of the civil law through performance of a civil juristic act, the occurrence of an act *de facto*, the occurrence of an event as provided by law, or by other lawful means.⑦ A person of the civil law enjoys his civil-law rights according to his own will and in accordance with the Constitution, the Civil Code, and the other laws free from any interference.⑧ Since the rights and obligations go hand in hand, when exercising civil law rights, a person of the civil law must perform his

---

① See Articles 102–108 of the Civil Code.
② See Article 102 of the Civil Code.
③ See Article 103 of the Civil Code.
④ See Article 104 and 105 of the Civil Code.
⑤ See Article 106 of the Civil Code.
⑥ See Article 107 of the Civil Code.
⑦ Article 129 of the Civil Code.
⑧ Article 130 of the Civil Code.

obligations provided by law or agreed with the other persons.① No one may abuse his civil-law rights and harm the interests of the State, the public interest, or the lawful rights and interests of other persons.②

Chinese law also grants protection to the minors, the elderly, the disabled, the women, or the consumers because the rights and interests of these groups of persons are vulnerable. The Civil Code provides that any laws particularly granting protection to these special groups must be followed.③

§2:3:1 Categorization of Civil Law Rights

Civil-law rights may be categorized by different ways.

§2:3:1:1 Proprietary Rights, Personal Rights, and Hybrid Rights

Based on its nature, a civil-law right may be a proprietary right, a personal right, or a hybrid civil-law right.

A Proprietary Right

A proprietary right is a right of property interest which may be transferred, abandoned, or inherited. A proprietary right can be a real right or a right *in rem*, *i.e.*, a right to directly and exclusively control a specific property against third persons,④ or a right based on an obligation, the right-holder of which may only request a specific obligor to do or not to do a certain act. For instance, if a person intends to buy a cell phone from an online store, after he has made payment, he has a claim against the online seller and may bring a litigation against the seller if the seller fails to deliver the cell phone to him within the specified time limit. Such a claim is a right based on an obligation and may only be alleged against the specific seller. Once the person has received the cell phone, he becomes the owner of it and, as an owner, his right over the cell phone is a real right so that he may use the cell phone in any manner as he wishes.

The categories and contents of real rights are provided by law and may not

---

① Article 131 of the Civil Code.
② Article 132 of the Civil Code.
③ Article 128 of the Civil Code.
④ Article 114 of the Civil Code.

be created by any person or persons upon agreement. ① A real right consists of the ownership, the right to usufruct, and security interests in the property, ② and its object may be either immovable property or movable property, and sometimes a right may also be treated as property over which a real right lies. ③ Real rights are protected by law and may not be infringed upon by any individual or organization, except that immovable or movable property may be expropriated or requisitioned for public interest, and it must be done within the scope of authority and in compliance with the procedure provided by law. Fair and reasonable compensation should also be paid for the expropriation or requisition. ④

A right based on an obligation is a right *in personam* which may arise from a contract, a tortious act, a *negotiorum gestio*, or unjust enrichment. ⑤ The law protects the parties to a contract, so each party has a contractual right to request the other party to perform the contractual obligations. ⑥ Where a person's civil-law rights and interests are infringed upon due to a tortious act, he has a right to request the tortfeasor to bear tort liability. ⑦ If a person voluntarily manages another person's property to prevent losses without a statutory or contractual obligation, he has a right to request the benefitted person to reimburse the reasonable expenses he has incurred. ⑧ On the other hand, if a person obtain unjust interests at the expense of another person's loss without a legal cause, the person thus harmed is entitled to request the enriched person to make restitution. ⑨

A Personal Right

A personal right is an interest which cannot be detached from a right-holder's person. It may be a right of personality or a relation-based right.

---

① Article 116 of the Civil Code.
② Article 114 of the Civil Code.
③ Article 115 of the Civil Code.
④ Article 117 of the Civil Code.
⑤ Article 118 of the Civil Code.
⑥ Article 119 of the Civil Code.
⑦ Article 120 of the Civil Code.
⑧ Article 121 of the Civil Code.
⑨ Article 122 of the Civil Code.

The rights of personality include a natural person's right to life, right to corporeal integrity, right to health, right to name, right to likeness, right to reputation, right to honor, right to privacy, and right to marital autonomy. A legal person or an unincorporated organization also has certain rights of personality such as the right to entity name, the right to reputation, and the right to honor.① The rights of personality are provided in a separate Book in the Civil Code, and will be further discussed in § 2:3:2. A relation-based right is a right arising from a marital or familial relationship,② including, *inter alia*, a right of kinship and a right to support.

The Civil Code has also provided protection to a natural person's personal information and prohibits any organization or individual from illegally collecting, using, processing, or transmitting such information, or illegally trading, providing, or publicizing such information.③

A Hybrid Right

A hybrid civil-law right has the nature of both personal and proprietary rights, such as an intellectual property right, an investor's right, and the right to succession. Intellectual property rights are the exclusive rights enjoyed by the right holders over the following subject matters as provided in Article 123 of the Civil Code:

(1) works;

(2) inventions, new utility models, or appearance designs;

(3) trademarks;

(4) geographical indications;

(5) trade secrets;

(6) layout designs of integrated circuits;

(7) new plant varieties; and

(8) the other subject matters as provided by law.

---

① Article 110 of the Civil Code.
② Article 112 of the Civil Code.
③ Article 111 of the Civil Code.

The nature of such a right is both proprietary and personal in that the right-holder may directly and exclusively control the intellectual property he creates or owns, sell or license it for use to others, and also enjoy certain rights closely related to the person of the right-holder, such as the right of authorship. Therefore, it is a kind of hybrid right.

An investor's right may be a shareholder's right or a membership right in a corporation or other investor's rights as provided by law.① A right to succession is the right of a natural person to inherit a deceased person's estate in accordance with law, and also the right of a natural person to transfer his estate through succession upon his death.② Likewise, these rights also are hybrid rights because they are based on the right-holder's relation-based status, and also involve proprietary interests.

§ 2:3:1:2 Rights to Control, Rights to Claim, Rights to Defense, and Rights to Affect a Juristic Relationship

Based on its function, a civil-law right may be a right to control and domination, a right to claim, a right to defense, and a right to affect a juristic relationship by a unilateral action.

A right to control and domination is an absolute right, and the right-holder may directly and exclusively control the object of the civil juristic relationship and enjoy a certain benefit and interest out of it. A proprietary right, such as an ownership right, is a typical right to control and domination; an intellectual property right, right of personality, and a relation-based right may also be a right to control and domination.

A right to defense and a right to claim are two opposite rights: without the right to claim there is no right to defense. This pair of rights exist between specific parties where one party may request the other party to do or not to do a certain act whereas the other party may fight against or deny the first party's claim. A right to claim is not an absolute right against the whole world, but a right *in personom*, because it may only be claimed against a specific obligor. For example, in a contract for sale of dictionaries between West Co. and East

---

① Article 125 of the Civil Code.
② Article 124 of the Civil Code.

Co., if East Co. is not satisfied with the quality of the dictionaries delivered by West Co. and therefore refuses to make payment, West Co. has a right to claim against East Co. for non-payment, and East Co. may raise a defense against West Co. for delivering nonconforming goods.

A right to affect a juristic relationship by a unilateral action is a right that the right-holder may unilaterally cause a civil juristic relationship to change by his own will. For example, if a party has a legal right to offset a debt he owes to another party, he may offset the debt in his own initiative and does not need any other party's permission or assistance. Once the party who has a right to affect a juristic relationship by a unilateral action decides to do so and so communicates to the other party, the civil juristic relationship will be thus created, altered, or extinguished. However, this right normally co-exists with another substantive right and may not be detached from the latter right or be independently transferred. Since the exercise of this right may have a significant impact on the other party, the law provides a prescription period beyond which the right-holder loses this right. For instance, if a debtor transfers his property at an unreasonably low price to a third person and, as a result, his ability to repay his creditor has been adversely affected, the creditor may request the court to revoke the debtor's act of transferring his property to the third person if the third person knows or should have known of this situation.[①] Such a right to revocation is a typical right to affect a juristic relationship by a unilateral action and the creditor may exercise this right unilaterally. However, such a right must be exercised within one year from the date on which the creditor knows or should have known that there exists a cause for revocation, and the right to revocation will be extinguished if the creditor fails to exercise such right within five years since the date on which the debtor transfers his property to a third person.[②]

§ 2:3:1:3 Absolute Rights v. Relative Rights

Based on whether there is a specified obligor, and based on the characteristics of the right, a civil-law right may be an absolute right or a

---

① See Article 539 of the Civil Code.
② See Article 541 of the Civil Code.

relative right.

An absolute right is also called "a right against the whole world," including, *inter alia*, the ownership right, the right of personality, and intellectual property right. A right-holder may exercise an absolute right without asking for anyone's permission. A relative right is one only against a specific obligor, not against the whole world. It is also called "a right against a specific person." A right based on an obligation is a typical relative right and the creditor must take an initiative to enforce his right.

The main differences between an absolute right and a relative right firstly lie in that the right-holder of an absolute right is specific whereas the obligor is not specific; however, both the right-holder and the obligor of a relative right are specific. In addition, in a legal relationship based on an absolute right, the right-holder only has rights and no corresponding obligations; however, in a juristic relationship based on a relative right, both parties have rights and obligations corresponding to each other. When an absolute right is infringed upon, the remedy would be restitution, and compensation will be granted only if restitution is impossible or if the right-holder makes such a special request. However, if a relative right is infringed upon, the general remedy would be monetary damages the main purpose of which is to compensate for the loss suffered by the right-holder.

§ 2:3:1:4 Other Categories of Civil Law Rights

A civil-law right may be a primary right or a secondary right. A primary right is a right that exists independently from the other rights. For example, in a surety contract, the secured interest is a secondary right and the right arising from the underlying contract is the primary right. A civil-law right may also be categorized as an executed right or an executory right; the former referring to a right which has been fully realized and the latter a right that may be realized in the future. Generally, most rights are executed rights.

§ 2:3:2 The Rights of Personality

One of the significant features of the Chinese Civil Code is that it has a separate Book on the rights of personality, which may be more accurately described as the rights of human dignity. It is quite an innovation because few civil codes have ever given the personality rights such a high status. It is conceivable that there had been lots of debates, disagreements, and discussions on it among the members of the legislature and the legal scholars during the deliberation of the draft, since the GPCL and the other related civil laws have already provided protection to a person's personality rights. Actually, a provision has already been included in the General Part of the Civil Code which clearly provides that the personal liberty and dignity of a natural person is protected by law.① Ultimately, the Civil Code has its Book Four as "Personality Rights" which is the shortest Book therein, and it is composed of six chapters. The first chapter lists the general rules, and the other chapters each focuses on a different category of personality rights, which are to be discussed in the following sub-sections.

In addition to the personality rights already included in the GPCL, *i.e.*, the right to life, the right to health, the right to name, the right to honor, the right to reputation, and the right to likeness, *etc.*, the Civil Code has added a few new personality rights such as the right to privacy, the right to credit standing, and the right to personal information, to correspond to the new issues, and expanded the definition of the personality rights to include the other rights and interests arising from personal liberty and human dignity.②

As a general rule, a personality right is protected by law but may not be detached from the person of the right-holder; therefore, it may not be waived, transferred, or inherited.③ Some of the objects of personality rights may be used by others with authorization. For example, a person may allow a company to use his picture to advertise their products; however, if the company uses his picture without his consent or authorization, the company infringes upon his right to personality, and specifically, his right to likeness. When a personality right is harmed, the right-holder of such right has a standing to sue the actor for civil liability. Some of the personality rights, such as the right to name, likeness, reputation, honor, privacy, remains, *etc.*, will survive the right-holder. When one of these rights is harmed by others after the right-holder

---

① Article 109 of the Civil code.
② See Articles 989 – 1001 of the Civil Code.
③ Article 992 of the Civil Code.

dies, the spouse, children, parents, or the other close relatives of the right-holder may sue the actor to bear civil liability. It is to be noted that the limitation periods do not apply to a case involving infringement of one's personality rights when the remedy requested is cessation of infringement, removal of nuisances, elimination of the danger or adverse effects, rehabilitation of reputation, or extension of apology.

§ 2:3:2:1 Rights to Life, Rights to Corporeal Integrity, and Rights to Health

The first category of personality rights includes the right to life, the right to corporeal integrity, and the right to health. [1] A natural person's right to life refers to the right to his life safety and dignity, the right to corporeal integrity refers to the right to his body integrity and freedom of movement, and the right to health includes the right to both his physical and mental health. A natural person enjoys these rights free from infringement by any organization or individual; in case such a right is endangered, any organization or individual who has the legal obligation to aid must extend rescue without delay, and the right-holder whose right is infringed upon may sue the actor for civil liability.

Such a right may be harmed by sexual harassment, false imprisonment, illegal search, or any form of purchase or sale of human cells, tissues, organs, or remains, which are therefore prohibited by the Civil Code. The scope of sexual harassment, as provided by the Civil Code, includes the harassing activities done by using oral words, written languages, images, or physical acts, *etc.*, and the State organs, enterprises, schools, and other organizations have a duty to take reasonable precautions and remedial measures to prevent or stop such an act. In addition, there are rules regulating voluntary donation of one's cells, tissues, organs, and remains. Generally, no one may force or induce a person to donate his cells, tissues, organs, or remains, but a person with full capacity for performing civil juristic acts may voluntarily do so by expressing his intent in writing. If a person has not made such a decision during his life, can his relatives make such a decision for him upon his death? The answer given by the Civil Code is a conditional yes, and the conditions are that

---

[1] See Articles 1002 – 1011 of the Civil Code.

the person has not opposed such a decision before he dies, and that after he dies, his spouse, adult children, and parents jointly decide to make such a donation in writing.

There are also rules regulating clinical trial and medical and scientific research on human genes, embryos, *etc*. Such trials and researches must be examined and approved by the relevant authorities and the ethics committee, and written consent of the participants or their guardians must also be obtained. The purposes, methods, and possible risks of the trial must be fully disclosed to the participants and no fee may be collected from them. Any medical and scientific research relating to human genes, embryos, *etc*. must be done in accordance with law and may not endanger human health, offend ethics and morals, or harm public interest.

Article 1011 of the Civil Code provides that a person whose freedom of movement has been deprived of or restricted by illegal detention, or whose body has been illegally searched, has a right to request the actor to bear civil liability. One of the following two cases involves illegal search and the other involves infringement upon a person's right to life. The first case happened in the early 1990s, when supermarkets just started to appear in China and many people were still used to shopping in traditional retail stores. The second case was decided in a more recent year, but before the Civil Code was enacted.

Case 7

Case 7: Ni & Wang v. China International Trade Center[1]

H Supermarket in China International Trade Center adopted a new open-shelf sale approach and allowed the customers to bring their own bags in, but posted an announcement in front of the entrance door providing that the cashier was required to check the bags brought in by the customers and requesting the customers to cooperate.

On December 23, 1991 at about 5 pm, Ni and Wang went to H Supermarket for shopping. After they stopped for a while before a candy

---

[1] See the SPC Gazette, Issue 1, 1993.

counter, they bought a photo frame from another counter and then checked out. When they walked out of the market for about 5–6 meters, two male employees of the supermarket chased out and called them back, asking them whether they had taken any unpaid items out of the store. They answered no. The two men asked again: Did you take anything out? Did you actually take anything out? They answered no, again. The two employees brought them back to the entrance door of the store and pointed to an announcement posted on the wall, saying that they had a right to check their bags. Then they brought the two girls to the office of the store where another female employee also joined in the questioning. Ni burst into tears, and Wang opened her purse, unbuttoned her coat, and took off her hat to let the three employees to check. They did not find anything belonging to the store, and one of the male employees said that he heard one customer saying that they took something away. The employee said sorry to them, and finally released them. The two girls wanted to talk to their manager, but they said the manager was not in. The girls sued.

Chaoyang District Court of Beijing Municipality firstly analyzes the rights owned by the supermarket: "Right" is an act that a citizen or legal person may exercise and a certain benefit that a citizen or legal person may enjoy. No one has a right to perform an act if without legal basis or incompliance with the provisions of law. The law never grants to the employees of a supermarket a right to question the customers or examine the customers' property, therefore the supermarket did not have a right to post the announcement by which requesting the customers to open their bags for the employees of the market to check.

Article 101 of the GPCL provides that the citizens and legal persons enjoy the right to reputation, and the human dignity of the citizens is protected by law, and no one may harm the reputation of the citizens or legal persons through insultation, defamation, or the like ways. The reputation of a citizen refers to the social evaluation on a citizen's integrity, talents, prestige, and trustworthiness based on the citizen's work, life, speech, and the like. Human dignity refers to a citizen's self-knowledge and self-evaluation of the social status and social value of himself. The right to reputation is a right of personality and is closely related to a citizen's reputation and human dignity.

If the employees of the supermarket suspected that the two girls had stolen some stuff from the store, they should have submitted it to the legally designated authority for investigation in accordance with the legal procedure; however, they did not do so, and instead they stopped the plaintiffs before the public without clear evidence, and asked them whether they had taken unpaid items out of the store. Although the question was tactful, it was apparently derogatory. Such a question not only made the plaintiffs felt that their social status had been degraded, but also actually adversely affected their reputation. Then the employees based on the invalid announcement of the store brought the plaintiffs into their office to continue the questioning. Although it seems that the plaintiffs voluntarily opened their bag, unbuttoned their coat, and took off their hat to let the employees to check, the nature of the employees' act was actually a search against the customers. Such a search could only be done by a legally designated authority.

Since the acts of the employees of the supermarket have severely harmed the plaintiffs' right to reputation, so the plaintiffs have the right to request the individual defendants to stop infringement, remove adverse effect, extend an apology, and may also make a request for compensation. Article 43 of the GPCL provides that an enterprise legal person assumes civil liability for the operational activities conducted by its legal representative or other employees. Therefore, the tort liability of the employees should be assumed by the defendant legal person.

After the court has clarified the facts and points out the faults, the defendant voluntarily decides to extend an apology to the plaintiffs and compensate to each plaintiff 1,000 yuan for economic damage and pains and suffering, and requests the plaintiffs to drop the case. The plaintiffs accept the compensation and agree to settle the case, so they submit to the court an application for withdrawal. After examining the application, the court determines that the application for withdrawal complies with Article 131 of the Civil Procedure Law, and there is no need to continue the proceeding. The case is thus withdrawn.

Chapter 2　General Part of the Civil Code

Case 8

Case 8: Liu & Guos v. Sun and L Co.[①]

Q Guo and Liu were spouses with two daughters (Guos). They lived in a residential complex in Xinyang City, Henan Province.

On September 23, 2019, at about 7:40 pm, Q Guo rode a bicycle inside the complex and hit H Luo, a 5-year-old boy who also lived in the same complex. Witnessing this, another neighbor Sun went to check H Luo and tried to call H Luo's parents through WeChat but no one answered. Sun then asked the other neighbors hanging around nearby to notify H Luo's mother Li, meanwhile asked Q Guo to stay and wait until H Luo's parents came. Q Guo said it was H Luo who hit him, and that he had something to do and needed to leave. Therefore, Q Guo and Sun had some verbal confrontations, and then Sun stood in front of the bicycle to block Q Guo's way to prevent him from leaving the scene.

At about 7:46 pm, Sun dialed 110 to call the police. Q Guo parked his bike and sat on a stone block, but in less than 2 minutes he fell on the ground. At about 7:48, Sun dialed 120 to call ambulance. When medical personnel came and tried to rescue Q Guo, they discovered that Q Guo died of cardiac arrest. The police also came over and questioned the relevant witnesses, also questioned H Luo with his parents present, and then questioned Sun again.

Q Guo's widow Liu and his two daughters sued Sun and L Co., the property management company hired by the owners of the said complex.

The court identifies the nature of this case as a dispute over Q Guo's right to life and the main issue of this case as whether Sun and the L Co. should assume tort liability.

Evidence shows that on September 4, 2019, Q Guo was admitted into the Central Hospital of Xinyang City and diagnosed with heart diseases and various other illnesses. The hospital issued a notice of serious illness in which stating that the patient's situation was critical and it could be

---

① See (2019) Yu 1503 Min Chu No. 8878, reprinted in the SPC's Guiding Cases No. 142.

further deteriorated and may endanger his life at any time. Later on, Q Guo requested to be released from the hospital, and the hospital agreed after a superior physician was consulted with.

Article 6 of the Tort Liability Law provides that an actor who harms other's civil-law rights and interests shall assume tort liability. In order to determine whether Sun is liable in tort, it is necessary to analyze whether Sun did a tortious act by preventing Q Guo from leaving the scene, whether there was a causal link between Sun's act and the death of Q Guo, and whether Sun was at fault.

Firstly, the court reasons that H Luo was a minor and needed adults to give him special protection. When H Luo was hit and injured by Q Guo, Q Guo did not reasonably check him but wanted to leave. For such kind of act against the health and the other lawful rights and interest of a child, any organization and individual may intervene or report to the relevant authorities. In order to protect H Luo's interests, Sun asked Q Guo to wait until H Luo's mother came, and her act was not illegal but with just cause and was in line with the common sense. Based on the evidence, Sun blocked Q Guo for 8 minutes, and during this period, Sun's languages were not outrageous, and Sun did not have any physical contact with Q Guo but only put her hand on his bicycle. The way and manner of the blocking were within the necessary limit. Therefore, there is no evidence showing that Sun committed any tortious act.

Second, although Q Guo's death happened subsequently after Sun's blocking, Sun's blocking itself could not have caused Q Guo's death, and the real reason for his death was his heart disease. Evidence shows that Q Guo suffered from various diseases and was admitted into the hospital in the same month of the accident, and was released from the hospital one week prior to the accident. After Sun blocked Q Guo from leaving, he sat down on a stone stool, and then fell on the ground and died of a heart attack. His death was a tragedy, and it is understandable that his family members were sad and then decided to bring this litigation. However, Sun's act was not the legal cause for Q Guo's death.

Third, although Sun did not allow Q Guo to leave which might have caused Q Guo emotionally excited, Sun did not know Q Guo, and had no knowledge that he had various diseases. The purpose of Sun's act was to protect the child and she had no intent or negligence to infringe upon Q Guo's interests. After Q Guo fell on the ground, Sun immediately dialed 120 to rescue him. Thus, Sun could not have foreseen Q Guo's death, and was not at fault either.

Regarding L Co.'s liability, Article 82 of the Real Rights Law provides that the property management enterprise should manage the buildings and their affiliated facilities within the construction zone entrusted to it by the owners, and are subjected to the owners' supervision. In this case, the place where Q Guo and H Luo collided was in a square within the residential complex under the management of L Co. The occurrence of the accident was not caused by L Co.'s negligence, and two security guards of L Co. went to the scene to conciliate them after it happened, and had performed the corresponding management duties. Q Guo's death was not legally caused by L Co.'s failure of performing its duties.

The plaintiffs' claims were dismissed.

§ 2:3:2:2 Rights to Name and Rights to Entity Name

A natural person enjoys the right to name and a legal person or an unincorporated organization enjoys the right to entity name, these rights are protected as part of the personality rights and no one may infringe upon other's rights to name or entity name by ways of interference, misappropriation, impersonation, or the like means. ① A natural person's name may be changed or used by other people with authorization; provided, however, public order and good morals should not be offended. Similarly, an entity may use, change, transfer, or allow others to use its entity name in accordance with law. In addition, changing one's name or entity name may need to be registered with the relevant authority if so required by law. These protections are also extended to cover a pseudonym, stage name, screen name, translated name, trade name, abbreviation of a name or entity name of a social

---

① See Articles 1012 – 1017 of the Civil Code.

popularity.

A natural person normally takes the surname of his father or mother. There were a couple giving birth to a child in a hospital who were required to name their baby before the baby was released from the hospital. They took a surname unrelated to the surname of either of them to name the baby, but the hospital refused to register the surname. Had it happened today, there would not have had any problem since the Civil Code clearly provides that a natural person may take a surname other than his father's or mother's as long as doing so does not offend public order or good morals.

While the right to name or entity name is protected by law, the law also allows a person to authorize the other persons to use his name unless the authorization is prohibited by law or the nature of the right determines that no authorization of use should be allowed. [1] If the right to name of a deceased person is harmed, the surviving spouse, children, parents, or other close relatives of the deceased person may request the actor to bear civil liability. [2] These rules are also applicable to any infringement of a person's right to likeness, reputation, honor, privacy, or remains.

§ 2:3:2:3 Rights to Likeness

The right to likeness is one of the personality rights protected by the Civil Code. [3] The "likeness" of a natural person is defined as an external image of the person reflected in video recordings, sculptures, drawings, or on other media by which the person may be identified. A natural person may make, use, publicize or authorize others to use his image in accordance with law, but no one may infringe upon other's rights to likeness by vilifying or defacing other's image, or make, use, or publicize the image of the right-holder without authorization. Nevertheless, the Civil Code provides five exceptional situations where a person's likeness may be used without authorization, including the use of a publicly available image of others for personal study, teaching and researching purposes, the use of an image of others for news reporting

---

[1] Article 993 of the Civil Code.
[2] Article 994 of the Civil Code.
[3] See Articles 1018 – 1023 of the Civil Code.

purposes, the use of the image by a State organ in performing its responsibilities, the use of other's image for demonstrating a specific public environment, or the use of other's image for protection of the public interest and the interests of the right-holder himself.

If a person's photo is lawfully kept by another person, can the latter person freely publish the photo? The rule is no, unless consent of the former person is obtained. In this situation, the former person holds the right to likeness over the photo, and the latter person holds an interest in the photo. The latter person is prohibited from publishing, duplicating, distributing, leasing, or exhibiting it without authorization of the holder of the right to likeness over the photo.

Can a hospital use a patient's photo to advertise its business? The following case involves such a circumstance.

Case 9

Case 9: Ye v. Anzhen Hospital, et al[①]

Ye was treated in X medical center for the bluish black marks on her face with good efficacy. In October 2001, she found an ad printed on the Beijing Tour Map advertising for Anzhen Hospital. The ad used Ye's facial pictures before and after the operation to advertise its business. After investigation, she found that her pictures had been printed on the map for more than a dozen times, and based on the information printed on the map, each edition of the map had been printed in 500,000 copies. Ye sued Anzhen Hospital, the publisher of the map, and the advertising company that designed the ad, requesting them to immediately stop infringement, remove adverse effect, extend an apology, and compensate 100,000 yuan for her loss.

The court identified the nature of this case as a dispute involving the right to likeness. After comparing the original pictures of Ye with the pictures used in the ad, the court was convinced that the pictures used in

---

① See the SPC Gazette, Issue 6, 2003.

the ad were the pictures of Ye.

The defendants did not challenge that the pictures they used on the map were Ye's pictures, but Anzhen Hospital alleged that the pictures only showed a part of Ye's face, and that the other part above her eyes were covered so that the images could not be recognized as Ye's. Furthermore, the ad only occupied a very small part of the map and it would not bring about severe impact on Ye. It also argued that the hospital had not gained any benefit from using the pictures, and therefore had not infringed upon Ye's right to her likeness. The publisher claimed that it was qualified to publish advertisements. The pictures published would not make the public to recognize the original person of the image, and the publisher performed its duty to examine the ad and there was no infringement upon Ye's right to likeness.

The court cited Article 100 of the GPCL which provided that citizens had the right to likeness and no one might use other's likeness for business purposes without authorization of the right-holder. The court also cited Article 120, which provided that a citizen whose right to name, right to likeness, right to reputation, or right to honor had been infringed upon might request the tortfeasor to stop infringement, restore his reputation, remove adverse effect, extend an apology, and compensate for his losses.

The court reasoned that the right to likeness was based on the image of citizens. Likeness referred to the portrait, picture, or the like of a person which might be formed through drawing, photographing, carving, recording, filming, or other artistic means to reflect the natural person's facial features. The likeness of a person was independent from the original person and was a complete, clear, visual, straight-forward, and identifiable representation of the original image so that the original person might be identified. If the image did not represent the comprehensive features of the original person so that the public might not recognize that it indicated a specific person or could not connect it with a specific person, it was not a likeness protected by law. If the picture could only be recognized or connected with a specific person by using high-tech means, then it was not the natural person's likeness. Under this circumstance, the natural person was only the original person in the picture, but not the one holding the right to likeness.

The court thus dismissed the case and requested Ye to pay the litigation cost of 80 yuan. Ye appealed.

On appeal, Beijing No. 2 Intermediate People's Court reasons that a picture showing part of a natural person's facial impression does not represent the features of the likeness of the natural person, neither does it constitute a likeness itself. Therefore, Ye's claim that the defendants infringed upon her right to likeness cannot be supported. The lower court's decision is affirmed, and Ye is requested to also pay the litigation cost of 80 yuan for the appeal.

§ 2:3:2:4 Rights to Reputation and Rights to Honor

A person's right to reputation is protected by law and no one may infringe upon other's right to reputation by insultation, defamation, or the like.① "Reputation" is defined as a social evaluation of the moral character, prestige, talent, and credit of a person of the civil law.

The Chinese law grants special protections to some persons and exempts their liabilities if they harm other's reputation when engaging in news reporting or supervising public opinions for the public interest, on the condition that the facts are not fabricated or distorted and they have verified the information in a reasonable manner. In addition, the language used may not be insulting or defame other's reputation. Nevertheless, if a person's right to reputation is harmed by news reporting, the person has a right to request the media to make corrections, delete the content, or adopt other measures in a timely manner. Otherwise the actor should assume liability.

In recent decades, there have appeared some fiction or non-fiction works which are sued by persons who believe that their rights of reputation have been harmed by them. The Civil Code distinguishes the works depicting real people and real events or one or more specific persons, and the works telling a story with only a part of it similar to the situation of a specific person. In the latter situation, the writer has no liability, whereas in the former situation, the

---

① See Articles 1024 – 1031 of the Civil Code.

writer is liable if the content is insulting or defamatory.

The right to credit standing is also recognized as one type of right to reputation in the Civil Code. A person has a right to check his own credit report and may raise objections and request correction, deletion, or other measures to be taken if he founds that his credit report is incorrect. Otherwise, the evaluators should assume liability. The right to honor is also a type of personality right that a person of the civil law may enjoy. Generally, the honorary title would be awarded and recorded by the State or the government at various levels, and it is protected by law.

In an era of internet, a person's reputation can be more easily harmed by the information posted on the internet, and because of its speed of spreading, the effect could be more severe. Therefore, the law on this subject has to be developed to respond to the new issues. Case 10 illustrates how a person's reputation was harmed by means of sending WeChat messages, and case 11 is a case involving infringement of a deceased person's right to reputation and right to honor.

Case 10

Case 10: L Co. & Huang v. Zhao[①]

L Co. owns a beauty shop in a residential complex named Fangtang in Shunyi District, Beijing Municipality. Huang is the shareholder and beautician, working in the shop. On January 17, 2017 at about 4 pm, Zhao, a resident living in Fangtang Complex accompanied her neighbor Xu to the beauty shop to do a facial. While Huang was servicing Xu, Zhao sat on a couch chatting with Huang about the freckle removing she did in the shop before. Somehow Zhao and Huang had some verbal confrontations on the service provided, and Zhao overturned a box on the table, with the items inside the box fell scattered. Huang called the police, and Zhao again overturned a cart and planned to leave. Huang grabbed her preventing her from leaving so that two of them fought

---

① See (2018) Jing 03 Min Zhong No. 725, reprinted in the SPC's Guiding Cases No. 143.

against each other until a male friend of Zhao came to separate them. Afterwards, the police arrived and took pictures of the scene. Huang went to see doctor and incurred 165 yuan for medical examination.

The police tried to mediate but failed. Later the police made a decision imposing administrative penalty on Zhao in accordance with law, and detained her for 3 days, from March 13 to 16, 2017.

Back to the day the incident occurred, right after the incident, someone posted several messages in a couple WeChat groups mainly composed of residents of Fangtang Complex. Based on the screenshots provided by Huang, in one of the WeChat groups, a member whose screen name was LengjingJunzhu posted a picture of the beauty shop with comments saying that Huang defrauded the customers, had mental problems, and pretended to be crazy, *etc*. Other members of the group asked what happened; in another neighbors' WeChat group, LengjingJunzhu posed a similar picture and comments. One of these two WeChat groups was organized by Zhao with 345 members, and the other was organized by the boss of the Complex's supermarket with 123 members. After the incident, Zhao de-friended Huang as a WeChat contact and removed Huang out of the WeChat group so that Huang could not receive messages anymore, but one of Huang's friends captured the relevant screenshots and sent them to Huang. Nevertheless, Zhao denied that she ever posted anything in the WeChat groups and denied that she was LengjingJunzhu.

Evidence shows that owing to Zhao's acts, the beauty shop could not operate normally between January 17, 2017 and March 17, 2017. Huang and L Co. sued Zhao.

Upon investigation with Shenzhen Tencent Co., the court found that the aforementioned WeChat screen name that sent messages defaming Huang belonged to Zhao, and that Zhao and Huang added each other as WeChat friends on March 4, 2016. Zhao admitted that the WeChat screen name was hers, but she no longer used it so she did not know who posted the messages about Huang and L Co.

The court reasoned that any citizen or legal person had the right to reputation, and a citizen's human dignity was protected by law, and no one might harm any citizen or legal person's reputation through insultation, defamation, or by other means. In this case, Zhao denied that the information sent in her WeChat screenname was sent by herself, but did not present any evidence to prove that. Therefore, the court determined that it was Zhao who published the aforementioned messages in the residents' WeChat groups and posted Huang's picture, used defamatory language on Huang and her beauty shop after the confrontations with Huang occurred on January 17, 2017. Neither did Zhao provide any evidence proving that the information she posted was true. Zhao subjectively had fault by publishing the inappropriate statements in the WeChat groups with numerous residents living in the residential complex so that these statements were spread. From the fact that the other group members had asked for further information, and considering the fact that information could be spread more conveniently and quickly through internet, the statements posted by Zhao could easily arouse conjecture and misunderstanding on Huang and her beauty shop, which resulted in adverse effect and degradation of their social evaluation. Therefore, Zhao's act infringed upon the right to reputation of Huang and L Co. and Zhao should assume tort liability.

The court thus held that (1) Zhao should post a statement, within 7 days after the judgment became effective, to extend an apology to Huang and L Co. on the beauty shop's entrance for 7 days, and the content of apology must be reviewed and approved by the court; if Zhao failed to do so, the court would post this judgment in front of the beauty shop's entrance; (2) Zhao must compensate L Co. 3,000 yuan's economic loss within 7 days after the judgement became effective; (3) Zhao should compensate Huang 2,000 yuan for pains and suffering; (4) the other requests of Huang and L Co. were dismissed.

Zhao appealed.

On appeal, Beijing No.3 Intermediate People's Court confirms the facts determined by the lower court, and affirms the lower court's judgment. Zhao should pay the litigation cost of 50 yuan for the appeal.

Case 11

Case 11: Peng v. *China Story* Magazine①

China Story is a bimonthly magazine mainly publishing fictions. In its Fourth Issue in 1998, it published a fiction *Huo Sui* written by Zhou Huang, which narrated a mega fraud case happened in Shanghai in 1928. In this fiction, General Peng Jiazhen was described as a negative character who had improper relationship with other women. Based on the records, the magazine conducted an initial review, a second review, and the last review on the fiction and the results of all three reviews were "publishable."

In October 2000, the magazine received faxes sent by the committee of the temple honoring General Peng Jiazhen and four relatives of Peng regarding the fiction's infringement of Peng's reputation. The magazine immediately requested the editor in charge to contact the author and responded to Peng's relatives that they were dealing with the problem. In early November, the magazine sent employees to Tianjin and Chengdu to verify the facts with the author and the relatives of Peng to know that the author Zhou Huang already died, and that there existed severe false information in the fiction. The magazine suspended the responsible person's work for further investigation, published an apology in the relevant media, and promised to publish a special article about the story of General Peng who died for the nation to correct the misunderstandings, if any.

However, unbeknownst to the magazine, General Peng's sister Peng Jiahui was still alive who brought a litigation against the magazine in July 2001. The magazine immediately sent an employee to Peng Jiahui's residence to visit and extend an apology.

The first instant court held that the magazine should pay 50,000 yuan for Peng Jiahui's mental distress. Both parties appealed.

One of the magazine's defenses was that the limitation period had run

---

① See SPC Gazette, Issue 6, 2002.

out when the litigation was brought up. Article 135 of the GPCL provided a two-year limitation period for protection of civil-law rights. Article 137 provided that the limitation periods started from the time the person knew or should have known that his right had been infringed upon.

The Fourth Issue of *China Story* in 1998 was formally published on July 1, 1998 in Chengdu, Sichuan Province; however, both its influence and scope of the publication were limited. Therefore, it was not reasonable to assume all social public should have known about the content of the fiction after its publication. To this end, the commencement of the limitation period should not start from the time the magazine was published. Peng Jiahui presented evidence showing that she learned about the content of the fiction *Huo Sui* only after her relative received a letter from a reader of the fiction in April 2000, and the magazine did not present any evidence proving that Peng Jiahui had learned about the fiction earlier than July 1999. Considering that Peng Jiahui was then over 90 years old and was illiterate, her claim was more trustworthy. After consulting with the magazine but without getting a satisfactory result, Peng Jiahui brought the litigation in July 2001, which fell within the limitation period provided by law.

While the case was pending appeal, Peng Jiahui died in April 2002, and the High People's Court of Sichuan Province ruled that the litigation be pending according to Article 136 of the Civil Procedure Law, and the case resumed after five of Peng Jiahui's children decided to join the litigation. Finally, the court holds that the magazine should compensate 50,000 yuan for Peng Jiahui's mental distress and other consequential costs, plus the litigation costs.

(Note that the Civil Code has expanded the limitation periods from 2 years to 3 years. [1])

§ 2:3:2:5 Rights to Privacy and Protection of Personal Information

The right to privacy refers to a right to enjoy an undisturbed private life, private space, private activities, and private information that a person does not

---

[1] See Article 188 of the Civil Code.

want to be known to others. No one may pry into, intrude upon, disclose, or publicize other's private matters.① The acts listed by law that may infringe upon other's rights to privacy include disturbing other's private life through making phone calls, sending text messages, using instant messaging tools, sending emails and flyers; entering into or taking photos of other's private space or body, eavesdropping or disclosing the private matters of others, or processing other's private information.

With the development of internet, a person's personal information could be more easily accessed and spread. The Civil Code expands its protection to the personal information and defines it as the information of a person, such as a person's name, date of birth, identification number, biometric information, residential address, telephone number, email address, health information, whereabouts, *etc.* that can be used to identify a natural person. There are also exceptions. The personal information may be used if the consent of the person involved has been obtained, or if it is used for protection of the public interest or the person's own lawful rights and interests. It may be okay to process in a reasonable manner the information disclosed by the natural person himself or the other information that has already been legally disclosed, unless expressly refused or objected by the person concerned, or if the processing of the information infringes upon a significant interest of the person.

Does the law protect a person from being exposed on the internet by another person's posting of a video which recorded the incident during which she was beaten by her husband? Does the law protect her husband from being so exposed? On the other hand, does the law protect a person's constitutional right to free speech by posting such a video on the internet? Are there any differences between a right to reputation and a right to human dignity, or between a right to reputation and a right to privacy? A recent case demonstrates these interesting points.

---

① See Articles 1032 – 1039 of the Civil Code.

Case 12

Case 12: Lin & Chen v. Cai[①]

Lin and Chen are spouses. On June 2, 2016, Lin and Chen had a quarrel and Lin slapped in Chen's face in front of a Shigong Temple. Seeing this, Cai, a passer-by, recorded the confrontation by his cell phone. Lin and Chen requested Cai to delete the video but was refused, and later the video was posted on the internet. The video did not take any technical measures to cover Chen's face, so they reported to police in the evening of June 3, 2016. Cai wrote a statement before the police, agreeing to delete the video to prevent it from being further spread. However, this video was broadcasted by the public channel of Anhui Province on June 25, 2016 under the title of "Real Shot of A Woman Slapped by Her Boyfriend," with over 61,934,000 hits. Lin and Chen sued Cai.

The court identifies the nature of this case as a dispute on natural persons' general rights of personality, and points out that this case actually demonstrates the tension between citizens' right to human dignity and the right to free speech.

The court reasons that citizens' human dignity and the freedom of speech are equally protected by law; however, the exercise of the rights must be within the scope of law. The law prohibits any right-holder from harming the lawful rights and interests of the other persons of the civil law while exercising their own rights.

In this case, Lin slapped in his wife's face by force in a public space and his act was illegal and infringed upon Chen's right of personality. When recording and publishing Lin's illegal act, Cai was exercising his right to free speech. However, Chen's right of personality had already been harmed by her husband's slapping her face in public, Cai's act had apparently further expanded the adverse impact on her right of personality and brought severe emotional distress on her. Cai's act

---

[①] See (2016) Yue 0512 Min Chu No. 217, reprinted in the SPC Gazette, Issue 11, 2020.

exceeded the necessary limit for him to exercise the right to free speech, and infringed upon Chen's right to human dignity. Therefore, Cai should assume the corresponding tort liability.

Chen alleged that Cai's act also infringed upon her right to reputation. The court reasons that reputation is a comprehensive evaluation of a citizen or legal person's integrity, prestige, image, and the like. A person's right to reputation is harmed if the actor insults or defames her reputation, and as a result, her social evaluation has been degraded. To the contrary, human dignity is the least social status that a person is entitled to and the least respect a person deserves from the society and the other persons. An act infringing upon other's right to reputation may harm a citizen's human dignity to a certain extent, but an act infringing upon a citizen's human dignity may not necessarily cause the victim's social evaluation to be degraded. Chen did not provide evidence proving that Cai's act had degraded her social evaluation, and Cai's act was not one of insulting or defamatory. Therefore, Chen's claim that Cai had infringed upon her right to reputation is untenable.

Lin also alleged that Cai infringed upon his lawful rights and interests. The court reasons that Lin's act of using force to insult others in a public place is illegal *per se* and is prohibited by law, and that Cai's publication of Lin's illegal act was an appropriate way to exercise his right to free speech. Furthermore, the video only showed Lin's back, and people may not be able to recognize that it was Lin who did the act; therefore, Cai's act did not infringe upon Lin's lawful rights and interests.

The court further reasons that an actor who infringes upon other's civil-law rights and interests should bear tort liability. A person whose right to dignity is infringed upon may request the actor to stop infringement, eliminate the adverse effect, extend an apology, and may also request compensatory damages. Cai published the video on the internet which had been broadcasted by the public channel, and the video was still in the Anhui Satellite TV channel. Cai had a duty to notify Anhui Satellite TV to delete the said video. Chen requested Cai to extend an apology, and the court concludes that such a request is reasonable. The way of extending an apology should be commensurate with the scope of the adverse impact. The court holds that Cai should extend an apology in writing and the content of the apology should be reviewed and approved by the court. Since Cai's act has caused emotional distress to Chen, it is also appropriate for Chen to request compensation for pains and suffering. Chen requested 20,000 yuan's compensation. Considering the scope of infringement, the impact and the degree of fault, the court determines that the compensation for Chen's pains and suffering should be 1,000 yuan.

Finally, the court holds that within 10 days after the judgment becomes effective, Cai should notify the public channel of Anhui TV station to delete the video concerned, and submit a letter of apology to Chen through the court, and the content of the letter should be approved by the court. If Cai fails to do so, the court will designate a nationally published newspaper or magazine to publish the main content of this judgment, with the expenses to be borne by Cai. In addition, Cai should compensate Chen 1,000 yuan for her pains and suffering. The other claims of Chen and the claims of Lin are dismissed. The litigation cost of 100 yuan should be paid by Cai.

It is to be noted that this case was decided prior to the enactment of the Civil Code when there were no systematic regulations on the personality rights. Based on the Civil Code, both the right to human dignity and the right to reputation are personality rights.

§ 2:3:2:6 Remedies and Liabilities

A person whose personality rights are infringed upon is entitled not only to compensatory damages, but also pains and suffering if he suffers severe mental distress as a result of the infringement. Even if such a person elects to request the tortfeasor to bear liability based on breach of contract, Chinese law allows him to claim for pains and suffering in addition to the compensatory damages. [1] Sometimes a person may want to enjoin an actor from committing an illegal act that infringes or will infringe upon his dignitary rights, he may

---

[1] Article 996 of the Civil Code.

request the court to order the actor to stop the act if he can prove that failure to timely stop the act will cause irreparable harm to his lawful rights and interests. ①

When determining the civil liability an actor is to bear for infringing upon other's personality rights, the court will consider the occupations of the actor and the injured person, the scope of impact of the act, the degree of fault of the actor, and the factors such as the purposes, methods, and consequences of the act. This rule does not apply to the situation where an actor infringes upon other's right to life, right to corporeal integrity, or the right to health. ② If an actor shall bear civil liability such as elimination of adverse effects, rehabilitation of reputation, or extension of apology for infringing upon other's personality rights, the liability must be commensurate with the specific way the act is done and the scope of its impact. ③ If the actor refuses to bear the above civil liabilities, the court may make an announcement or publish the final judgment through newspapers, periodicals, or online websites and any expense thus incurred should be borne by the actor. ④

As mentioned earlier, the Civil Code has provided some special protections to the persons who infringe upon other's personality rights. For example, the name, entity name, likeness, or personal information of a person of the civil law may be reasonably used by those who are engaged in news reporting, supervision of public opinions, or similar conducts for the public interest. However, these uses must not unreasonably harm the personality rights of the person, otherwise the actor or actors must still bear civil liability. ⑤

§ 2:4 Juristic Acts

§ 2:4:1 Juridically Significant Facts

Juridically significant facts (also called "legal facts") refer to the objective facts to which legislation attaches legal consequences. A juridically

---

① Article 997 of the Civil Code.
② Article 998 of the Civil Code.
③ Article 1000 of the Civil Code.
④ Article 1000 of the Civil Code.
⑤ Article 999 of the Civil Code.

significant fact may cause the creation, alteration, or termination of a civil juristic relationship. Sometimes two or more judicially significant facts are working together to bring about the expected legal consequence, but other times one such fact is sufficient. A juridically significant fact may be an event or act.

An event refers to a natural event, *i.e.*, an objective phenomenon that does not involve any human being's will but may cause a legal consequence. For example, a person's death is such an event and it brings about the consequence that the decedent's heirs since then obtain the right to inherit the decedent's estate. An act, to the contrary, is an activity conducted and controlled by human being, which may be either a behavior or a juristic act. A behavior is an act unrelated to human being's subjective will, such as finding a lost property; whereas a juristic act is an act aimed to create, alter, or terminate a civil juristic relationship.① The fundamental difference between a behavior and a juristic act is whether the party has made an expression of intent and whether this expression has a binding effect.

§ 2:4:2 Juristic Acts

Juristic acts are the most important juridically significant facts. A juristic act must be purported to bring about a legal consequence, which includes the creation, alteration, or termination of a civil juristic relationship and the consequence must be anticipated by the parties.②

When a person of the civil law, through conducting a juristic act, creates or forms a certain relationship in law so that the parties to such relationship may exercise civil-law rights and must perform civil-law obligations thereunder, a civil juristic relationship is said to be created. A juristic act is effective upon its completion and once the juristic act is completed, it cannot be changed or revoked without authorization unless done in compliance with law or as consented to by the other party.③ When a person of the civil law decides to change the content of an existing civil juristic relationship and has actually done

---

① Article 133 of the Civil Code.
② Article 133 of the Civil Code.
③ Article 136 of the Civil Code.

so, the juristic relationship is said to be altered. If the alteration is so significant and actually terminates the original juristic relationship and creates a new relationship, then the juristic relationship is said to be terminated.

Signing a contract is such a juristic act. For instance, after negotiation, West Co. and East Co. decides to sign a contract for sale of 100,000 E-books. Upon both parties' execution of the sales contract, a contractual relationship is created between West Co. and East Co.. Afterwards, if East Co. decides to purchase 2,000 more of the dictionaries, it may not unilaterally change the contract term, but may only do so after obtaining West Co.'s consent. Upon consent of the West Co., they may modify the quantity term of the contract, and thus alter the contractual relationship. In addition, either company may decide to terminate the contract according to law or according to the contract, in which case the contractual relationship between them will be terminated.

A juristic act must be done by a person of the civil law, so an act such as making a judgment or arbitral award by a court or an arbitration tribunal is not a juristic act. A juristic act must be lawful to be protected, and it will be invalid if it violates the mandatory provisions of law or administrative regulations. Juristic acts may be categorized in different ways.

§ 2:4:2:1 Categorization of Juristic acts

A juristic act may be a unilateral act, a bilateral act, or a common act. ① A unilateral act may be done by one party's expression of intent and a bilateral act requires two parties to have a meeting of minds, whereas a common act, which is also called a concord act, requires the meeting of three or more minds. A unilateral act sometimes only involves one person's right. For example, when Mr. White buys a new cell phone and decides to throw away his old cell phone, as the right-holder of the old cellphone, he is actually abandoning a property he owns. Such an act is a unilateral one and it will only bring about a consequence to himself. However, other times, a unilateral act may also affect another person's right. For example, Mr. White writes a will under which he decides to give all his estate to his mother. Such an act will affect not only himself, but also the other persons including at least his mother and the other

---

① Article 134 of the Civil Code.

heirs of his. Granting authority to an agent, revoking an agency relationship, granting a right of disposition of property to another person, making a will, abandoning a right to succession, and exercising a right to rescind a contract are all unilateral acts, but they will affect the creation, alteration, or extinguishment of another person's rights. A bilateral act can only be done when two parties have a meeting of minds, but when conducting a common act, the parties are pursuing a common interest and the expression of the common will needs to observe the procedure specially provided by law. When Mr. White represents West Co. to sign a sales contract with Ms. Zhang, the legal representative of East Co., the act of making such a contract is a typical form of a bilateral act. If West Co., East Co., and South Co. decide to form a joint venture company in China engaging in the production and sales of the E-Books, the formulation of the articles of association (also called articles of incorporation) of the joint venture is a typical example of a common act.

Based on whether the parties need to exchange considerations, a juristic act may be a gratuitous act or a non-gratuitous act. A non-gratuitous juristic act requires one party to confer certain interests to the other party through performing the duty provided by law, and the other party should pay consideration in order to receive this interest. It is a typical legal form for exchange of commodities. In practice, most juristic acts reflecting transactional relationships are non-gratuitous acts. A gratuitous juristic act does not require the party that receives interests to pay any consideration in return. For instance, Mr. White decides to donate 100,000 yuan to support a Chinese girl from a remote mountain area to go to college, such an act of gifting is a typical gratuitous juristic act.

A juristic act may be effectuated by making promises or by performance. If one party's expression of intent (promise), once consented to by the other party, immediately brings about a legal consequence, the act is effectuated by the promises. When the parties have a meeting of minds, but the legal consequence will not be brought about unless the subject matter is delivered or performed, then the act is to be effectuated by performance. Thus, in the previous examples, the contract for sale of the E-books between West Co. and East Co. is a juristic act effectuated by making promises, and it becomes valid right after both parties sign the contract; whereas the donation made by Mr.

White to the child from a poor family normally is a juristic act effectuated only by performance, and will not be effective unless after Mr. White has actually delivered the money to the child.

A juristic act may be one with form requirement or one without form requirement based on whether the act must be conducted in a certain way. A juristic act with form requirement is an act that should be conducted in a way as required by law or agreed upon by the parties. For example, a mortgage contract must be registered in order to be effective against a third person, and signing such a contract is an act with form requirement and consequently, the contract will only be effective upon being registered. For a juristic act without form requirement, the parties are not required by law to adopt any specific form, so the parties may conduct it orally, in a written form, or by any other means. ①

Based on the relationship between the juristic acts, an act may be a primary juristic act or a secondary juristic act. A primary juristic act is one that may independently exist, while a secondary juristic act is one the existence of which must be conditioned upon the existence of another juristic act. A typical example is a surety contract: while the formation of the underlying contract is a primary juristic act, the execution of the surety contract is a secondary juristic act.

Based on whether the effectiveness of a juristic act is conditioned upon the existence of a cause, an act may be a causative act or a non-causative act. For example, the issuing of a bank draft is a non-causative act because the validity of the draft will not be affected by the underlying legal relationship. Even if the underlying legal relationship is declared as invalid, the commercial paper is still valid. While most of the juristic acts are causative acts, Chinese law grants protection to some non-causative acts in order to protect the security of transactions.

A juristic act may be valid, effectiveness-pending, revocable, or void depending on its effectiveness. In order to be effective, a juristic act must satisfy the elements required by law.

---

① Article 135 of the Civil Code.

§ 2:4:2:2 Elements for A Valid Juristic Act

For a juristic act to be effective, the person of the civil law who conducts the act must have the required capacity for performing civil juristic acts, the expression of the person's intent must be true, and the act must not violate law.

Capacity Requirement

A valid juristic act must be done by a person of the civil law who has full capacity for performing civil juristic acts,① thus, a juristic act conducted by a person with no such capacity is void.② However, if a person who conducts a juristic act only has limited capacity for performing civil juristic acts, the effectiveness of the act will depend on whether the act is solely beneficial to him or considered appropriate to his age, intelligence, or mental status. If the act is solely beneficial to the person, or considered to be appropriate to his age, intelligence, or mental status, the act is valid; otherwise the act will be valid only if prior consent or subsequent ratification is obtained from the legal representative of the person.③

True Expression of Intent

A person of the civil law conducts a juristic act by making an expression of intent. An expression of intent may be made either expressly or implicitly, and either orally or through other means. Silence is generally not deemed as an expression of intent unless it is so provided by law, agreed upon by the parties, or if silence has been deemed as an expression of intent based on the course of dealing between the parties. The expression of intent must be true in order for the juristic act to be valid.

An expression of intent may be made in different scenarios and the timing when an expression becomes effective is very critical for a juristic act to be effective.④ Firstly, the situations must be distinguished where an expression is made through real-time communication or not through real-time communication considering the fact that in a real-time communication, the

---

① Article 143 of the Civil Code.
② Article 144 of the Civil Code.
③ Article 145 of the Civil Code. Also see Article 47 of the Contract Law of 1999.
④ Articles 137–142 of the Civil Code.

counterparty would be able to immediately receive the information and respond to it. Therefore, such an expression of intent becomes effective from the time the counterparty is aware of its content. On the other hand, if an expression of intent is made in a form other than a real-time communication, there may be a time difference between the time the expression is made and the time the expression is awared of by the counterparty. Under such a circumstance, the expression of intent becomes effective only when it reaches the counterparty. Sometimes an expression of intent is not made to any specific person, and it becomes effective when the expression is completed. If the expression is made through public notice, then it becomes effective when the notice is posted. The Civil Code also considers the development of new technologies and provides, for example, for the situation when an expression of intent is made through an electronic data message. An expression of intent may be withdrawn as long as the notice of withdrawal reaches the intended party prior to or at the same time when the expression reaches the intended party.

A juristic act conducted by a party and a counterparty based on a false expression of intent is void. If an expression of intent deliberately conceals a civil juristic act, the concealed act may or may not be valid and its validity will be determined in accordance with the relevant laws governing the specific act.① If a person fails to express his true will when conducting a juristic act, the act is revocable and the person may request the court or an arbitral tribunal to revoke the act. The grounds for revocation include misunderstanding, unconscionability, fraud, duress, or undue influence.② The right to revoke such a civil juristic act does not exist forever, and will be extinguished under the following circumstances as specified in Article 152 of the Civil Code:

> (1) the party has failed to exercise the right to revocation within one year from the date when it knows or should have known of the cause for revocation, or within 90 days from the date when the party who has performed the act with serious misunderstanding knows or should have known of the cause for revocation;

---

① Article 146 of the Civil Code.
② Articles 146-151 of the Civil Code; also see Article 54 of the Contract Law of 1999.

(2) the party acting under duress has failed to exercise the right to revocation within one year from the date when the duress ceases; or

(3) the party who becomes aware of the cause for revocation waives the right to revocation expressly or through its own conduct.

No Violation of Law

A juristic act may not violate any mandatory provision of laws or administrative regulations, or offend public order and good morals;① otherwise it is void, unless such mandatory provision does not lead to invalidity of such a civil juristic act.② A civil juristic act is also void if it is conducted through malicious collusion between the actor and a counterparty and as a result, the lawful rights and interests of another person is harmed.③

If a juristic act is held void or be revoked, it does not have any legal force from the beginning,④ so that any property obtained by a person as a result of such act must be returned, or, if impossible to return, compensated based on the appraised value of the property to its original owner, and any loss incurred as a result of such act must be compensated by the party at fault.⑤ However, if a civil juristic act is divisible, the invalidity of one part of the act will not affect the other part, so the other part of the act will remain valid.⑥

In the following case, an exculpatory clause contained in a labor contract was held as an invalid juristic act for violating the law.

Case 13

Case 13: Zhangs v. Zhang⑦

Zhang signed a labor contract with the defendant in which there was an exculpatory clause exempting the defendant's liability for Zhang's

---

① Article 143 of the Civil Code.
② Article 153 of the Civil Code.
③ Article 154 of the Civil Code.
④ Article 155 of the Civil Code.
⑤ Article 157 of the Civil Code.
⑥ Article 156 of the Civil Code.
⑦ See the SPC Gazette, Issue 1 (1989).

injury suffered during his work for the defendant. When working for the defendant, Zhang hurt his ankle, which led to his death after two weeks. Medical report showed that his death was solely caused by the injury. When Zhang's parents Zhangs requested the defendant to compensate the loss of 17,600.40 yuan, the defendant refused based on the exculpatory clause in the contract.

The Tanggu District People's Court of Tianjin Municipality reasons that the exculpatory clause in the labor contract is invalid. The Constitution requires the employers to grant protection to the employees. Such an exculpatory clause is in violation of the Constitution and the relevant labor laws, and is also against the socialist public ethics. Therefore, it is an invalid juristic act. In this case, Zhang's death was caused by the defendant's negligence, and the defendant should be liable for compensation.

Later the parties agreed to settle the case under the court's direction, and the defendant agreed to pay to the plaintiff 18,000 yuan plus the litigation costs.

§ 2:4:2:3 Juristic acts Subject to a Condition or Term

A juristic act may be one subject to a condition, or one subject to a term.

A Juristic Act Subject to a Condition

Where the parties agree that the effectiveness of a juristic act will depend on the satisfaction of a specific condition, the act is one subject to a condition.① The condition must be a fact that may or may not happen in the future and that will cause the juristic act created or terminated. Normally such a condition is not required by law but is agreed upon by the parties, but it must be lawful and cannot be incompatible with the main purpose of the juristic act. A condition attached to a juristic act may be a condition precedent or a condition subsequent.

A condition precedent is also called a suspensive condition and a juristic act

---

① Article 158 of the Civil Code; Article 62 of the GPCL.

with such a condition will not be valid until the condition is fulfilled. ① In this situation, the effectiveness of a juristic act is temporarily suspended, and the obligee may not request the obligor to perform his obligation until after the attached condition is satisfied. For instance, if there is a clause in the contract for sale of E-books between West Co. and East Co. which provides that the contract will only be deemed effective after West Co. has obtained the patent certificate of the dictionary, then the contract is one subject to a condition precedent, and is not effective until after the patent certificate has been presented.

A condition subsequent is also called a resolutory condition, satisfaction of which will terminate the validity of the act. ② For example, if there is a clause in the contract between West Co. and East Co. providing that the contract will be ineffective if there is any patent infringement claim filed against East Co. regarding the sale of E-books, this clause imposes a condition subsequent, and once such condition is satisfied, the contract becomes invalid. However, the contract will always be effective if there is no patent infringement claim arisen.

It is illegal for a person to improperly obstruct or facilitate the fulfillment of a condition. Where a party improperly obstructs the fulfillment of a condition for his own benefit, the condition is deemed to have been fulfilled, and where a party improperly facilitates the fulfillment of a condition, the condition is deemed not to have been fulfilled. ③

A Juristic Act Subject to a Term

A juristic act may be subject to a term, *i.e.*, a certain period of time within which the parties should accomplish the juristic act, and the term is used as the basis of effectuating or terminating the juristic act. ④ Therefore, a term of a juristic act may be a term of effectiveness or a term of termination.

A juristic act subject to a term of effectiveness becomes effective when the term begins, while a juristic act subject to a term of termination becomes ineffective when the term expires. For example, if the parties agree that Party

---

① Article 158 of the Civil Code.
② Article 158 of the Civil Code.
③ Article 159 of the Civil Code.
④ Article 160 of the Civil Code.

A will rent Party B's house for two years and that this contract will take effect since January 1, 2025, this juristic act is one subject to a term of effectiveness and the contract will not be effective until January 1, 2025. A juristic act may not be subject to a term if the nature of the act determines that there should be no term attached.

Sometimes a condition and a term could be confusingly similar, but the main difference between a condition and a term is whether the juridically significant fact is certain to happen or appear in the future. A condition is something may or may not happen in the future, but a term is something that is bound to happen for sure.

The following case involves a contract subject to a condition precedent and the court determined that the condition had not been fulfilled and therefore the contract was not valid.

Case 14

Case 14: Disputes Regarding Transfer of a Land Use Right[1]

An Australian company, N Co., signed a contract for transfer of a right to use a lot of State-owned land (approximately 152,702 square meters) on January 6, 2003 with the Land Bureau of Laoshan, Qingdao City, Shandong Province, for the purpose of developing a project named "Australian Garden." The land-use term is 50 years, and the land use fee is 369.15 yuan per square meter with a total of 56,369,943.2 yuan. Article 5 of the contract provided that Laoshan Land Bureau would transfer the land use right at the time when the contract was approved. Article 6 of the contract provided that the contract would become effective since it was executed by both Laoshan Land Bureau and N Co.

The City Planning Bureau of Qingdao City, Shandong Province issued a permit (No. 3, 2003) to N Co. on January 13, 2003 to allow it to develop the lot of land, and clarified that the Australian Garden project complied with the city planning requirements. N Co. had actually paid off

---

[1] See (2004) Min Yi Zhong Zi No. 106, reprinted in the SPC Gazette, Issue 3 (2007).

the land-use fee according to the contract between September 28, 2001 and May 29, 2003.

On March 1, 2004, the Legislative Affairs Office of Qingdao City Government and the Land Resources and Housing Bureau of Qingdao City co-issued a document regarding the Australian Garden Project stating that the said lot of land could not be transferred as agreed with N Co. on January 6, 2003, and that the parties should rescind the contract, the paid land use fee should be refunded, and the lot of land should be put back into the government's land reserves.

On April 12, 2004, Laoshan Land Bureau notified N Co. to rescind the contract on the ground that the contract both parties signed earlier was invalid and it could not perform the contractual obligations. It requested N. Co. to collect the refund within 30 days after receiving this notice. On June 18, 2004, the Land Bureau sent another letter to urge N Co. to go through the procedure. N Co. brought this litigation to the High People's court of Shandong Province on June 28, 2004.

The court decided that Laoshan Land Bureau should continue to perform the contract and facilitate N Co. to apply for the title certificate of the land use right concerned. Laoshan Land Bureau appealed the case to the SPC. During the period the case was pending appeal, the director of Laoshan Land Bureau was convicted of receiving bribery from unrelated parties.

The main issue before the SPC is whether the contract for transfer of the land use right is valid.

First, the defendant alleges that the contract is one subject to the condition that it must be approved by the government. Article 45 of the Contract Law provides that the condition attached to a contract must be one agreed by the parties and in compliance with law. The power and authority of a government agency regarding the review or approval of a matter or a contract originate from the statutes and administrative regulations and are not something that the parties may agree otherwise. Therefore, it is not a condition attached to the contract.

Second, the defendant alleges that the contract signed by the parties is in violation of the local legislation made by the standing committee of the people's congress of Shandong Province. The court reasons that according to Article 52 of the Contract Law and Article 4 of the SPC's Interpretation I Concerning Certain Issues on Application of the Contract Law, the ground for invalidating a contract should be based on laws and administrative regulations instead of local legislations or local regulations. Therefore, this allegation is invalid.

Third, Article 6 of the GPCL provides that the persons of the civil law, when conducting civil activities, must abide by the State policies in addition to the laws. The State Council has issued various rules regarding adjustment of the market for land-use rights and these rules are State policies. According to one of these policies, a lot of land, as the subject matter in a land-use contract that has not been approved by the city or county government or if no written contract on the development of the land-use project was signed prior to July 1, 2002, should change the way of its transfer to transfer through bidding or auction. The changes to the bidding or auction procedure should be regarded as modification or rescission of the contract, but would not affect or restrict the validity of the contract. Because of this policy, the disputed contract involves a right to use the lot of land which may not be enforced since there was no written agreement on the development of the project prior to July 1, 2002, and thus, according to the policy, the right to use the lot of land may only be transferred through bidding or auction. To this extent, the contract could be performed by Laushan Land Bureau. The failure of Laushan Land Bureau to strictly implement the State policy causes such result, so that the contract could not be performed. The procedural requirement does not make the contract concerned in this case invalid, but has made the contract not performable any more.

Based on these reasons, the SPC reverses the first instance court's decision, dismisses N Co.'s request for performance of the contract, but orders Laushan Land bureau to pay all the litigation costs totaling of 865,569.16 yuan, on the ground that the fundamental reason for this litigation and for the N Co.'s failure to obtain support from the court is owing to Laushan Land Bureau's acts; therefore, it should pay for it.

The SPC thus reverses the decision and dismisses N Co.'s claims.

§ 2:5 Agency Relationship

§ 2:5:1 Agency Relationship in General

Agency relationship[①] is a special kind of civil juristic relationship under which one party, an agent, independently deals with a third person in the name of the other party, the principal, within the scope of authority granted by the principal, and any legal effect of such act will be directly binding on the principal.[②] Since the purpose that a principal hires an agent is to increase his own benefit, it is essential that the legal effect of the agent's act is directly borne by the principal, which means that the legal effect does not need to be assigned or delegated by the agent to the principal; instead, once the authorized juristic act is completed, the principal will enjoy all legal benefits and assume all legal liability arising from the authorized act. These rules apply not only to an agent authorized by a natural person, but also to an agent authorized by an organization. Article 170 of the Civil Code especially provides that a juristic act performed by an agent for fulfilling his responsibilities assigned by a legal person or an unincorporated organization within the scope of authority and in the name of the legal person or the unincorporated organization is binding on the legal person or unincorporated organization.

An agent must have capacity to independently perform juristic acts on behalf of the principal by utilizing his knowledge and skills. The juristic acts that an agent may conduct on behalf of a principal may include concluding a contract, performing an obligation, accepting payment, or requesting damages. A typical example is to authorize an agent to make a contract. Where an agent is authorized to sign a contract in the principal's name, the agency relationship thus created involves two contracts and three relationships. The two contracts include an agency agreement between the principal and the agent, also called an "entrustment contract," and a contract signed by the agent and a third person. The legal effect of the latter contract is to be assumed by the principal. The three relationships involved are the relationships between the principal and the agent, between the agent and a third person, and between

---

① Agency relationship is regulated in Articles 161-175 of the Civil Code.
② Article 162 of the Civil Code.

the third person and the principal. The first relationship is an internal relationship of the agency while the latter two relationships are external relationships. Any restriction imposed by a principal on the scope of authority of an agent is only effective between the two parties and not effective against a *bona fide* third person.

A person may not authorize an agent to do everything. For example, an agent may not be authorized to conduct an act in violation of law, because the purpose of recognizing the agency system is to facilitate the parties to realize their lawful rights and interests. If an act must be performed by the principal himself in accordance with law, as agreed by the parties, or based on the nature of the act, the principal may not authorize an agent to conduct such act.① The situations include performance of an obligation based on a fiduciary relationship or the person's intelligence, skills, know-how, or equipment, *etc.*, and performance of an obligation conditioned upon a specific person's status. An agent may not represent a principal to do an act that will significantly alter the party's relation-based status, such as getting married or divorced, or establishing or terminating an adoption relationship. Neither may an agent represent a principal to do an act that is personal in nature, such as making a will or accepting a testamentary gift.②

The Chinese law recognizes the direct agency relationship in which an agent acts in the name of a principal instead of in his own name. Historically, indirect agencies also existed in China but only in the foreign trade area. Foreign trade had been controlled by a limited number of State-owned enterprises in China which were granted an exclusive power to engage in export and import businesses. The other enterprises that needed to import or export commodities had to sign an entrustment agreement with such a State-owned enterprise and the latter would act as the former enterprise's agent to deal directly with foreign companies in its own name. After China's accession to the WTO, this practice had been abolished. Today all of the enterprises in China, upon application and approval, may engage in import or export businesses,③ so

---

① Article 161 of the Civil Code.
② Article 161 of the Civil Code.
③ Article 8 of the Foreign Trade Law of the PRC.

indirect agency no longer exists in the foreign trade area.

§2:5:2 Categorization of Agency

Based on the form of creation, an agency relationship may be one created by agreement or one created by operation of law.[①] An agency created by agreement is one created based on a principal's authorization and the scope of the agent's authority is determined by the principal. An agency created by operation of law is a statutory agency (or legal agency) which is created based on a personal relationship between an agent and a principal with a wide scope of authority provided by law.

Based on the scope of authority, an agency may be a general one or a special one. A general agency refers to an agency relationship without specific limitations on the authority granted to an agent and the agent may conduct a wide range of juristic acts on behalf of the principal. Generally, an agency relationship created by operation of law, i.e., a legal guardian of a minor, is a general one. A special agency is one with limited authority and is also called limited agency. An agent in a limited agency relationship can only act strictly within the scope of the authority. The agency relationship created by agreement is generally a limited one.

Based on whether an agent may independently conduct an authorized act, an agency may be an independent agency or a joint agency. In an independent agency relationship, an agent may independently conduct an act within his authority, and even if there are two or more co-agents concurrently hired by the same principal, each of the agents may independently act within their specific authorities. In a joint agency relationship, however, there are two or more co-agents who are jointly responsible for the principal to handle the same matter, so they must collectively act within their authorities. If one agent independently acts without consulting with the other co-agents and causes harm to the principal's rights and interests, the agent who thus acts will bear civil liability.[②] Whether a co-agency is an independent agency or a joint agency should be determined in accordance with law or based on the

---

① Article 163 of the Civil Code.
② Article 166 of the Civil Code.

principal's authority. If the law or the authority is not clear, the agency is presumed to be a joint agency and the agents must collectively conduct an authorized act.

Based on whether an agent needs to use his skills or expertise to conduct an authorized act, an agency may be an active one or a passive one. An agent in an active agency should actively act on behalf of the principal, and may need to use his skills or expertise to complete the authorized matter. However, an agent in a passive agency may simply follow the principal's instruction to do the authorized act.

Based on who selects the agent, an agency may be a primary agency or a sub-agency. A primary agency is one created by the principal's authority or directly provided by law. A sub-agency is one created by the agent based on an entrustment agreement. In a sub-agency relationship, an agent, based on a power of re-authorization and in its own name, elects a sub-agent who will deal with a third person on behalf of the principal, while the legal effect of which will be borne by the principal instead of the agent. Issues of sub-agencies will be discussed in § 2.5.5.1.

Based on whether a principal is disclosed to a third party, an agency may be a disclosed agency or an undisclosed agency. A disclosed agency is one where an agent discloses the existence and the status of the principal and then act in the name of the principal. An undisclosed agency is one where an agent does not disclose the existence or the status of the principal. [1]

Based on the existence of authority, an agency may be one with authority or one without authority. An agency with authority may be further categorized as an agency with actual authority and an agency with apparent authority. An agency with actual authority is one established on the principal's authority or directly on the provisions of law. The effect of such an agent's act will be borne by the principal. An agency with apparent authority will be discussed in § 2.5.5.2 of this Book.

An agency without authority is not a real "agency" and a holding-out "agent" acts without actual authority or apparent authority. The effect of an act of such an "agent" will not be borne by the principal; instead, it is an

---

[1] Article 926 of the Civil Code.

effectiveness-pending act and only creates a specific civil liability relationship among the principal, the holding-out "agent", and the third person. For example, if a holding out "agent" signs a contract in the name of a principal when he does not have any actual authority as an agent, his act exceeds the authority he has, or he acts after the authority is terminated, unless his act meets the apparent authority standard, the contract does not have any legal effect on the principal. However, such a contract may be valid if it is ratified by the principal. Otherwise, the holding out "agent" is liable for any damage arising from the contract. The third person may urge the principal to ratify the contract within thirty days after receiving the demand, and may rescind the contract before it is ratified, unless the third person knows or should have known that the holding out "agent" has no authority. ①

§2:5:3 Creation and Termination of an Agency Relationship

§2:5:3:1 Agency Created by Agreement

An agency created by agreement is a typical form of agency which is formed based on an authority granted by a principal to an agent. An entrustment agreement is the legal basis of the authority and the agency relationship; however, the formation of an entrustment agreement does not necessarily create an authority in the agent. Only after a principal has unilaterally authorized an agent to do a certain act will the authority be granted. Therefore, an entrustment agreement is a mutual consent and will be effective only between the two parties, *i.e.*, the principal and the agent; however, granting an authority is a unilateral act which, once completed, will be effective against a third person. Therefore, an entrustment agreement and the authority granted to an agent are two different things.

An authority may be made orally or in a written form, unless it is required by law to be made in writing. A power of attorney (letter of authorization) is a written document proving that a principal grants an authority to an agent based on an entrustment agreement. However, an entrustment agreement only reflects the internal relationship between a principal and an agent, which

---

① Article 171 of the Civil Code.

cannot affect a third person's interests. A third person does not need to know anything about the entrustment agreement and only needs to know the power of attorney based on which he may deal with the agent.

Since an authority is independent from an entrustment agreement, even after the latter has been rescinded, if the power of attorney is not taken back, the effect of the transactions done between a third person and the agent will still be directly binding on the principal. This rule is designed to protect a *bona fide* third person's interests and protect the security of transactions. Therefore, a principal who fails to well manage the power of attorney or take back the power of attorney after the agency relationship ceases to exist will bear legal liability.① When a principal rescinds or cancels an entrustment agreement, he is suggested to revoke the authority at the same time.

A power of attorney should be signed by the principal, and contain the name of the agent, the matters the agent is authorized to do, the scope of authority, and the duration (term) of the authority. In practice, a letter of reference may be used as a power of attorney. If a power of attorney is not clear as to the scope of authority, the principal is liable to the third person and the agent bears joint and several liability.② The reason is that an unclear power of attorney may lead the agent to do something in violation of the principal's intent and therefore cause harm to a third person. In case it happens, both the principal and the agent will be jointly and severally liable for the third person's damage. The legal basis for the principal to assume liability is because he negligently makes the power of attorney, whereas the legal basis for the agent to bear liability is that he should have discovered the defect of the power of attorney but fails to do so. In order to avoid disputes, a principal is suggested to make the power of attorney as detailed as possible.

An agency created by agreement may be terminated upon expiration of the term of authority or completion of the authorized tasks stated in the power of attorney. If a power of attorney does not specify a term of the authority, then the principal may determine the term at any time by making a unilateral expression of intent. An agency relationship may also be terminated upon

---

① Article 172 of the Civil Code.
② Article 172 of the Civil Code.

revocation by the principal or resignation by the agent. Since the agency relationship is created based on a fiduciary relationship, once the trust has been lost, the principal may revoke the authorization and the agent may resign from his capacity as an agent. Upon resignation, an agent has a duty to complete the authorized tasks and continue to do the authorized thing before a new agent has taken his place. When the principal or agent dies or loses his capacity for performing civil juristic acts, the agency relationship will be automatically extinguished,[1] except that an act performed by the agent after the principal dies is valid under the following circumstances as provided in Article 174 of the Civil Code:

> An act performed by an agent under agreement after the principal deceases remains valid under any of the following circumstances:
> (1) the agent does not know or should not have known of the death of the principal;
> (2) the act is ratified by the heirs of the principal;
> (3) it is clearly stated in the letter of authorization that the agency is terminated only upon completion of the authorized tasks; or
> (4) the agent has started the act before the principal deceases and continues to act in the interests of the heirs of the principal.
> The preceding paragraph shall be applied *mutatis mutandis* where the principal who is a legal person or an unincorporated organization is terminated.

§ 2:5:3:2 Agency Created by Operation of Law

An agency relationship created by operation of law is to protect the interests of a special group of persons under special circumstances and to secure the transactions. It mainly applies when a person has no or limited capacity for performing civil juristic acts. A statutory agent will be designated to represent such a person in accordance with law. For example, a guardian of a minor is the statutory agent (also called "legal representative") of the minor who does not have full capacity for performing civil juristic acts. Under certain

---

[1] Articles 173 and 174 of the Civil Code.

circumstances, a social organization may become a statutory agent of its members. For example, a trade union may be the statutory agent of its members so that it may sign a collective labor contract or participate in a litigation related to employment disputes on behalf of its members. An agency relationship created by operation of law may be extinguished if the principal has obtained, regained, or resumed his capacity for performing civil juristic acts, upon death of the principal or the agent, or upon the agent's loss of capacity for performing civil juristic acts. ①

§ 2:5:4 Duties of Agent

§ 2:5:4:1 Duty of Care

The agency system as a whole is established for the benefit of the principal, and one of the principal's purposes of creating an agency relationship is to utilize the knowledge and skills of an agent to serve himself. Thus, an agent has a duty of care to use his knowledge and skills to act as authorized for the principal's benefit in order to realize the latter's objectives, and, unless consented to by the principal, or unless under special circumstances, an agent must perform the authorized act by himself and should not re-delegate it to another person.

An agent should also report to the principal about any and all significant information relating to the authorized matter so that the principal will know the development of the authorized matter as well as any gain or loss of his benefit. The report must be true and accurate and shall not include any false or misleading information. Upon completion of an authorized act, an agent should also report to the principal about the process and the outcome of the authorized act and submit any necessary document or material to the principal. In addition, an agent may not disclose any confidential information about the principal to anyone, or utilize the information to unfairly compete against the principal.

If an agent fails to perform or fully perform his duties and thus causes

---

① Article 175 of the Civil Code.

harm to the principal, the agent must bear civil liability. ①

§ 2:5:4:2 Duty of Loyalty

An agent owes a duty of loyalty to his principal. In this sense, an agent may not conduct an authorized act in a principal's name with himself; such a self-dealing is prohibited by law unless it is consented to or ratified by the principal. ② The reason is that when an agent represents a principal's interests and at the same time deals with himself as "a third person," the conflict of interests is obvious and cannot be overcome.

Neither may an agent act as an agent for both parties to a transaction because the interests of both parties to a same transaction have a conflict. Where an agent concurrently represents two or more principals, if he conducts an authorized act in the name of one principal with another principal he represents, the two principals have conflicting interests and the balance of their interests will never be achieved through bargaining. Thus, unless prior consent or subsequent ratification is obtained from both principals, such a transaction is invalid. ③

An agent is prohibited from maliciously conspiring with a third person to harm the interests of the principal since such an act is seriously against the fiduciary nature of the agency relationship. If it happens, the agent and the third person will be jointly and severally liable for the principal's losses thus caused. ④

An agent is prohibited from conducting an illegal act through the agency relationship. Illegal acts are never allowed to be included in the scope of authority in an agency relationship. Where an agent knows or should have known that handling an entrusted matter is illegal but still conducts the act as authorized, or, if a principal knows or should have known that an act conducted by the agent is illegal but does not make any objection, then the agent and the principal will bear joint and several liability. ⑤

---

① Article 164 of the Civil Code.
② Article 168 of the Civil Code.
③ Article 168 of the Civil Code.
④ Article 164 of the Civil Code.
⑤ Article 167 of the Civil Code.

§2:5:5 Specific Issues on Agency Relationship

§2:5:5:1 Sub-agency Relationship

Generally, the selection of an agent is based on the trust and reliance of a principal on the knowledge, skills, and honesty of the agent, and the internal relationship of an agency is featured on its personal fiduciary relationship. Normally an agent must personally perform his obligations based on the authority granted to him by the principal and should not re-authorize it to anyone else. If an agent cannot fulfill his obligations in such capacity, the principal may revoke the authorization and the agent may also resign; afterwards, the principal may authorize another agent to perform the act. In this sense, an agent generally may not re-authorize a sub-agent to handle an authorized matter; nevertheless, an agent may delegate part or all of his authority to a sub-agent if prior consent or subsequent ratification is obtained from the principal or under an emergency situation in order to fully represent the principal and protect the principal's interests. ① An emergency situation may include a situation where an agent is sick and can neither perform his obligations nor timely notify the principal. Thus, the power of re-authorization will only be granted according to a specific provision of law or under a special authorization of the principal. If an agent decides to delegate his authority to another person, a sub-agency relationship is established. The sub-agent acts in the name of the principal and the principal assumes the legal effect of the sub-agent's act.

A sub-agency must be based on the existence of a primary agency relationship and is the continuance of the primary agency; however, it is different from the primary agency in that it is created only by agreement and cannot be created by operation of law. A sub-agent is selected by the agent not the principal so that the relationships in a sub-agency are more complicated. In a sub-agency, there is an entrusting relationship between the principle and the agent, a delegation relationship between the agent and the sub-agent, an agency relationship between the principal and the sub-agent, a legal relationship between the sub-agent and the third person, as well as an allocation of the legal consequences

---

① Article 169 of the Civil Code.

between a third person and the principal. The scope of the delegation of authority may not exceed the scope of the original authorization. However, the delegation of authority does not mean that the authority of the primary agency relationship has been transferred because the agent is still responsible to the principal's for the authorized matter.

A re-authorization must be clear and specific. If a third person's interests are harmed owing to an ambiguous re-authorization, the third person may ask the principal to compensate for his damage; afterwards, the principal who has fully compensated the third person has a right to indemnification against the agent. A sub-agent who is at fault will be jointly and severally liable.

Sub-agency will bring about significant legal effects. A sub-agent becomes the agent of the principal who may act in the name of the principal and the legal effect of the act will be assumed by the principal. A sub-agent is also obligated to appropriately perform the entrusted act and bears liability if he fails to perform the authorized act and thus causes harm to the principal. In a sub-agency consented to or ratified by a principal, the principal may directly instruct the sub-agent to do the authorized task, and the agent is only liable to the principal for his selection and supervision of the sub-agent and the instructions given to the sub-agent by himself. If an agent is not at fault in selecting or supervising the sub-agent and the loss is caused solely by the sub-agent's fault, then the principal can only claim damages against the sub-agent. However, if the sub-agency is not consented to or ratified by the principal, the agent is liable for the acts performed by the sub-agent unless he re-delegates his authority to the latter in an emergency situation in order to protect the interests of the principal. An agent may remove a sub-agent who fails to perform his obligations. ①

The relationship between the agent and the principal does not cease upon selection of a sub-agent because re-authorization is not a transfer of the power of attorney, and the agent still has the authority to perform the entrusted acts.

---

① Article 169 of the Civil Code.

§ 2:5:5:2 Apparent Authority

Generally speaking, when a person (a "fake" agent), while without actual authority, deals with a third person on behalf of another person (a "fake" principal), there is no agency relationship established. However, if a third person has a reason to believe that the holding out "agent" has authority, then the law recognizes such a relationship as an agency and the "agent" is deemed to have apparent authority to perform an act on behalf of the "principal,"[①] so that the act conducted by the "agent" is binding on the "principal." The purpose of this rule is for protecting the interests of the "principal" and the *bona fide* third person, as well as protecting the security of transactions.

In order for the apparent authority to be recognized, the following conditions must be satisfied: (a) it must otherwise have the basic legal characteristics of an agency relationship; (b) there must be an objective reason for a third person to believe that an agent does have authority; and (c) the third person must be in good faith and without fault. A third person is in good faith when he does not know or should not have known that the agent acts without authority.

The situations where apparent authority may be established include: (a) an authority made by a principal is unclear, so that a third person mistakenly believes that the act exceeding the authority is an act within the scope of the authority; (b) in a joint agency relationship, where one or more of the agents without consulting with the other agents conduct an act so that a third person believes that the agent or agents have authority to act; (c) after an authority is revoked or the agency relationship expires, the principal has not adopted any necessary measure to publicize or notify the third person of the termination of the authority, so that the third person does not know that the agency relationship is terminated; (d) owing to inappropriate internal management, the "agent" holds a document certifying that he has the authority so that a third person mistakenly believes that the agent does have the authority; (e) a principal has expressly stated to a third person that he will grant authority to an agent but has not actually granted the authority; and (f) because a specific relationship between a "principal" and an "agent" exists and they have not

---

① Article 172 of the Civil Code.

announced to the public that they are actually independent of each other so as to mislead a third person to misunderstand their relationship.

An apparent authority once established creates the same effect as an agency with actual authority and the legal effect of the agency relationship will be directly assumed by the principal. After bearing the legal liability, the principal may request the "agent" to indemnify him. If both the principal and the agent have faults, they will share the damage based on the extent of their faults. The law imposes heavier liability on the principal in this situation in order to maintain the security of transactions and the social order.

When representing a client, a lawyer acts as an agent of the client. The following case involves the malpractice of such a lawyer.

Case 15

Case 15: Wang Baofu v. Law Firm[①]

In 2001, Wang and San Xin Law Firm signed an entrustment contract for dealing with non-litigation matters under which the Law Firm agreed to designate Zhang, a lawyer in the Law Firm, to be Wang's attorney at law. Wang signed his name on the contract, and the Law Firm sealed with its official stamp on it, but the contract did not indicate the date of execution. In September 10 of the same year, Wang and the same Law Firm signed an authorization letter on non-litigation matters. The Letter stated that Wang entrusted Zhang as his agent to witness his will. On September 17, the Law Firm prepared a letter of witness, with Wang's will attached.

The first matter in Wang's will was to devise his rights and interests in a residential apartment to his eldest son Wang Baofu. The letter of witness stated that "Wang personally signs his name before us on his will, and that the signature of him is the true expression of his intention, and thus is true and valid according to Article 55 of the GPCL." Zhang signed his name in the end of the document, with the Law Firm's official seal

---

① See the SPC Gazette, Issue 10, 2005.

followed. Wang received the letter of witness on September 19, 2001.

Wang died in December 2002, and Wang Baofu went to court in January 2003 requesting the court to allow him to inherit the said apartment according to Wang's will. The first instance court held in June 2003 that although the will was signed by Wang, witnessed by his attorney Zhang, and sealed by the Law Firm, it did not conform to the legal requirements for a holographic or allographic will, therefore Wang's estate should be distributed as an intestate succession. Wang Baofu sued in court requesting the Law Firm to compensate his loss.

Article 27 of the Lawyers' Law provides that a lawyer who serves as an agent for dealing with litigation or non-litigation matters shall protect the principal's lawful rights and interests within the scope of authority. The purpose that Wang hired the lawyer to witness his will was to make his will legally valid through accepting the legal service provided by a person specialized in legal matters. Unless the Law Firm can prove that the principal only asked the lawyer to "witness" his execution of his will and to prove the authentication of his signature was true, and that the Law Firm had also exercised its duty of disclosing this information to the client, the Law Firm shall assume the adverse consequence.

Article 49 of the Lawyers' Law provides that where a lawyer causes damage to his client owing to his practicing in violation of law or owing to his negligence, the law firm that he is associated with shall assume compensation liability. After the law firm has made compensation, it has the right of indemnification against the lawyer who intentionally or by gross negligence committed the malpractice.

In this case, the reason that the plaintiff did not get the estate was that the lawyer and the law firm failed to provide appropriate legal service and perform their duties, and thus the plaintiff's rights and interests have been harmed. Therefore, the Law Firm is liable for compensation to the extent of the estate that the plaintiff should have inherited had the will been upheld.

Finally, the court holds that the Law Firm should compensate 114,318.45 yuan to the plaintiff.

§ 2:6 Limitation Periods

§ 2:6:1 Overview

A limitation period[1] is a time limit beyond which an obligee (the aggrieved party) may lose his right to request the court to protect his civil-law rights.[2] This period is a legal limitation imposed by law and may be suspended, discontinued, or extended according to law, but may not be excluded or changed by the parties.[3] Apparently, the law on limitation periods encourages an obligee to timely claim his rights, and to this end, grants limited protection to an obligor, *i.e.*, if an obligee claims his rights after such period expires, the obligor may defend the claim on the ground that the limitation period has expired.

The limitation periods apply to a right that will not permanently exist. A limitation period generally applies to a right to claim against a person whereby requesting the person to do or not to do a certain act. It especially applies to a right to claim against an obligor for the performance of his obligation, such as a debt incurred under a contract, in a tort scenario, or in the situation of *negotiorum gestio*[4] or unjust enrichment. If an obligee fails to make his claim within the limitation period, the obligor will have a defensive right against the obligee's right to claim. It also applies to a right to claim for succession, including a right to request for confirmation of an heir's qualification and restitution of the estate. The heirs must exercise such a right to claim within the limitation period; otherwise their rights will not be protected. For example, no dispute relating to a right to succession may be litigated after twenty years since the beginning date of the inheritance.[5]

The limitation periods generally do not apply to a right to control, a right to affect a juristic relationship by a unilateral action, or a right to defense. Even for the rights to claim, it does not apply to those arising from a natural

---

[1] Also called "limitation of action" or "period of prescription"; *c.f.*, "statute of limitations" at common law.
[2] Article 188 of the Civil Code.
[3] See Articles 188 – 199 of the Civil Code.
[4] "*Negotiaorum gestio*" is also translated as "management of another's affairs."
[5] Article 188 of the Civil Code.

person's personality or, sometimes, a relation-based status, such as a claim for cessation of infringements, removal of nuisances, or elimination of perils. In addition, the limitation periods do not apply to a claim for restitution made by a person who has a right *in rem* over a real property or a registered personal property, a claim for payment of support or alimony, or any other claim to which a limitation period is not applicable in accordance with law. ①

For example, a person has a right to request a tortfeasor to stop infringement, remove nuisances, or prevent infringement when his right to personality has been infringed or will be potentially infringed upon and such a right to claim is based on a natural person's personality, so that it will not be barred by the expiration of the limitation period. A right to claim based on a natural person's relation-based status that involves pecuniary payment, such as determination of paternity relationship or cohabitation of spouses, will not be barred by expiration of the limitation period, either. As a general rule, a limitation period does not apply to a right to child support or parental support. Other rights that are not subject to a limitation period include a right to claim on a real right and a right in State-owned property which has not been entrusted to citizens or legal persons to operate or manage.② The relevant provision is as follows:

Article 196

The limitation period does not apply to the following rights to claim:

(1) a claim for cessation of the infringement, removal of the nuisance, or elimination of the danger;

(2) a claim for return of property of a person who has a real right in immovable or registered movable property;

(3) a claim for payment of child support or support for other family members; or

---

① Article 196 of the Civil Code.
② Article 170 of the SPC's Opinions on Certain Issues on Implementing the General Provisions of Civil Law of the PRC (hereinafter referred to as "SPC's Opinions on the GPCL") which was issued by the SPC on January 26, 1988.

(4) any other claim to which the limitation period is not applicable in accordance with law.

Upon expiration of the limitation period, an obligor has a defense against a claim of non-performance. However, an obligee's substantive right is not extinguished in that the obligor may still voluntarily perform the obligation after the limitation period expires. Specifically, an obligor who agrees to perform his obligations after the limitation period expires may not later on use expiration of the period as a defense for non-performance, and the obligor who has voluntarily performed his past due obligation may not later on demand for restitution.① The court shall not invoke the limitation period on its own initiative,② so that an obligor must raise this defense in the litigation; otherwise such defense is deemed to be waived.

The period of limitation, the counting method of the period, and the grounds for suspension and interruption of the period are all provided by law, and any arrangement otherwise agreed upon between the parties is void. An anticipatory waiver of the limitation period made by the parties is also void.③

§2:6:2 Specific Limitation Periods

A limitation period within which an obligee may request the court to protect his civil-law rights may be a general period or a special period. The GPCL provided some special limitation periods for different civil juristic relationships,④ but the Civil Code has replaced them by providing a unified general limitation period of three years⑤ applicable to most civil juristic relationships, with a number of exceptions. For example, the limitation period for litigation or arbitration of a dispute arising out of an international contract

---

① Article 192 of the Civil Code.
② Article 193 of the Civil Code.
③ Article 197 of the Civil Code.
④ For example, Article 136 of the GPCL provided a one-year special limitation period for cases involving compensation for bodily harm, sales of substandard goods without proper notice, delayed or refused payment for rent, and the loss of or damage to the property on consignment.
⑤ Article 188 of the Civil Code; it replaced Article 135 of the GPCL which provided for a 2 years' limitation period.

for sales or technological import and export contract is four years. ①

Since the Civil Code only provides a general limitation period, some special limitation periods provided in other laws preempt such general period. For instance, Article 257 of the Maritime Law provides a one-year special limitation period for the right-holder to sue the carrier of sea cargo transportation. The limitation periods provided in the Civil Code are also applicable to arbitration unless a different limitation period is provided for arbitration in other laws. ②

The Chinese civil law also provides a maximum period of limitation which is twenty years since an injury occurred, and the people's court may not enforce a right if twenty years have passed since the date the right is infringed upon. However, this maximum limitation period may be extended by court in special situations. ③

§ 2:6:3 Commencement of Limitation Periods

It is important to determine when a limitation period starts to run. Generally, a limitation period commences from the time when an obligee knows or should have known that his right has been harmed and that who is the obligor. ④ The Civil Code provides rules governing different situations thereof. For example, if the parties stipulate that a same obligation should be performed by installments, the limitation period commences from the time when the last installment is due. ⑤ If a person with no or limited capacity for performing civil juristic acts has a claim against his legal representative, then the limitation period will run from the time when the statutory agency is terminated. ⑥ The limitation period for a sexual molestation claim by a minor runs from the date when the minor reaches the age of 18 in order to fully protect the minor's interests. ⑦

---

① Article 594 of the Civil Code.
② Article 198 of the Civil Code.
③ Article 188 of the Civil Code.
④ Article 188 of the Civil Code.
⑤ Article 189 of the Civil Code.
⑥ Article 190 of the Civil Code.
⑦ Article 191 of the Civil Code.

§ 2:6:4 Suspension, Interruption, and Extension of the Limitation Period

A limitation period may be suspended. Upon presence of a legal cause, an obligee who has not yet urged his claim against an obligor may request the limitation period be suspended until after the legal cause that obstructs the running of the period has been removed; and then the counting of the period will be continued. *Force majeure* is one of the causes for suspension of the limitation period.① It refers to an objective circumstance which is unforeseeable, unavoidable, and which cannot be overcome, such as war or earthquake.② However, even if a *force majeure* event occurs, a limitation period may not be suspended if the alleged *force majeure* event does not adversely affect the right-holder's ability to exercise his rights.

A limitation period may also be suspended if an obligee has no or limited capacity and does not have a legal representative, or his legal representative dies, is no longer qualified to be a representative, or has lost capacity for performing civil juristic acts. Still, if the heirs or administrator of an estate has not been determined after succession opens, the limitation period for succession will be suspended. If an obligee is controlled by the obligor or another person so that he cannot exercise the right to claim, the limitation period will also be suspended. A limitation period may only be suspended if an obligee cannot exercise the right to claim within the last six months of the limitation period with a legal cause, and it will be continued for another six months since the date the cause that suspended the period has been removed.③ A limitation period may be re-suspended if a legal cause presents again.

A limitation period may be interrupted upon the time an obligee requests an obligor to perform his obligations, an obligor agrees to perform his obligations, an obligee initiates a lawsuit or arbitration proceeding, or other circumstances with the similar effect as initiating a lawsuit or arbitration proceeding by an obligee.④ If a limitation period is interrupted, it will recommence from the time of interruption or the time when the relevant

---

① Article 194 of the Civil Code.
② Article 180 of the Civil Code.
③ Article 194 of the Civil Code.
④ Article 195 of the Civil Code.

proceeding is completed. ①

A limitation period may also be extended by the people's court in special situations upon request of an obligee. The obligee needs to show just cause, and then the court will make an investigation and determine whether it is necessary to extend the limitation period. ② The purpose of the extension is to avoid an unfair consequence and protect the right-holders who for some special reasons could not timely urge their claims. The SPC has the power to extend the limitation period.

However, the period within which an obligee may exercise certain rights such as a right to revocation or a right to rescission provided by law or agreed upon by the parties runs from the time when the obligee knows or should have known that his rights exist, and the limitation period for such a claim may not be suspended, interrupted, or extended; consequently, upon expiration of the limitation period, such a right ceases to exist. ③

Article 199

The time period within which a right-holder may exercise certain rights, such as the right to revocation and the right to rescission, which are provided by law or agreed by the parties shall begin, unless otherwise provided by law, from the date when the right-holder knows or should have known that he has such a right, and the provisions on the suspension, interruption, or extension of the limitation period are not be applicable. Upon expiration of the time period, the right to revocation, the right to rescission, and the like rights are extinguished.

Case Review

Case 11 summarized in § 2:3:2:4 involves a dispute on infringement of the rights of personality of a late General Peng. One of the claims alleged by the defendant was that the limitation period expired. Read the relevant part again.

---

① Article 195 of the Civil Code.
② Article 188 of the Civil Code.
③ Article 199 of the Civil Code.

Case 11: Peng v. *China Story* Magazine①

One of the magazine's defenses was that the limitation period had run out when the litigation was brought up. Article 135 of the GPCL provides a two-year limitation period for protection of civil-law rights. Article 137 provides that the limitation period started from the time the person knows or should have known that his right has been infringed upon.

The Fourth Issue of *China Story* in 1998 was formally published on July 1, 1998 in Chengdu, Sichuan Province; however, both its influence and scope of publication were limited. Therefore, it is not reasonable to assume all social public should have known about the content of the fiction after its publication. To this end, the commencement of the limitation period should not start from the time the magazine was published. The Plaintiff Peng Jiahui presented evidence showing that she learned about the content of the fiction *Huo Sui* only after her relative received a letter from a reader of the fiction in April 2000, and the magazine did not present any evidence proving that Peng Jiahui had learned about the fiction earlier than July 1999. Considering Peng Jiahui was then over 90 years old and was illiterate, her claim was more reasonable. After she consulted with the magazine but did not get a satisfactory result, Peng Jiahui brought the litigation in July 2001, which fell within the limitation period provided by law.

§ 2:7 Counting of the Periods of Time

The determination of a period and its starting and ending dates is important for determination of a civil-law right. "A period" means a period of time which may become a juridically significant fact if its expiration may cause the creation, alteration, or termination of a civil juristic relationship, and it is counted in terms of year, month, day, and hour according to the Gregorian calendar.② The period will affect the legal status of a person of the civil law or

---

① See SPC Gazette, Issue 6, 2002 (by the High People's Court of Sichuan Province).
② Article 200 of the Civil Code.

a civil-law right, as well as the actual performance of a certain right and obligation.

The ways of counting the periods of time are provided by law. Where a period is counted in terms of year, month, and day, the day on which an event occurs is not counted in, and the period commences from the following day. Where a period is counted in terms of hour, the period commences from the hour as provided by law or agreed upon by the parties. ① Where a period is counted in terms of year or month, the corresponding date of the due month is the last day of the period; if without such a corresponding date, the last day of the month is the last day of the period. The ways of counting the periods can be adjusted by law or by the parties' agreement. If the parties agree that a period will not start from the first day of the month or year, then one month would be presumed to have 30 days, and a year 365 days. ② Where the last day of a period falls on a legal holiday, the day after the legal holiday is the last day of the period. If the last day of the period was a Sunday or a legal holiday, and if the Sunday or legal holiday was adjusted by the government, then the following day of the actual holiday would be the last day of the period.

The last day of a period ends at 24:00 hours; where a business hour is applied, the last day ends at the time the business is closed. ③

§ 2:8 Civil Liability and Defenses

§ 2:8:1 Civil Liability

A person of the civil law shall perform civil-law obligations in accordance with law or the agreement he has with another person; otherwise he should assume civil liability. ④ Civil liability is the adverse consequence that a person will be held for if he fails to perform his civil-law obligations. Civil liability could be mandatory or discretionary, and the parties may agree on how to share civil liability through consultation as long as there is no violation of any mandatory provisions of law. Without such an agreement, civil liability will be

---

① Article 201 of the Civil Code.
② Article 202 of the Civil Code.
③ Article 203 of the Civil Code.
④ Article 176 of the Civil Code.

shared according to the civil law.

Civil liability may be based on tort law or contract law. Tort liability is one to be borne by a tortfeasor who infringes upon other's proprietary or personal interests because of his fault, or regardless of his fault if the law so provides. For example, civil liability is imposed on a person who infringes upon the name, likeness, reputation, or honor of a person such as a hero or a martyr and thus harms the social public interest. Contractual liability is a liability that a party to a contract may be held for if he fails to perform his obligations as provided in a contract. Where a party's breach of contract causes harm to the other party's personal or proprietary rights or interests, the damaged party may elect to request the former party to assume either contractual liability or tort liability.①

Civil liability may be a fault liability or a non-fault liability.

Fault liability is a liability to be assumed by a person who breaches his duties or fails to perform his obligations imposed by the civil law and causes harm to another person owing to his fault.② In other words, when determining the liability issue, a court will not only examine the illegal act, but also examine the subjective fault of the person who conducts the act. If the party does not have any fault, he will not be liable even if harm is caused. In some special situations, the tortfeasor shall bear liability unless they can prove that they were not at fault.③ The basis for this type of liability is rebuttable presumption of fault. It is also a fault liability, except that the tortfeasor is presumed by law to be at fault unless he may disprove it. To this end, the burden of proof is shifted from the plaintiff to the defendant.

When the element of fault is immaterial in determining civil liability, the liability is a non-fault liability, and it mainly applies to contractual disputes and some special types of tort disputes.④ Generally, fault is not an element in determining the breach of contract; therefore, the breaching party will be exempt from liability only if he can prove that the breach occurs owing to a *force majeure* event or if there is a special clause agreed upon by the parties

---

① Article 186 of the Civil Code.
② Article 1165 of the Civil Code.
③ Article 1165 of the Civil Code.
④ Article 1166 of the Civil Code.

which exempts the breaching party from the liability.

Sometimes an accident occurs and damage is caused but neither party is at fault, the court may order the tortfeasor and the victim to share the losses in accordance with law.① The predecessor of this article is article 132 of the GPCL, which provided that a court should order the tortfeasor to compensate the victim's loss considering the financial situations of the tortfeasor and the victim as well as other relevant factors. This kind of liability has been called fair liability because it is regarded as "fair" to both parties. However, this liability is actually based on "balancing of interests" which is more like a kind of "moral obligation," because when imposing this liability, the court is balancing the interests of both parties but not considering each party's fault.

A civil liability may be a shared liability or a joint and several liability. Where two or more persons share a liability, each person's liability is in proportion to their respective share of fault if such share can be determined, or in equal share if such share cannot be determined.② Where two or more persons assume joint and several liability, an obligee may request that some or all of them assume the liability. The share of liability of each such person subjected to the joint and several liability shall be determined by each person's respective share of fault; where such share cannot be determined, each such person shall assume the liability in equal shares. The person who has thus assumed the liability more than his own share of fault has a right to indemnification against the other person(s) subjected to the joint and several liability. Joint and several liability may be imposed by law or agreed upon by the parties.③

The main forms of civil liability that are provided by Chinese civil law include, *inter alia*, cessation of the infringement, removal of the nuisance, elimination of the danger, restitution, restoration to the original condition, repair, redoing, or replacement, continuance of performance, payment of compensation for losses, payment of liquidated damages, elimination of adverse effects and rehabilitation of reputation, and extension of apology.④

---

① Article 1186 of the Civil Code.
② Article 176 of the Civil Code.
③ Article 178 of the Civil Code.
④ Article 179 of the Civil Code.

These forms of civil liability may be applied separately or concurrently, and in addition, punitive damages may also be granted in accordance with law. ①

Where a person of the civil law concurrently assumes civil, administrative, and criminal liabilities as a result of a same act, the assumption of administrative or criminal liabilities shall not affect such person's ability to assume the civil liability. In other words, if a person, who is concurrently subjected to administrative, criminal, and civil liabilities, does not have sufficient assets to discharge all of these liabilities, he should satisfy his civil liability first. ②

The following case illustrates how a court determines civil liability, especially regarding the application of the fair liability rule.

Case 16

Case 16: Li & Gong v. May Flower Co. ③

On October 24, 1999 at about 6 pm, Li and Gong took their 8-year-old son to dine with other friends in May Flower Restaurant, and were arranged to sit outside a private dining room on the second floor. At about 6:30 pm, there was an explosion occurred inside the private room, the wall of the room fell, causing death of their son, and severe injury of Li and Gong. Later Li was determined to be with a second-degree disability. They sued.

The restaurant defended that this explosion was planned by a criminal suspect. Evidence shows that one of the customers who was a physician sitting inside the private dining room of the restaurant brought a bottle of alcohol to the restaurant without knowing that the bottle of alcohol, given to him by a person not involved in this litigation as a gift, was actually a disguised explosive, and he could not foresee that it would explode, neither could the restaurant have foreseen the explosion. The person who sent it to the physician was caught by police and the criminal case was under

---

① Article 179 of the Civil Code.
② Article 187 of the CCGP (Article 187 of the Civil Code).
③ See the SPC Gazette, Issue 2, 2002.

investigation. Therefore, the restaurant alleged that the explosion was an accident to both the restaurant and the customers. The restaurant did not have subjective fault, and objectively it did not perform any infringing act either. The explosion also caused death of one of the waiters, and the inside decoration as well as certain equipment of the restaurant was damaged. The restaurant suffered various direct or indirect damage almost reaching 1 million yuan. In sum, the restaurant believed that itself was also a victim, so the plaintiff might only claim against the real tortfeasor, not the restaurant.

The Intermediate People's Court of Zhuhai City reasoned that a relationship between consumers and a service provider had been formed when Li and Gong went to the restaurant to eat, under which relationship the May Flowers Restaurant had a duty to protect the personal safety of Li and Gong. Whether it had performed its duty should be determined on the nature, character, and the requirements of the restaurant business, and other factors as a whole. In this case, the personal injury of Li and Gong, and the death of their son were caused by the explosion occurred inside the May Flowers Restaurant, and the explosion was caused by a third person's criminal act, which did not have any direct causal link with the restaurant's own service. Under the then circumstance, the restaurant would not have foreseen the explosion through reasonable care, and it had performed its duty of providing security protection to the customers.

Li and Gong alleged that the wood wall of the restaurant did not conform to the standard so that it imposed potential risks on customers, and for which the restaurant should assume civil liability. The court held that the nonconforming wood wall may have contributed to Gong and Li's injury and their son's death, but it was not the direct cause thereof and did not have any causal link with their damage.

Article 22 of the Law on Protection of the Rights and Interests of Consumers provides that an operator shall guarantee that the commodity or service it provides have the required quality, nature, usefulness, and shelf life during normal use of the commodity or normal acceptance of the service, unless the consumer knows the existence of defects before he buys the commodity or accepts the service. According to the law, the restaurant only has the duty to guarantee the quality of the commodity they provide, not the commodity brought in by the customers. In this case, the customer brought in the explosive disguised as a bottle of alcohol, which was unrelated to the commodities or services provided by the restaurant. The court reasoned that allowing customers to bring in their own alcohol into the restaurant was both a need of the customers and the practice of the food industry, which were not prohibited by laws, administrative regulations, or trade practices. Therefore, the restaurant was not at fault for allowing customers to bring in alcohol.

According to Article 106 of the GPCL, a citizen or legal person who infringes upon the property of the State or collective, or infringes upon the person or property of other persons owing to his or its fault shall assume civil liability. Accordingly, the following elements must be satisfied to find a general tort: (1) objectively there must have damage, (2) there must be a causal link between the tortious act and the damage, (3) the actor must have fault, and (4) the act must be in violation of law. However, under certain circumstances of a special tort, even if all the four factors do not present, the actor may also assume liability if the law so provides. The laws on special torts adopt different fault theories such as presumption of fault, non-fault liability, or fair liability, but the precondition is that the law must expressly so provide.

The tort liability alleged by Li and Gong did not fall within the special torts, and liability for general torts may only be based on fault. In this case, since the accident was caused by a third person tortfeasor, fair liability rule could not be applied either. Since the restaurant had performed its duty of care and it was also one of the victims in this incident, it did not have any fault and should not be liable for Li and Gong. Furthermore, the restaurant did not have any other interested relationship with the tortfeasor, it should not bear vicarious liability for the tortfeasor. Li and Gong should request the direct tortfeasor to compensate for their loss. Finally, the court dismissed the case and requested the two plaintiffs to pay the litigation cost of 30,160 yuan.

Li and Gong appealed to the High People's Court of Guangdong Province. The High Court reasoned that according to Article 122 of the

Contract Law, where a party's breach of contract caused harm to the other party's personal or proprietary rights and interests, the latter party may elect to request the former to bear liability either for breach of contract or for commission of tort. During both the first and second instance proceedings, Li and Gong claimed that the restaurant breached the contract and committed torts, but did not elect a legal basis from the two. Therefore, the court had to make a decision after comprehensively considering the case in accordance with the principle of favoring the right-holder.

Li and Gong alleged that the wood wall of the private dining room of the restaurant did not conform to the fire protection requirements. Even if it was true, Li and Gong were not injured because of fire, and their son was not killed because of fire. Since there was no law providing mandatory provisions regarding the anti-explosion requirement of the wood wall, the restaurant should not assume the liability for having improperly maintained the wood wall.

Regarding the breach of contract claim, after the restaurant accepted Li and Gong's family to eat inside the restaurant, there formed a contractual relationship of consumption and service providing between the two parties. Article 60 of the Contract Law provides that the parties shall comply with the principle of good faith, and perform such obligations as sending notification, rendering assistance, and keeping confidentiality in accordance with the nature and purpose of the contract and the course of dealing. The restaurant should completely perform the agreed obligations under the contract, as well as the collateral duties such as the duty to protect the consumers' person and property free from illegal infringement. In order to perform these collateral duties, an operator must protect the consumers' personal and property safety based on the nature, character, and condition of the trade practice. In this case, owing to the sudden occurrence of a crime and the difficulties in discovering the disguised alcohol, even if the operator had performed its duty of care or prevention, it might not completely avoid the infringement of the consumer's person and property by the criminal suspect. Once such an infringement occurs, whether the operator breaches the contract could only be determined by whether it has reasonably performed its duty of care. The restaurant allowed customers to bring in alcohol because of the trade practice. According to the social custom of the country, it is not necessary or not possible to require the operators to perform a security check as strictly as the airport to passengers. Since the package of this explosive looked exactly like a real bottle of alcohol, ordinary people may not be able to recognize it. Even the customer who brought it in had placed it in his home for quite some time and did not find the danger; therefore, it is not reasonable to require the waiter to tell whether there was danger upon opening the bottle lid. Since the restaurant had performed reasonable duty of care, and could not have recognized the explosive disguised as alcohol, it did not breach the contract.

Regarding whether the restaurant committed a tort, according to the consumer protection law, an operator should be liable for the commodities or services it provides, which excludes the articles brought in by the customers. When Li and Gong family dined at the restaurant, they were injured and killed by the wood wall, which fell because of the explosion caused by a criminal suspect, and the liability should be borne by the third person. The restaurant was not in collusion with the third person, did not perform a common tortious act either, therefore it cannot be held to have committed a tortious act tort according to the consumer protection law.

The court concludes that neither party was at fault in this case. However, it could not be said that the restaurant had nothing to do with Li and Gong family's losses. Although both parties suffered losses in this accident, Li and Gong family suffered loss of life and health when they dined in the restaurant, which actually benefited the restaurant; whereas the restaurant's loss was mainly economic interests. Comparing the two, Li and Gong family's losses were more severe than the restaurant's damage. The restaurant, as well as the public, has expressed deep sympathy to Li and Gong family. Article 157 of the SPC's Tentative Opinion on Certain Issues on Implementation of the GPCL provides that where neither party is at fault for the damage caused, if one party suffers loss during the activity for the benefit of the other party or for the common benefit of the two parties, the court may order the other party or the beneficiary to give certain economic indemnification to the first party. According to this article, and considering Li and Gong family's financial situation, it is appropriate to ask the restaurant to indemnify part of the economic loss suffered by Li and Gong family. Finally, the High People's Court holds that the restaurant should indemnify Li and Gong 300,000 yuan, and each party should share half of the litigation cost of the two instance proceedings (60,320 yuan in total).

§ 2:8:2 Defenses

An obligor may be exempt from civil liability. For example, a person who fails to perform his civil-law obligations owing to *force majeure* assumes no civil liability.[①] A person who causes harm to another person with a justifiable defense or when seeking to avoid peril in response to an emergency assumes no civil liability. These are the legitimate defenses that an obligor may use to counter the claim against himself.

Justifiable Defenses

A person who causes harm to another person (the tortfeasor) assumes no civil liability if he can establish a justifiable defense. A justifiable defense may be established when a person causes harm to an aggressor who is infringing upon the public interest, the personal or other interests of the person himself, or the personal or other interests of another person.[②] It is a legitimate act encouraged by law and a private remedy in its nature. However, the law imposes restrictions on justifiable defenses. There must be an illegal act that is actually happening to infringe upon the interests of the person himself, other persons, or the public, and there must be a necessary and urgent need to protect oneself or other persons. In addition, the act must be against the illegal aggressor and the purpose must be to protect the lawful rights and interests of oneself or other persons. In a word, a justifiable defense may not exceed the

---

① Article 180 of the Civil Code.
② Article 181 of the Civil Code.

limit necessary to achieve the goal. ①

Necessities in an Emergency

Necessities in an emergency may be established when a person harms another person's rights or interests when he tries to protect the public interest or the lawful rights and interests of himself or others free from an actual and emergent peril. The peril may come from human being's activities or from natural forces. If a person causes harm to others when seeking to avoid a peril in response to an emergency, the person who creates the peril, not the said person, shall bear civil liability. However, where a peril is caused by natural forces, although the person who causes harm by seeking to avoid the peril assumes no civil liability, he may need to give appropriate compensation. ② When seeking to avoid a peril in an emergent situation, one may not exceed the necessary limit and should try every effort to protect a greater legal interest and cause less harm. If a person adopts improper measures or exceeds the necessary limit in seeking to avoid peril in response to an emergency and causes unreasonable harm to others, such person shall assume appropriate civil liability. ③

Good Samaritan Law

Helping others has been regarded as a meritorious value in Chinese tradition. However, in recent decades, people have been discouraged to do so owing to the worry that they may incur civil liability by doing so. In order to eliminate such a worry, the Civil Code has clarified that a person who voluntarily rescues another person in an emergency situation and causes harm to the latter person assumes no civil liability. ④ A related question is who is going to compensate the loss suffered by a person who is injured in protecting the civil-law rights and interests of another person. If a tortfeasor who has caused the peril leading to the injury can be identified and located, he shall assume the civil liability. If the tortfeasor cannot be located, upon request of the injured

---

① Article 181 of the Civil Code.
② Article 182 of the Civil Code.
③ Article 182 of the Civil Code.
④ Article 184 of the Civil Code.

person, the beneficiary who has been rescued from the peril shall give the injured person appropriate compensation. ①

The following excerpt is translated from a police announcement regarding a potential criminal case involving justifiable defense. The reasoning could also be applied in a justifiable defense in a civil case.

Case 17

Case 17: Yu's Case②

On August 27, 2018 at 9:30 pm, Liu drove a BMW sedan along Zhenchuan Road of Kunshan City, Jiangsu Province under the influence of alcohol with three other persons in the car. When they approached the intersection with Shunfan Road, the car forced into the bicycle lane and almost hit Yu, who was riding a bicycle in the same direction. One of the guest passengers got off the car and had some verbal confrontations with Yu. After persuaded by someone inside the car, he returned, but the driver Liu suddenly got off and pushed and hit Yu. Later on, he returned to his car and took out a 59 cm-long chopper with 43×5 cm double blades from the car and continuously hit Yu on his neck, waist, and legs by the chopper. During the fight, the chopper was shaken off so that Yu snatched it, and stabbed Liu in his abdomen and hips, and slashed him in his right chest, left shoulder, and left elbow. The fight lasted for 7 seconds. Liu was injured and ran to the car, then Yu chased him and slashed two more strikes on him but both failed. Liu ran in the north-eastern direction from his car, and Yu went to the car and took out Liu's cell phone and put it into his own pocket. After police arrived, Yu gave the cell phone and the chopper to the police, and said that he took Liu's cell to prevent him from calling other people to come to revenge on him.

After Liu fled away, he fell in the green belts 30 meters from his car, and died on the same day after being rescued and sent to the hospital.

---

① Article 183 of the Civil Code.
② See the announcement published by the Public Security Bureau of Kunshan City, Jiangsu Province on September 1, 2018.

Evidence shows that Liu had been stabbed and slashed for five strikes, and died of hemorrhagic shock. Yu was injured in his neck and left part of his chest.

The police investigated the case for determining whether or not to indict Yu.

Article 20 of the Criminal Law provides that a person who takes defensive measures against an illegal aggressor who is committing a violent crime such as criminal battery, murder, robbery, rape, kidnap, or the like, and causes injury or death to the latter person is not regarded to have exceeded the limits of justifiable defense and shall not assume criminal liability.

Firstly, Liu was committing a criminal battery regulated by the criminal law. According to Article 20 of the Criminal Law, the core requirement for determining whether a person has committed a criminal battery is whether the act has severely endangered another person's safety. In judicial practice, it is unreasonable to require the person who is seeking justifiable defense to make a rational judgment in emergency situation regarding whether the aggressor's act actually constitutes a criminal battery, and it is even more unreasonable to require that the person who defends himself has actually suffered an injury. Instead, determination should be made according to the specific situation and the average cognitive level of the common people. In this case, Liu initiated the fighting by his hands, and then by a chopper to continuously strike Yu, which activity had already severely endangered Yu's personal safety and should be regarded as committing a criminal battery.

Secondly, Liu's illegal act was a continuous process. After the confrontations between one guest passenger and Yu had almost come to an end, Liu provoked troubles under the influence of alcohol by firstly punching and kicking Yu, then taking a chopper from his car and continuously slashing Yu, and the infringement grew more violent. After the chopper fell on the ground, he still tried to snatch it. Evidence shows that he did not give up even after he was injured, so Yu's personal safety had always been under Liu's violent threats.

Lastly, Yu's act was defensive in nature. In this case, after Yu snatched the chopper, he stabbed and slashed Liu for 5 strikes within 7 seconds, although afterwards he tried two more strikes (both failed) when he was chasing Liu, the strikes constituted one continuous act with the earlier strikes. In addition, Yu went to the car to seek Liu's cell phone for the purpose of preventing Liu from calling more people to come over to revenge on him and protecting his own personal safety, and it was in line with his intent to defend himself.

Therefore, the police determined that Yu's act was a justifiable defense and Yu should not assume criminal liability. The case was withdrawn.

Chapter 3
Real Rights Law

§ 3:1 General Introduction

The GPCL had been playing an important role in regulating the civil juristic relationships arising out of the attributes and utilization of property between the persons of the civil law until the first Chinese Real Rights Law was enacted by the NPC on March 16, 2007. The enactment of the Real Rights Law symbolized the effort of the Chinese legislature to establish a complete civil law system and had actually laid a foundation for the codification of the civil law. The legislative purpose of the Real Rights Law, as stated in its Article 1, was to maintain the fundamental economic system and the socialist market order, to clarify the attributes of the property, to fully utilize the property, and to protect the right-holder's real rights. [1] After the Real Rights Law has been integrated into the Civil Code, the purpose of the Book Two (Real Rights) of the Civil Code is stated as "to regulate the civil-law relations arising from the attributes and utilization of things."[2]

§3:1:1 Principles of the Real Rights Law

Equal protection is the most fundamental principle of Chinese real rights law, under which the real rights owned by the State, the collectives, the

---

[1] Article 1 of the Real Rights Law.
[2] Article 205 of the Civil Code. It is to be noted that "thing" or "property" are used interchangeably through this book, unless otherwise indicated.

individuals, or other right-holders are equally protected by law. For example, Article 207 of the Civil Code provides that the real rights of the State, collectives, private individuals, and other right-holders are protected by law, and no organization or individual may infringe upon these rights. It also means that the real rights law equally applies to all of the civil participants, *i.e.*, the State, the collectives, private individuals, and other right-holders. For example, the law provides that an owner has a right to possess, use, profit from, and dispose of the real or personal property legally owned by him. ① This provision equally applies to the State, the collectives, and individuals. The law also provides that the creation, alteration, transfer, or extinguishment of a real right in immovable property must be registered in order to be effective, and, unless otherwise provided by law, will not take effect without registration. ② Therefore, when engaging in civil activities, the State as a person of the civil law should also observe this rule when creating a real right in immovable property, unless the law has a special provision to exempt it from such requirement. Article 209 of the Civil Code is one of such special provisions which provides that the ownership registration is not required for natural resources that are provided by law to be owned by the State.

Another important principle of the real rights law is *numerous clausus*, which means that the categories and content of each real right must be provided for by law, and the parties may not create any new type of real rights that the law does not recognize. ③ For example, Chinese law provides for three types of secured interests: mortgage, pledge, and lien, and pledge only includes pledge on rights and pledge on personal property. The parties may not create any new type of secured interest other than these three types provided by law, neither may they create a pledge on real property. The content of the real rights is also determined by law and the parties may not change it upon agreement. For example, in order to secure performance of a debt, a debtor or a third person (mortgagor) may mortgage the property to a creditor (mortgagee) but the mortgagor does not need to transfer the property to the mortgagee. ④ Since a

---

① Article 240 of the Civil Code.
② Articles 208 and 209 of the Civil Code.
③ Article 116 of the Civil Code.
④ Article 394 of the Civil Code.

mortgagee's rights provided by law does not include the right to possess the collateral, the parties may not change this provision by stipulating in the agreement that the mortgagor should surrender the possession of the collateral to the mortgagee.

The third principle of the real rights law is the principle of public notice. [1] The principle of public notice of real rights requires that whenever a real right is altered, the legal consequence of the alteration, *i.e.*, the nature and attributes of the right on the property after the alteration, must be publicized; otherwise the change will have no legal effect. The public notice is posted mainly through registration of real property and possession (and delivery) of personal property.

The fourth principle is the principle of good faith. [2] While public notice of a real right brings about the effect of the real right's transfer (which is against the whole world), the good faith principle, which is about the good faith acquisition of personal or real property, protects the rights and interests of a *bona fide* third person in the transaction. Article 311 of the Civil Code provides protections to the good faith acquisition of both real and personal property:

> Where a person with no right to dispose of immovable or movable property transfers it to another person, the owner has the right to recover it; unless otherwise provided by law, the transferee acquires the ownership of the immovable or movable property under the following circumstances:
>
> (1) the transferee is in good faith at the time when the immovable or movable property is transferred to him;
>
> (2) the transfer is made at a reasonable price; and
>
> (3) the transferred immovable or movable property has been registered as required by law, or has been delivered to the transferee where registration is not required.
>
> Where a transferee acquires the ownership of the immovable or movable property in accordance with the provisions of the preceding paragraph, the

---

[1] The relevant articles include Articles 208, 209 and 224 of the Civil Code.
[2] See Article 311 of the Civil Code.

original owner has the right to claim damages against the person who disposes of the property without a right.

Where a party acquires, in good faith, a real right other than ownership, the provisions of the preceding two paragraphs shall be applied *mutatis mutandis*.

The fifth principle of the Chinese real rights law is the principle of specificity, which means that real rights must be specific, [1] *i.e.*, the object of a real right is required to be specific. The specificity requirement is satisfied even if the object is not specific upon creation of the real right, as long as it will be specified when the right is realized. For example, the collateral of a mortgage of inventories [2] may not be specified upon creation of the mortgage because it may include all of the production equipment, raw materials, work in process, or even the products that the mortgagor does not own at the moment of creation of the mortgage but may own them in the future. However, the mortgaged collateral must be specified upon realization of the mortgagee's rights. [3]

Another principle of the Chinese real rights law is that the acquisition and enjoyment of the real rights are not without limitation. When acquiring and enjoying a real right, a right-holder must observe the law, respect social ethics, and may not infringe upon the public interest or other's lawful rights and interests. [4] This is actually one of the basic principles of the Chinese civil law.

§ 3:1:2 Thing/ Property

"Property" or "thing" is defined in various ways under different laws in China. For example, the first section of Chapter 5 of the GPCL defined "property" as a tangible thing, but Article 3 of the Succession Law provided that property included both tangible things and rights. The later enacted Real Rights Law clearly limited the concept of "property" to a tangible thing,

---

[1] Article 114 of the Civil Code.
[2] See Article 396 of the Civil Code.
[3] Article 411 of the Civil Code.
[4] Articles 8 of the Civil Code.

including both personal and real property.① Therefore, the intangible things, such as rights in written works, trademarks, inventions, electricity, wind powers, *etc.* were not regulated by the real rights law, but by special laws such as the Copyright Law, Patent Law, or Trademark Law. However, some intangible things that might be exclusively controlled and disposed of by the persons of the civil law were also regulated by the Real Rights Law. For example, the proprietary rights in the intellectual property, account receivables, fund shares, the right to use a lot of land for construction purposes, *etc.* might be pledged or mortgaged. Article 2 of the Real Rights Law thus clarified that if there was a law providing that certain rights should be the object of the real rights, then these rights would be recognized as property to be regulated by the Real Rights Law. The Civil Code has unified the definition of the property, and provides that property consists of immovable and movable property, as well as rights, as long as the law provides that the right shall be treated as property over which a real right lies.②

Accordingly, property includes both real property and personal property. The standard to distinguish the two is whether the property is movable or not: the property that is movable is personal property, and the property that is immovable is real property.③ Real property includes the land and the other property attached to the land which may not be moved according to its nature, or once moved, the economic value of which will be decreased. Since in China the land is owned by the State or collectives, no individual owns the land. However, a person of the civil law may own a right to use a lot of land, and the land-use right may be transferred according to law. To this end, a right to use land is regarded as an interest in the real property. The Security Law provided that the real property referred to the land and the other fixtures on the land, such as houses and trees.④ The Opinions on the GPCL provided that the land, the buildings and the other fixtures on the land, and the auxiliary facilities of the buildings were real property.⑤ Thus, in China, the land, the

---

① Article 2 of the Real Rights Law.
② Article 115 of the Civil Code.
③ Articles 115 and 205 of the Civil Code.
④ Article 92 of the Security Law.
⑤ Article 186 of the Opinions on the GPCL.

buildings constructed on the land, and other fixtures or auxiliary facilities of the buildings are real property. Among them, the land and the buildings constructed on the land cannot be detached from each other; therefore, Chinese law has established a principle that a right-holder of the right to use a lot of land and a right-holder of the ownership in buildings on the lot of land must be the same person, *i.e.*, upon transfer, the buildings constructed on the lot of land will go with the land, and *vice versa*. ①

§3:1:3 Real Rights

A real right is an absolute right of control, which is defined as a right to directly control the property and a right of exclusivity in a specific property, which consists of ownership, right to usufruct, and security interests in the property.② On the one hand, a real right-holder may directly control and dispose of the specific property he owns without any other person's act or consent. On the other hand, the right-holder has a right to exclude any other person from infringing upon his rights. The nature of a real right is not a relationship between human beings and the property, but a relationship between and among human beings.

The creation, alteration, alienation, or extinguishment of a real right in immovable property must be registered to satisfy the public notice requirement, whereas the creation and transfer of a real right in movable property must be subject to the delivery of the movable property in accordance with law. ③

The first facet of real right is a right of control, the scope of which is determined by the categories of the real rights. For example, an ownership right-holder (an owner) has the completest and broadest right to control the property, whereas a right-holder of another type of real rights may only control part of the property. The control referred to herein could be a physical control or a non-physical control, depending on the provisions of law. For instance, a mortgagee may not physically control the property and must follow a certain legal procedure when realizing his right in the collateral. A holder of

---

① See Articles 356 and 357 of the Civil Code.
② Article 114 of the Civil Code.
③ Article 208 of the Civil Code.

a right to control the property may manage, receive, or dispose of the property, and he also has a right to prohibit an obligor from doing a certain act. For example, an obligee of a passive easement has a right to prohibit the owner or user of the servient land from conducting a certain act on the land, such as building constructions.

A real right as an absolute right is also called a right against the whole world. All of the other persons have a duty not to infringe upon or obstruct the real right-holder's rights. This is a passive duty of non-action. In this sense, the real rights are strictly protected by both the real rights law and the tort law. However, it does not mean that the right-holder may exercise his rights freely without any limitation.

§3:1:4 Acquisition of Real Rights

§3:1:4:1 Original Obtainment v. Subsequent Obtainment

A real right may be acquired through original obtainment or subsequent obtainment. If a real right is obtained not through transfer by its original owner, but directly by operation of law, it is said to be acquired through an original obtainment (also called obtainment inherent). In this scenario, the property has not been owned by any person of the civil law before the right-holder obtains the original real right in it, such as in a situation that a property is obtained by occupancy; or although the property had been owned by a person of the civil law, the owner later on abandoned it or lost his rights in it for some reasons. An original obtainment may also occur in the situation of the State's expropriation. In order to satisfy the demands of the public interest, the State may expropriate the land owned by the collective and the houses and other real property owned by an organization or individual within the scope of authority provided by law and according to the legal procedure. [1] An original obtainment of a real right will extinguish all encumbrances on the property. For example, after the State has lawfully expropriated the land owned by a rural collective, the ownership of the collective in the land is extinguished, and the other real rights in the land, such as the right to contract and manage the rural land, or

---

[1] Article 243 of the Civil Code.

the right to use the house site, are also extinguished. The original right-holder cannot claim any right on the property, and the new right-holder may not ask the original right-holder to bear any warranty liability either.

Subsequent obtainment, also called successive obtainment, is an obtainment of a real right based on transfer or grant of a real right. If a real right is transferred from the original right-holder, such as in a sale or gift situation, the property's conditions remain unchanged. A subsequent obtainment may also occur when a real right is created on the property, such as in a mortgage or easement situation.

§ 3:1:4:2 *Bona Fide* Acquisition Doctrine

An ownership may be acquired through *bona fide* acquisition, which refers to a situation where a possessor of real or personal property who does not have a right to dispose thereof, transfers such property to a third person, or creates another real right in such property for a third person's benefit. The third person who acts in good faith will receive the ownership over, or otherwise a real right in, the property. The purpose of this system is to maintain the security of transactions. Before the Real Rights Law was enacted, the *bona fide* acquisition rule was scattered in various laws and judicial interpretations, such as Article 12 of the Commercial Paper Law, Article 89 of the Opinions on the GPCL, and Article 84 of the Interpretations of the Security Law. These provisions had been integrated into Articles 106 - 108 of the Real Rights Law, and now have been integrated into Articles 311-313 of the Civil Code, which apply to *bona fide* acquisition of both ownership and the other real rights. ①

In order to apply the *bona fide* acquisition doctrine, several requirements must be satisfied.

First, the property to be acquired may be either real or personal property, but its transfer must not be prohibited by law. For example, an ownership over real or personal property that the law provides to be exclusively owned by the State may not be obtained through *bona fide* acquisition doctrine. ②

---

① Article 311 of the Civil Code.
② Article 242 of the Civil Code.

Second, the transferor must be a person who has no right to dispose of the property, no matter whether this person possesses the property lawfully or not in the first place. The transferor could be a lawful possessor if he possesses the property based on a right in *personam*, as a lessee, borrower, or custodian, *etc.* who has a right only to possess the property but no right to dispose of the property, or, based on a right to usufruct or a secured interest in the property where his rights do not include the right to dispose of the property. The transferor is also regarded as a lawful possessor if he has ownership over the property but his ownership right is restricted. A typical example is in the case of a co-ownership situation where one of the co-owners disposes of the property without the other co-owners' consent.

Third, the transferee must be a *bona fide* purchaser, or a person acts in good faith, which means that the transferee did not know the fact that the transferor did not have the right to dispose of the property, and that the transfer must be conducted at a reasonable price. [1] If the transferee knew that the transferor did not have the right to dispose of the property, or should have known it but owing to gross negligence did not know it, the transferee is not protected by this doctrine because he has failed to perform the duty of diligence.

Fourth, the transfer must satisfy the public notice requirement, if any, *e.g.*, registration for alteration of the real right; otherwise, the transaction is not regarded as being done in good faith.

Finally, the contract between the transferor who does not have the right to dispose of the property and the transferee is not otherwise invalid or revocable.

However, the *bona fide* acquisition doctrine does not apply to lost property. [2] Generally, an owner or a holder of another right in the lost property has a right to request the lost property to be returned. If the lost property is possessed by another person through transfer, the right-holder has a right to ask the transferor who does not have the right to dispose of the property to pay damages. Alternatively, a right-holder may, within two years since the date when he knows or should have known about the transferee, ask

---

[1] Article 311 of the Civil Code.
[2] Article 312 of the Civil Code.

the transferee to return the property, except that the right-holder may need to pay the price the transferee has paid when purchasing the property if the transferee purchases the lost property through auction, or from a qualified seller. After the right-holder has paid the price to the transferee, he has a right to indemnification against the transferor, who does not have the right to dispose of the property in the first place.

The system of *bona fide* acquisition may affect the various relationships between different parties. For example, an ownership over the property transferred by a person without a right to dispose of it is obtained by the transferee, and the true right-holder has no right to ask the transferee to return the property. ① However, if the property is encumbered, *e.g.*, mortgaged or pledged, then things are different. Since a secured interest in a real property is required by law to register, even if a *bona fide* transferee of the property may obtain ownership over the real property, the obtainment of ownership right will not extinguish the encumbrances on the property because it is presumed that the transferee has knowledge about the existence of such encumbrances. Furthermore, during the period of the mortgage, without the mortgagee's consent, the mortgagor may not transfer the mortgaged property unless the transferee agrees to repay the debts so as to extinguish the mortgage. ② The rule for personal property is different. If personal property is obtained by a *bona fide* transferee, the encumbrances on the property will be extinguished unless the transferee knew or should have known the existence of such encumbrance. ③

The *bona fide* acquisition doctrine will also affect the relationship between the true right-holder and the person without the right to dispose of the property. Although the true right-holder may lose his right in the property under the doctrine, he still has a right to claim against the person who disposes of the property without a right to do so based on either contract or tort law theories. ④

---

① Article 311 of the Civil Code.
② Article 406 of the Civil Code.
③ Article 313 of the Civil Code.
④ Article 311 of the Civil Code.

§ 3:1:4:3 Obtainment by Occupation

Occupation doctrine allows a person to obtain ownership over personal property that does not have an owner by possessing it. This doctrine only applies to personal property that has no owner, such as wild plants and animals, except for those expressly protected by the Law on Protection of Wild Animals and Plants and the similar laws and regulations. It may also be applied to the abandoned personal property. The personal property that may be obtained by occupation must be transferrable according to law. For example, medical wastes may not be obtained by occupation because the law prohibits transfer or sale of the medical wastes.① A person must establish his intent to own the property in order to obtain ownership over the property through occupation.

§ 3:1:4:4 Obtainment by Find of Lost Property

Some countries recognize obtainment of real rights in lost property by find, but Chinese law does not. Lost property is personal property that has an owner but is not possessed by anyone at the moment when it is found. Sometimes it is hard to determine whether a property is a lost property or a property without an owner. In this situation, the Chinese law presumes that the property is lost property in order to better protect the ownership rights and to avoid the situation that a true right-holder loses his right owing to the occupation system.

The Chinese law grants various rights to and imposes various duties on the finders of lost property. A finder of lost property has a general duty to timely notify and return it to the true owner.② Where a finder of lost property, floating property, or a lost domesticated animal returns it to the owner, the owner is responsible for the expenses thus incurred by the finder.③ If the owner is unknown, the finder should send it to the police or another relevant department. Before returning it or submitting it to the relevant department, the finder has a duty to well keep the property. If the lost property is damaged or destroyed owing to an intentional or grossly negligent act of the finder or the

---

① Article 14 of the Regulations on Management of Medical Wastes.
② Article 314 of the Civil Code.
③ Article 319 of the Civil Code.

relevant department responsible for keeping it, the finder or keeper shall bear civil liability. ①

No specific institution is designated by law as being responsible for accepting and keeping lost property, but some local legislations or departmental rules designates such an institution like one in a railway station, the local airport, a police station, or a notary public office to take the charge. The relevant department that has received the lost property must notify the known owner, or otherwise its right-holder to take it back, or make a timely public notice if the owner is unknown. ② A finder who refuses to return the property to its right-holder upon request is liable for returning the benefit unjustly obtained or liable under tort law. ③ A finder who has illegally possessed the lost property as his own, if the amount is large and if he refuses to return, will bear criminal liability for committing a conversion. ④

A finder does have certain rights, though. First, a finder has a right to ask for reimbursement. A right-holder who takes back the lost property should pay the necessary expenses incurred by the finder or the relevant department for keeping the lost property. ⑤ If a right-holder of the lost property refuses to pay the above expenses, the finder or the keeper may retain the property under a lien. ⑥ If a right-holder has posted a reward for finding the lost property, upon taking back the property, the finder may ask for the reward. ⑦ However, a finder who illegally converts the lost property has no right to any compensation or reward. If no one claims ownership over the lost property within one year after the date the public notice is posted, the property will be escheated to the State. ⑧

§ 3:1:4:5 Obtainment by Discovering Buried or Hidden Property

Buried property is personal property that is buried inside another thing and

---

① Article 316 of the Civil Code.
② Article 315 of the Civil Code.
③ Article 94 of the Opinions on the GPCL.
④ Article 270 of the Criminal Law.
⑤ Article 317 of the Civil Code.
⑥ Article 447 of the Civil Code.
⑦ Article 317 of the Civil Code.
⑧ Article 318 of the Civil Code.

the owner is unclear, such as jewelries buried under the earth. Hidden property is personal property that is hidden in another thing and its owner is unclear. When it is hard to determine whether the found property is buried or hidden property, or lost property, the Chinese law presumes that it is lost property. The provisions on finding lost property also apply to the find of floating property, buried property, or hidden property, except that if the law on protection of cultural relics or other laws that have special regulations thereon, the latter prevails.① For example, the cultural relics buried under the ground are owned by the State and may not be privately excavated by any organization or individual; therefore, the regulations on find of buried or hidden property do not apply to cultural relics.②

Since the law applicable to lost property applies to buried and hidden property, a person who discovers buried or hidden property also has the same rights and duties as a finder of lost property, and the property may be escheated to the State if its owner cannot be located within one year after a public notice is posted.③ In this sense, Chinese law does not recognize the doctrine of obtainment by discovering buried or hidden property. However, what will happen if the property was known to be buried by a person? The following case may give out an answer.

Case 18

Case 18: Wangs v. Huai An Museum④

Bingcheng Wang and the other five people (collectively Wangs) have been living in Room 306 of Dong Chang Street of Huai An City. In April 2007, their house was included in the area of demolition. Before the house was demolished, Wangs notified the project office and the local residents' committee that their grandfather buried ancient coins under the ground below the house. During the demolition, Wangs and the demolition

---

① Article 319 of the Civil Code.
② Article 5 of the Law on Protection of Cultural Relics.
③ Article 318 of the Civil Code.
④ See (2011) Huai Zhong Min Zhong Zi No. 1287, reprinted in the SPC Gazette, Issue 5, 2013.

department could not reach agreement regarding the amount of subsidy for the demolition and settlement. On September 27, 2009, while the demolition personnel were discussing with Wangs about the demolition matters in another place, Wangs' house was demolished. On October 13, 2009, when the demolition personnel dug out some ancient coins from under Wangs' house, the people hanging around looted some of the coins. Later on, the coins were cleaned up and collected by the City Museum. After an appraisal, it was determined that these coins were culture relics with certain historical and cultural value. The coins were made of copper during the late Qing Dynasty until early 1910s. On April 14, 2010, Huai An City Police and the Culture Relics Bureau of Huai An City made an announcement requesting all people who looted the coins to voluntarily cooperate with the recovery of the cultural relics.

On October 19, 2009, the local residents' committee issued a certificate stating that Wang family reported for several times that there were certain ancient coins buried under their house since April 7, 2007. There were also some people testifying that Wangs' grandfather engaged in wine business and that Wangs' report was true. On October 20, 2009, the demolition office issued a certificate to the same effect. Regarding the amount of the ancient coins, Wangs claimed that there were 13 bags and approximately 150,000 – 160,000 coins; the museum admitted that there were 13 bags, but it argued that after cleaning, there were only about 55,000 coins. The court inspected the temporary warehouse of the museum and sealed up the two cardboard boxes that contained all of the coins cleaned up by the museum.

After trial, the Qinghe District People's Court of Huai An City holds that the evidences are sufficient to prove that these coins belong to the ancestors of the Wangs. Regarding whether these coins should be returned to Wangs, the court holds that Chinese law does not prohibit citizens from lawfully owning the cultural relics although their transfer may be restricted.

According to Article 93 of the SPC's Tentative Opinion on Certain Issues Concerning the Implementation of the GPCL, where a citizen can prove that a buried or hidden property dug out or discovered belongs to him, and where according to the current laws and policies it may be owned by him, such a right should be protected. Article 6 also provides that regarding cultural relics belonging to collectives or private individuals, their ownership rights are protected by law. Therefore, the law allows private persons to own cultural relics. The coins involved in this case were buried by Wangs' grandfather and thus are cultural relics with an owner, so that Wangs can lawfully inherit and possess them. Finally, the court requests the museum to return the two boxes of ancient coins to Wangs.

The museum appealed to the Intermediate People's Court of Huai An City. The appellate court affirms the lower court's decision.

§3:1:5 Change to Real Rights

A change to a real right includes alteration and loss of the real right.

§3:1:5:1 Alteration of Real Rights

In a narrower sense, alteration of a real right means the changing of the content of a real right. For example, a mortgagee and a mortgagor may agree to change the priority order of repayment of the mortgagee or the amount of debts secured by the collateral, provided that the alteration of the mortgage does not adversely affect the rights of the other mortgagees without the latter's written consent. ① The alteration of a real right is to be effectuated on either delivery or registration of the property concerned. Generally, the creation, alteration, transfer, or extinguishment of a right in real property must be registered, and alteration of a right in personal property will not be effective unless after being delivered. ②

In China, all land belongs to the State or collectives, and any right created in the land must be registered in order to be effective. However, the law has provided various exceptional situations. For example, in rural areas, a person of the civil law may obtain a right to manage a lot of the rural land through contracting with the local collective. Such right (hereinafter "the right to use rural land") is a land use right, which is a type of right to usufruct in real

---

① Article 409 of the Civil Code.
② Articles 209 and 224 of the Civil Code.

property. However, such a right is created upon effectiveness of the land use contract, not upon registration. ① If a right-holder of the right to use rural land exchanges or transfers such right with or to the other persons, they may request registration for alteration with the local people's government at or above the county level. ② Without registration, the alteration will not be effective against a *bona fide* third person. Similarly, the creation of a right to easement is also effective upon effectiveness of the easement contract, ③ and it is only an option for the parties to register the right with the local government; provided, however, if without registration, the easement is not effective against a *bona fide* third person.

Some property like automobiles, boats, aircrafts, and similar transportation vehicles are personal property in nature, but they are treated as quasi-real property. Therefore, the alteration of the real rights in such property is also subject to registration. For example, the obtainment, transfer, and extinguishment of the ownership right in civil aircrafts should be registered with the department under the State Council responsible for civil aviation; without registration, the alteration will not be effective against a third person. ④ In order to create a mortgage in a civil aircraft, both the mortgagor and the mortgagee must register with the civil aviation department; without registration it is not effective against a third person. ⑤ The obtainment, transfer, and extinguishment of ownership of a ship must be registered with the ship registration authority; otherwise it is not effective against a third person. ⑥ Upon creation of a mortgage in a ship, the mortgagee and the mortgagor should register with the registration authority for ships; otherwise it is not effective against a third person. ⑦ The alteration of real rights in automobiles should be registered with the relevant authority, but the

---

① Article 333 of the Civil Code.
② Article 335 of the Civil Code.
③ Article 374 of the Civil Code.
④ Article 14 of the Civil Aviation Law, which was enacted by the NPC on October 30, 1995 and effective on March 1, 1996.
⑤ Article 16 of the Civil Aviation Law.
⑥ Article 9 of the Maritime Law, which was enacted by the NPC on November 7, 1992 and effective on July 1, 1993.
⑦ Article 13 of the Maritime Law.

registration is not a legal element for the effectiveness of the alteration of the right.① These provisions have been integrated into Article 225 of the Civil Code which provides that the creation, transfer, alteration, or extinguishment of the real rights in ships, aircrafts, and automobiles are not effective against a *bona fide* third person without being registered.

§ 3:1:5:2 Extinguishment of Real Rights

A real right in property will extinguish if the property does not exist anymore. For example, if A's house is burned to the ground by B, A's ownership in the house also extinguishes. However, A has a right to ask B to compensate his loss; in this sense, A's ownership right in the house has turned from a real right to a right in *personam* against the debtor B. Sometimes a real right will extinguish even if the property is not totally destroyed. For instance, if A throws away a cell phone that does not work anymore, the ownership of A over the cell phone extinguishes even though the cell phone itself still exists after the abandonment.

§ 3:1:6 Public Notice of Real Rights

§ 3:1:6:1 Registration of Real Property
In General

The creation, alteration, transfer, or extinguishment of a right in real property must be registered in order to be effective against a third person. Registration of real property is actually the registration of the rights in the real property. The rights that are required to be registered include a right to use a lot of land for construction purposes, the ownership right in a house, a mortgagee's right, a right to use a lot of rural land, and a right to easement, *etc*. The registration authority is the administrative authority responsible for regulating the specific type of property. For example, the registration authority for a right to use a lot of land for construction purposes is the land administration; the registration authority for a real right in a building is the

---

① Article 12 of the Road Traffic Safety Law, which was promulgated by the NPC on October 28, 2003, and effective on May 1, 2004.

administrative department responsible for buildings. Upon registration, the registration authority will not only record the rights in the real property on the register of immovable property, but also issue a corresponding real right certificate to the right-holder.

Types of Real Property Registration

Registration of real property includes initial registration, registration for creation, registration for transfer (alienation), registration for alteration, and registration for extinguishment (deregistration).

Initial registration is the first-time registration of an ownership right in a newly constructed building, or the first-time registration of an ownership in the land owned by a collective. The State does not need to register its rights in real property because the natural resources that belong to the State are not required by law to be registered. ①

Registration for creation is the registration of the rights in real property other than the ownership rights, such as a right to use a lot of rural land, a right to use a lot of land for construction purposes, a mortgage right, a right to easement, and the like. A right to use a lot of land for construction purposes is created upon registration and the registration authority will issue a certificate of such to the right-holder. ② The mortgage of certain rights in property must also be registered. ③

Registration for transfer includes registration of transfer of a land use right, an ownership right in a house, and other real rights in property arising from sales, exchanges, capital contribution, or gift. Without being registered, such a transfer is not effective. ④

Registration for alteration refers to the situation where the content of a right or the real property itself changes so that the same party must register the change with the authority. For example, if the street, the number, or the name of a house has been changed, or if the area size of a house increases or decreases, the right-holder of the house should register the change with the

---

① Articles 210 and 208 of the Civil Code.
② Article 349 of the Civil Code.
③ Article 402 of the Civil Code.
④ Article 355 of the Civil Code.

authority. A mortgagee and a mortgagor may through an agreement change the priority order of repayment of the mortgagee and the amount of debts secured. Such alteration is not effective until being registered. ①

Deregistration is also called registration for writing off the real right. When a right in real property extinguishes owing to a legal cause or an agreed reason, the right-holder should file for deregistration of the right. For example, when a right to use a lot of land for construction purposes extinguishes, the grantor should timely file for deregistration. ② If the registered right to use a house site extinguishes, the user should timely file for deregistration. ③ Upon deregistration, the registration authority should take back the real right certificate.

Effect of Registration

The creation, alteration, transfer, or extinguishment of a right in real property is effective upon the time it is registered on the real property register if the law so requires. ④ Generally, once registration is completed, the change of the real right becomes effective, ⑤ and it is presumed that the recorded information on the register truly reflects the actual situation of the real property. Anyone who challenges the registration must prove that the matter recorded in the register is wrong. A third person who relies on the register and conducts transactions with the recorded right-holder is protected by law. ⑥

However, a transaction involving transfer of an unregistered right in real property is not necessarily ineffective, although it had been the long-standing practice in Chinese judicial practice to confuse the registration of real property with the effectiveness of the transaction involving the real property.

The Chinese Contract Law provided a general rule, which has been integrated into the Civil Code, that a contract formed according to law is effective upon formation, and that if the contract is required by law or

---

① Article 409 of the Civil Code.
② Article 360 of the Civil Code.
③ Article 365 of the Civil Code.
④ Article 214 of the Civil Code.
⑤ Articles 208, 209 and 214 of the Civil Code.
⑥ Article 311 of the Civil Code.

administrative regulations to be approved or registered before taking effect, the contract should be so approved or registered.① The SPC made an interpretation on this provision which specifically provided that if there was a law or regulation providing that a contract would not be effective without being approved or registered, then the contract would not be effective if the party had not received the required approval, or had not been approved or registered before the end of the court argument phase of the first instance trial. On the other hand, if the law or administrative regulation only required the contract be registered, but did not say that the effectiveness of the contract would be conditioned only upon registration, then the effectiveness of the contract would not be affected if the parties had not registered the contract, but the transfer of ownership rights and other rights in the real property as the subject matter of the contract should not be effective.② If, according to law, a contract is not effective unless it has been approved or registered, failure to obtain approval or registration does not affect the validity of the contract clauses concerning performance of the obligation of filing for approval and the like procedures and the other relevant clauses, and the party obligated to complete application for approval or other procedures shall bear default liability for breach of such obligation.③

The Real Rights Law integrated this judicial interpretation in its Article 15, which has been subsequently included in the Civil Code. The law provides that a contract signed between the parties on creation, alteration, transfer, or extinguishment of a right in real property becomes effective upon formation of the contract, unless it is otherwise provided by law or agreed upon by the parties. It further provides that the fact that a real right has not been registered will not affect the effectiveness of the contract.④

Registration Authorities

The authorities for property registration include the land administration department, house administration department, agricultural administration

---

① Article 44 of the Contract Law (Article 502 of the Civil Code).
② Article 9 of the Judicial Interpretations I of the Contract Law.
③ See Article 502 of the Civil Code.
④ Article 215 of the Civil Code.

department, forestry administration department, ocean administration department, *etc*. Different provinces have different practices regarding the administration of real property and its registration. Some provinces/cities have unified the registration of houses and land, such as Shanghai, Chongqing, Shenzhen, and Guangzhou; while most of the other cities have not unified them. Article 210 of the Civil Code requires that the State implement a unified registration system for real property. ① A right-holder should register the real property with the registration authority of the place where the property is located.

The specific jurisdiction over real property registration is regulated by the land administration law and the urban real estate administration law. The Land Administration Law② provides that the land owned by the rural collectives should be registered with the local government at the county level, which will determine the ownership right and issue a real right certificate over the property. If a lot of collective-owned land is used for non-agricultural purpose, it must be registered with the government at the county level; if an organization or individual lawfully uses a lot of State-owned land, they should register it with the local government above the county level.

The specific registration and certificate-issuing authority for the State-owned Land used by the State agencies of the Central Government are determined by the State Council. The determination of the right to own and the right to use the forests and grasslands or the right to use the water surface or tidal flats should be in accordance with the Law on Forests, the Law on Grasslands, and the Law on Fishery. The Urban Real Estate Administration Law③ provides that the housing administration department of local government above the county level is responsible for examining the initial registration, registration for alteration, registration for transfer, and registration for mortgages of the real rights, and issuing the real right certificate accordingly.

---

① Article 210 of the Civil Code.
② The Land Administration Law was enacted by the NPC on August 29th, 1998, and effective on January 1st, 1999.
③ The Urban Real Estate Administration Law was promulgated by the NPC on July 5, 1994, and effective on January 1, 1995.

Real Right Register and Certificate

The register of real property is established by the State and kept by the registration authority. It is the basis for determining the attributes and coverage of real rights.① A right-holder or an interested person may apply to the registration authority to retrieve and make copies of the registration materials,② and if a matter recorded on the register is mistaken, it must be corrected.③

A real right certificate of real property is a proof of a right-holder's rights in the real property.④ The main purpose of issuing the real right certificate is to guarantee the priority order of registration and the security thereof. An applicant must pay a fee for the real property registration, and such fee is based on each entry instead of a percentage of the area, size, or purchase price of the real property.⑤ The matters recorded on the real right certificate should be consistent with those recorded on the real property register; if there are any discrepancies, the real property register shall prevail unless there is evidence proving that the real property register has a clear error.⑥ If a person's interests are harmed owing to the registration's clerical error in registering the real property in the register, the registration authority is liable for compensation.⑦ However, if a mistake was made owing to the applicant's provision of false materials upon application for registration and thus causes damage to another person, the applicant is liable for compensation.⑧

If the register's recordation is mistaken or omits some important information, the parties may apply to the registration authority to correct the error and have the information recorded in the register be rectified. The registration authority may also do it on its own initiative. A right-holder or an interested person who believes that the matter recorded on the real property

---

① Article 216 of the Civil Code.
② Article 218 of the Civil Code.
③ Article 220 of the Civil Code.
④ Article 217 of the Civil Code.
⑤ Article 223 of the Civil Code.
⑥ Article 217 of the Civil Code.
⑦ Article 222 of the Civil Code.
⑧ Article 222 of the Civil Code.

register is mistaken may apply for rectification. ① The registration authority should correct it if the right-holder as recorded in the register consents in writing to the correction, or if there is evidence proving that the registration is clearly wrong. If the right-holder as recorded in the register does not agree to the correction, an interested person may apply for a registration of demurrer, which is a temporary registration for protecting the lawful rights and interests of the true right-holder by temporarily cutting off the public notice power of the register and sending a warning to the third person of the transaction. If the registration authority registers the demurrer, the applicant must file a lawsuit within 15 days after the demurrer is registered; otherwise the registration of demurrer becomes invalid. If the registration of demurrer is inappropriate and thus causes damage to the right-holder, the right-holder may request compensation from the applicant of the registration of demurrer. ②

Priority Registration

If the parties sign an agreement for the sale of a house or any other real right in real property, the parties may, upon agreement, apply to the registration authority for registration of a priority notice (vormerkung) for the purpose of securing the realization of the real right in the future. After a priority notice is registered, no one may dispose of the registered real property without consent of the right-holder as registered. However, the applicant who registers a priority notice must register the real right in the real property within 90 days from the date on which the creditor's claim extinguishes or the real property is eligible for registration; otherwise the registration of the priority notice becomes ineffective. ③ The registration of a priority notice mainly applies to a pre-purchased house, a mortgage in a pre-purchased house, or a mortgage of a project being constructed, and the transfer thereof.

§ 3:1:6:2 Delivery of Personal Property

While a right in real property needs to be registered, a right in personal

---

① Article 220 of the Civil Code.
② Article 220 of the Civil Code.
③ Article 221 of the Civil Code.

property needs to be delivered according to Chinese law. Specifically, the creation, alteration, transfer, or extinguishment of a right in movables will not be effective unless it is delivered.① Delivery originally means actual delivery, i.e., the actual transfer of the possession of the personal property from one person to another, so the delivery of a real right in personal property can only refer to the creation and transfer of the ownership right in personal property and pledge on personal property.

Sometimes actual delivery is not necessary and simple delivery is enough. For example, if the subject matter of a contract has been possessed by the buyer before the contract is formed, delivery is completed upon the time the contract becomes effective. Similarly, if a right-holder has lawfully possessed the personal property before a real right in the property is created or transferred, delivery is deemed to be completed upon the time the juristic act creating or transferring the real right becomes effective.② In short, simple delivery does not require the property to be actually delivered from one person to another.

Delivery may be done through *constitutum possessorium*, which means that a person transfers the ownership right in the specific property he owns to another person while the property is still under the transferor's control. In other words, upon transfer of the real right in personal property, if the parties agree that the transferor will continue to possess the personal property, the real right will be effectively transferred to the transferee upon the time the agreement becomes effective, and no delivery is required.③ Since the transferee does not actually possess the property, it is also called "indirect possession."

Delivery may also be achieved through instructions, which is also called "transfer of the right to restitution." If a third person lawfully possesses the personal property before a right in the property is created or transferred, the person who has a duty to deliver the property may transfer his right to request a third person to return the property in lieu of delivering it.④ For example, A rented a car to B, and then sold the car to C. A may transfer his right against B to C, so that C will receive the ownership right in the car.

---

① Article 224 of the Civil Code.
② Article 226 of the Civil Code.
③ Article 228 of the Civil Code.
④ Article 227 of the Civil Code.

§ 3:2 Ownership Rights

An ownership right is a complete right over real property or personal property, and a right-holder (owner) may completely control the real right of the subject matter, including possessing, using, profiting from, and disposing of the real or personal property he owns.① An owner also has a right to create a right to usufruct or a security interest in the real or personal property he owns,② and the holder of the right to usufruct or the holder of the security interest thus created may not harm the rights and interests of the owner of the property. However, the ownership right is not without limitation, and a person, when obtaining or exercising the ownership right, must abide by law, respect social ethics, and may not harm the public interest or other's lawful rights or interests.

The ownership rights include both active rights and passive rights. An active right may include a right to possess, use, profit from, and dispose of the property, while a passive right is a right that an owner may exclude other's unjust interference with his right. The main way to exclude this interference is to exercise a right to claim on real rights.③ In China, the ownership right is an exclusive right.

§3:2:1 Ownership of the State, Collectives, and Private Individuals

One of the fundamental policies of the Chinese Constitution is that at the primary phase of the socialism, the State implements an economic system under which the public ownership is in a dominant position, with various other types of ownership co-existing.④ Accordingly, there exist public ownership and non-public ownership, and the public ownership includes State ownership and collective ownership.

§ 3:2:1:1 State Ownership

Under the Chinese Constitution, State-owned economy, *i.e.*, "the

---

① Article 240 of the Civil Code.
② Article 241 of the Civil Code.
③ Article 241 of the Civil Code.
④ Article 6 of the Constitution.

socialist economy of ownership by the whole people," is the predominant force in Chinese national economy, and the State guarantees the consolidation and development of it.① The State ownership refers to the right that the State has to possess, use, profit from, and dispose of the State-owned property, which is regarded as an ownership by the whole people. The property that the law provides to be owned by the State belong to the State.②

The State ownership covers a broad range of rights. Chapter 5 of Book Two of the Civil Code lists the property that the law provides to be exclusively owned by the State, including the land, mineral deposits, waters, sea areas, *etc*. The most important production materials also generally belong to the State. See the following Articles:

Article 247

Mineral deposits, waters, and sea areas are owned by the State.

Article 248

Uninhabited islands are owned by the State, and the State Council exercises the ownership rights over the uninhabited islands on behalf of the State.

Article 249

Urban land is owned by the State. Land in rural and urban suburbs that is provided by law to be owned by the State is owned by the State.

Article 250

Natural resources, such as forests, mountain ridges, grasslands,

---

① Article 7 of the Constitution.
② Article 246 of the Civil Code.

unreclaimed land, and mudflats, other than those provided by law to be collectively-owned, are owned by the State.

Article 251

The wild animal and plant resources that are provided by law to be owned by the State are owned by the State.

Article 252

Radio-frequency spectrum resources are owned by the State.

Article 253

The cultural relics that are provided by law to be owned by the State are owned by the State.

Article 254

The assets for national defense are owned by the State.

Infrastructures such as railways, roads, electric power facilities, telecommunication facilities, as well as oil and gas pipelines that are provided by law to be owned by the State are owned by the State.

The State ownership will be exercised by the State Council on behalf of the State.① If the law provides that the real or personal property exclusively belong to the State, then no organization or individual may obtain ownership rights over tit.② The public property is stated to be "sacred and inviolable,"③ which fully reflects the predominant position of public ownership in China.

---

① Article 246 of the Civil Code.
② Article 242 of the Civil Code.
③ Article 12 of the Constitution.

§ 3:2:1:2 Collective Ownership

Collective ownership is a type of ownership under which the people within each collective organization collectively have the right to possess, use, profit from, and dispose of the property owned by the collective. ① The State protects the lawful rights and interests of the urban and rural collective economic organizations, encourages, guides, and helps the development of the collective economy. ② In China, collective ownership includes rural collective ownership and urban collective ownership. It is an important ownership form in the rural areas in China because most of the rural lands are owned by the rural collectives. The Constitution allows the rural collective economic organizations to adopt a two-tier management system, with household contractual management as the basis, integrated with the collective management of the rural lands. ③ The various forms of cooperative economy, such as hand crafting, production, construction, transportation, commercial, and service industries in the urban areas may also be owned by collectives. ④ The collective-owned property, as part of the public property, is also "sacred and inviolable" under the Constitution, ⑤ and no organization or individual may misappropriate, loot, secretly distribute, or destruct the property. ⑥

§ 3:2:1:3 Non-Public Ownership

Private ownership is a type of ownership under which private individuals own their lawful income, houses, articles for daily use, production tools, raw materials, and other personal and real property in accordance with law. ⑦ The Constitution grants protection to private ownership. Private economy, along with the individual economy, is categorized as non-pubic economy in China, which is regarded as an important component of socialist market economy. The State protects the private ownership, ⑧ encourages, supports, and guides the

---

① Articles 260–263 of the Civil Code.
② Article 8 of the Constitution.
③ Article 8 of the Constitution; also see Article 330 of the Civil Code.
④ Article 8 of the Constitution.
⑤ Article 12 of the Constitution.
⑥ Article 265 of the Civil Code.
⑦ Article 266 of the Civil Code.
⑧ Article 11 of the Constitution.

development of non-public economy, and supervises and administers such according to law. ①

While the Constitution provides that public property is "sacred and inviolable," ② it also states that private property lawfully owned by the citizens is "inviolable." ③ The Civil Code specifies the details about how to protect private real rights. ④ For instance, the lawful savings, investment, and income of private individuals are protected by law, and the State protects the individuals' right to succession and other lawful rights and interests. ⑤ In addition, the law expressly states that the lawfully-owned property of private individuals are protected by law, and no organization or individual person may misappropriate, loot, or destroy such property. ⑥

§ 3:2:1:4 Expropriation and Requisition

Private ownership is protected by the Chinese Constitution and the Civil Code, but the State may expropriate or requisition private property under certain circumstances. ⑦

Expropriation

Expropriation is a way that the State may acquire real property from collectives or private owners for the need of the public interest and in accordance with the legal procedure. ⑧ The legal requirements for expropriation are very strict.

First, both the Constitution and the Civil Code provide that the property may only be expropriated for the needs of the public interest. Under the Constitution, the State, for the needs of the public interest, may expropriate or requisition the private property of the citizens according to law and must give compensation

---

① Article 11 of the Constitution.
② Article 12 of the Constitution.
③ Article 13 of the Constitution, also see Articles 267-270 of the Civil Code.
④ Articles 267-270 of the Civil Code.
⑤ Articles 124 and 1120 of the Civil Code.
⑥ Article 267 of the Civil Code.
⑦ Article 13 of the Constitution; also see Article 117 of the Civil Code.
⑧ Article 243 of the Civil Code.

therefor.① The Civil Code also provides that for the purpose of the public interest, the State may expropriate the collectively-owned land and the houses and other real property owned by an organization or individual within the scope of authority and according to the procedure provided by law.②

Second, expropriation of arable lands is highly restricted. Since the total areas of the arable lands in China have been decreased in recent decades, China implements a special protection on the arable lands, and strictly restricts the transform of arable lands into lands for construction purposes.③

Third, expropriation must be done by the State within the scope of authority and in accordance with the procedure provided by law.④ Only the laws promulgated by the NPC may authorize expropriation and its procedure because regulating the expropriation of non-State-owned property is exclusively within the legislative powers of the NPC and its Standing Committee under the Law on Legislations.⑤

Fourth, the Constitution requires the State to pay compensation for expropriation.⑥ Accordingly, the Civil Code provides that when expropriating the collectively-owned land, the State should fully compensate the collective in the way of paying land compensation fees, resettlement subsidies, and compensation fees for rural villagers' dwellings and other ground attachments, as well as young crops on the ground, and arrange social security premiums for the farmers affected by the expropriation and secure their livelihood and lawful rights and interests.⑦ When expropriating a house or other immovable property owned by a private organization or individual, compensation for resettlement must be made and the lawful rights and interests of the affected person must be protected.⑧ If the expropriated house is the residence of its original owner, the living condition of the affected person must be guaranteed.⑨ Furthermore, no

---

① Article 13 of the Constitution.
② Article 243 of the Civil Code.
③ Article 244 of the Civil Code.
④ Article 243 of the Civil Code.
⑤ Article 8 of the Law on Legislations.
⑥ Article 13 of the Constitution.
⑦ Article 243 of the Civil Code.
⑧ Article 243 of the Civil Code.
⑨ Article 243 of the Civil Code.

organization or individual may embezzle, misappropriate, secretly distribute, intercept, or default on the payment of the expropriation fees. ①

Requisition

Requisition refers to a situation in which the private property owned by a private organization or individual is used by the State for the needs of the public interest. The State may, within the scope of authority and in accordance with the procedure provided by law, requisition the real or personal property owned by a private organization or individual in response to an emergency, such as for providing disaster relief or preventing and controlling pandemics. ② The requisitioned property must, after its use, be returned to the affected owner, and the State must pay compensation to such owner during or after the requisition. If the requisitioned property is destructed, damaged, or lost after being requisitioned, compensation shall also be made. ③

Distinction between Expropriations and Requisitions

The differences between an expropriation and a requisition are quite obvious. The object of expropriation is the land owned by the collective, or the houses or other real property owned by the organizations or individuals, while the object of requisition may be either real property or personal property. The conditions for the application of expropriation and requisition are different. Expropriation must be for the public interest in general, while requisition must be for the public interest in disaster relief or rescuing others, and the need must be emergent so that the State does not have time to purchase or produce the property from the market.

In addition, the legal effects of the two are different. The consequence of expropriation is that the ownership over the land owned by the collective, and the ownership on the real property owned by an organization or individual extinguishes, and the State obtains the ownership rights; however, requisition only deprives the original owner of the right to use the real or personal

---

① Article 243 of the Civil Code.
② Article 245 of the Civil Code.
③ Article 245 of the Civil Code.

property that has been requisitioned, but the ownership right is still held by the organization or individual as long as the property has not been destructed. Consequently, after the purpose of the requisition has been achieved, the property should be returned to its original owner.

Since expropriation extinguishes the ownership right of the organization or individual over the real property, the other affiliated real rights on the real property will also be extinguished. Therefore, a person holding a right to use the real property which is expropriated is also entitled to compensation.① However, requisition does not necessarily lead to extinguishment of the ownership, and the property that has been temporarily requisitioned will be returned to its original owner.② Compensation will only be granted if the property has been damaged or lost. Accordingly, a person holding the right to usufruct in the requisitioned property will only be compensated if the requisition leads to extinguishment of the right to usufruct or affects the exercise of such a right.③

§3:2:2 Ownership of a Building's Units

Ownership over a building's units is a special type of real estate ownership newly recognized by Chinese Law. Such a right exists when a building is composed of various units each separately owned by a different owner, while all the owners co-own the common areas of the building. Chapter 6 of Book Two of the Civil Code provides detailed regulations on such right. Basically, the unit owners each has a right to exclusively own his unit, *i.e.*, his residence or premise inside the building, and has a right to co-own and co-manage the common area within or attached to the building other than the unit exclusively owned by them.④ This special type of ownership right is a combination of three different rights, *i.e.*, an independent ownership of each unit owner over the unit exclusively owned by him, a co-ownership over the other parts of the building, and the right to manage the building arising from the joint ownership.

---

① Article 327 of the Civil Code.
② Article 245 of the Civil Code.
③ Article 327 of the Civil Code.
④ Article 271 of the Civil Code.

§ 3:2:2:1 An Independent Ownership over A Unit

An owner of a unit of a building (unit owner) has an independent ownership right over the unit exclusively owned by him as his residence or business premise.① Such a unit refers to the part of the building that in its structure and utility is independent from each other and may be used and disposed of by each owner independently.② In other words, an exclusive unit must be independent in structure and independent in utility. Independency in structure means that each unit of the building is completely isolated from the other units of the building, i.e., there are four walls which may shelter the owner's space from others. Generally, the developer of a building uses clear dividing walls to make sure that each unit is independent from the other units and the structure is independent. Independency of utility means that each unit may be independently used by the owner as a residence, office, or warehouse.

The ownership right in a building's unit is not different from the ownership right in any other house, so that it also includes the right to possess, use, profit from, and dispose of the unit.③ Since each unit is a part of the building, the creation, alteration, transfer, or extinguishment of the right in the building's unit must be registered to be effective.④ Therefore, a unit owner must file registration in order to obtain such right. The right of a unit owner is not absolute because he may not change the purpose of the building by his own will. Therefore, a unit owner is prohibited from changing his residence into a commercial premise in violation of law unless the owner has obtained consent from all of the other interested unit owners and must not violate the law, regulations, or covenants.⑤

§ 3:2:2:2 A Co-Ownership over the Common Areas

The unit owners of a building jointly own the common areas of the building in addition to their exclusive units. It is a special type of co-ownership which is

---

① Article 271 of the Civil Code.
② See Article 114 of the Civil Code; also see local legislations such as Article 47 of Regulations on Administration of Residential Buildings by Shanghai Municipality, and Article 92 of the Regulations on Administration of Buildings by Chongqing Municipality.
③ Article 272 of the Civil Code.
④ Articles 208 and 209 of the Civil Code.
⑤ Article 279 of the Civil Code.

different from a joint ownership or an ownership by shares. It is different from a joint ownership because the allocation of the expenses on the building and its attached facilities and the distribution of the income gained therefrom should be agreed upon by all unit owners; without such an agreement, or if the agreement is unclear, it will be determined according to the proportion of the area of each unit owner's exclusive unit to the total area of the building. ① It is also different from an ownership by shares, because the unit owners may not partition or dispose of the co-owned common areas, and may only transfer such right upon transferring the unit he owns. ②

The common areas include the lot of land under the building. When a building, construction, and their attached facilities are transferred, exchanged, contributed as capital, or gifted, the right to use the lot of land (for construction purposes) that is occupied by the building, construction, and their attached facilities will be disposed of concomitantly. ③ In other words, a right to use a lot of land for construction purposes will follow the buildings and constructions above the land. Consequently, when a unit owner obtains a right in the building, he also obtains a right to use the lot of land under the building. In this sense, the land under the building is part of the common areas of the unit owners.

The green lands and roads within the residential area are also part of the common areas. The green lands within the construction zone are co-owned by all unit owners, except for the public green lands which are owned by the city or town, or the green land which is expressly indicated to belong to a private owner. ④ The roads within the construction zone are also co-owned by all unit owners, except for the public roads that belong to the city or town. ⑤ However, the infrastructure facilities such as railroads, public roads, electronic facilities, telecommunication facilities, or gas pipes within the construction zone may be owned by the State if so provided by law. ⑥

---

① Article 283 of the Civil Code.
② Article 273 of the Civil Code.
③ Article 357 of the Civil Code.
④ Article 274 of the Civil Code.
⑤ Article 274 of the Civil Code.
⑥ Article 254 of the Civil Code.

Common areas also include the other public areas and premises used for public utilities and property services.① These may include the areas and facilities that are for use of all unit owners, including the elevator, firefighting facilities, street lamps, pumps, heating, water pipes, drainpipes, public lighting, mail boxes, garbage collection facilities, *etc.* which are within the building, and parks, ponds, spring fountains, gate, playground, football court, cultural and sports facilities for public benefits, and garbage cans, *etc.* which are in the open area. The premises used for property services may include the offices, cleaning room, storage room, activities room for the owners committee, *etc.*

In addition, parking lots and garages may also be part of the common areas. Parking lots and garages may be treated in different ways under the Chinese law. If the parking lot occupies the roads or other areas that are co-owned by all unit owners, it is part of the common areas and is co-owned by all unit owners. If the parking lot is located in a planned area and does not occupy any common area, then it is not part of the common areas, and the parties may decide on the ownership of the parking lot upon agreement made on sale, gifting, or renting of each parking space.② The parking lots or garages that are planned to be used for this purpose within the construction zone must firstly satisfy the needs of the owners.③

§ 3:2:2:3 Right to Co-Manage the Common Areas

The unit owners have both the right and duty to co-manage the part of the building co-owned by all unit owners, and may not avoid performing their duties under the pretext of abandoning their rights.④ Generally, a unit owner has a duty to observe the law, administrative regulations, and the covenants, and follow the decisions made by the owners' assembly or the owners' committee.⑤ The covenants are the self-management rules made by all unit owners in writing through legal procedures which is binding to all unit owners. The unit owners may establish an owners' assembly and elect an owners'

---

① Article 274 of the Civil Code.
② Articles 275 and 276 of the Civil Code.
③ Articles 275 and 276 of the Civil Code.
④ Article 273 of the Civil Code.
⑤ Articles 286 and 280 of the Civil Code.

committee. The relevant departments of the local people's government are responsible for providing guidance and assistance in establishing and selection of the owners' committee.① A unit-owner who believes that his rights and interests are infringed upon by the decision made by the owners' assembly or owners' committee may request the court to revoke it.②

The unit owners have a right to co-manage the common areas of the building which are co-owned by them. The unit owners' right to co-management includes the right to co-own and co-use the public maintenance funds. The maintenance funds for the building and its attached facilities are co-owned by all unit owners. The owners may co-decide on using the funds to maintain the public areas or facilities like elevators or water closets. The information about raising and using of the maintenance funds should be publicized to all unit owners.③ The unit owners also have the right to decide on the allocation of the cost for the building and its attached facilities and the distribution of the income. The share of cost for the building and its attached facilities and the distribution of income obtained from the building should be determined based on agreement; if there is no such agreement or if the agreement is unclear, it will be determined in proportion to the area of each unit owner's exclusive unit to the total area of the building.④

In addition, the unit owners may co-manage the building and its attached facilities by themselves, and may also entrust a property management service enterprise or a manager to manage them. The unit owners have a right to change the property management enterprise or manager hired by the developer.⑤

The unit owners also have a right to co-decide on certain significant matters, as provided in the Civil Code:

Article 278

The following matters shall be jointly decided by the unit owners:

---

① Article 277 of the Civil Code.
② Article 280 of the Civil Code.
③ Article 281 of the Civil Code.
④ Article 283 of the Civil Code.
⑤ Article 285 of the Civil Code.

(1) to formulate and amend the procedural rules of the owners' assembly;

(2) to formulate and amend the covenants on management;

(3) to elect or replace members of the owners' committee;

(4) to employ and remove the property management service enterprise or other managers;

(5) to use maintenance funds for buildings and auxiliary facilities thereof;

(6) to raise maintenance funds for buildings and auxiliary facilities thereof;

(7) to renovate and reconstruct buildings and auxiliary facilities thereof;

(8) to change the intended use of the co-owned space or making use of the co-owned space to engage in business activities; and

(9) to handle other major matters relating to co-ownership and the right to joint management.

To decide on a matter subject to co-management, the quorum is two thirds or more of the exclusive units both by area and by number of unit owners. Generally, a simple majority vote is required for deciding the matters listed above, except that when deciding on the matters listed as (6)-(8) above, i.e., the raising of the maintenance funds, reconstructing or renovating the building and its attached facilities, and changing the intended use of the common areas, there must be consent from the unit owners representing three quarters or more of the participating exclusive units both by area and by number of unit owners. [1]

Case 19

Case 19: Great Wall Broadband Network v. China Tietong[2]

Great Wall Broadband Network (Great Wall) and QT Co., a property management company, signed a cooperative operation agreement on broadband service on September 18, 2013, providing that both parties

---

[1] Article 278 of the Civil Code.
[2] See (2014) Jiangning Min Chu Zi No. 3935, reprinted in the SPC Gazette, Issue 12, 2019.

would co-construct the community broadband network in the South Garden Complex, and Great Wall may use the existing network and facilities. Later on, Great Wall installed cable inside and outside the residential buildings within the South Garden Complex.

In September 2014, the employees of China Tietong cut off over 6,000 meters optical cable installed by Great Wall in the said Complex and took away the twisted pair wire. The employees of Great Wall called the police on September 27, 2014, and then brought litigation.

In addition to the above facts, the court found that J Co., the real estate developer of the complex concerned delivered the buildings in the South Garden Complex to the owners in 2009, and signed a preliminary property management contract with Q Co., with a term from July 1, 2011 to June 30, 2014, under which J Co. selected Q Co. to provide the preliminary property management services, and Q Co. was responsible for managing the property owned by all owners of the complex, and the income, after deducting the relevant operational expenses and costs, shall be used as the property service fees. The contract was sealed by the owners' committee of the South Garden Complex.

In October 2001, China Tietong Jiangsu Branch signed a contract with J Co., agreeing that Jiangsu Tietong would be responsible for installation, maintenance, and operation of telephones for the residents within the complex, and J Co. would be responsible for installing the outdoor and indoor lines for its own account. It was further agreed that during the cooperation period, the right to use the lines belonged to Jiangsu Tietong, and Jiangsu Tietong also was responsible for installing the outdoor cables the ownership of which belonged to Jiangsu Tietong. The term of the contract was 20 years within which South Garden Complex promised not to cooperate with any other company for the same or similar services; in case any party incurred a change of ownership or management which might affect the cooperation and operation of this project, the party with such change should notify the other party in writing within 60 days before the change happened, and deliver this contract to the transferee of the ownership or management. On July 17, 2002, China Tietong Nanjing Branch was established and Jiangsu Tietong transferred the relevant contractual rights and obligations to Nanjing Tietong.

The first instance court emphasizes that the proprietary rights of a legal person are protected by law. The contract between Jiangsu Tietong and J Co. which grants Tietong an exclusive right to use the telecommunication cables within the South Garden Complex prevents the other telecommunication companies from connecting their cable into the complex which undermines the fair competitive market environment, restricts the rights of the unit owners to freely select telecommunication services, and harms the interests of the unit owners within the complex. Therefore, the contract is invalid.

According to the Real Rights Law, the public spaces, public utilities, etc. within the construction zone of the complex are co-owned by all owners. The telecommunication cables are one type of the public utilities and should be co-owned by all owners after the units are delivered to the owners. Q Co. is responsible for providing preliminary property management services and may dispose of the telecommunication cables co-owned by the owners. Based on the contract signed by the Great Wall and Q Co., Great Wall has the right to install cables within the South Garden. Nanjing Tietong cut off the cables installed by Great Wall, which infringes upon the proprietary rights of the Great Wall and should assume tort liability. Finally, the court holds that Nanjing Tietong should restore Great Wall's cables to its original status within 30 days after this judgment becomes effective. Neither party appeals within the legally provided period and the judgment has become effective.

§3:2:3 Contiguous Relationship

Contiguous relationship, also called adjacent relationship, is a relationship of rights and duties between or among the right-holders who live in an adjoining area. A contiguous relationship requires the owners of adjacent real property provide convenience for each other in possessing, using, profiting from, or disposing of their real property.[1] The right-holders must be the owners of real property that are adjacent to each other, including the right-

---

[1] Article 288 of the Civil Code.

holders of the ownership rights or other real rights, and the persons who have a creditor's right to possess the real property. The adjacent properties do not need to be directly next to each other, and as long as they can affect each other, the relationship is established. The right-holders in a contiguous relationship are required to deal with each other according to the principles of being beneficial to production, convenience for living, unity and mutual assistance, and fairness and reasonableness.① The aggrieved party in a contiguous relationship has a right to request the other party to remove obstructions and to eliminate dangers. When there is no law or regulation regulating the contiguous relationship, the local customs should be applied.②

The main contiguous relationships include a relationship in supplying water usage and drainage,③ in using other's property as a passage,④ in using the adjacent land,⑤ in using the wind-passage and day-lighting,⑥ in environmental protection,⑦ and in risk prevention.⑧ The right-holders should endeavor to avoid any damage to the right-holder of the adjacent property when using the adjacent property for the above purposes; compensation must be made for any damage thus caused.⑨

Case 20

Case 20: Xinhua Daily Pres v. H Co.⑩

H Co. and Xinhua Daily Pres (Xinhua Daily) are adjacent neighbors. In April 1991, H Co. started a construction work and stopped the construction after one month upon discovering land subsidence on the nearby ground. In June 1991, the construction resumed after the construction plan was

---

① Article 288 of the Civil Code.
② Article 289 of the Civil Code.
③ Articles 290 and 296 of the Civil Code.
④ Article 291 of the Civil Code.
⑤ Articles 292 and 296 of the Civil Code.
⑥ Article 293 of the Civil Code.
⑦ Article 294 of the Civil Code.
⑧ Article 295 of the Civil Code.
⑨ Article 296 of the Civil Code.
⑩ See the SPC Gazette, Issue 3, 1996.

modified. In mid-October the same year, Xinhua Daily discovered that there were cracks on the walls of its printing plant and the ground, three printing machines imported from Germany worked irregularly which made the printing quality decreased significantly. It entrusted the relevant institutions to identify the reason which turned out to be that H Co. significantly pumped out the groundwater. After failing to obtain compensation from H Co., Xinhua Daily sued in court.

The High People's Court of Jiangsu Province held that, when H Co., as the neighbor of Xinhua Daily's printing plant, constructed the building, it did not fully consider the safety of the adjacent buildings and significantly pumped out the groundwater, and did not timely adopt necessary protective measures after discovering the problem, so that Xinhua Daily suffered damage. The facts were clear, the evidences were sufficient, and H Co. violated Article 83 of the GPCL (Article 288 of the Civil Code) which provides that the neighboring parties of real estate shall properly deal with the adjacent relationship based on the principles of facilitation to production, convenience for daily lives, solidarity and mutual assistance, and fairness and reasonableness. H Co. should bear full liability for compensation. The court held that H Co. should compensate Xinhua Daily for its losses of 13,883,580.28 yuan in total, as well as the litigation fee of 79,428 yuan and preservation fee of 70,520 yuan.

H Co. appealed to the SPC which affirmed the case.

§3:2:4 Co-Ownership

Real or personal property may be co-owned by two or more natural persons or organizations.① Generally, there are two types of co-ownership: joint ownership and ownership by shares,② with the co-ownership by all unit owners over the common areas of a building as a special type of co-ownership.

Joint ownership is created based on a joint relationship but the ownership by shares does not require such a joint relationship. In a joint ownership

---

① Article 297 of the Civil Code.
② At common law, joint ownership is called "joint tenancy" while ownership by shares is called "tenancy in common."

situation, the right of the joint owners is in the total of the jointly-owned property and not limited to any part of it, and the owners have equal rights and assume equal duties in the property. ① However, in a situation of ownership by shares, the owners each has the rights and assumes the duties based on the shares he holds. ② During the existence of the co-ownership, without a prior agreement, the joint owners generally may not request a partition of the jointly-owned property unless with a compelling reason; however, the co-owners by shares may partition the property at any time. ③ Without a prior agreement, the disposal or significant repair of the co-owned property should be consented to by all of the joint owners in a joint ownership situation, but only needs the consent from 2/3 or more co-owners in a case of ownership by shares. ④

When determining whether a co-ownership is one by shares or a joint ownership, the Opinions on the GPCL adopted a presumption of joint ownership if there was no evidence proving that the property was owned by shares. ⑤ However, the Real Rights Law provided a different rule which has been integrated in the Civil Code. If the parties do not have an agreement regarding whether a co-ownership is a joint ownership or an ownership by shares, or if such an agreement is unclear, a co-ownership by shares will be presumed, except that when the co-owners are family members, the presumption will be in favor of a joint ownership. ⑥ The reason for the change is that a joint ownership is based on the existence of a joint relationship; lacking such a relationship, it is more appropriate to assume that the ownership is one by shares.

Co-ownership does not only involve the ownership rights, but may also involve other rights, such as a right to usufruct or a secured interest in the property. For example, if two or more persons own a mortgagee's right on the property jointly or by shares, then there is also a co-ownership, which may be

---

① Article 299 of the Civil Code.
② Article 298 of the Civil Code.
③ Article 303 of the Civil Code.
④ Article 301 of the Civil Code.
⑤ Article 88 of the Opinions on the GPCL.
⑥ Article 308 of the Civil Code.

called quasi-co-ownership. The subject matter of quasi co-ownership must be a real right other than the ownership rights; it may include a right to usufruct such as a right to use a lot of State-owned land or a right to easement, a secured interest such as a mortgage right, an intellectual property right, or a creditor's right. It may be an ownership by shares or a joint ownership depending on the relationship of the parties. If there are no special regulations on the relationship, the provisions of the Civil Code on the co-ownership rights are applicable. ①

§ 3:2:4:1 Co-Ownership by Shares

In a co-ownership by shares, the rights and duties of each co-owner are based on his shares in the property. ② A co-ownership by shares may be created by agreement of the parties or by operation of law. For example, if A and B decide to buy an apartment together and A contributes 70% of the purchase price while B contributes the rest, then A and B co-own the apartment by shares according to the proportion of their capital contribution. On the other hand, co-ownership by shares may also be created by improvement on the real property.

A co-ownership of real property must be recorded in the register, and the registration authority will issue a co-ownership certificate to each co-owner. Each co-owner's shares in the property are determined by agreement among the co-owners, or by the amount of capital contribution made by each co-owner if there is no such an agreement or if the agreement is unclear. If the amount of capital contribution is not determinable, then each owner will have equal shares. ③

Each co-owner has a right to partition his own shares, and transfer, mortgage, lease, or abandon the shares, while the other co-owners have the first right of refusal. ④ When transferring the shares in the co-owned property, the co-owners must file registration for alteration with the registration authority if the property is real property, or complete delivery if the property

---

① Article 310 of the Civil Code.
② Article 298 of the Civil Code.
③ Article 309 of the Civil Code.
④ See Articles 303 – 306 of the Civil Code.

is personal property. However, since the shares of a personal property could be intangible, the transferee may not actually possess any specific part of the co-owned property. When a co-owner transfers his shares in the property to another person, the other co-owners have a priority right to buy it under the same condition. ①

Although each co-owner by shares may partition and transfer his shares at any time, if the co-owners clearly agree to maintain the co-ownership relationship and not to allow partitioning, the co-owners are bound by this agreement and cannot partition the property unless there is a compelling reason for partition. If the partition of the co-owned property causes damage to the other co-owners, the co-owner requesting the partition will be held liable for compensation. ② The act of requesting partition is a unilateral juristic act, and is effective right after it is completed. The method of partition should be firstly determined by the parties through consultation. If the parties cannot reach an agreement, where the property is divisible and its value will not be depreciated by the partition, then the property can be divided in kind and each co-owner will get the part based on his shares. If the property is not divisible or the division may depreciate its value, then the property should be sold at an auction or sale, and the purchase money received will be divided among the co-owners; alternatively, the property may be appraised and one of the co-owners may get the property, and the other co-owners will get monetary compensation based on the appraisal and on their shares. ③ Where the immovable or movable property acquired by a co-owner by means of partition is defective, the other co-owners shall share the losses.

The co-owners by shares are jointly and severally entitled to claims and are jointly and severally obligated to perform obligations arising from the co-owned property, unless it is otherwise provided by law or the third person is aware that the co-owners are not in a relationship of joint and several claims and obligations. Internally, unless otherwise agreed by the co-owners, the co-owners by shares are entitled to claims and obligated to perform obligations in

---

① Articles 305 and 306 of the Civil Code.
② Article 303 of the Civil Code.
③ Article 304 of the Civil Code.

proportion to their shares they each own, and if a co-owner by shares has performed the obligation in excess of his shares, he has a right to contribution against the other co-owners. ①

§ 3:2:4:2 Joint Ownership

In a joint ownership, the ownership right in one property is co-owned by several owners based on a joint relationship created by operation of law or based on a contract. ② For example, the heirs of a deceased person have joint ownership on the estate before it is partitioned and distributed. This is a joint ownership created by law. If the spouses agree that during the existence period of their marital relationship, the property received by either spouse will be jointly owned by the two spouses, a joint ownership is created by agreement. Once a joint relationship is created, the joint owners have equal rights and undertake equal duties in the co-owned property as a whole. ③ In other words, the joint owners have the right to possess, use, profit from, or dispose of the co-owned property as a whole instead of by shares, and undertake duties on the co-owned property as a whole. The joint owners generally cannot make a request for partitioning the jointly-owned property, unless the basis for the joint ownership is lost, or there is a compelling reason to partition the property. ④

Most of the joint ownerships are based on a spousal relationship, family and cohabitation relationship, partner relationship, and succession. The salaries, bonuses, and other income that the spouses receive during the period when the marital relationship exists are jointly owned by the spouses, unless otherwise agreed upon by the spouses in an agreement. ⑤ So the spouses have equal rights to deal with the jointly-owned property. Family members jointly own the property that is co-created and received by them during the period when they live together and used to maintain the family members' co-production and living. During the period that a partnership enterprise exists, the capital contribution made by the partners, the income received in the name

---

① Article 307 of the Civil Code.
② Article 299 of the Civil Code.
③ Article 299 of the Civil Code.
④ Article 303 of the Civil Code.
⑤ Articles 1062 and 1065 of the Civil Code.

of the partnership enterprise, and the other property that has been received according to law are property of the partnership enterprise. The partners jointly own the partnership property, co-manage the property, and may not request partition of the property before liquidation of the partnership unless otherwise provided by law.① A joint ownership may also be created among the heirs of the deceased before the estate is partitioned, and then all of the heirs jointly own the estate.

In a joint ownership, the joint owners are jointly and severally entitled to claims and are jointly and severally obligated to perform obligations arising from the jointly-owned property against a third person, unless it is otherwise provided by law or where the third person is aware that the joint owners are not in a relationship of joint and several claims and obligations. However, for the internal relationship, the joint owners are jointly entitled to claims and obligated to perform obligations.②

A joint ownership may be extinguished if the basis for the joint ownership is lost. For example, if the spouses divorce, the joint ownership based on marriage is extinguished. If a partnership is dissolved, the joint ownership based on the partner relationship is also extinguished. In addition, a joint ownership will also be extinguished if the co-owned property is transferred, expropriated, or destructed. However, if after the property is transferred, expropriated, or destructed, consideration, compensation, or insurance payment has been received, then the owners jointly own these compensations in lieu of the original property.

Case 21

Case 21: Yu v. Tian & Liu③

Yu and Tian married in December 1988 and are still married with two daughters. Tian and Liu had a daughter who was born in 2009 out of wedlock.

---

① Articles 1062 and 1065 of the Civil Code.
② Article 307 of the Civil Code.
③ See (2015) Hu Er Zhong Min Er (Min) Che Zhong Zi No.1, reprinted in the SPC Gazette, Issue 7, 2018.

In October 2007, Tian bought a house in Jiading District, Shanghai Municipality and paid 10,180,000 yuan as purchase price. Upon priority registration, the house was firstly registered in the name of a third person Li, and later changed to be under the name of Tian on June 6, 2008. On June 8, 2008, Tian and Liu signed a cooperative agreement under which both parties agreed to buy the house. Both of them would jointly own the house but the title of it would be registered in the name of Liu.

In January 2009, Tian wrote a receipt confirming that he had received 2,700,000 yuan as part of the purchase price paid by Liu, and that the future taxes and property management fees would be paid by Liu. It also stated that the house was co-owned by the two parties, and Tian owned 60% whereas Liu 40%. The parties also agreed that they would not use the house for the moment, and once it was sold, the proceeds would be applied to firstly refund each party's contribution, and then each party would get 50% of the profit, if any. It was also stated that unless consented to by the parties, the house might not be disposed of. Then in April 2009, the priority registration of the house had been transferred to Liu. In July 2011, Tian wrote a statement confirming that the house had been gifted to Liu in April 2009. In November 2011, Tian explained the process of purchasing the house in writing, stating that he bought the house firstly in the name of Li, and then in his own name, and in March 2009 he gave the house to his girlfriend Liu, and that Liu had not made any actual payment of the purchase price.

In December 2011, Tian's wife Yu brought a litigation to the Intermediate Court of Dalian City, claiming that during their marriage, Tian secretly transferred large amount of community property to buy property for Liu, and that she tried but failed to ask them to refund, therefore she requested the court to order the two defendants to refund 25,000,000 yuan. Liu challenged the court's jurisdiction and requested the case to be removed to a court in Shanghai since the real property involved in this case was located in Shanghai. After consideration, the Intermediate Court of Dalian ruled that the nature of this case was not about a real estate dispute, but a case about the validity of a gift, and therefore overruled Liu's challenge. Liu appealed, and the High People's Court of Liaoning

Province affirmed the first instance court's decision.

During the period the case was appealed to the High People's Court, Tian sued Liu in the Jiading District People's Court of Shanghai Municipality requesting the court to confirm his 60% ownership over the disputed house. Tian and Liu concealed the fact that Yu had already sued in the Intermediate People's Court in Dalian City, the identity of Yu, and the relationship between themselves. The Jiading District People's Court made a judgement in August 2012, declaring that Tian owned 60% of the disputed house. This judgment became final since neither party appealed.

In August 2012, Dalian Intermediate People's Court held a hearing during which Yu modified her claims and requested the court to declare that the gift between Tian and Liu were invalid, and requested Liu to return the gifted house and change the registration of the house as coowned by Yu and Tian. On the same day, Liu presented the Shanghai Jiading District Court's decision as evidence to the Dalian court. On July 4, 2013, Dalian court made a judgment holding that Tian's gifting of the house to Liu was invalid, and the house should be registered in the name of Tian or Yu. On July 20, Liu appealed to the High People's Court of Liaoning Province. The High Court explained to Yu that her rights and interests were adversely affected by the Shanghai Jiading Court's decision, therefore she brought a litigation with Shanghai Jiading District People's Court on September 26, 2013, requesting the court to revoke the disputed judgment. Meanwhile, In October 2013, the Liaoning High Court dismissed Yu's litigation.

After investigation, Jiading Court found that the purchase price that Liu said she had paid were actually paid by Tian, and Liu had paid nothing, that neither the defendants had used the disputed house, and that the disputed house was still registered under the name of Liu. During the litigation, upon Yu's request, Jiading Court froze the disputed house.

The main issue is whether the original judgment should be revoked. Tian's purchase of the disputed house occurred during the period when the spousal relationship between Tian and Yu existed, so that the purchase money was community property according to the marriage law. After

Tian purchased the house and had obtained the priority registration, he transferred it to Liu without Yu's consent or Liu's payment. This act harmed the ownership and equal right of disposal of the community property that Yu had as a spouse. The original judgment was based on the fact that the house was registered in Liu's name and that both Tian and Liu confirmed about their proportional right in the house, and the declaration of the ownership over the disputed house harmed Yu's civil-law rights and interests and therefore should be revoked.

The court also held that while Yu had already brought litigation in Dalian regarding the gift of the disputed house, Tian filed with the Jiading Court requesting a declaration of his proportion of the disputed house (60%), and deliberately concealed to the court the litigation Yu had already brought in Dalian, Yu's identity, and the relationship between Tian and Liu. The purpose of Tian was to prevent Dalian court from hearing the relevant case through bringing the litigation in Shanghai, and it infringed upon Yu's lawful rights and interests. Therefore, Tian conducted malicious litigation.

Finally, Jiading Court made a decision, according to Articles 56 and 112 of the Civil Procedure Law and Article 17 of the Marriage Law, on October 22, 2014. Among other things, it revoked the original judgment. Liu appealed to Shanghai No.2 Intermediate People's Court which affirmed this part of the Jiading Court's decision.

§ 3:3 Rights to Usufruct

A right to usufruct is a real right owned by a person other than the owner of the property. While an ownership right is a complete right, a right to usufruct is a limited real right because the holder of a right to usufruct only has a right to possess, use, and profit from the real or personal property which is actually owned by others. ①

A right to usufruct is also different from a secured interest. The purpose of a right to usufruct is to obtain the use value of other's property, which cannot

---

① Article 323 of the Civil Code.

be realized without actually possessing the property. However, the purpose of a secured interest is to control the exchange value of the property owned by others and the priority right to be paid from the sales price of the property. A secured interest may be created in a real property, personal property, or even in a right, but a right to usufruct generally may only be created on a real property. Furthermore, a right to usufruct is an independent real right and does not need to be accompanied by any obligee's right. However, the creation of a secured interest is mainly for securing the realization of an obligee's right; therefore, it is secondary to the obligee's right.

This subsection will introduce the various types of rights to usufruct recognized in China.

§3:3:1 The Rights to Use Land for Construction Purposes

A right to use land for construction purposes is a right to use a lot of State-owned land defined in the Land Administration Law and the Law on Administration of the Urban Real Estate. The person with the right to use land for construction purposes has the right to possess, use, and profit from the lot of State-owned land, and may build buildings, constructions, and its attached facilities on the lot of land according to law.[1]

Urban lands in China are owned by the State. The rural lands or the lands in suburban areas are owned by the collectives, except that these lands may be owned by the State if so provided by law.[2] So the right to use land for construction purposes is a type of right to usufruct on the State-owned land. A right-holder has the right to possess, use, profit from the lot of State-owned land, and also has the right to dispose of this right, *e.g.*, a right-holder may transfer, lease, or mortgage such right within the prescribed limit, or use it for other economic activities.[3]

A right to use a lot of land for construction purposes may be created on the ground of the land, below the land, or above the land, provided that the newly created land-use right may not harm any existing rights to usufruct.[4] The

---

[1] Article 344 of the Civil Code.
[2] Article 10 of the Constitution; Article 6 of the Land Administration Law.
[3] Article 353 of the Civil Code.
[4] Articles 345 and 346 of the Civil Code.

procedure of obtaining a right to use a lot of land for construction purposes is provided by law. A land-use right may be obtained through gratuitous grant, grant, or transfer. The first two happen in the primary market of the land use right, which is strictly regulated by law. According to the Land Administration Law and the Law on Administration of Urban Real Estate, the grant of a right to use a lot of land for construction purposes must comply with the overall planning of the land use, the city planning, and the annual planning for land used for construction.

A right to use land for construction purposes is not permanent. The term of the grant for a land use right is determined by the State Council.① The maximum term for the grant of land-use right is 70 years if it is for residential use, 50 years for industrial use, 50 years for lands used for development of education, technologies, culture, public health, and sports, 40 years for lands used for commercial, tourism, and entertainment purposes, and 50 years for comprehensive or other types of land use.②

A land use right may be created through gratuitous grant or grant.③ Before granting the right to use a lot of land for industrial, commercial, tourism, or entertainment purpose, or for commercial residences, or if there are two or more applicants applying for the same land, the land-use right should be granted through public bidding.④ Since the State requires the user of the natural resources to pay consideration for them,⑤ the creation of a land-use right through gratuitous grant is highly restricted by law. Upon transfer, exchange, contribution as capital, or gifting of a land-use right, the constructions, buildings and the attached facilities on the land will be disposed of concomitantly with the land-use right, and *vice versa*.⑥ The following sections introduces some specific issues arising from creating or transferring a right to use a lot of land for construction purposes.

---

① Article 13 of the Law on Administration of Urban Real Estate.
② Article 13 of the Interim Regulations on Grant and Transfer of the Right to Use Urban Land for construction purposes.
③ Article 347 of the Civil Code.
④ Article 347 of the Civil Code.
⑤ Article 325 of the Civil Code.
⑥ Articles 356 and 357 of the Civil Code.

§ 3:3:1:1 Ways to Obtain a Right to Use Land for Construction Purposes

Grant of a Right to Use Land for Construction Purposes

Only the State may grant a right to use a lot of land for construction purposes. The State as the owner of the land may grant a right to use land to a land user for a certain period of time, and the land user pays consideration to the State. There are various ways to grant a right to use a lot of land for construction purposes, such as through making an agreement, through bidding or auction, or through listing the lot of land on the land exchanges.

A land-use right may be granted through an agreement between the parties. Since this procedure is not open to the public and thus not transparent, the law imposes restrictions on this type of grant. For example, a right to use a lot of land for industrial, commercial, tourism, or entertainment purposes may not be granted upon agreement, but must be granted through public biddings such as bid invitation or auction. If there are two or more applicants for the right to use the same lot of land, the land-use right may not be granted upon agreement either.① A land-use right may also be granted through listing the lot of land on the land exchanges. If the right to use land for construction purposes is created through bidding, auction, or agreement, the parties should sign a written contract.②

The grant of a land-use right is not permanent and the term of use may expire. Upon expiration of the term of a right to use a lot of land for residential purposes, the grant will be automatically renewed.③ The renewal of a right to use a lot of land for non-residential purposes should be in accordance with special laws and regulations. Upon returning the land use right, the ownership over the houses or other real estate on the land should be determined in accordance with the agreement; if there is no agreement or if the agreement is unclear, the issue should be resolved according to law or administrative regulations.

Gratuitous Grant of a Right to Use Land for Construction Purposes

The government at or above the county level may gratuitously grant a land-

---

① Article 347 of the Civil Code.
② Article 348 of the Civil Code.
③ Article 359 of the Civil Code.

use right to a land user who does not need to pay consideration, but sometimes the user may need to pay some forms of compensation or re-location fee.

The land-use rights gratuitously granted are mainly in the land for government use, for military use, for city infrastructure and public utilities, or for projects of energy, transportation, or water conservancy. A gratuitous grant could be permanent because the purpose of the gratuitous grant generally is not for profit. ① However, such a land use right cannot enter into the land market, neither can it be transferred, mortgaged, or leased. The government may take back the land-use right thus granted for purposes of city development and construction. ②

Transfer of a Right to Use Land for Construction Purposes③

A right to use a lot of land for construction purposes may also be obtained through transfer of the land-use right by the current right-holder to a subsequent right-holder. The land-use right may be transferred through buying and selling, exchanges, and gifting.

§ 3:3:1:2 **Registration**

A right to use a lot of land for construction purposes is created upon registration of such right by the owner or the prior land user of the lot of land with the registration authority. ④ The registration authority issues a certificate for the land-use right. The registrants should also file for modification of the registration if the land-use right is transferred, exchanged, offered as capital contribution, or given away as a gift, ⑤ and file for de-registration upon extinguishment of the land-use right. ⑥

A land-use right may be taken back for various reasons. The public interest may be one of the grounds, provided that the State shall pay compensation for the houses and the other real property on the land because it is an expropriation

---

① Article 22 of the Law on Administration of Urban Real Estate.
② Article 23 of the Law on Administration of the Urban Real Estate.
③ Article 353 of the Civil Code.
④ Article 349 of the Civil Code.
⑤ Article 355 of the Civil Code.
⑥ Article 360 of the Civil Code.

in nature.① The land administration department should also return the corresponding grant fee when taking back the land-use right for the public interest.② Upon expiration of the term for the land-use right, where the application for renewal is not approved, the land-use right will be taken back. A land-use right gratuitously granted will be taken back if the organization is dissolved or relocated, or if the land is no longer in use. A land-use right will also be taken back if the public roads, railroads, airports, or mines on or under it have been discarded or abandoned upon approval. Breach of a grant contract by the land user is also a ground for a land-use right to be taken back.

§3:3:2 The Rights to Use Rural Land③

As previously mentioned, all lands in China are owned by the State and collectives. An ownership right in land may not be transferred in China, but a right to use land, as a type of right to usufruct, may be obtained and transferred.④ Rural lands include the arable lands, forest lands, grasslands, and other lands used for agricultural purposes that are either owned by the rural collectives, or owned by the State but used by the rural collectives.⑤ A right to use rural land is one of the important rights to usufruct which derives from the ownership right in the collective-owned lands.

China implements a system of contracted management of rural lands, *i.e.*, through contracting, individuals and organizations may use the arable lands, forestlands, grasslands, and other lands used for agricultural production purposes that are owned by the rural collectives, or owned by the State but used by the rural collectives.⑥ Accordingly, a right to use rural land is a right in using and profiting from the lot of rural land obtained by the contractor through a contract.⑦ In other words, such a right-holder has a right to possess,

---

① Article 327 of the Civil Code.
② Article 358 of the Civil Code.
③ "土地承包经营权" may be translated in different ways, such as "the right of contracted management of land" or "the right to contract and manage the land," in this book, "the right to use rural land" is used to refer to this special kind of right to usufruct in China.
④ Article 10 of the Constitution.
⑤ Article 2 of the Law on Contracted Management of Rural Land.
⑥ Article 330 of the Civil Code; also see Article 9 of the Land Administration Law.
⑦ Article 331 of the Civil Code.

use, and profit from the lot of rural land that has been contracted to them, and may engage in plantation, forestation, livestock farming, and other agricultural productions thereon.

There are two ways to obtain a right to use the rural land: through a family-based contract, or through other methods, such as bidding, auction, or agreement upon consultation with all members. Only the members of a rural collective economic organization may obtain a right to use the rural land through a family-based contract,① while any organization or individual outside the rural collective economic organization may only use the rural land through other methods.② The rural lands that may be used through family-based contracting include the arable lands, forestlands, and grasslands, as well as the four wastes, i.e., the waste mountains, waste ditches, waste hills, and waste flats (collectively, "four wastes"). However, the persons outside the rural collective organization may only obtain the right to use the four wastes through the methods provided by law.③

The term for a family-based contract is 30 years for arable lands, 30-50 years for grasslands, and 30-70 years for forest lands. The term for the use of a special lot of forest lands may be further extended upon approval by the forestry administration under the State Council.④ However, the term for a contract to use other rural lands may be agreed upon by the parties on a case by case basis. The rural land contracted to the families within the collective may be circulated only through limited ways, such as sub-contracting, leasing, exchanging, or transferring,⑤ but the land contracted through the methods other than family-based contract may be circulated in more ways, such as through capital contribution or creation of mortgage, as long as the contract is registered according to law.⑥ Therefore, a lot of rural land contracted through

---

① Article 5 of the Law on Contracted Management of Rural Land.
② Article 48 of the Law on Contracted Management of Rural Land.
③ Article 3 of the Law on Contracted Management of Rural Land.
④ Article 27 of the Law on Contracted Management of Rural Land and Article 126 of the Real Rights Law.
⑤ Article 32 of the Law on Contracted Management of Rural Land; Article 133 of the Real Rights Law.
⑥ Article 49 of the Law on Contracted Management of Rural Land.

family-based contract may not be mortgaged or used to set off debts. ① If the parties mortgage the land use right or use it to set off debts regardless and thus cause harm, the party at fault will bear civil liability.

§ 3:3:2:1 Contracted Management of Rural Land through Family-Based Contract

Upon creating a right to use a lot of rural land, the contract must be consented to by 2/3 or more members or villager-representatives in the villagers meeting of the local collective economic organization, in compliance with Article 12 of the Law on Rural land Contracting. ② The members of the same collective economic organization have an equal right to get the land-use right or to voluntarily give up the right. The contracting procedure must be lawful, fair, and reasonable, and go through a democratic consultation procedure. In this process, the collective is the grantor, and the members of the collective are the grantees, i.e., the right-holder of the right to use the rural land.

A contract for use of a lot of rural land is effective upon formation, and the contracting party (grantee) obtains the land use right upon effectiveness of the contract. ③ After such a right is created, the local people's government at or above the county level will issue a certificate for the lot of land, forest, or grassland contracted to the grantee, and register it on the register. ④ After the contract becomes effective, the grantor may not modify or revoke the contract owing to the changes of its person in charge, or owing to the division or merger of the collective economic organization. The State department and their staff may not take advantage of their position to interfere with the contracting of rural land, or modification or revocation of the contract.

A grantee has a right to use and profit from the lot of land contracted, a right to transfer such land-use right, and a right to independently produce, manage, and dispose of the products on the land. If the contracted lot of land

---

① Article 15 of the Supreme People's Court's Interpretations on the Law application Issues Arising from Dealing with Cases Involving disputes on Contracted Management of Rural Land.
② Article 18 of the Law on Contracted Management of Rural Land.
③ Article 22 of the Law on Contracted Management of Rural Land.
④ Article 333 of the Civil Code.

has been expropriated, the grantee has a right to receive compensation.① Within the contract term, a grantee may voluntarily return the land to the grantor, but should give the grantor a 6-month prior written notice and may not re-contract any lot of land within the residual term of the original contract. If a grantee returns the contracted land, or if the grantor takes back the land within the contract term, the grantee has a right to receive compensation for his investment in the lot of land which has improved the production capacity of the land. The profits that the grantee is entitled to receive may be inherited according to the Succession Law. If the grantee of a forest land dies, his heirs may continue to manage the forest within the contract term. On the other hand, a grantee has a duty to use the lot of land for agricultural purposes and may not use it for non-agricultural development. A grantee must protect and reasonably utilize the land, and may not bring any permanent harm to the land. Once such a grantee has become a non-rural resident, he should return the contracted arable land or grassland to the grantor.

A grantor of a right to use rural land has a right to contract out the collective-owned rural land, or the land owned by the Stated but authorized to be used by the collective, and supervise the grantee to ensure that the contracted lot of land is reasonably used and protected according to the purpose agreed upon in the contract. A grantor also has a right to prohibit a grantee from doing anything to harm the contracted land or the agricultural resources. On the other hand, a grantor has an obligation to protect the grantee's right in the land, and may not illegally change or revoke the contract. A grantor should respect the grantee's right to independently engage in production, and should not interfere with the grantee's normal production and management activities. In addition, a grantor should provide services of production, technology, and information according to the contract, and implement the general land-use plan of the county or town, and organize the construction of agricultural infrastructure within the collective economic organization.

A grantee may, according to the Law on Contracted Management of Rural Land, transfer the right to use rural land through sub-contracting, exchanging,

---

① Article 338 of the Civil Code.

leasing, or transferring.① The term of a sub-contract should not exceed the residual term of the original contract. Without being approved, a grantee may not use the contracted land for non-agricultural construction purpose. The parties should sign a written contract when sub-contracting a right to use rural land, and should obtain consent from the grantor. If a land-use right is sub-contracted through exchanging and transfer, it may not be against a *bona fide* third person if it is not registered.②

The law imposes certain restrictions on the transfer of a right to use rural land. First, the transfer must not change the nature of the ownership and the agricultural use of the land. Second, the term of transfer should not exceed the residual term of the original contract. Third, the transferee must be a member of the same collective economic organization if the right is exchanged; in other situations, the transferee must be a farmer engaging in agricultural production and operation. Lastly, under the same conditions, the members of the same collective economic organization have a priority right to sub-contract the lot of land.

§ 3:3:2:2 Contracted Management of Rural Land through Other Methods

Sometimes the members of a collective would not like to work on the "four-wastes" through family-based contract or because they do not have full capacity to manage all of these lands, then these lands may be offered to members of other collective organizations or even persons who are not rural residents through bidding, auction, or agreement upon consultation with all members. Such a contracting process must be based on the principles of voluntariness, openness, and fairness. Under the same conditions, the members of the collective have a priority right to make a contract.

When a grantor decides to contract out the four-wastes to an organization or individual outside the collective, consent must be obtained from 2/3 or more of the members or villager-representatives of the collective or the villagers meeting, and it must report to the county or town government for approval. Before such a contract is signed, the credit standing and management capacity

---

① Article 334 of the Civil Code.
② Article 335 of the Civil Code.

of the proposed grantee must be carefully examined.

If a grantor has contracted out the same lot of land to two or more grantees and all of the grantees claim their rights to use the lot, the grantee who has registered will get the right. If no contract is registered, the grantee whose contract becomes effective first in time will get the right. Otherwise, the grantee who has possessed and used the lot of land according to the contract will get the right, except that if one grantee forcibly possesses the lot of land after the dispute arises, the grantee may not use this fact as a basis for determining the right. [1]

A right holder may sub-contract a right to use a lot of rural land that has been obtained through bidding, auction, or agreement upon consultation with all members through transferring it, contributing it as capital, mortgaging it, or other ways according to the laws and regulations. Obviously, a right-holder who has obtained such right through these methods has more rights than a right-holder of the right to use rural land through family-based contract. [2] For example, the arable lands, home-based lands, and home-based mountains generally may not be mortgaged. [3]

§3:3:3 The Rights to Use House Site

A right to use house site is a right that a member of a rural collective organization may possess and use part of the collective-owned land according to law and build a dwelling and auxiliary facilities thereon. [4] This is an independent right to usufruct on land and serves for the purpose of providing social welfare to the rural residents. The rural residents' basic livelihood and living conditions are secured through obtaining the right to use a house site.

The laws and regulations on land administration apply to the obtainment and transfer of the rights to use a house site. [5] Since the rural residents may get the house site at a very low price or even at no cost, only qualified villagers

---

[1] Article 20 of the Supreme People's Court's Interpretations on the Law Application Issues Arising from Dealing with Cases on Contracted Management of Rural Land.
[2] Article 342 of the Civil Code.
[3] Article 399 of the Civil Code.
[4] Article 362 of the Civil Code.
[5] Article 363 of the Civil Code.

may obtain the house site through an approval procedure, which includes the examination by the town government and the final approval by the county government. Each villager may only have one house site, and the total acreage of the house site that each villager may obtain must not exceed the standard set by the province, autonomous region, or the municipality directly under the State Council where the village is located in. A house site may also be obtained through inheritance.

The right to use house site is very important for the rural residents, the Civil Code expressly prohibits the right to use the house site from being mortgaged.① However, it does not prohibit the transfer of the right to use a house site. Therefore, a house site may be transferred within the collective organization between its members. If a person wants to transfer his house site to a person outside the collective organization, the transferee must from then on reside in the village and must comply with the other conditions for applying for the house site. The total acreage of a house site obtained by the transferee is restricted.

§3:3:4 The Rights of Habitation

In order to protect some special groups of persons, the Civil Code creates a new type of right to usufruct — the right of habitation in Chapter XIV of its Book Two (Real Rights)②. A right of habitation is a right of a person to possess and use another person's dwelling to meet his own needs. Such a right may be created by the owner of the dwelling during his life based on a written contract, or upon his death based on his will.③

For instance, a senior couple who have sold their own house and used the money to purchase a bigger house for their son intending to live therein with their son for the rest of their lives may become homeless if someday their son doesn't allow them to live in. In this situation, the Civil Code provides a solution whereby the couple may urge their son to create a right of habitation for them. For another example, after a father dies, he would like his son to

---

① Article 399 of the Civil Code.
② Articles 366-371 of the Civil Code.
③ Articles 366 & 371 of the Civil Code.

inherit their residence, but would like his spouse to continue to live in the residence for the rest of her life. He can write a will and states such intent therein. A right of habitation will be created for the mother upon the father's death.

The written document creating a right of habitation should indicate the name and address of the owner of the dwelling and the person holding the right of habitation, the location of the dwelling, the conditions and requirements for the habitation, the duration of the right of habitation, and the means of dispute resolution.① A right of habitation may be created gratuitously, but must be registered with the registration authority.② After a right of habitation is created, it may not be transferred or inherited, and the dwelling subjected to the right of habitation may not be let on lease, unless otherwise agreed by the parties.③

A right of habitation is extinguished if the term of the right expires, or if the person entitled to the right deceases. Upon extinguishment, the right of habitation must be deregistered in a timely manner.④

§3:3:5 The Rights to Servitudes

A right to servitudes recognized in Chinese law mainly refers to a right to easement, which means a right of one person to use another's immovable property in order to enhance the efficiency of his own immovable property.⑤ The first person's land that is to be benefitted by the easement is called dominant tenement or dominant land and the second person's land that is subject to the easement right is called servient tenement or servient land.⑥ This right may be created or obtained by the party through performing a juristic act recognized by law.

A right to easement is a secondary right because it cannot be transferred or mortgaged independently from the dominant land.⑦ When a right to use a lot

---

① Article 367 of the Civil Code.
② Article 368 of the Civil Code.
③ Article 369 of the Civil Code.
④ Article 370 of the Civil Code.
⑤ Article 372 of the Civil Code.
⑥ Article 372 of the Civil Code.
⑦ Articles 380 and 381 of the Civil Code.

of rural land or a right to use a lot of land for construction purposes is transferred, the right to easement connected to the land is also transferred, unless otherwise agreed in the contract.

A right to easement is different from the contiguous relationship. Contiguous relationship is not an independent real right, but it does not have a term, nor needs to be registered. The parties to a contiguous relationship do not need to pay anything to the other party. However, a right to easement is created by the parties through an easement agreement, while the parties should voluntarily consult with each other regarding whether consideration needs to be paid.① Thus in China, an easement may only be created through the parties' written agreement, and created at the time the easement contract enters into effect. The parties may choose to register the easement; if not registered with the registration authority, an easement is not effective against a *bona fide* third person.②

If a right to usufruct, such as a right to contractual management of land, a right to use a lot of land for construction purposes, or a right to use a house site, has been created on a lot of land, without consent of the usufructuary, the owner of the lot of land may not create an easement on the lot.③ If a land owner (mainly referring to the collective land owner) is entitled to an easement or has an obligation to provide an easement to others, upon creation of a right to usufruct, the usufructuary will continue to be entitled or be encumbered with the easement thereon that has already been created.④ The term of the easement may be freely agreed upon by the parties; however, since the land-use right in China are not permanent, the term of easement may not exceed the term of the land-use right.⑤

A right to easement may be extinguished upon expiration of the term of easement if the parties have not applied for a renewal. When the dominant land and the servient land have been owned by the same owner, or the usufructuary of the dominant land and the usufructuary of the servient land

---

① Article 373 of the Civil Code.
② Article 374 of the Civil Code.
③ Article 379 of the Civil Code.
④ Article 378 of the Civil Code.
⑤ Article 377 of the Civil Code.

have become the same person, the easement will be extinguished. Other grounds for extinguishment of a right to easement include the expropriation of the servient land, the abandonment of the easement by the right-holder, the occurrence of a cause which, as provided in the contract, may lead to extinguishment of the easement, when the person who has the right in the servient land rescinds the easement contract on the ground that the right holder of the easement violates the provisions of law or the contract, or, in case of a paid use of the servient land, if the right holder of the easement fails to pay the relevant fees despite of receipt of two warning notices within a reasonable period of time after the payment is due according to the agreement. [1]

§ 3:4 Security Interests

§ 3:4:1 The Security System in General

The security system is established to secure a claim of a creditor or otherwise an obligee in a commercial transaction such as lending or buying and selling. [2] When a debtor fails to perform his obligation due, or there occurs any event upon the occurrence of which a security interest is to be enforced as agreed upon by the parties, the person holding the security interest has priority to be paid from the collateral in accordance with law. [3] This system may help promote financing and commodity transfer, and benefit the development of market economy.

A security interest can be created by the parties through entering into a security contract (or a security agreement) in accordance with law, such as a mortgage contract, a pledge contract, or otherwise a contract with the function of security. [4] Therefore, there are two contracts involved in a secured transaction, one is a primary contract (also called a principal contract or an underlying contract), the other is a security contract, which is secondary to the primary contract. As a general rule, if the primary contract is invalid, the

---

[1] Article 384 of the Civil Code.
[2] Article 387 of the Civil Code.
[3] Article 386 of the Civil Code.
[4] Article 388 of the Civil Code.

security contract is also invalid.① If a security contract is determined to be void, if the debtor, the security provider, or the creditor are at fault, they shall each bear civil liability in proportion to their fault.②

The scope covered by a security interest includes the principal claim and its interests based on the primary contract, liquidated damages, compensatory damages, and the expenses arising from safekeeping the collateral and enforcing the security interests, unless otherwise agreed by the parties.③

A security provider may be either a debtor or a third person. In a situation that a security is provided by a third person, if the creditor allows the debtor to transfer all or part of the secured obligations without the security provider's written consent, the third-person security provider is no longer liable for securing the part of the obligations so transferred.④ A debt may be secured by both a collateral and a surety. In this situation, if the debtor fails to perform his obligation due or any event upon which a security interest is to be enforced as agreed upon by the parties occurs, the creditor may enforce his claim in accordance with the agreement. Where there is no agreement or the relevant agreement is unclear, if the collateral is provided by the debtor himself, the creditor shall first enforce the claim against the collateral, and if the collateral is provided by a third person, the creditor may elect to enforce the claim against the collateral or request the surety to assume liability. After the third-person security provider has assumed such liability, he has a right to indemnification against the debtor.⑤

A security interest will be extinguished if the claim arising from the underlying contract extinguishes, the security interest has been enforced, the creditor waives his security interest, or the interest extinguishes as provided by law.⑥

Before the Civil Code was enacted, the laws governing secured transactions in

---

① Article 388 of the Civil Code.
② Article 388 of the Civil Code.
③ Article 389 of the Civil Code.
④ Article 391 of the Civil Code.
⑤ Article 392 of the Civil Code.
⑥ Article 393 of the Civil Code.

China included the GPCL, Security Law① and the judicial interpretations on it,② as well as the Real Rights Law. Now the provisions of these laws have been integrated into Part Four of Book Two of the Civil Code. In addition, some special laws also govern the secured transactions, such as the Negotiable Instruments Law and Maritime Law. Many administrative regulations or departmental rules are also part of the legal framework governing secured transactions in China. The main principles of the Chinese security system are the principles of equality, voluntariness, fairness, and honesty, which are identical to the principles of the general civil law. There are five types of securities recognized in China, three of them, *i.e.*, mortgage, pledge, and lien, relates to real rights. The following sections will introduce these three types of secured real rights.

§ 3:4:2 Mortgage

Mortgage is a type of security whereby a debtor or a third person uses his property as collateral, without relinquishing the possession of the property, to secure a principal debt owed by the debtor. When the debtor fails to perform his obligation due, the creditor has priority to be paid out of the proceeds of the collateral. The debtor or the third person is the mortgagor, the creditor is the mortgagee.③ A mortgagee's right is a real right.

§ 3:4:2:1 Creation and Extinguishment of a Mortgage

A mortgage is created on a mortgage contract entered into by a mortgagor and a mortgagee.④ A mortgage contract must be in writing and generally contains the clauses as set out in Article 400 of the Civil Code:

> To create a mortgage, the parties shall enter into a mortgage contract in writing.

---

① The Security Law was enacted by the Standing Committee of the Eighth NPC on June 30, 1995 and effective from October 1, 1995.
② The Interpretations of the Supreme People's Court on Certain Issues of the Security Law was made by the Supreme People's Court of the PRC on September 29, 2000 (hereinafter referred to as "Interpretations on Security Law").
③ Article 394 of the Civil Code.
④ Article 400 of the Civil Code.

A mortgage contract generally contains the following clauses:

(1) the type and amount of the secured claim;

(2) the term during which the debtor shall perform obligations;

(3) such particulars as the name and quantity of the mortgaged property; and

(4) the scope of the security interest covered.

Where a mortgagor and mortgagee do not induce the contract in writing but one of the parties has performed the principal obligations under the contract (e.g., filing a mortgage registration) which has been accepted by the other party, the mortgage contract is also valid according to Article 490 of the Civil Code. A mortgage contract, once formed, is effective between the mortgagor and the mortgagee. In order for a mortgage contract to be effective against a third person, it must be registered with the registration authority.①

A mortgage will be extinguished if the principal debt is fully discharged;② if the principal debt is only partially discharged, the mortgagee still has a right against the whole collateral. If the principal debt is discharged upon satisfaction made by a third person, the third person obtains the right to compensation based on subrogation, so the mortgagee's right is not extinguished either. A mortgage will be extinguished if the principal debt has been transferred without being consented to by a third person mortgagor.③ A mortgage will also be extinguished if the collateral is totally destructed, but the mortgagee's right against the proceeds of the collateral is not extinguished. Where a mortgagee's right is extinguished owing to the destruction of the collateral, the compensation obtained for the destruction of the collateral is deemed to be collateral④ and the mortgagee may request the court to adopt preservation measures against the insurance compensation, damages, or other remedies obtained by the mortgagor.⑤ However, if the collateral has been transferred to a third person during the term of the mortgage, the mortgagee's

---

① Articles 395 and 403 of the Civil Code.
② Article 393 of the Civil Code.
③ Article 39 of the Interpretations of the SPC on Security System under the Civil Code of the PRC.
④ Article 390 of the Civil Code.
⑤ Article 42 of the Interpretations of the SPC on Security System under the Civil Code of the PRC..

right will not be affected. ①

If, in addition to the mortgage, a debtor also provides collateral to secure the debt, or a surety provides guarantee to secure the debt, if the creditor waives or exempts the debtor or the surety's liability, the mortgage will be extinguished. A mortgage may also be extinguished upon expiration of the mortgage term, or upon realization of the mortgagee's right.

§ 3:4:2:2 The Parties to a Mortgage

A mortgagor may be a debtor or a third person who has full capacity for performing civil juristic acts. A mortgage created by one of the joint owners on the jointly-owned property without being consented to by the other joint owners is invalid. A legal person's capacity to be a mortgagor is limited by law. For example, the provision of security for others by a corporation must be in accordance with its articles of incorporation, or with the resolutions made by the board meeting or shareholder meeting. A bankrupt enterprise's capacity of providing a mortgage is also restricted. If a mortgage is provided by such an enterprise within the period starting from one year prior to the date the bankruptcy petition is filed with the court, to the date of declaration of the bankruptcy is made, it is invalid on the ground that during this period the bankrupt enterprise has no right to dispose of its assets.

A mortgagee is a creditor, including a creditor of a future interest, whose right is secured by the mortgage. Since the mortgagee is a party who does not have any obligation but will receive pure benefit from the mortgage contract, the mortgage contract is valid regardless whether the mortgagee has full capacity for performing civil juristic acts, as long as he is the creditor of a valid debt.

A Mortgagor's Rights

After a mortgage becomes effective, the mortgagor is still the owner of the collateral of the mortgage and still has a right to possess the collateral, utilize and profit from it, and dispose of it in accordance with law. However, this right is restricted by law in that the interests of the mortgagee cannot be harmed. To a certain extent, a mortgagor's rights are actually the limitations

---

① See Article 406 of the Civil Code.

imposed on the mortgagor so that the mortgagor should not harm the mortgagee's right when exercising its ownership right.

A mortgagor may continue to possess the collateral or may allow others to possess it. Nevertheless, a mortgagor's possession of the collateral is different from his possession of the other property he owns in that it is not only a right but also an obligation for the mortgagor to possess the mortgaged collateral. Once the mortgagor's possession of the collateral is infringed upon, he must request for remedies, and meanwhile, during the period of possession, the mortgagor must properly keep the collateral and will be liable if the collateral is damaged.

Although a mortgagor may still exercise his right to dispose of the collateral as an owner of the property, Article 406 of the Civil Code imposes certain restrictions:

> A mortgagor may transfer the mortgaged property to another person during the term of the mortgage unless otherwise agreed by the parties. The transfer of the mortgaged property does not affect the mortgage.
>
> A mortgagor who transfers the mortgaged property to another person shall notify the mortgagee in a timely manner. The mortgagee may request the mortgagor to apply the proceeds of the transfer to pay off the obligation before it is due, or place such proceeds in escrow where he may establish that the transfer of the mortgaged property may impair his right to the mortgage. The portion of the proceeds obtained from the transfer in excess of the amount of the obligation owed shall belong to the mortgagor, whereas any deficiency balance shall be paid by the debtor.

A mortgagor may lease the collateral as long as he notifies the lessee that the leased property has been mortgaged so that the lessee knows the existence of the mortgagee's right prior to the lease. If the mortgagor can prove that the lessee knew that the leased property has been mortgaged but still wants to lease it, any loss suffered by the lessee owing to the realization of the mortgagee's right will be borne by the lessee.[①] However, if the collateral has been let to

---

① Article 54 of SPC's Interpretations on the Security System under the Civil Code.

and possessed by a lessee prior to creation of the mortgage, then the lease relationship is not affected by the mortgage. ①

A mortgagor may create other security interests in the collateral. Article 35 of the Security Law required that only when the value of the collateral exceeded the secured debt would the mortgagor create other security interests in it. However, this requirement has not been included in the Civil Code. Then a question may arise as to the order of repayment under the different security contracts. If a collateral is both mortgaged and pledged, the priority order of repayment with the proceeds obtained from auction or sale of the collateral will be based on the priority in time of registration and delivery of the property. ②

A mortgagor may also create a right to usufruct on the collateral; however, the right to usufruct thus established is not effective against the mortgagee's right. Upon realization of the mortgagee's right, the right to usufruct is not effective against the purchaser of the collateral.

A Mortgagee's Rights

After a mortgage is created, a mortgagee has several rights to protect its own interests. First, a mortgagee has a right to preserve the value of the collateral. During the term of the mortgage, if any act of the mortgagor may decrease the value of the collateral, the mortgagee may request the mortgagor to refrain from performing such act. If the value of the collateral has been decreased, the mortgagee has a right to request the mortgagor to restore the value of the collateral, or provide additional security to the extent of the decreased value of the collateral. If the mortgagor neither restores the original value of the collateral, nor provides additional security, the mortgagee has a right to request the debtor to pay off the debt before it is due. ③

Where two or more mortgages are created on the same property, different mortgagees have different priority orders to be satisfied. Article 414 of the Civil Code provides the priority order:

---

① Article 405 of the Civil Code.
② Article 415 of the Civil Code.
③ Article 408 of the Civil Code.

Where a property is mortgaged to two or more creditors, the proceeds obtained from auction or sale of the mortgaged property shall be applied to repay the debts in accordance with the following provisions:

(1) where the mortgages have all been registered, the priority order of payment is based on the priority in time of registration;

(2) a registered mortgage has priority over an unregistered mortgage to be paid; and

(3) where none of the mortgages are registered, payment shall be made on a *pro rata* basis against the claims.

The preceding paragraph shall be applied *mutatis mutandis* with regard to the priority order of payment for other security interests that are registrable.

A mortgagee may waive or transfer his right in the collateral, and may also waive or transfer his priority right to be satisfied. When a mortgagee waives his right on the collateral, he automatically gives up his right to be paid prior to the other creditors. Article 409 of the Civil Code provides the general rule:

A mortgagee may waive his right to the mortgage, or waive his priority order in the line of the mortgagees. A mortgagee and the mortgagor may reach an agreement to change such things as the mortgagee's priority order in the line of the mortgagees and the amount of the secured claim, provided that any change to the mortgage may not adversely affect the other mortgagees without their written consent.

Where a debtor creates a mortgage on his own property, and the mortgagee waives his right to the mortgage and his priority order in the line of mortgagees, or changes the mortgage, the other security providers shall be exempted from the security liability to the extent of the rights and interests of the mortgagee that are forfeited owing to the waiver of his priority to be paid from the mortgaged property, unless the other security providers are committed to still provide security.

§ 3:4:2:3 Mortgageable Property

The collateral is the property that a security provider uses to create a security interest. In a mortgage scenario, the collateral is the mortgaged property. All property are not mortgageable. Article 395 of the Civil Code provides a list of property that may be mortgaged, whereas Article 399 provides a list of property that may not be mortgaged:

Article 395

The following property, which the debtor or a third person is entitled to dispose of, may be mortgaged:
(1) buildings and other things attached to the land;
(2) the right to use a lot of land for construction purposes;
(3) the right to use the sea areas;
(4) production equipment, raw materials, work in process, and finished products;
(5) buildings, vessels, and aircraft under construction;
(6) vehicles for transport; and
(7) any other property not prohibited by laws or administrative regulations from being mortgaged.

A mortgagor may mortgage the property listed in the preceding paragraph concurrently.

Article 399

The following property may not be mortgaged:
(1) land ownership;
(2) the right to use the land owned by a collective, such as house sites, land and hills retained for household use, unless it may be mortgaged as provided by law;
(3) educational facilities, medical and health facilities, and other public welfare facilities of non-profit legal persons established for public welfare purposes, such as schools, kindergartens, and medical institutions;
(4) property of which the ownership or right to the use is unclear or disputed;
(5) property that has been sealed up, detained, or placed under custody

in accordance with law; and

(6) any other property that may not be mortgaged as provided by laws or administrative regulations.

It is to be noted that the predecessor of item (7) of Article 395 was "any other property that the law or administrative regulations allows to be mortgaged."[①] Apparently, the Civil Code has expanded the scope of property that may be used as collateral in a mortgage relationship.

In China, land is owned by the State and rural collectives. Generally, the State-owned land and the rural land may not be mortgaged but a land use right may be mortgaged in accordance with law. A right to use the State-owned land is a right lawfully obtained to develop, utilize, and operate a lot of the State-owned land. As stated in §3:3:1:1, there are three ways to obtain a right to use a lot of land, including grant, transfer, and gratuitous grant.[②] As the owner of the State-owned land, the State may grant the right to use a lot of State-owned land to a land user within a specified period on the conditions that, *inter alia*, the land user pays the land use fees. The State may also gratuitously grant a land use right to a land user who does not need to pay any land use fee. A land user may transfer the right to use a lot of land he has obtained from the State to another person by way of sales, exchanges, or making a gift. A land use right obtained through grant or transfer may be mortgaged, whereas a land use right obtained through gratuitous grant may not be mortgaged unless it is approved by the land management and real estate management departments of the government above the county level, and the land user has paid the land use fee or used the proceeds received from the mortgage to set off the land use fee.

Since only land use rights may be mortgaged in China, mortgages on immovable property typically involve buildings on and other fixtures to land only. However, when a building is mortgaged, the right to use the lot of land under the building must be mortgaged concomitantly, and *vice versa*.[③]

---

① Article 34 of the Security Law.
② The Provisionary Regulations on Grants and Transfers of the Right to Use the Urban State-owned Land made in 1990.
③ Article 397 of the Civil Code.

However, a right to use a lot of land for construction purposes owned by a township or village enterprise may not be mortgaged separately. When a factory premise or any other building of such an enterprise is mortgaged, the right to use the lot of land for construction purposes in the area occupied by the premise or building should be mortgaged concomitantly. ①

Likewise, all rights to use rural land are not mortgageable. For example, arable land which is used for agricultural production purposes according to the Land Administration Law is not allowed to be mortgaged because the State adopts a strict system to protect the arable land and prevent the function of the arable land to be changed. Generally, a house site may not be mortgaged either. A house site is a lot of land used by a rural family to build their residence. According to the Land Administration Law, each rural household can only have one house site and its acreage may not exceed the standard set by the relevant province, autonomous region or the municipality directly under the central government. Since the function of a house site is for a specified villager to build his residence, the villager who has obtained the house site may only build his own residence on the house site and he may not mortgage his right to use the house site. Home-based land and home-based mountains are collective-owned land that is distributed to the villagers in order to protect the villagers' basic livelihood. Actually, a right to use home-based land or mountains serves for providing social security to the villagers, and it will remain unchanged for quite a long term. Therefore, such land use rights may not be mortgaged.

Traditionally, mortgage mainly involves immovables; however, mortgage on movables becomes increasingly important today because the movables such as machines or transportation vehicles have greater value and can be used as collateral. Moreover, an enterprise, an individual-run industrial and commercial household, or an agricultural production operator is allowed to mortgage their inventories currently owned or after-acquired, including their production equipment, raw materials, work in process, or finished products. If a debtor fails to perform his obligation due, the creditor has priority to be paid from the movable property determined at the time when the mortgaged property is ascertained.

---

① Article 398 of the Civil Code.

The collateral in a mortgage transaction must be the property that the mortgagor has the right to dispose of. In addition to the land ownership and certain right to use the land by a collective, the facilities of some non-profit legal persons established for public welfare purposes may not be mortgaged. These non-profit institutions or social organizations are aimed at providing public benefits and their facilities are established to serve their purposes, therefore the law prohibits these facilities from being mortgaged. However, these institutions and social organizations may mortgage their facilities that are not established for public welfare purposes to secure their own debts.

If the ownership of or right to use the property is not clear or is disputed, it would be difficult to determine who has the right to dispose of the property, and therefore the property may not be mortgaged. To determine whether the ownership of or right to use the property is unclear or disputed, whether the mortgagor can provide a formal title proof may be a *prima facie* evidence. If a mortgagor mortgages property that the title paper of which has not been issued, the mortgage may be valid if the mortgagor can provide the title paper or complete registration of the collateral before the end of the argument phase in a court hearing of the first instance trial. The property that has been sealed up, detained, or placed under custody in accordance with law may not be mortgaged.

A debtor or a third person may also create a maximum mortgage for floating claims by providing a collateral for future claims that will arise consecutively within a certain period of time to secure the debtor's performance of his obligations. In this case, if the debtor fails to perform his obligation when it is due, the mortgagee has priority to be paid from the collateral up to the maximum amount of his claims.① Since the claims to be secured are not ascertained upon creation of the mortgage, the ascertainment of the claims are important in such a mortgage. Article 423 of the Civil Code provides the situations in which the claims of a mortgagee are ascertained:

> The claims of the mortgagee are ascertained under any of the following circumstances:

---

① Article 420 of the Civil Code.

(1) where the agreed period of time for the claims to be ascertained expires;

(2) where there is no agreement on the period of time for the claims to be ascertained or the relevant agreement is unclear, and the mortgagee or the mortgagor requests ascertainment of the claims after the lapse of two years from the date of the creation of the mortgage;

(3) where it is impossible for a new claim to arise;

(4) where the mortgagee knows or should have known that the mortgaged property has been sealed up or detained;

(5) where the debtor or the mortgagor is declared bankrupt or dissolved; or

(6) there exists any other circumstance under which the claims are to be ascertained as provided by law.

Before the claims secured by the maximum mortgage for floating claims are ascertained, the mortgage may not be transferred even when part of the claims is transferred, unless otherwise agreed by the parties.① However, the mortgagee and the mortgagor may change by agreement the period of time for the ascertainment of the claims, the scope of the claims, and the maximum amount of the claims, provided that such changes may not adversely affect the other mortgagees.②

§3:4:3 Pledge

A debtor or a third person may deliver their property to a creditor as collateral to secure a transaction. Where the debtor fails to perform his obligations, the creditor has a priority right to be satisfied from the proceeds of the collateral. This is called a pledge, the debtor or the third person is the pledgor while the creditor is the pledgee.③ A pledge is effective upon delivery of the collateral to the pledgee.

Pledges may be divided into different categories according to different

---

① Article 421 of the Civil Code.
② Article 422 of the Civil Code.
③ Article 425 of the Civil Code.

standards. Based on the nature of the pledged collateral, it may be a pledge on movable property or pledge on rights and interests. Real property may not be pledged under Chinese law.

§ 3:4:3:1　A Pledge on Movables

If a debtor delivers his movable property to his creditor to secure a principal transaction, a pledge on movables is created. The debtor is the pledgor and the creditor is the pledgee. If the debtor fails to perform his obligation when it is due, the creditor has priority to be satisfied from the proceeds of the collateral, through appraisal, auction, or sale. Article 427 of the Civil Code requires that the parties must conclude a written contract to create a pledge, and it also sets out some clauses that a pledge contract may need to contain:

> To create a pledge, the parties shall enter into a pledge contract in writing.
> A pledge contract generally contains the following clauses:
> (1) the type and amount of the secured claim;
> (2) the term for the debtor to perform the obligation;
> (3) such particulars as the name and quantity of the pledged property;
> (4) the scope of the security covered; and
> (5) the time for and the mode of the delivery of the pledged property.

Although a pledge contract is required to be in writing, if a pledgor has delivered the collateral to the pledgee and the pledgee has accepted it, even if there is no writing, the pledge contract is still formed and the pledgee has obtained the interests on the collateral under the contract law.[①] A pledge is effective only upon delivery of the collateral to the pledgee by the pledgor.[②]

Under a pledge contract, a pledgor may be the principal debtor or a third person who has a right to dispose of the collateral. A pledgee is the principal creditor who does not need to have full capacity for performing civil juristic

---

① Article 490 of the Civil Code.
② Article 428 of the Civil Code.

acts. However, after a pledge is created, since the collateral must be possessed by the pledgee and the pledgee has an obligation to properly keep the collateral, the pledgee needs to have the ability to understand the nature of his rights and obligations; otherwise he may not sign a pledge contract with the pledgor unless it is signed by his legal representative on his behalf, or it is consented to by his legal representative.

A collateral pledged must be a specific movable property that is transferable and that its transfer is not prohibited by law. ① If the collateral is not specific, it must be specified before the pledge becomes effective. For instance, money is not specific and generally cannot be used as collateral of a pledge. However, the parties may specify it through depositing the money into a special account. The parties may also create a maximum pledge for floating claims upon agreement. ②

A pledgee has an obligation to properly keep the collateral and is liable for compensating any damage or loss caused to the collateral owing to his improper safekeeping of it. If a pledgee unilaterally decides to use or dispose of the collateral or repledges the collateral to a third person without the consent of the pledgor, the pledgee is liable for any damage thus caused to the pledgor. ③ On the other hand, a pledgor has a right to request the pledgee to place the collateral in escrow, or to allow him to discharge his obligation prior to its due date and return the collateral if the pledgee's act is likely to cause the collateral to be destructed, damaged, or lost. ④

Nevertheless, if the collateral is likely to be damaged or significantly diminished in value owing to a cause not attributable to the pledgee, the pledgee may request the pledgor to provide additional security, and, if the pledgor fails to provide additional security, may have the pledged property sold at auction or in a sale and may apply the proceeds to discharge the obligation before it is due or place such proceeds in escrow. ⑤

A pledgee may waive his right to the pledge. Under this circumstance, if

---

① Article 426 of the Civil Code.
② Article 439 of the Civil Code.
③ Article 431 of the Civil Code.
④ Articles 432 & 434 of the Civil Code.
⑤ Article 433 of the Civil Code.

the collateral is provided by the debtor, the other security providers will be exempted from their security liability to the extent of the rights and interests of the pledgee that are forfeited owing to the waiver of his priority to be paid from the collateral, unless the other security providers are committed to still provide security. ①

If a debtor has performed his obligation or a pledgor has paid the secured claim before it is due, a pledgee should return the collateral to the pledgor. However, if a debtor fails to perform his obligation when it is due, or there occurs an event upon the occurrence of which a pledge is to be enforced as agreed upon by the parties, the pledgee may, by agreement with the pledgor, appraise and accept the collateral as satisfaction of his claim, or have priority to be paid from the proceeds obtained from auction or sale of the collateral. The appraisal or sale of the collateral should be based on the market price. ②

Where a pledgee and a pledgor agree that the creditor may own the collateral in the event that the debtor fails to perform the obligation due, Chinese law only allows the pledgee to have priority to be paid from the pledged property instead of owning the collateral. ③ After the collateral is appraised or is sold at auction or in a sale, where the value of the collateral as appraised or the proceeds obtained from auction or sale is in excess of the amount of the obligation owed, any excess must belong to the pledgor, whereas any deficiency balance must be paid by the debtor. ④

A pledge may be extinguished upon extinguishment of the collateral, upon the satisfaction of the secured debt, upon the transfer of the debt by the debtor without consent of the third person pledgor, upon waiver or the returning of the collateral to the pledgor by the pledgee, upon the loss of the possession of the collateral by the pledgee, upon realization of the pledgee's right, or upon expiration of the term of the pledge.

§ 3:4:3:2 A Pledge on Rights

Where the pledged collateral is the rights and interests other than the

---

① Article 435 of the Civil Code.
② Article 436 of the Civil Code.
③ Article 428 of the Civil Code.
④ Article 438 of the Civil Code.

ownership rights or rights to usufruct in the property, it is called a pledge on rights. A pledge on rights also needs to be concluded in writing. Article 440 of the Civil Code provides the rights that may be pledged:

> The following rights, which a debtor or a third person is entitled to dispose of, may be pledged:
> (1) bills of exchange, promissory notes, and checks;
> (2) bonds and certificates of deposits;
> (3) warehouse receipts and bills of lading;
> (4) transferable fund shares and equity;
> (5) transferable proprietary rights consisted in intellectual property such as the right to the exclusive use of registered trademarks, patent rights, and copyrights;
> (6) existing and after-acquired accounts receivables; and
> (7) any other proprietary right that may be pledged in accordance with the provisions of laws and administrative regulations.

Since the rights and interests that may be used as collateral in a pledge are diversified, the timing of the creation of a pledge on different rights is various.[①] A pledge on a bill of exchange, promissory note, check, bond, certificate of deposits, warehouse receipt, or bill of lading is created at the time when the certificate of such a right is delivered to the pledgee, or, where there is no such a certificate, at the time when the pledge is registered. If the maturity date for the payment or the delivery of goods against a pledged bill of exchange, promissory note, check, bond, certificate of deposit, warehouse receipt, or bill of lading precedes the due date of the principal claim, the pledgee may cash the certificate or take delivery of the goods, and, upon agreement with the pledgor, apply the purchase price or the goods accepted to discharge the obligation before it is due or place it in escrow.

On the other hand, a pledge on fund shares, equity, a proprietary right in intellectual property, or an account receivable is created upon registration of the pledge. Once a pledge is created, the pledgee has a right to possess the

---

① Articles 441 – 446 of the Civil Code.

collateral and also has a duty to properly keep it. Before the secured debt has been fully discharged, a pledgee may refuse to return the collateral to the pledgor or other people. Neither may the collateral be transferred, unless the pledgor and the pledgee both agree, and the proceeds from the transfer must be applied to pay to the pledgee to discharge the obligation before it is due or be placed in escrow in order to protect the pledgee's interests.

The Civil Code and other relevant laws and regulations may impose restrictions on certain rights and interests to be used as collateral. For example, the stocks to be pledged must be one that are allowed to be transferred by law. For example, since the stocks owned by an incorporator of a joint stock limited company may not be transferred within one year after the corporation is established,① an incorporator may not pledge his shares within the specified period.

Upon creation of a pledge, the parties need to either deliver the certificate of the rights or interests or file registration with different institutions. For example, if stocks or shares in funds are the collateral, the pledge should be registered with the securities registration and clearing institutions. If the other equity rights or account receivables are the collateral, the parties need to register it with the administration of industry and commerce or other relevant departments.

If a pledgee is not fully satisfied upon expiration of the term of performance of the debt, he has priority to be paid from the proceeds obtained from disposing of the collateral. The proceeds may be represented by an appraised value or obtained through auction or sale; except that if the pledged stocks are those of a listed company, it can only be assessed through trading in the stock market. Based on the principle of honesty and good faith, a pledgee must timely exercise such right. If a pledgee has not timely enforced the pledge after expiration of the term of performance of the obligation so that the value of the stocks or shares depreciate, the pledgor may request the court to have the collateral sold at auction or in a sale to discharge his obligation. If any damage is caused to the pledgor owing to the pledgee's indolence in doing so, the pledgee will be liable for compensation.

---

① Article 141 of Corporation Law.

A pledgor may only pledge his real rights in the shares, and the other rights of a shareholder shall not be affected by the pledge. Therefore, a pledgee of stocks may not have the decision-making right of a shareholder.

§3:4:4 Lien

Where movable property of a debtor has been lawfully possessed by a creditor, if the debtor fails to perform his obligation relating to this movable property owed to the creditor upon expiration of the term of performance, the creditor may keep the movable property according to law and has priority to be paid from it. In this situation, a lien is created and the creditor is the lienholder and the movable property in his possession for this purpose is the collateral retained under lien. ①

A lien is a security created by operation of law and not by the parties' expression of intent. A lien is created only upon satisfaction of certain conditions. On the one hand, the lienholder must have lawfully possessed the retained property owned by the debtor, and the retained property must be in the same legal relationship as the underlying claim, unless the lienholder and the debtor are both enterprises. ② On the other hand, the term of performance of the debt must have expired. However, the parties may exclude a lien through a prior agreement. ③

The creation of a lien may not be against public policy. For example, withholding a debtor's necessaries may be against the public policy or the public interest. If the property retained under a lien is a divisible thing, the value of the retained property may only be equivalent to the amount of the obligation. ④

After a lien is established, the owner of the retained property still has the ownership right over the property except that his right is limited. The lienholder (also called lienee) has a right to withhold the property and has an obligation to properly keep it, and will be liable for compensation if it is destroyed, damaged, or lost due to his improper custody. ⑤ After the property

---

① Article 447 of the Civil Code.
② Article 448 of the Civil Code.
③ Article 449 of the Civil Code.
④ Article 450 of the Civil Code.
⑤ Article 451 of the Civil Code.

is retained under a lien, the lienholder and the debtor should reach an agreement on the period of performance of the obligation. If no agreement has been reached, or if the agreement is unclear, the lienholder should give the debtor a period of 60 or more days to perform the obligation, unless the retained property is fresh, living, or perishable so that it is hard to keep it for long. If the debtor still fails to perform his obligation upon expiration of such term, the lienholder may, upon agreement with the debtor, appraise the retained property, or be paid with priority from the proceeds obtained from auction or sale of the retained property. ① If the value of the retained property or the proceeds obtained from auction or sale of the retained property is in excess of the amount of the obligation owed, any excess should belong to the debtor whereas any deficiency balance should be paid by the debtor. ②

After the period of performance of the obligation expires, if the lienholder fails to timely enforce the lien, the debtor may request the court to have the retained property sold at auction or in a sale to satisfy his obligation. ③

If the property retained under lien has already been mortgaged or pledged, the lienholder has priority to be paid. ④

A lien is extinguished if the lienor provides a new collateral, if the lienholder loses possession over the retained property or accepts another form of security provided by the debtor, ⑤ or if the performance term of the debt has been extended.

Case 22

Case 22: CCB v. Zhongyi Co. & China Export Co. ⑥

On August 19, 1996, China Construction Bank Shanghai Pudong Branch (CCB) and China Zhongyi International Trade Development Co. (Zhongyi Co.) signed a contract for a loan of foreign currency. Under

---

① Article 453 of the Civil Code.
② Article 455 of the Civil Code.
③ Article 454 of the Civil Code.
④ Article 456 of the Civil Code.
⑤ Article 457 of the Civil Code.
⑥ See (2001) Min Er Zhong Zi No. 155, reprinted in the SPC Gazette, Issue 7, 2004.

this contract, CCB would provide US $4,500,000 to Zhongyi Co. as working capital loan from August 19, 1996 to August 18, 1997 with the annual interest as CCB's interest for 1-year foreign exchange working capital loan floating by six months, and the pay days would be March 20, June 20, September 20, and December 20. If Zhongyi could not repay the due amount, CCB would charge an overdue interest based on 1.3 times the loan interest rate. On the same day, CCB transferred US $4,500,000 to Zhongyi's account. Afterwards, Zhongyi defaulted. Up to January 20, 1998, Zhongyi owed the principal of US $4,500,000 and the interests of US $307,330.08 (including overdue interests).

China Export Commodity Base Construction Corporation (China Export Co.) issued an irrevocable guarantee to CCB, guaranteeing the repayment of the above principal loan and the interests and relevant fees, as well as overdue interests and fees. It promised to repay CCB the principal and interests owed by Zhongyi Co. to CCB within 14 days after the written notice of CCB had been received. This guarantee provided a continuous surety and became effective since it was executed, until the guaranteed amount had been fully repaid by Zhongyi Co. or China Export Co.. On this guarantee, there was signature of Xue Zhao, the chairman of the board of directors of China Export Co., and the official stamp of China Export Co.. However, the official stamp of China Export Co. on this guarantee letter is different from the official seal impression it left with the State Administration of Industry and Commerce (SAIC).

Zhongyi Co. was invested and established in 1995 by China Export Co. and Zhongyi Group. When registering Zhongyi Co. with the SAIC Shanghai Pudong Branch (Pudong SAIC), China Export Co. as one of its investors, used the official stamp concerned in this case in multiple materials for registration. It also used this stamp in the materials involved in two loans it borrowed from the ABN AMRO Bank Shanghai Branch (ABN).

CCB sued in Shanghai High People's Court on February 28, 1998 requesting Zhongyi Co. to return the principal and interests, and requesting China Export Co. to assume joint and several liability for the guarantee. The court held for CCB. China Export Co. appealed to the SPC.

The SPC ruled that the facts found by the lower court was not clear, and the evidences were not sufficient, so that it made a ruling on Feb. 3, 2001, remanding the case to Shanghai High People's Court.

On retrial, Shanghai High People's Court reasoned that this was a case involving a dispute on the loan contract between CCB and Zhongyi, which contract was lawful and valid, and both parties should perform the contract. Zhongyi apparently breached the contract and should assume the corresponding civil liability. Although China Expert Co.'s stamp used in the guarantee letter is not in compliance with the seal impression it left with the SAIC, the stamp was recognized by China Export Co. since it had used it in other transactions for many times. Therefore, providing guarantee for the loan involved in this case was the true expression of intent of China Export Co., and it should perform the surety obligations. Since the guarantee letter involved did not clearly stipulate the way of guarantee, China Export Co. should assume joint and several liability. After China Export Co. assumed the liability, it would have the right to indemnification against Zhongyi Co. The court finally held that Zhongyi Co. should repay principal and interests including the overdue interests to CCB within 10 days after the judgment becomes effective, and China Export Co. assumes joint and several liability as to the above payment obligations. The litigation fee of 209,021.45 yuan shall be jointly assumed by Zhongyi Co. and China Export Co.

China Export Co. appealed again to the SPC. The main issue of the second appeal was whether the guarantee letter was valid.

Article 32 of the Contract Law provides that where the parties conclude a contract in the form of a written agreement, the contract is formed at the time when the parties sign or stamp on the written agreement. The SPC reasons that this article means that either the signature or the official stamp would make a contract formed.

The signature of the parties includes the signature of a natural person or of his legal representative, or of the legal representative of a legal person or other economic organization. Article 38 of the GPCL provides that the person with the responsibility of representing a legal person in conducting civil activities in accordance with law or the legal person's articles of association is the legal representative of the legal person. Article 43 provides that an enterprise is liable for the operational activities conducted by its legal representative and other personnel. The guarantee letter involved in this case was signed by its legal representative; however, the signature was forged, and therefore, Xue Zhao, the legal representative of China Export Co., should not be labile for this signature. Accordingly, it cannot draw a conclusion that the guarantee letter was the true intention of China Export Co., so China Export Co. should not be liable for this guarantee letter based on the forged signature. The stamp may also make a contract formed. However, the official stamp on the guarantee letter was not the true stamp of China Export Co., and thus the guarantee letter did not express the intent of China Export Co. either.

In sum, the SPC finds that the signature on the guarantee letter was not the true signature of the legal representative Xue Zhao, and the official stamp thereon was an altered one.

The court reasons that whether China Export Co. is liable based on the Guarantee letter will need to be determined based on the overall situation. If the alteration of the official stamp was done by China Export Co. itself, even if the stamp was altered, it could represent China Export Co.'s true intention, and accordingly, China Export Co. should assume the guarantee liability. However, there is no evidence to prove it. Thus, the lower court improperly determined that China Export Co. used the altered official stamp for many times.

Furthermore, CCB, as a specialized financial institution, failed to exercise its duty of care and did not find that the stamp was altered so that it accepted the guarantee letter with the altered stamp. China Export Co. did not have any fault, and should not assume the liability under the guarantee letter.

Finally, the SPC holds that Zhongyi Co. is liable for repayment of the loan's principal and interests, but China Export Co. was not liable. It further holds that the first instance litigation fee of 209,02.45 yuan should be paid by Zhongyi Co., and the second instance litigation fee of 209,021.45 yuan should be paid by CCB.

Case 23

Case 23: Yangtze River Delta Commodity Exchange Co., Ltd v. Lu[①]

A Jetta car (license plate BXXXXX), registered under the name of Yangtze River Delta Commodity Exchange Co., Ltd (Delta Co.), was bought by the company on September 6, 2013, and was delivered to Lu for his use. Lu was the Deputy General Manager of Delta Co. On Feb. 21, 2014, Delta Co. delivered a notice to Lu, notifying him that he had been absent without just cause consecutively for 13 days and refused to report after the company had notified him for several times, and that he misappropriated and refused to return the company car. The notice also stated that Lu was fired because his activities were in violation of the employee handbook and constituted severe delinquent behavior. Lu believed that the termination was illegal, and that the company needed to pay him the salary in arrears, social security benefits and economic compensation, so he refused to return the said car.

The court found that Lu had applied for labor arbitration to the employment disputes arbitration committee of Binhu District, Wuxi City on June 9, 2014, and the committee made an arbitral award on July 25, 2014 ordering the Delta Co. to pay to Lu 120,600 yuan's salary in arrears between January 2013 to January 2014, and 80,000 yuan's economic compensation for illegally terminating the employment contract.

The first instance court determined that Lu's possession and use of the Delta Co.'s car was lawful because the company allocated the car to Lu since he acted as the deputy GM of the company. Since Lu alleged that the company owed him salary and economic compensation, Lu had the right to retain the car. The company appealed.

The Intermediate People's Court of Wuxi City reasons that the right to retain property is a way to guarantee the realization of an obligee's rights between the persons of the civil law equal in status. Except for the retainment of property between enterprises, the movable property

---

① See (2014) Xi Min Zhong Zi No. 1724, reprinted in the SPC Gazette, Issue 1, 2017.

retained under a lien by an obligee should be in the same legal relationship with the underlying claim.

However, the parties to an employment relationship are in an unequal relationship in that one party is under the management of the other party. An employee may not claim his right to retain the tool or other property provided by the employer as a lien on the ground that the employer owes him salary, since these movables are not the subject matter of the employment contract, and does not fall within the same legal relationship. Chinese labor law has already provided protection to the employees and they may protect their right arising from the employment through the means provided by law. If they are allowed to use private protective measures to protect such right, the order of labor and management will be disturbed, and inequality in the protection of the obligee's right will be caused. On the other hand, a lienholder has priority over the other obligees such as a mortgagee or pledgee; however, a labor dispute arises between an employer and an employee, the nature of which is an internal dispute within the economic organization, so that such a right should not be exercised in priority over the other external obligees.

In addition, the disputed car is not the subject matter of the labor relationship, the retention of which does not comply with the law which requires that the property retained under a lien must fall within the same legal relationship. A same legal relationship means that the possession of the movable by an obligee must be based on the same legal relationship under which the obligee's right arises. In other words, the movable and the occurrence of the obligee's right must have a close connection. In this case, the car is unrelated to the employment relationship so that the company may take it back at any time without affecting the original labor relationship. The company requested Lu to return the car based on its ownership rights and not based on the labor relationship.

Furthermore, since the labor relationship between the two parties has been dissolved, Lu has lost the basis of lawfully possessing the disputed car. The benefit that Lu, as a senior management officer, may enjoy is limited by time and restricted by certain conditions. These conditions no longer exist after the dissolution of the labor relationship; therefore, Lu should return the car to the company.

Finally, the court holds that the facts found by the first instance court were accurate, but the application of law was wrong and should be corrected. It holds that the judgment below should be reversed, and Lu should return the disputed car to the company within 10 days after the judgment becomes final, and Lu should also pay the litigation fees for both proceedings.

§ 3:5 Legal Remedies

Real rights are protected by law. The protection of real rights is reflected in the liabilities imposed on a person who infringes upon another person's real rights and the remedies granted to the person whose real rights are infringed upon by another person. Such protections are provided by both public laws, *i.e.*, the administrative law, criminal law, *etc.*, and private law — the civil law. Chapter III of Book Two of the Civil Code, specifically Articles 233 – 239, provide the remedies to a real right holder.

Article 233

Where a real right is infringed upon, the right-holder may have the problem solved by means of settlement, mediation, arbitration, litigation, and the like.

Article 234

Where a dispute arises over the attribution or contents of a real right, an interested person may request a confirmation of the right.

Article 235

Where immovable or movable property is possessed by a person not entitled to do so, the right-holder may request a restitution.

Article 236

Where there is a nuisance or a potential nuisance against a real right, the right-holder may request a removal of the nuisance or elimination of the danger.

Article 237

Where immovable or movable property is destructed or damaged, the right-holder may request repair, redoing, replacement, or restoration to the original condition in accordance with law.

Article 238

Where a real right is infringed upon and damage is thus caused, the right-holder may, in accordance with law, request the infringing person to pay damages or bear other civil liabilities.

Article 239

The forms of real right protection provided in this Chapter may be applied either separately or concurrently according to the circumstances of the infringement of a right.

Chapter 4
Contract Law

§ 4:1 General Introduction

§ 4:1:1 Historical Development and the Sources of Chinese Contract Law

Until the end of the 1970s, China had been featuring its planned economy and most, if not all, of the enterprises were State-owned and the purchase and sale of their products were all based on the State planning. Therefore, any business dispute would be resolved internally between or among the government departments governing the involved enterprises. It explains why there had been no contract law in China for quite a long time. In the early 1980s, the State implemented a policy of reform and openness to develop its economy and to transform the planned economy to a market economy. Accordingly, there began to have new market participants and more transactions between and among State-owned enterprises and non-State-owned enterprises or even individuals. The new situation required new laws. In order to meet this need, the Fifth National People's Congress (NPC) enacted the Economic Contract Law in 1981 to regulate the legal relationship arising from the economic contracts. It had been amended for three times and the last revision was made in 1993. It regulated the formation, performance, alteration, and termination of domestic economic contracts, the liability of the parties in default, as well as the dispute resolution.

It soon proved to be insufficient given the fact that there started to have more foreign investors involved in the economic transactions in China. Although attracted by the huge market of China, many foreign investors worried about the legal protection they might get from the Chinese legal system. This concern, to some extent, discouraged them from actively investing in the Chinese market. In 1985, the Sixth NPC enacted the Foreign-Related Economic Contract Law for the purpose of protecting the lawful rights and interests of the parties to foreign-related economic contracts. This law applied where one or more parties to a contract were enterprises with legal person status, other economic organizations, or individuals of foreign countries, the subject matter of the contract was located outside the territory of China or the contract required a cross-border performance by the parties, or the judicially significant facts which caused the creation, alteration, or extinguishment of a contractual relationship occurred outside the territory of China. Two years later, the SPC issued the Answers to Certain Questions Relating to the Foreign-Related Economic Contract Law. From then on, the parties to both domestic contracts and the contracts with foreign elements could seek legal protection from the above two contract laws.

Meanwhile, in order to re-construct the Chinese legal system which had almost been completely abolished during the Cultural Revolution period, Chinese government decided to make new laws governing the various aspects of the social and economic life and as a result, the early 1980s witnessed the bulk legislation of China. One of the important laws enacted during that period was the General Provisions of the Civil Law of the PRC (GPCL), which was the first general law to regulate the contractual relationship in China. It was enacted by the Sixth NPC in 1986 and become effective on January 1, 1987. Chapter 5 of the GPCL protected three types of civil-law rights: ownership rights, the obligee's rights, and the intellectual property rights. The second section within this chapter focuses on the creditor's rights which in effect are the rights arising from contracts.

Another important law at one time governing contracts in China was the Law on Technology Contracts, which was enacted by the Sixth NPC in June 1987. It regulated the legal relationships of the parties to the contracts relating to the development, transfer, consultation, and service of technologies. These contracts were regulated by the Economic Contract Law before the Law on Technology Contracts was enacted. The then State Committee of Science and Technology, upon approval by the State Council, made the Implementing

Rules on the Law on Technology Contracts and the Temporary Provisions on the Management of the Technology Contracts. These regulations not only interpreted the Law on Technology Contracts, but also supplemented and expanded its scope of application.

In the late 1980s, a complete framework of contract law had been established. While the Economic Contract Law, the Foreign-Related Economic Contract Law, and the Law on Technology Contracts provided specific regulations on different types of contract, the GPCL provided the default rules if the above laws were silent. In addition, a contract shall also comply with the administrative regulations enacted or approved by the State Council. The judicial interpretations made by the SPC, including the opinions, notices, responses, and other types of answers are also part of the legal framework of contract law.

The enactment and implementation of the 1999 Contract Law by the Ninth NPC had actually concluded the era when three different contract laws applied to different contracts in China. The Contract Law applied to all of the contracts other than those relating to marriage, adoption, or guardianship.[①] The unification of the contract law had successfully avoided the conflicts the former laws presented in legal practice and had provided a complete set of legal rules which fully representing the principles of freedom of contract and encouragement of transactions. Its purpose was to improve the efficiency of transactions, maintain the social public interest, and protect the lawful rights and interests of the consumers. The legislature had fully studied the successful legislation experience and precedents of both the civil law and common law systems when making the Contract Law, and had integrated various new rules and systems of the modern contract law into it. Most of the provisions of the Contract Law have now been integrated into Book Three of the Civil Code.

Now Book Three of the Civil Code, the Civil Procedure Law, Arbitration Law, Foreign Investment Law, Patent Law, Trademark Law, and the other relevant laws enacted by the NPC or its Standing Committee and the relevant regulations made by the State Council and the other committees or departments under the State Council form the basic legal framework of the Chinese contract

---

① Article 2 of the Contract Law.

law. The judicial interpretations made by the SPC are also part of this legal framework. In addition, the laws and regulations regulating import and export, inspection, and custom may also apply to the contracts as well. The sources of Chinese contract law also include the international conventions such as the United Nations Convention on Contracts for International Sale of Goods (CISG) which has taken effect since January 1st 1988, for which China is a party, as well as the international customs and practices, like the International Rules for the Interpretation of Trade Terms, Warsaw-Oxford Rules, and the Uniform Customs and Practice for Documentary Credits. When people talk about Chinese contract law, they refer to the system formed by all of the laws and regulations mentioned above.

§ 4:1:2 General Rules

A contract is defined as an agreement made by two parties on the establishment, modification, or termination of a civil juristic relationship between the persons of the civil law. ① Generally, an agreement on establishing a marriage, adoption, guardianship, or other personal relationships are not governed by the contract law rules, but the contract law rules may be applied *mutatis mutandis* according to the nature of such an agreement. ② The Civil Code reiterates that a contract formed according to law is protected by law, and legally binding on and only on the parties to the contract, unless otherwise provided by law. ③ The general principles discussed in Chapter 1 are applicable to a contractual relationship.

The Civil Code provides the rules of interpretation of a contract clause. If the parties to a contract have a dispute on the understanding of a contract clause, the meaning of the disputed clause should be interpreted according to the words and sentences used, with reference to the relevant clauses, the nature and purpose of the contract, the custom, and the principle of good faith. ④ In a contract involving a cross-border transaction, the parties may come from different countries and use different languages. If such a contract is made in

---

① Article 464 of the Civil Code.
② Article 464 of the Civil Code.
③ Article 465 of the Civil Code.
④ Article 142 of the Civil Code.

two or more languages and both texts are agreed to be equally authentic, the words and sentences used in each text are presumed to have the same meaning. If there is any inconsistency between the different texts, interpretation should be made in accordance with the related clauses, the nature, and the purpose of the contract, and the principle of good faith. ①

Book Three of the Civil Code is composed of three parts, Part One is about the general provisions applicable to contracts, Part Two introduces 19 kinds of nominate contracts, including sales contracts, gift contracts, loan contracts, suretyship contracts, and partnership contracts, *etc.*, and Part Three is about quasi-contracts. This Chapter will mainly focus on the general provisions of the contract law with a very brief introduction to the quasi-contracts in the end to conclude this Chapter. The nominate contracts are to be discussed in a different book.

§ 4:1:3 Types of Contract

A contract may be categorized by different ways under Chinese law.

Based on whether the two parties to a contract owe to each other an equivalent obligation, a contract may be a unilateral-obligation contract or a bilateral-obligation contract. A unilateral-obligation contract refers to a contract whereby only one party owes an obligation to the other party, such as a loan-to-use contract under which only the borrower has an obligation to properly use and duly return the loaned tool or facility to the lender. On the other hand, in a bilateral-obligation contract, the right of one party is the obligation of the other party. Examples include sales contracts or lease contracts. It is to be noted that the distinction between a unilateral-obligation contract and a bilateral-obligation contract under Chinese law is different from the distinction between a unilateral contract and a bilateral contract under common law. For example, a loan contract is a bilateral contract under common law but a unilateral-obligation contract under Chinese law.

Based on whether the parties may get benefit from the contract, a contract may be a for-consideration (non-gratuitous) contract or a gratuitous contract. Different from the common law, consideration is not a necessary element for

---

① Article 466 of the Civil Code.

the formation of a contract under Chinese law. Therefore, a gift is a contract under the Civil Code. Most of the bilateral-obligation contracts are for-consideration contracts; however, all unilateral-obligation contracts are not gratuitous contracts. Some unilateral-obligation contracts are not for consideration such as a gift contract, while others are for consideration, such as a loan contract.

Based on whether a contract is enumerated by the Contract Law, a contract may be a named (nominate) contract or an un-named contract. The 1999 Contract Law named fifteen types of contract, such as sales contract, contract supplying electricity, water, gas, or heating, gift contract, loan contract, lease contract, financing lease contract, processing contract, construction engineering contract, transport contract, technology contract, consignment contract, warehousing contract, entrustment contract, as well as broker and dealer contract. The Civil Code expands the list as to cover 19 types of contract. The newly added types of nominate contracts are surety contracts, factoring contracts, contracts for property management service, and partnership contracts. These nominate contracts are sometimes referred to as "typical contracts" because the law expressly provides the basic requirements as to the terms of such contracts, although the parties may change these terms by mutual assent. Un-named contracts are the contracts that have not been listed in the Contract Law. Since the parties to a contract has a freedom to determine the terms of the contract, even if a contract signed by the parties is not a nominate contract, it is still valid as long as it does not violate the prohibitive regulations of law or against the social public interest. When a dispute arises from a contract, the judges need to consult with written statutes in resolving the legal issue. Where a disputed contract is a named contract, the specific legal rules on that type of contract provided by the Civil Code will be applied to the case; however, if a disputed contract is an un-named contract, Article 467 of the Civil Code allows the judges to firstly apply the general principles of the contract law as set out in Book Three of the Civil Code, and then apply the other rules provided in the same Book as well as other laws on a contract which are most similar to the said contract by analogy. For example, a tourism contract is an un-named contract; however, it may cover various named contracts such as transport contract and lease contract, therefore, the rules governing those named contracts may be applied to the tourism contract *mutatis mutandis*.

A contract may be a contract formed on promises or a contract formed on delivery. A contract on promises is similar to a bilateral contract at common law, which requires the parties' promises to form a contract. A contract on delivery is similar to a unilateral contract at common law, which will not be formed until the parties deliver the subject matter or perform the required act. Most of the contracts in China are contracts on promises and the contracts on delivery are specifically provided by law. For example, a gift contract will not be formed until the gift has been delivered to the donee and the donor may revoke the gift prior to the transfer of the rights in the gifted property. ①

A contract may be one with form requirement and one without form requirement. If a contract is required by law to be formed in a certain way or through a certain procedure, or by satisfying some other specific requirements, then the contract is one with form requirement. An example of a contract with form requirement is a mortgage contract which is legally required to be made in writing. But the general rule is that the parties may conclude a contract in writing, orally, or in any other forms. ② As to what may constitute "a writing," the law has developed with the development of the digital economy. Generally, a writing can be any form as long as its content can be represented in a tangible form. In this sense, a written agreement, a letter, a telegram, a telex, or a facsimile will be sufficient to be a writing. In the digital world, people are using data messages more often, so the Civil Code has expanded the coverage of a writing to include a data message in any form, as long as its content can be represented in a tangible form, such as electronic data interchange and emails. ③

There are other ways to categorize a contract. For example, a contract may be a primary contract or a secondary contract based on whether it is an independent contract or its existence relies on the existence of another contract. A surety contract is a contract secondary to the underlying sales

---

① Article 658 of the Civil Code.
② Article 469 of the Civil Code.
③ Article 469 of the Civil Code.

contract. Sometimes a contract is made for the benefit of the parties, and such a contract is a contract for the parties; if a contract is for the benefit of another person, then it is a contract for third person beneficiaries.

§ 4:2 Concluding a Contract

Determining whether a contract has been formed is very important in determining the parties' rights and interests when a dispute arises from an alleged contract or a quasi-contract. Suppose East Co. believes that West Co. has delivered nonconforming dictionaries and sues West Co. in court for breach of contract, it must firstly prove that there is a contract already formed between East Co. and West Co. Whether a contract has been formed will determine whether the contract exists. However, formation of a contract does not necessarily mean that the contract is valid and enforceable. The effectiveness of a contract will be discussed in the next sub-section.

When determining whether a contract has been formed, Chinese law considers whether there are two or more independent parties and whether the parties have reached a mutual agreement on the main terms of the contract. Article 470 of the Civil Code provides the general terms of a contract to be included in a contract:

> The content of a contract shall be agreed by the parties and generally includes the following clauses:
> (1) name or entity name and domicile of each party;
> (2) objects;
> (3) quantity;
> (4) quality;
> (5) price or remuneration;
> (6) period, place, and manner of performance;
> (7) default liability; and
> (8) the means of dispute resolution.
> The parties may use the various types of model contracts for reference when concluding a contract.

Different from the common law under which offer, acceptance, and consideration are deemed as the basic elements required to form a contract, in China, the parties may conclude a contract by making an offer and acceptance, or through other means.① Apparently, consideration is not a required element for a contract to be formed in China, and a contract may also be formed by a way other than making an offer and acceptance by the parties.

§4:2:1 Offer

"Offer" is a manifestation of intention of an offeror to form a contract with an offeree who accepts the offer. The terms of an offer must be specific and definite and the offeror must intend to be bound by the terms of the offer once it is accepted.②

§4:2:1:1 Effectiveness of Offer

An offer must be distinguished from an invitation to offer. Generally, an auction or bidding announcement, a prospectus of stock, bond, or fund, a commercial advertisement or promotion, a mailed price catalog, *etc.* is only an invitation to offer; however, a commercial advertisement or promotion may be regarded as an offer if its content complies with the requirements for an offer.③ If a person makes an announcement promising to pay a reward to anyone who has completed a particular act, such a promise is recognized as an offer, and anyone who has completed the act may request the rewarder to pay the reward.④

An offer will not be effective until it reaches the offeree. Suppose Mr. White asks the manager of the promotion department of West Co. to print some leaflets advertising "Electronic English-Chinese Dictionary, price low during the promotion period!" and place them inside the Hualian Supermarket for the potential customers to pick up. This is a commercial advertisement but not an offer under Chinese law because it does not contain any specific or definite term that may bind the offeror. If Ms. Wang, the manager of the

---

① Article 471 of the Civil Code.
② Article 472 of the Civil Code.
③ Article 473 of the Civil Code.
④ Article 499 of the Civil Code.

Hualian Supermarket happens to see West Co.'s leaflets, and calls Mr. White saying that she is interested in the electronic dictionaries and asks Mr. white to send specifications and quotations to her. This phone call again is not an offer for the same reason and it is only an invitation to make an offer. However, if Mr. White subsequently mails Ms. Wang a letter in which he writes, "See the attached catalogue for the specifications and prices of the dictionaries," then this letter may be an offer, unless there is a line at the end of the catalogue saying, "the prices in this catalogue are only for your reference and subject to changes without further notice." Consider whether it makes any difference if Mr. White also writes in his letter "5% discount will be given if order placed during the promotion period which is thirty days from now." Suppose the catalogue Mr. White sends to Ms. Wang does not contain the "subject to" sentence but does contain the "5% discount" sentence, most probably, the letter and the catalogue will be otherwise regarded as an offer.

Generally, an offer becomes effective once it is received by an offeree, but it is not always easy to determine when an offer is received. Article 474 of the Civil Code provides that this issue should be resolved in accordance with Article 137 of the Civil Code, which specifies how to determine the timing of effectiveness of an expression of intent in the following scenarios. If an offer is made through real-time communication, such as a face-to-face conversation or a telephone conversation, the offer becomes effective from the time the offeree is aware of the content of the offer. If an offer is made in a form other than real-time communication, such as an offer made through a facsimile or a letter, there will be a time difference between when the offer is made and when the offer is received. In this situation, Chinese law adopts the civil law tradition of the receipt doctrine, which is different from the dispatch doctrine adopted by the common law countries. Therefore, an offer becomes effective upon the time the offer reaches the offeree. If an offer is made through an electronic data message such as an email letter, if the offeree has designated a specific email address, the offer becomes effective when the email message enters the offeree's email system. If no specific email address has been designated, then the offer becomes effective when the offeree knows or should have known that the email letter has entered the system. The parties may also agree otherwise on the effective time of such an offer made in the form of an electronic data message.

§ 4:2:1:2 Termination of Offer

An offer may be terminated by the offeror or by the offeree.

An offeror may terminate an offer through withdrawing or revoking the offer. An offer may be withdrawn only before it becomes effective, and may be revoked only after it becomes effective. Upon withdrawal, an offeror must send a notice to the offeree and such notice must reach the offeree prior to or at the same time with the offeree's receipt of the notice of withdrawal. ① Generally speaking, an offer may be revoked before it is accepted; however, an offer may not be revoked if the offeror has expressly indicated in the offer that it is irrevocable by specifying a time limit for acceptance or in any other manner, or if the offeree has reasons to believe that the offer is irrevocable and has made reasonable preparations for performing the contract. ② The former situation resembles the option under common law of contracts; however, no consideration is required for such an option, which strongly reflects the civil law practice. The latter situation resembles the *promissory estoppel* doctrine at common law. If a revocation notice is made through real-time communication, then the revocation must be known to the offeree before he makes an acceptance; otherwise the revocation must reach the offeree before he makes an acceptance. ③

For instance, if Mr. White, after he has deposited a letter containing a specific catalogue of West Co.'s dictionaries to Ms. Wang of Hualian Supermarket, receives a large order from Wal-Mart Shanghai so that his company will not be able to fill in any order for at least six months, so he write another letter to Ms. Wang on the second day explaining that West Co. will not be able to sell Hualian any electronic dictionaries now and sends it by express mail. If Ms. Wang receives the express mail before or at the same time when she receives the first letter (the catalogue) sent by Mr. White, the offer made by Mr. White is successfully withdrawn. On the other hand, if Ms.

---

① Articles 475 and 141 of the Civil Code.
② Article 476 of the Civil Code.
③ Article 477 of the Civil Code.

Wang has already received the first letter (catalogue) sent by Mr. White, and when she is just about to write back to Mr. White to accept the offer, the second letter arrives. Now the offer is successfully revoked, unless Mr. White wrote in his first letter that "this offer is open and irrevocable for one month."

An offer may also be terminated by the offeree. An offeree may terminate an offer simply by doing nothing so that the time limit for acceptance as provided in the offer will expire. An offeree may also terminate the offer by directly rejecting it, or materially alters the content of the offer.① For instance, Mr. White writes a letter to Ms. Wang stating that "We will offer our electronic English-Chinese dictionaries 'E-Books' at 999 yuan each, and 899 yuan each for an order of more than 5,000 dictionaries, and this offer is only good during the promotion period which is thirty days from today." After receiving the letter, Ms. Wang checks with her staff to find that their customers do not have a large demand for electronic dictionaries, so she has not responded within the thirty-day period. The offer is thus revoked owing to the lapse of time. Nevertheless, Mr. White cannot write to Ms. Wang to revoke the offer before the 30-day period expires. If Ms. Wang changes her mind and writes a letter accepting Mr. White's offer on the 31st day, this is a new offer made by Ms. Wang but not an acceptance because the original offer has already been terminated.

Suppose Ms. Wang writes a letter back to Mr. White during the one-month period telling the latter that they are not interested in purchasing the dictionaries, the offer is terminated by direct rejection. However, if Ms. Wang is interested in the dictionaries but believes that the unit price is not competitive, so she writes to Mr. White asking him to lower the price to 888 yuan . Such a letter constitutes a material alteration of the offer and meanwhile also terminates the offer. In the last scenario, Ms. Wang's letter is a counter offer or a new offer, which may be accepted by Mr. White.

§4:2:2 Acceptance

Acceptance is a manifestation of intent of an offeree to accept an offer,②

---

① Article 478 of the Civil Code.
② Article 479 of the Civil Code.

which implies that once an acceptance is made, the offeree would be bound by the terms of the offer. The content of an acceptance must be consistent with the terms of the offer. Where an acceptance materially alters the main terms of the offer, it is not an acceptance but a counter offer. Any change to the object of the contract, the quantity, quality, price or remuneration, period of performance, place and manner of performance, default liability, or the means of dispute resolution constitutes a material alteration. ① In other words, if an acceptance has only made a minor change which has not materially altered the offer, the acceptance is deemed to be effective and the terms of the acceptance will become the terms of the contract, unless the offeror timely objects or if the offer expressly indicates that an acceptance may not make any change to the terms of the offer. ②

Thus, if Ms. Wang writes to Mr. White asking for a lower unit price for the dictionaries, then the price term is changed which constitutes a "material alteration." Accordingly, Ms. Wang's letter is not an acceptance but a counter offer or a new offer. However, if Ms. Wang writes to accept the offer, but requires that the packages of the dictionaries be a kind of environment-friendly material that can be reused and recycled, then the acceptance is valid unless Mr. Smith timely objects the additional requirements after receiving the acceptance notice.

A contract is formed at the time when an acceptance becomes effective, unless otherwise provided by law or agreed by the parties. ③ Therefore, it is important to determine when an acceptance becomes effective. Under common law of contracts, an acceptance is effective once it is made, and a contract has been formed at that time even if the offeror has not yet received the acceptance. ④ However, under Chinese contract law, an acceptance is not valid until it is received by the offeror. Generally speaking, an offeree may make an acceptance by giving notice or by performing a juristic act according to the

---

① Article 488 of the Civil Code.
② Article 489 of the Civil Code.
③ Article 483 of the Civil Code.
④ See the "mailbox rule" discussed in Robert W. Hamilton, CONTRACTS: CASES AND MATERIALS 444 (2nd Ed. West Publishing Co. 1992).

parties' course of dealing or as required by the offer itself. ① If an acceptance is made by means of notice, then the acceptance notice must reach the offeror within the time limit specified in the offer in order for it to be effective. Where an offer does not specify such a time limit for acceptance, if the offer is made through real-time communication, the acceptance must be made instantly; otherwise it must reach the offeror within a reasonable period of time. ② Where notice is not required for making acceptance, an acceptance becomes effective when an act of acceptance is performed according to the parties' course of dealing or as indicated in the offer. ③

If an offeree makes an acceptance beyond the time limit for acceptance, or an acceptance is made within the time limit but it cannot reach the offeror in time under normal circumstances, such an acceptance constitutes a new offer unless the offeror timely notifies the offeree that the acceptance is effective. ④ However, where an offeree makes an acceptance within the time limit for acceptance, if it would have reached the offeror in time under normal circumstances but reaches the offeror beyond the time limit for other reasons, the acceptance shall be effective unless the offeror timely notifies the offeree that the acceptance is not accepted as it exceeds the time limit for acceptance. ⑤

Problems may arise if the parties are from different countries under different legal systems. For example, Chinese law applies to East Co. since it is a company established under Chinese law, while US law applies to West Co. which is established under the law of the New York State. Based on the US law, a contract is formed upon acceptance is made and deposited into the mailbox. However, under Chinese law, a contract is formed only after an acceptance notice has reached the offeror. The offeree may withdraw his acceptance as long as the notice of withdrawal reaches the offeror before or at the same time when the notice of acceptance reaches the offeror. ⑥ Suppose West Co. decides to sign a contract with East Co., both need to study the US

---

① Article 480 of the Civil Code.
② Article 481 of the Civil Code.
③ Article 484 of the Civil Code.
④ Article 486 of the Civil Code.
⑤ Article 487 of the Civil Code.
⑥ Articles 141 and 485 of the Civil Code.

law and the Chinese law to see how to avoid the problem. It is suggested to add some specific and definite language to the offer or notice of acceptance regarding the revocability and the term of the offer within which it may be accepted. In addition, the United Nations Convention on Contracts for International Sale of Goods (CISG) may be consulted with since both the US and China are parties to the Convention.

§4:2:3 Formation of Contract

The principle of freedom of contract allows the persons of the civil law to freely choose the form to conclude a contract. The Civil Code provides that a contract may be formed orally, in writing, or by other means.[①] If it is required by law or agreed by the parties that a contract must be concluded in writing, then the contract must be concluded in writing; however, if such a contract is not concluded in writing but one party has performed his principal obligation and the other party has accepted the performance, the contract is also regarded as formed.[②] Sometimes a contract may be required to be approved by the government. Article 502 of the Civil Code provides the relevant rules in this regard:

> A contract formed in accordance with law becomes effective upon its formation, unless otherwise provided by law or agreed by the parties.
>
> Where there are laws or administrative regulations providing that a contract shall be subject to approval or other procedures, such provisions shall be followed. Where failure to complete the approval or other procedures is to affect the effectiveness of the contract, the validity of the clauses concerning the performance of the obligation of filing for approval and the like procedures and the other relevant clauses in the contract are not affected. Where the party obligated to complete application for approval or other procedures fails to do so, the other party may request the said party to bear the liability for breach of such obligation.
>
> Where there are laws or administrative regulations providing that

---

[①] Article 469 of the Civil Code.
[②] Article 490 of the Civil Code.

modification, assignment, or rescission of a contract shall be subject to approval or other procedures, the provisions of the preceding paragraph shall be applied.

Where the parties conclude a contract in the form of a written agreement, the contract is formed at the time when the parties all sign, stamp, or put their fingerprints on the written agreement. Prior to signing, stamping, or putting their fingerprints thereon, where one of the parties has already performed the principal obligation and the other party has accepted the performance, the contract is formed at the time of the performance is accepted. However, if the parties conclude a contract in the form of a letter, data message, or the like, and a confirmation letter is required to be signed, the contract is not formed until the confirmation letter is signed.① This also features the civil law tradition because at common law, after an acceptance becomes effective, a contract is formed and no party may refuse to perform the contract on the ground that a confirmation letter has not been signed.

With online shopping becomes more popular, disputes arising from online shopping are not uncommon. Article 491 of the Civil Code provides a rule for resolving these disputes. Where the information about goods or services published by a party *via* information network, such as internet, satisfies the conditions for an offer, unless otherwise agreed by the parties, a contract is formed at the time when the other party selects such product or service and successfully submits the order.

Sometimes the determination of the place of the contract, *i.e.*, the place where a contract is formed, is also important. Generally, the place where an acceptance becomes effective is the place where a contract is formed. If a contract is concluded in a form of data message, then the recipient's principal place of business or, if the recipient does not have a principal place of business, the recipient's domicile is generally the place where the contract is formed. If a contract is concluded in the form of a written agreement, the place where the written agreement is finally signed, stamped, or fingerprinted is the place

---

① Article 491 of the Civil Code.

where the contract is formed. ①

Case 24

Case 24: Time Group v. Land Bureau of Yuhuan County, Zhejiang Province②

On November 7, 2002, the Land Bureau of Yuhuan County, Zhejiang Province published an announcement on the local newspaper *Yuhuan Newspaper* about the listing of a lot of land to be transferred. Specifically, the announcement says that upon approval of the Yuhuan County people's government, the Land Bureau will list, from 8:00 am on November 21, 2002 to 3:00 pm on December 4, 2002, a lot of land with an area of 25.9434 hectares to be used as commercial and residential purposes for 70 years. In addition to some specific requirements the announcement also indicated that the starting land-use price would be 43,000,000 yuan, and 40% of the purchase price should be paid upon execution of the contract with the balance to be paid according to the schedule agreed in the contract. All companies, enterprises, or other organizations in or outside China that have sufficient funds and will be capable of completing the project within the specified period of time may compete against each other to buy it. The registration period will be from November 1, 2002 to 3:00 pm on November 20, 2002 at 3:00 pm, and 20,000,000 yuan's bond must be paid upon registration.

Article 13 of the rules on such listing sale of Yuhuan County Land Bureau provides that the conclusion of the transaction will be based on the following rules: (1) where there is only one potential purchaser makes an offer, if the offering price is higher than the bottom price and the other requirements are satisfied, the transaction is concluded; (2) where there are two or more potential purchasers making an offer, the one who offers the highest price will have the contract; where the offering prices are the same, the one who makes the offer first will have the contract, unless the

---

① Article 493 of the Civil Code.
② See (2003) Min Yi Zhong Zi No. 82, reprinted in the SPC Gazette, Issue 5, 2005).

price is below the bottom price; (3) where there is no one making an offer, or the offering prices are all below the bottom price or the other requirements are not satisfied, the listing fails; (4) where there are two or more potential buyers intending to offer a price upon expiration of the listing period, the transferor may decide to have an on-site bidding or may have an auction at another time, and the one who offers the highest price will get the offer.

On November 20, 2002, the Land Bureau received an application from Time Group, and on the same day, Time Group wired 20,000,000 yuan's bond to the Land Reservation Center of Yuhuan County. The Land Bureau issued a certificate confirming receipt of this amount of money. The following day, the Time Group offered a price of 50,000,000 yuan.

On November 21, 2002, Yuhui Co. offered a price of 51,000,000 yuan to the Land Bureau. The story here was a bit interesting. On December 14, 2001, Yuhui Co. signed a draft contract with the Land Bureau regarding the transfer of a lot of land basically similar to the lot listed in the announcement for a price of 44,000,000 yuan. Yuhui had paid 17,200,000 yuan by several installments and somehow the money would be refunded. On November 14, 2002, it provided a report to the Land Bureau about transforming the land use fee to be refunded into a bond securing the listed lot of land as announced on November 7, 2002. On November 18, 2002, Wang, the legal representative of the Land Bureau, agreed in writing to this proposal, and then Yuhui Co. had paid 2,800,000 yuan and the Land Bureau provided the receipt to Yuhui Co. On November 22, 2002, the money was transferred to the account of the Land Reservation Center of Yuhuan Country, and afterwards, Yuhui Co. made an offer of 51,000,000 yuan.

Actually, on November 20, 2002, the Land Bureau deposited a letter of the bottom price of 57,000,000 yuan with Yuhuan County's Notary Public Office.

On the same day, the Department of Land and Resources of Zhejiang Province received a complaint alleging that the Land Bureau conducted irregular activities in the listing of the disputed land-use right, and discovered that the application for listing of this lot of land was still under consideration and had not yet been approved, so it requested the Land Bureau to stop the listing before the listing was approved.

On November 22, 2002, the Land Bureau notified Time Group and Yuhui Co. that the listing was cancelled owing to the fact that the listing had not been approved. The notice also said that if the lot of land was to be listed in the future, a new notification would be publicized. Meanwhile, the Land Bureau refunded 20,000,000 yuan to Time Group.

On December 6, 2002, Time Group replied to the Land Bureau, stating that the public announcement and the acceptance of the bond and its offering price were civil juristic acts which were binding to both parties. The unilateral termination of the listing violated the relevant laws and regulations and was ineffective. In the correspondence, the Time Group requested the Land Bureau to resume the listing and transfer the right to use the lot of land in accordance with law; otherwise, it requested the Land Bureau to refund twice the amount of the deposit, and pay compensation. In the end, it requested the Land Bureau to give a response within 5 working days, otherwise it would bring a litigation against the Bureau.

In the litigation, Time Group alleged that the 20,000,000 yuan's bond was earnest money, and according to Articles 89 and 90 of the Security Law, the Land Bureau should return twice amount of it.

The first instance court reasoned that the 20,000,000 yuan was performance bond instead of earnest money, therefore Time Group's claim in this regard was not supported.

Regarding the nature of the announcement of the listing, the court held that it was not an offer, but an invitation to offer.

The court held that the listing was not approved by the provincial government, therefore the listing was invalid. Before the listing was cancelled, the Land Bureau did not confirm that Time Group won the bidding, did not accept Time Group's offer, and thus, the contractual relationship between the two parties had not been established. The 20,000,000 yuan was not earnest money, so the request for double refund was not supported either. Finally, the court dismissed the case and held that Time Group should pay for the litigation costs of 360,010 yuan.

Time Group appealed to the SPC.

The SPC reasons that that a contractual relationship had been established between the Time Group and the Land Bureau is the prerequisite for requesting the Land Bureau to continue to perform the contract. The determination of whether such a relationship had been established should be based on the legal nature of the announcement of the listing, whether there existed acceptance, and what the legal basis is for the Land Bureau to assume liability.

Article 15 of the Contract Law provides that the legal nature of an auction and bidding announcement is an invitation to offer. The listing announcement published on newspaper in this case was an expression of intent to attract or invite the unspecified persons to make an offer. Its nature was to expect the potential buyers to offer the price, therefore it is an invitation to offer. The offering price given by Time Group on November 21, 2002 was an the offer. The law does not imposed restrictions on withdrawal of invitation to offer. As long as it will not harm the reliance interests of a *bona fide* third person, the withdrawal of invitation to offer is valid and will not incur any liability. Therefore, Time Group's request for the Land Bureau to continue to perform the contract should not be supported. However, when publishing the listing announcement, even by the time the hearing of the appeal at the SPC is to be ended, the Land Bureau has not received approval for the listing of the lot of land, and it was the main cause that Time Group's expectation was not realized. The Land Bureau was at fault and should assume the pre-contracting liability. The loss suffered owing to the loss of the reliance interests must be compensated through an independent claim. During the second instance trial, the Land Bureau agreed to assume the pre-contracting liability, but Time Group still insisted on requesting it to assume the liability of continuance of performance or returning twice amount of the earnest money, and did not request the Land Bureau to make compensation based on its pre-contracting liability. Therefore, the SPC decides not to entertain this claim.

Regarding the nature of the 20,000,000 yuan's bond, it is not earnest money since it was indicated as the performance bond in the announcement, and the parties did not agree that it was earnest money, therefore it is not earnest money.

Finally, the SPC affirms the lower court's decision. Regarding the litigation cost of 360,010 yuan for the appeal, Time Group assumes 240,010 yuan and the Land Bureau assumes 120,000 yuan.

§ 4:3   Effectiveness of Contract

The formation, effectiveness, and enforceability of a contract mean different things. A contract that has been validly formed may or may not be immediately effective and an effective contract may or may not be enforceable. Generally speaking, a contract is effective upon its formation unless otherwise provided by law or agreed upon by the parties. For instance, if it is required by law or administrative regulations that a specific type of contract must be approved by a government department, then the contract is not effective until and unless it has been so approved.① Likewise, an effective contract may be unenforceable in court if the limitations period expires.

§4:3:1   Limitations on Effectiveness of Contract

There have been discussions on the conditions and terms attached to a juristic act in § 2:4:2:3. Since concluding a contract is a typical juristic act, it is necessary to review the rules regarding the conditions and terms in a contract scenario. The parties to a contract may impose a condition or a term to limit the effectiveness of the contract. Upon the occurrence or non-occurrence of the condition, or upon the beginning or expiration of the term, the contract may become effective.

A condition may be a condition precedent or a condition subsequent. A contract subject to a condition precedent becomes effective when the condition is fulfilled, whereas a contract subject to a condition subsequent becomes invalid when the condition is fulfilled. Imposition of a condition on the enforceability of a contract does not make the contract invalid, but only limit the enforceability of the contract and put the contract under a special situation.② Using the same example, if West Co. signs a contract for sale of

---

① Article 502 of the Civil Code.
② Article 158 of the Civil Code.

the E-books with East Co. and the contract contains a clause providing that the contract will not be effective unless West Co. has obtained and presented a certificate of patent for the dictionaries. Such a contract is one subject to a condition precedent and is not effective until after the certificate has been obtained and presented; however, it is not invalid and both companies are bound by the other terms of the contract even before the required certificate is obtained and neither party may unilaterally alter or revoke the contract.

The law also imposes certain restrictions on a condition. A condition must be an event that may or may not happen in the future. Any past event cannot be set as a condition to the enforceability of a contract. If the parties impose a condition which is known to the parties to be a past event, then it will be presumed that there is no such condition attached on the contract if the satisfaction of the condition will make the contract enforceable, or it will be presumed that the contract is ineffective if the satisfaction of the condition will make the contract unenforceable. In addition, a condition must be an event the occurrence or non-occurrence of which is not ascertainable. If the parties know at the time of concluding the contract that the condition will never be met, then it is presumed that the parties do not intend to conclude the contract at all. A condition must be imposed by the parties voluntarily and mutually, and must be lawful, in accordance with the law and public ethics. An illegal condition may or may not lead the whole contract invalid and the court will consider whether the contract without the condition is a complete, lawful, or independent one. A condition may not contradict with the main terms of the contract; otherwise the contract is invalid. After a condition is attached to a contract as a limitation of its effectiveness, if a party, for the sake of its own interests, improperly obstructs the fulfillment of the condition, the condition is deemed as having been fulfilled; if a party improperly facilitates the fulfillment of the condition, the condition is deemed as not having been fulfilled. [1]

The parties to a contract may also stipulate a term in the contract unless the nature of the contract determines that such a term should not be attached. A term may be a term of effectiveness or a term of termination. A contract subject to a term of effectiveness becomes effective when the term begins, and

---

[1] Article 159 of the Civil Code.

a contract subject to a term of termination becomes ineffective upon expiration of the term. [1] If the parties impose a condition on a contract which the parties have known to be happening for sure in the future, then it is not a condition, but a term. Case 14 in § 2:4:2:3 illustrates a contract subject to a condition subsequent which deserves a revisit.

§ 4:3:2 Basic Elements for Effectiveness of Contract

Whether a contract is effective is very important because an effective contract is binding on the parties to the contract so that the parties are obligated to perform their contractual obligations in accordance with the contract and may not alter or revoke the contract at their will. [2] A lawfully formed contract does not bind a third person who is not a party to the contract, but an effective contract would grant the parties a right to be free from illegal intervention and infringement by any third person.

A contract must satisfy several requirements in order for it to be effective. According to Article 143 of the Civil Code, there are three basic elements for a contract to be effective. First, the parties to a contract must have the required capacity for performing civil juristic acts. Second, the expression of intention manifested by each party must be true. Third, the contract does not violate any mandatory provisions of laws or administrative regulations, nor offend public order or good morals. In addition, some special requirements may also need to be satisfied for certain special types of contract to be effective. The following subsections will examine the most important issues relating to the effectiveness of a contract.

§ 4:3:2:1 Capacity Issue

The Civil Code requires that the parties to a contract have the required capacity for performing civil juristic acts. The rationale is that a contract involves both parties' interests, and the law seeks to balance these interests by granting special protection to the party who does not have the capacity to sign a contract with others, while granting appropriate protection to the expectation

---

[1] Article 160 of the Civil Code.
[2] Article 465 of the Civil Code.

interests, reliance interests, and the restitutionary interests of the other party. Generally, a party must have full capacity for performing civil juristic acts to sign a contract; however, if the party only has a limited capacity, the contract he signs may also be valid if his legal representative consents to or ratifies the contract. In addition, if a contract is purely beneficial to the party with limited capacity, or if a contract is deemed appropriate considering the age, intelligence, or mental status of the party, then the contract is valid.① The rules on a natural person's capacity for performing civil juristic acts have already been discussed in § 2.2.1.2.

A legal person or unincorporated organization may also be involved in a contractual relationship, and likewise, it must have the required capacity for contracting. For a long time, Chinese judicial practice regarded a contract signed by a corporation beyond its business scope, *i.e.*, *ultra vires*, as invalid. For example, the SPC once said that when determining the validity of a contract, the court would examine the content of the contract to see whether it exceeded the business scope of the corporation. If the answer was yes, then the contract was invalid.② This practice had discouraged people to engage in commercial transactions and did not give sufficient protection to a *bona fide* third person. Later on, the SPC changed its position and recognized that a contract should not be declared as invalid solely because a party signed a contract *ultra vires*, provided that the contract did not violate any prohibitive provision of laws or administrative regulations.③ This rule has been integrated into the Civil Code. If a legal person concludes a contract beyond its scope of business, the contract will not be determined as invalid solely on the ground that it is *ultra vires*.④ An unincorporated organization, such as a social organization or a branch office of a foreign company, also has the capacity to make a contract because it is a person of the civil law under the Civil Code. Where the legal representative of a legal person or the responsible person of an

---

① Article 145 of the Civil Code.
② See the Opinion of the Supreme People's Court on Certain Issues in Implementing the Economic Contract Law issued by the Supreme People's Court in 1984.
③ See Article 10 of the Interpretation of the Supreme People's Court on the Application of the Contract Law of the PRC issued by the Supreme People's Court on December 1, 1999.
④ Article 505 of the Civil Code.

unincorporated organization concludes a contract *ultra vires*, such an act is effective and the contract is binding on the legal person or the unincorporated organization unless the other party knows or should have known that the legal representative or the responsible person acts *ultra vires*.①

§ 4:3:2:2 Manifestation of the True Intention

The essence of a contract is the meeting of the minds of the parties; therefore, the parties must express their true intention and induce it into the letter of the contract. In other words, an effective contract must represent the true intention of the parties to bind them. Section 3 of Chapter VI of Book One of the Civil Code provides rules governing the effect of a civil juristic act, which are also applicable to the contracting act performed by the persons of the civil law. For example, a party's expression of intent may be tainted by fraud, duress, undue influence, *etc.* so that the contract thus made may be void or voidable. The relevant rules have already been discussed in § 2:4:2:2 for reference. We will discuss the legal issues arising from a form contract or a standard clause contained in a contract in this sub-section.

A form contract or a standard clause refers to a contract or a contract term that is prepared by one party prior to the making of a contract for repeated use in order for it to be accepted by the other party and which is not the result of a negotiation between the parties, nor is it to be changed by the other party.② Such a form contract or a standard clause (hereinafter collectively referred to as "a standard clause") is convenient for the standardization and the commercial transactions; however, it may not be conscionable if it is unjust or unreasonable. For instance, West Co. presented a prepared contract to East Co. for it to sign, and among the terms of the contract, there is a clause providing that any dispute must be resolved by submitting it to the New York International Arbitration Center for arbitration. If this clause has been integrated into the contract without being negotiated with East Co., it is a standard clause. Whether such a clause is valid depends on different situations. Because a standard clause may affect the expression of intent manifested by the

---

① Article 504 of the Civil Code.
② Article 496 of the Civil Code.

parties, such a clause is generally held void if a party providing the standard clause unreasonably exempts or alleviates himself from liability, imposes heavier liability on the other party, or restricts the main rights of the other party; or if a party providing the standard clause deprives the other party of his main rights. ① So the law imposes on the provider of such a clause a duty to be just and reasonable and a duty to warn and explain to the other party upon conclusion of the contract.

A court will examine whether a party providing a standard clause has allocated the parties' rights and obligations in compliance with the principle of fairness. If such clause actually concerns the other party's major interests and concerns, e.g., it exempts or alleviates the liability of the party providing the standard clause, the party providing the clause must call the other party's attention to the clause in a reasonable manner, and give explanations of such clause upon request of the other party. If the party providing the standard clause fails to call attention of or give explanations to the other party, thus resulting in the other party's failure to pay attention to or understand the clause concerning his major interests and concerns, the other party may claim that such clause is not part of the contract. ②

If a standard clause is included in a contract, where a dispute arises over the understanding of its meaning, it should be interpreted in accordance with its common understanding. Where there are two or more interpretations of a standard clause, it should be interpreted against the party providing the standard clause. If a standard clause is inconsistent with a non-standard clause, the non-standard clause shall prevail. ③

§ 4:3:2:3 Not in Violation of Law or Against Social Public Interest

Another element for a contract to be effective is that the contract must not violate the mandatory provisions of law or be against the social public interest. The Civil Code as well as the other laws contain both mandatory and voluntary provisions and the parties to a contract must comply with the mandatory

---

① Article 497 of the Civil Code.
② Article 496 of the Civil Code.
③ Article 498 of the Civil Code.

provisions and should not change them by agreement. However, the voluntary provisions are mainly aimed at guiding the parties in concluding contracts and do not require the parties to strictly comply with them. The content of a contract, including the main terms and conditions of the contract, must be in accordance with law. Any term or condition that violates law may lead the contract to be invalid, except that under certain circumstances, some of the terms of a contract may be declared invalid while the other terms may still be valid. ①

For example, Article 506 of the Civil Code provides that an exculpatory clause in a contract exempting the liability arising from physical injury inflicted on the other party, or the liability arising from losses caused to the other party's property due to an intentional act or by gross negligence is void. Suppose the contract prepared by West Co. contains a clause providing that West Co. is not liable for any physical injury caused by the electronic dictionaries it produces to any consumer of East Co., such a clause apparently violates Article 506 of the Civil Code and thus is void.

A contract may not be against the social public interest either. Certain contracts that have not violated any prohibitive provision of law may materially harm the interests of the public and disturb the social economic order. Since there is no clear definition of the "social public interest," the judges have discretion in determining this issue.

§4:3:3 Status of Contracts

A contract may or may not be enforced by court. A contract may be unenforceable for various reasons including that it violates the law, it has been formed under frauds or undue influence, or the parties had a significant misunderstanding about the main content of the contract. The enforceability of a contract may be affected by the fact that the contract is void, revocable, or effectiveness-pending.

§4:3:3:1 Void Contracts

The Civil Code lists the situations when a contract is void, and a void

---

① Article 156 of the Civil Code.

contract does not have any legal effect from the beginning (*ab initio*); however, if invalidation of a part of a contract does not affect the validity of the other part, the other part of the contract remains valid.① Generally, a contract is void under the following circumstances.

A contract formed by a person who has no capacity for performing civil juristic acts is void.② If a contract is formed by a person with limited capacity, the contract is also void unless the contract is purely beneficial to the person, considered appropriate to the age, intelligence, or mental status of the person, or a consent or ratification is obtained from the person's legal representative.③

A contract formed by a person and another person based on a false expression of intent is void.④ This kind of contract is also described as a contract with an illegal purpose covered by a lawful form. In other words, if judged by its appearance, the acts of the parties to a contract are lawful; however, the content and purpose of the contract are illegal. When concluding such a contract, the purpose of the parties is not the purpose stated in the contract, but an illegal one under the color of the lawful purpose. For example, the parties sign a contract for sale which is lawful from its appearance; however, the true purpose of the parties is to conceal the property by illegally transferring it. Such a contract is void although its form is lawful because its underlying purpose is to infringe upon the interests of the State, collective, or other individuals.

If the form or content of a contract violates any mandatory provision of laws or administrative regulations, or is against the social public interest, the contract is a void contract which does not have any legal effect from the beginning, unless the mandatory provision of laws or administrative regulations does no lead to invalidity of such a contract.⑤ The mandatory provisions of laws and administrative regulations include mandatory regulations and prohibitive regulations, which are the regulations that everyone must comply with and may not exclude their application. These regulations are aimed at

---

① Articles 155 and 156 of the Civil Code.
② Article 144 of the Civil Code.
③ Article 145 of the Civil Code.
④ Article 146 of the Civil Code.
⑤ Article 153 of the Civil Code.

maintaining the social public interest and the State's interests by limiting the parties' freedom of contract. Therefore, the parties may not violate these provisions when making a contract; otherwise the contract is void. If a contract is formed through malicious collusion between one of the parties and a third person, thus harms the lawful rights and interests of another party, the contract is void. ①

A form contract or a standard clause of a contract is void if the party providing the form contract or the clause unreasonably exempts or alleviates itself from liability, imposes heavier liability on the other party, or restricts the main rights of the other party, or the party providing the contract or the clause deprives the other party of its main rights. ② Sometimes a contract term other than a standard clause may also be void. For example, a disclaimer in a contract exempting one party from the liability arising from physical injury inflicted on the other party caused by the performance of the contract or the liability arising from losses caused to the other party's property due to an intentional act or by gross negligence of the first party is void. ③ Such an exculpatory clause often appears in a contract signed by the manufacturers, wholesalers, or retailers of a product and the customers. The invalidity of these terms may not affect the effectiveness of the other terms of the contract.

§ 4:3:3:2 Revocable Contracts

If a contract is formed based on the expression of one or two parties' untrue intention, the contract is revocable in accordance with law. The grounds for revocation include serious misunderstanding, fraud, duress, unconscionability, *etc*. ④

Specifically, if a party signed a contract owing to a serious misunderstanding of the major content of the contract, this party may have a right to revoke it. Sometimes a party to a contract has a mistaken belief on the main terms of the contract owing to his own negligence. If the mistake is made by a party's intentional act or gross negligence, then the law does not allow the party to

---

① Article 154 of the Civil Code.
② Article 497 of the Civil Code.
③ Article 506 of the Civil Code.
④ Articles 147–151 of the Civil Code.

revoke the contract on the ground that the performance of the contract is adverse to his benefit. For example, if a party did not even read the contract document provided to him before executing the contract, then the party may not revoke the contract thus signed. To apply this rule, the party's execution of the contract must be caused by the misunderstanding, *i.e.*, the party would not have made the contract without such misunderstanding.

If a party by fraudulent means induces the other party to form a contract against the latter party's true intention, the defrauded party may revoke it. Where a party knows or should have known that a contract performed by the other party is based on a third person's fraudulent act and is against the other party's true intention, the defrauded party may revoke it. Fraud exists when a party intentionally conceals the true situation or makes false statement to defraud the other party and the other party signs the contract in reliance on such statement. To find a fraud, a court will examine whether the defendant had the intention to defraud the other party, *i.e.*, whether the party knew that the information to be disclosed to the other party was false and that the false information would lead the other party to mistakenly rely on it. The defrauding party must have actually implemented the defrauding act; in other words, the defrauding party has actually concealed the true information or disclosed the false information to the other party. The other party thus mistakenly believed in the false information, and, in reliance thereon, signed the contract.

When a party to a contract directly threatens to harm the other party or use a future event to threaten the other party, and the other party feels frightened and thus signs the contract, the contract is made under duress or undue influence. Where a party signs a contract against his true intention owing to duress or undue influence of the other party or a third person, the coerced party may revoke the contract.

Where one party takes advantage of the other party that is in a desperate situation or lacks the ability of making judgment, and as a result, the contract thus signed is obviously unfair and unconscionable, the damaged party may revoke it. Such an unconscionable contract is signed either because one party is at an advantageous position, or the other party is lack of experience or acts negligently. As a result, the terms of the contract unreasonably allocate the rights and obligations between the parties so that it is obviously unequal and unjust. A contract will be determined as unconscionable only when the benefit obtained by one party exceeds the reasonable limit provided by law and that the public would regard it as unjust.

A revocable contract must be valid and effective before it is revoked. The party with a right to revocation may only exercise such right through litigation or arbitration, i.e., through requesting the court or an arbitral tribunal to revoke the contract. In addition, a right to revocation must be exercised within a certain period of time, otherwise it will be extinguished. [1] The party holding such right of revocation may waive it expressly or through his own conduct. Otherwise, the general limitation period within which a right to revocation must be exercised is one year, with exceptions applicable in different situations. For example, in a case of serious misunderstanding, the right holder must exercise the right to revocation within 90 days from the date when he knows or should have known of the cause for revocation. In a case of duress, the right holder must exercise the right to revocation within one year from the date when the duress ceases. Such a right to revocation is extinguished if the party fails to exercise it within five years from the date when the contract has been formed.

If a party fails to exercise a right to revocation within the specified period, or, if the party only requests a rectification of the contract, the contract is still valid and the parties must perform the obligations under the contract. It is to be noted that a party who has a right to revoke such a contract is the one whose rights and interests have been infringed upon by signing the contract against his true intention, whereas the other party does not have such a right, neither may the court or arbitral tribunal revoke such a contract on its own initiative.

§ 4:3:3:3 Effectiveness-Pending Contracts

An effectiveness-pending contract is a contract the enforceability of which is unclear at the time of concluding the contract. Such a contract is not void because it neither violates any prohibitive regulation of law nor is against the

---

[1] Article 152 of the Civil Code.

social public interest, and that the manifestations of intention of the parties are not untrue. However, because one of the parties does not have the required legal capacity to make the contract, the contract is not valid unless it is ratified by the legal representative or lawful agent of that party. In case a minor or a person with mental deficiency signs a contract with another party, the latter party may ask the legal representative of the person to make ratification within 30 days from receipt of the notification. Inaction of the legal representative is deemed as refusal of ratification. Before such a contract is ratified, a *bona fide* third person may revoke the act, and the revocation must be made by notice. ① As discussed earlier, if a contract is one that grants pure benefit to the party with deficient capacity, or if a contract is one that is considered appropriate with regard to the age, intelligence, and mental status of the party with deficient capacity, the contract is valid and does not need to be ratified.

One of the important features of an effectiveness-pending contract is that it must be ratified to be effective and enforceable, and the ratification must be made by the legal representative of the party without full capacity. It distinguishes an effectiveness-pending contract from a revocable contract in that the latter contract is effective and enforceable before it is revoked, but the former contract is not effective and enforceable before it is ratified. It is to be noted that both contracts may be called "voidable contracts" at common law and are effective but may or may not be enforceable in different situations. Furthermore, at common law, a contract signed by a person without full capacity may be either ratified or disaffirmed by the legal representative of the person depending on the nature of the contract. The US law uses a reasonable time after the minor reaches the majority age as a time limit within which the legal representative of the minor may disaffirm the contract, and beyond which the contract will be enforceable. ② However, the Chinese law is silent about it and does not consider the fact that a minor may reach the majority age someday and may want to enforce the contract.

---

① Article 145 of the Civil Code.
② See the text and notes in John Edward Murray, Jr., CONTRACTS: CASES AND MATERIALS 300-01 (5th Ed. Lexis Publishing 2000).

Case 25

Case 25: Xu v. Z Co. [1]

Xu signed a lease contract with Z Co. under which she leased an apartment from Z Co. Based on the contract, the term of lease started from Oct. 8, 2003 and ended on Oct. 7, 2004, and the monthly rent was 1,600 yuan. The contract provided that Xu should pay 1,600 yuan as deposit which would be returned to Xu within one month after the contract expired if Xu had paid the utilities bills in full. It also provided that where Xu decided to cancel the contract prior to its expiration day, Xu should give Z Co. a written notice one month ahead of time and it would not be regarded as a breach of the contract. Otherwise it would be deemed as a breach. Xu paid the deposit, but decided to end the lease. She applied to Z Co. for early termination of the contract on December 5, 2003, and on January 7, 2004, the parties checked the apartment and signed a checking-out sheet and an agreement of early termination of the contract. On the checking-out sheet, it stated that Xu still owed 28 yuan's utilities fee, and under the agreement of early termination, there was a clause stating that "the parties will have no leasing or economic relationship ever since." On January 14, 2004, Xu paid 28 yuan to Z Co. as the owed utilities fee, evidenced by a receipt issued by Z Co.

Later on, Xu requested Z Co. to return the deposit but was refused. Xu sued in Haidian District People's Court in Beijing, and the court held that the lease contract and the agreement on termination of the contract between Xu and Z Co. reflected the expression of both parties' intention and did not violate any law, and therefore were both lawful and valid. Since both parties agreed in the agreement on termination of the lease contract that both parties had no leasing or economic relationship, Xu's request to Z Co. for returning the deposit was not supported by any fact and law. The first instance court dismissed Xu's case on December 20, 2004.

---

[1] See the SPC Gazette, Issue 9, 2005.

Xu appealed to Beijing No. 1 Intermediate People's Court. On appeal, the court finds that the lease contract, agreement on termination of the lease contract, as well as the checking out or other documents were all pre-printed by Z Co. and filled by the parties upon execution. The main issue of the appeal is whether the clause "both parties will have no leasing or economic relationship ever since" contained in the agreement on termination of the lease contract is valid.

The court reasons that the deposit paid for a lease contract is the property of a lessee delivered to a lessor for the purpose of guarantee that the lessee would perform her obligations under the lease contract. After the lessee has performed her contractual obligations, the lessor should return the deposit to the lessee. After considering all the evidence presented by both parties, the court determines that upon termination of the lease contract, Xu did not damage the leased apartment or any property inside the apartment, and did not owe any unpaid fees. Furthermore, she did not express her intention to give up the deposit. Under this circumstance, Z Co. did not return the deposit solely based on the ground that there existed the aforementioned clause in the agreement on termination of the lease contract.

According to a common understanding, a deposit involves an economic relationship. If the parties do not have any economic relationship, they do not have any "deposit relationship". However, the payment and collection of the utilities fees are also a kind of economic relationship. After the parties signed the agreement stating that they would not have any economic relationship, Xu still paid and Z Co. still collected the utilities fees, which means that their understanding of this clause is against the common understanding. Xu claimed that this clause did not include the deposit relationship, whereas Z Co. argued that it included the deposit relationship, but excluded the payment and collection of the utilities fees. Apparently the two parties understood this clause in completely opposite ways.

The court finds that the lease contract and the termination agreement were both form contracts provided by Z Co. to Xu. Except for the different understanding on the disputed clause, the parties had no problem regarding the other clauses. Therefore, the other clauses of these two contracts are lawful and valid. Article 3 of the Contract Law provides that the parties to a contract are equal in legal status and no party may impose its own will on the other party. Article 41 further provides that where there is a dispute arising on the understanding of a form clause, the clause shall be interpreted based on the common understanding. Where there are two or more interpretations on the form clause, interpretation shall be made against the party providing the form clause. Where a form clause is inconsistent with a non-form clause, the non-form clause should be adopted. In this case, upon execution of the termination agreement, Z Co. knew that the deposit had not been returned and that the receipt of the deposit was still in Xu's hand. As the provider of the form clause, Z Co. had a duty to warn Xu or indicate in the agreement that the disputed form clause meant that the deposit would not be returned after this agreement was signed and the receipt of the deposit would become invalid. However, Z Co. failed to perform such duty. Since the termination agreement did not mention anything about the deposit or the receipt of the deposit, it cannot be inferred from the disputed form clause that Xu had expressed her intention to voluntarily give up her deposit. Therefore, Z Co. infringed upon Xu's proprietary right by refusing to return the deposit on the ground that Xu had signed the termination agreement.

Finally, the court holds that the facts found by the first instance court are accurate; however, the application of law was in error so that the judgment was not proper. The second instance court holds that the judgment of the court below was reversed and Z Co. should return 1,600 yuan to Xu within 10 days after the judgment becomes effective. In addition, Z Co. should pay for the litigation fees for both the first instance trial and the second instance appeal.

§ 4:3:4 Legal Effect of a Revoked or Voided Contract

After a contract is revoked or declared as void, the legal effect expected by the parties upon execution of the contract no longer exists. Instead, the parties will be required to return the benefit received under the revoked or voided contract, or even pay damages to the aggrieved party.

A revoked or voided contract has no legal force from the beginning of its conclusion. Once a contract is revoked or declared as void, the contractual relationship is extinguished and the contract is not or no longer binding on any of the original parties. Neither may the parties claim any right or enjoy any benefit based on the original contract. If the contract has not been performed yet, the parties do not have any contractual obligations to perform it, and the party who has obtained any property based on the revoked contract is obligated to return it to its original owner, or pay damages based on the appraised value of the property if it is impossible or meaningless to return it. The loss thus incurred upon the other party must be compensated by the party at fault, or if both parties are at fault, by the parties proportionally.① The purpose is to restore the parties to their original status they were in prior to the conclusion of the contract.

In order to receive the compensation as described above, the aggrieved party must first prove that he has suffered actual damage owing to the revocation or the invalidation of the contract. The actual damage may include the damage suffered during the process of making the contract and during the process of performing the contract. The aggrieved party then must prove that the other party was at fault, and that there is a causal link between the fault and the damage. Even if one party is at fault, if there is no causal relationship between the fault and the damage, the party does not need to compensate the other party for his loss.

Since the contractual relationship between the parties no longer exists after a contract has been revoked or declared as void, the damages to be paid is obviously not based on the contract law, but based on the negligence in concluding the contract, which actually resembles the quasi-contract theory at common law. It is also called pre-contractual obligations.

Case 26

Case 26: Zhang v. H Co.②

Zhang bought a Shanghai GM Chevrolet (car) on Feb. 28, 2007 at

---

① Article 157 of the Civil Code.
② See (2008) Er Zhong Min Zhong Zi No. 00453, reprinted in the SPC's Guiding Cases No. 17.

138,000 yuan from H Co. Article 7 of the contract between the parties stipulated that the seller guaranteed that the purchased car was a new car and had been inspected and cleaned before delivery, and that the mileage was 18 km, and that it complied with all specifications and standards listed in the documents delivered to the buyer with the car. On the same day of execution of the contract, Zhang paid 138,000 yuan plus taxes and other fees, and H Co. delivered the car to Zhang. On the same day, Zhang registered the car. On May 13, 2007, when Zhang sent the car to H Co. for maintenance, she discovered that the car had been repaired on Jan. 17, 2007. Zhang brought a litigation.

During the trial, H Co. said that the car was scratched during transportation and had been fixed on Jan. 17, 2017. H Co. said that it had notified Zhang, upon selling the car, of the repair of the car, and said that the original price of the car was 151,900 yuan, and owing to the repair, the selling price of the car was 138,000 yuan. H Co. provided a receipt signed by Zhang and dated on Feb. 28, 2017, and in the "remarks" column, it wrote that the car had been repaired and sold as the agreed price. H Co. also said this receipt was kept by the company and Zhang did not have a copy of it. Zhang acknowledged that she signed the receipt, however, H Co. did not notify her that the car had been repaired, and when she signed the receipt, there was no statement in the "remarks" column.

The trial court reasoned that the contract between Zhang and H Co. was based on the expression of the parties' true intent and did not violate any mandatary provision of laws or administrative regulations, and therefore the contract was valid and both parties should perform the contract.

The court reasoned that the main issue in this case was whether H Co. told Zhang at the time she bought the car about the fact that the car had been repaired. Based on Article 7 of the contract, H Co. promised that the car was a new car, and the contract did not include any stipulations on the fact that the car had been repaired. Now H Co. alleged that Zhang had been notified of the defect of the car based on the receipt kept by itself. Zhang denied this allegation, and H Co. had no other evidence to prove that Zhang knew about the defect of the car, so the receipt could not prove that H Co. had performed its duty of notification. Although H Co. presented evidence proving that the selling price and the free decoration inside the car were the result of the negotiation of the parties, it could not prove that Zhang knew about the defect of the car. Therefore, the court held that H Co. concealed the defect of the car when it sold it, which constituted a fraud on Zhang.

H Co. alleged that the car belonged to luxury goods which should not be governed by the Law on Protection of the Rights and Interests of Consumers (Consumer Protection Law). The court reasoned that Zhang bought the car because she needed it for daily life, and H Co. did not have any evidence to prove that Zhang bought this car for operational activities; therefore, Zhang's purchase of the car was a consumption for daily life, and the Consumer Protection Law should be applied. Now Zhang requested the court to rescind the contract and requested H Co. to refund the purchase price and compensate for her loss, such requests were in compliance with law and should be supported.

However, since the car had been possessed and used by Zhang after delivery, the court held that Zhang should be liable for the depreciation of the car. Zhang did not agree to appraise the value of the car, so the court determined that the depreciation would be 10% of the car, i.e., 13,800. As a result, H Co. should deduct such amount and then refund the purchase price to Zhang.

Finally, the court held that the contract for purchase of the car was rescinded, and Zhang should return the car to H Co. and H Co. should refund Zhang the purchase price of 124,200 yuan within 7 days after the judgment became effective. H Co. should also compensate for the other taxes and fees that Zhang had paid for the car; in addition, H Co. needed to pay 138,000 yuan as punitive damages.

H Co. appealed the case to Beijing No. 2 Intermediate People's Court. The court affirms the original judgment and requests H Co. to pay both proceedings' litigation costs (3,004 yuan for the first instance trial and 6,008 yuan for the appeal).

§ 4:4 Performance

After a contract has been concluded, each party to the contract is obligated to completely perform his contractual obligations so that the other party's contractual interests can be fully realized. An act to perform a contract may be either a positive act, such as delivery of the subject matter of the contract, completion of the agreed work, provision of the agreed services, or payment of the price, or inaction of a party under special circumstances. The formation and effectiveness of a contract is the prerequisite of the performance thereof.

§ 4:4:1 The Principles of Performance

The principles of performance of a contract under the Chinese contract law include, *inter alia*, the principle of full performance, the principle of honesty and good faith, the principle of efficiency and reasonableness, and the principle of environmental protection. [1]

Principle of Full Performance

The parties to a contract must fully perform their respective obligations as agreed in the contract, because the contract terms are made upon the agreement by the parties and effective between the parties once the contract has been formed. Partial performance may result in default liability. In addition to performing the principal obligation, an obligor should also pay to the obligee interests and other expenses related to the enforcement of the obligation. If the payment is not sufficient to discharge all of the obligations, unless otherwise agreed upon by the parties, the payment should be applied firstly to pay the relevant expenses incurred by the obligor for enforcing the claim, then to pay the interests, and lastly to the principal obligation. [2]

Under the principle of full performance, the parties should also perform their contractual obligations by themselves and cannot ask any third person to perform the obligations for them, unless otherwise agreed by the parties.

---

[1] Article 509 of the Civil Code.
[2] Article 561 of the Civil Code.

Principle of Good Faith and Honesty

The parties to a contract must comply with the principle of good faith, and perform such obligations as sending notification, rendering assistance, and keeping confidentiality in accordance with the nature and purpose of the contract and the course of dealing between the parties. The parties are required to be cooperative when performing the contract. For instance, when one party makes payment, the other party must accept the payment or facilitate the other party for his performance. If one party fails to perform or fully perform the contract for a cause, the other party is obligated to adopt measures to avoid or mitigate the damage; otherwise the other party will be liable for any aggravated damage. Nevertheless, this principle does not require the parties to overlook their own independent interests in the contract. A party may refuse to cooperate in performance if the cooperation would increase the burden on the party.

Principle of Efficiency and Reasonableness

The principle of efficiency and reasonableness requires the parties to pursue economic efficiency by minimizing the cost and maximizing the contract benefits when performing the contract. Under this principle, the parties may choose the method and time of performance which may bring the best economic benefit to themselves. One party may refuse the other party's request for performing his obligations prior to the specified time unless the prior performance does not harm his interests.[1] The law also allows the parties to change the location and the subject of the performance in order to pursue economic efficiency, but it requires that such a change may not cause loss to or increase the burden on the other party; otherwise the party who proposes such change will be liable for any increased cost or the damage thus caused.

Principle of Environmental Protection

The parties should also avoid wasting the resources, polluting the environment, or damaging the ecology in the course of performance of the contract.

---

[1] Article 530 of the Civil Code.

§ 4:4:2 Defenses to Non-Performance

A non-performing party may allege several defenses under Chinese contract law. The defenses may include defense of concurrent performance or later performance, the defense of insecurity, as well as other defenses.

The defense of concurrent performance is a civil law concept which refers to a situation that any party to a contract may refuse to perform its obligations prior to the other party's corresponding performance. It is actually similar to the concurrent condition at common law. According to Article 525 of the Civil Code, where the parties mutually owe obligations to each other and the contract does not provide for a priority order of performance, then the parties should concurrently perform their obligations and either party may refuse to perform the contract before the other party performs. Either party may reject the other party's request for the corresponding performance if the other party's performance does not conform to the agreement. ①

The defense of later performance refers to the situation in which one party has an obligation to perform the contract only after the other party has completed the performance; which is an obligation to perform "later" than the other party. If the other party's performance does not comply with the contract, the first party may refuse to perform the corresponding obligations. Article 525 of the Civil Code provides that where the parties mutually owe obligations to each other and the contract provides for a priority order of performance, if the party obligated to perform first fails to perform the obligation, the party obligated to perform later may reject the request for performance made by that party. Where the performance of the party obligated to perform first does not conform to the agreement, the party obligated to perform later may reject the request made by the former party for the performance of the corresponding obligations.

Defense of insecurity refers to a situation in which one party is obligated to perform the contractual obligation before the other party performs and the time of performance is approaching; however, the ability of the other party to perform the contract has been obviously decreased after the contract is signed, and there is an actual risk that the other party may not be able to perform the

---

① Article 525 of the Civil Code.

contract. Under this circumstance, the first party may withhold its performance on the ground of insecurity. Article 527 of the Civil Code lists the situations whereby the defense of insecurity may be used, which include that the other party's business operation has seriously deteriorated, the other party transfers property or withdraws funds in order to evade debts, the other party has lost its goodwill, and any other situation in which the other party has lost or is losing its ability to perform the obligation. However, if the first party does not have sufficient evidence to prove that the other party is in one of the above situations, the first party is liable for the default.[①] If a party decides to suspend performance on the ground of insecurity, he should promptly notify the other party, and, if the other party provides a bond to secure the performance, he must resume performance. If the other party fails to restore his ability to perform the obligation and fails to provide an appropriate security within a reasonable period of time, the other party is deemed to indicate by act that it will not perform the principal obligation, and the party that suspends the performance on the ground of insecurity may rescind the contract and may request the other party to bear default liability.[②]

The defense of insecurity looks similar to the anticipatory repudiation. Repudiation originally is a common law concept and has been integrated into Article 563 of the Civil Code. There are significant differences between the defense of insecurity and anticipatory repudiation. First, the prerequisite conditions are different. In order to apply the defense of insecurity, there must be an order of performance by the two parties stated in the contract. However, such an order is not required under the doctrine of anticipatory repudiation. Secondly, the defense of insecurity requires that the financial status of the party must be deteriorated after the contract is made and there is an actual risk that the party may not be able to perform the contract, whereas anticipatory breach only requires an express or implied intent of the party not to perform the contract, which may not involve the financial status of the party. Thirdly, the defense of insecurity may be applied disregarding whether the party is at fault, whereas anticipatory repudiation requires the breaching party has a

---

① Article 527 of the Civil Code.
② Article 528 of the Civil Code.

subjective intent to breach the contract. ①

§ 4:4:3 Securing Contractual Debts

Under the Chinese contract law theories, after a contract becomes effective, a party to the contract should use all of his assets to secure the performance of his contractual obligations. If a party illegally transfers all or part of his assets to another person, he may not have sufficient assets to perform the contract; and if he defaults, even if the other party obtains a judgment against him, his assets may not be enough to pay the judgment creditor. In other words, if a party to a contract illegally transfers part or all of his assets to another person, there is a potential risk that the other party's interests may be harmed. In order to preserve the obligor's assets for the future enforcement of the contract, Chinese civil law adopts a system of securing contractual obligations by granting the obligee of a contract the right to revocation and the right to subrogation. We use "obligor" and "obligee" to refer to the two parties to a contract in this sub-section. An obligor is the party obligated to perform the contractual obligations while an obligee is the other party with the right to request the obligor to perform.

§ 4:4:3:1 The Right to Revocation

If an obligor's act harms an obligee's rights and interests arising from a contract between the obligor and the obligee, the obligee has a right to request the court to revoke the obligor's act and such act, once revoked, does not have legal effect from the beginning. ② The obligor's acts that may be revoked mainly include an act of gratuitously disposal of his proprietary rights and interests or maliciously extending the period of performance of his due claim so that the enforcement of the obligee's claim is adversely affected. Specifically, if an obligor waives his claims, waives the security for his claims, or transfers his assets without consideration, or extends the period of performance of his

---

① For more about anticipatory repudiation at common law, see RESTATEMENT (SECOND) OF CONTRACTS § 250 et seq. and the Note in John Edward Murray, Jr., CONTRACTS: CASES AND MATERIALS 696 (5th Ed. Lexis Publishing 2000).
② Article 542 of the Civil Code.

due claim with a bad faith, the obligee whose rights and interests are adversely affected has a right to revocation against his act.① In addition, if an obligor transfers his assets at an obviously unreasonably low price, takes a third person's assets at an obviously unreasonably high price, or provides security for a third person's obligation, so that the obligee's claim is adversely affected, the obligee may request the court to revoke the obligor's act if the third person knows or should have known such circumstance.②

In order to exercise the right to revocation, an obligee must establish that he has a lawful and effective contractual claim against the obligor and that the obligor has, successfully but inappropriately, disposed of his assets either through giving up his claim against a third person, gratuitously transferring his assets to a third person, or transferring its assets at an obviously unreasonable price to a third person, and the other acts with the same effect. The above acts of an obligor must have caused harm to the obligee's interests. Malice of the obligor and the third person must also be present in order for the obligee to exercise his right to revocation. The holder of the right to revocation can only be the aggrieved obligee.

An obligee's right to revocation should not exceed the extent of the obligee's claim against the obligor.③ The right to revocation is an important measure to secure an obligor's performance of contract and to protect an obligee's rights and interests. An obligee must exercise the right to revocation within one year from the date on which he knows or should have known the cause for revocation; and in any event, a right to revocation is extinguished if the obligee does not exercise such right within five years since the date on which the obligor conducts the relevant act.④

§ 4:4:3:2 The Right to Subrogation

While the purpose of granting the right to revocation to an obligee is to secure the performance of the contract through preventing the obligor's assets from being shrunk, the purpose of the right to subrogation is to effectively

---

① Article 538 of the Civil Code.
② Article 539 of the Civil Code.
③ Article 540 of the Civil Code.
④ Article 541 of the Civil Code.

increase the property of the obligor so that the obligor can better perform the contract. Specifically, if an obligor fails to claim against a third person owing to his indolence so that the enforcement of the obligee's due claim is adversely affected, the obligee may request the court to allow him to exercise by subrogation the obligor's claim against the third person in his own name, unless such claim belongs exclusively to the obligor himself. The scope of the right to subrogation is also limited to an obligee's due claim, and the third person's defenses against the obligor, if any, may also be asserted against the obligee. ①

If, prior to the due date of an obligee's claim, the limitation period for the obligor's principal claim against a third person is to expire, or the obligor fails to timely declare his claim in a bankruptcy proceeding, so that the enforcement of the obligee's claim is adversely affected, the obligee may exercise a right of subrogation to request the third person to perform his obligation to the obligor, declare the obligor's claim to the bankruptcy administrator, or conduct other necessary acts. ②

When exercising a right to subrogation, an obligee acts in his own name. Although there is no contractual relationship between the obligee and the third person, the obligee's right to subrogation actually binds the third person because the obligee takes the position of the obligor against the third person. However, the obligee may only request the third person to perform his obligation to the obligor instead of the obligee.

In order to exercise the right to subrogation, an obligee must establish that there are two valid and effective contractual relationships existed, one is between the obligee and the obligor, and the other is between the obligor and a third person. Further, where an obligation owed by a third person to the obligor is due, if the obligor fails to exercise his right against the third person, the inaction of the obligor may cause actual damage to the obligee in that the obligor does not have sufficient assets. Nevertheless, an obligee may not exercise the right to subrogation if the right owned by the obligor against a third person belongs "exclusively to the obligor himself," *e.g.*, a claim arising

---

① Article 535 of the Civil Code.
② Article 536 of the Civil Code.

from a relationship of support or inheritance, which may include a right to remuneration, retirement compensation, pension, damages, settlement fee, life insurance compensation, or a right to personal injury compensation.

If the court determines that a right to subrogation has been established, the counterparty of the obligor should perform the obligation he owed to the obligee, and afterwards, the corresponding rights and obligations between the obligee and the obligor, and those between the obligor and the counterparty, are both terminated. ①

§ 4:4:4 Third Parties Involved

The performance of a contract is normally done by the parties to the contract; however, under certain circumstances, a contract may also be performed by a third person, provided that it does not violate the provisions of law and the contract, and the performance is not against the nature of the contract. It may involve different situations.

§ 4:4:4:1 Third-Person Beneficiaries

The first situation involves third-person beneficiaries. Where the parties agree that the obligor shall perform the contractual obligation to a third person, if the obligor fails to perform the obligation to the third person or the performance does not conform to the agreement, the obligor is liable to the obligee. In this case, the third person may also directly request the obligor to perform the obligation to him if it is so provided by law or agreed upon by the parties and if the third person does not explicitly reject it within a reasonable period of time. However, when exercising this right, the defenses that the obligor has against the obligee may be asserted against the third person. ②

§ 4:4:4:2 Third-Person Performance

The second situation involves third-person performance. Where the parties to a contract agree that a third person shall perform the contractual obligation to the obligee, if the third person fails to perform the obligation or the

---

① Article 537 of the Civil Code.
② Article 522 of the Civil Code.

performance does not conform to the agreement, the obligor is liable to the obligee. ①

All third persons may not perform a contract for the benefit of the obligor, and all kinds of obligations may not be performed by a third person. A third person who is to perform contractual obligations for the benefit of the obligor of a contract must be a qualified third person who has an independent status, and the nature of the contract must be such that it may be performed by a third person. There must be no adverse agreement between the obligee and the obligor regarding the third-person performance. The third-person performance should not violate law or be against the social public interest. Third-person performance will result in certain legal effects between and among the obligee, obligor, and the third person.

First, the third-person performance discharges all or part of the obligation of the obligor, and the obligee shall not require the obligor to re-perform that part of the obligation under the contract. Based on the same theory, if the third person fails to perform or the performance is defective, the obligee may claim for default liability against the obligor because the third-person performance does not make the third person a party to the contract between the obligor and the obligee.

Between the obligor and the third person, the legal effect of the third-person performance may depend on the relationship between the two. The third-person performance may be based on the requirement of law, under an entrustment contract, or based on the quasi-contract theory. In the first situation, the law that imposes such a requirement will govern; in the second situation, the terms of the entrustment contract between the obligor and the third person will govern. In the last situation, the law on unjust enrichment will be applied to the legal effect of the third-person performance.

If a third person performs the contractual obligation based on a legal requirement or the agreement between the obligor and the obligee, then the obligee should not refuse to accept the third person's performance. However, if a third person performs purely based on the obligor's unilateral intent, then the obligee may refuse to accept the third person's performance if the contract

---

① Article 523 of the Civil Code.

is personal in nature and not suitable for third-person performance, if the obligee and the obligor previously agree that the contract cannot be performed by any third person, or, if the law provides that the contract shall not be performed by a third person. Third-person performance may also be refused if it increases the burden on the obligee.

§ 4:4:4:3 Third-Person Performance on Subrogation

The Civil Code has added a new article providing for third-person performance on subrogation. Where a third person has a lawful interest in the performance of the obligation under a contract and the obligor fails to perform the obligation, the third person may perform the obligation to the obligee on behalf of the obligor, unless the obligation may only be performed by the obligor based on the nature of the obligation, as agreed by the parties, or as provided by law. After the obligee accepts the performance of such obligation by the third person, his claim against the obligor is assigned to the third person, unless otherwise agreed upon by the obligor and the third person. [1]

Case 27

Case 27: Sinochem International (Overseas) Pte Ltd v. Thyssen Krupp Metallurgical Products GmbH [2]

The Sinochem Holding Company is the parent company of Sinochem International (Overseas) Pte Ltd (Sinochem). On April 11, 2008, Sinochem and Thyssen Krupp Metallurgical Products GmbH (German Co.) signed a contract for sale, under which Sinochem agreed to purchase 25,000 tons (with 10% more or less) of fuel grade petroleum cokes with the typical value of 36 - 46 HGI. The port of loading was Pittsburgh, California, and the destination was a port in China, with the specific port to be determined by Sinochem. Both parties agreed, among other things, that an independent inspector confirmed by both parties would take

---

[1] Article 524 of the Civil Code.
[2] See (2013) Min Si Zhong Zi No. 35, reprinted in the SPC's Guiding Cases No. 107.

samples in the port of loading and issue an inspection certificate, and the result of the inspection would be final and binding on both parties. Sinochem could inspect the amount and quality of the petroleum cokes in the port of discharge, and the German Co. could entrust an independent inspector to witness the inspection at its cost. If Sinochem discovered that the quality or amount of the petroleum cokes does not conform to the quality or amount as inspected in the port of loading, it may issue a notice to the German Co., and may claim damages within 60 days after the goods arrived at the port of destination. The contract also stipulated that the then effective laws of the New York State of the United States were the governing laws of the formation, jurisdiction, and interpretation of the contract.

On August 8, 2008, A. J. Edmond Co., the inspector approved by both parties issued an inspection certificate in the port of loading stating that the HGI index of the petroleum cokes is 32. On August 11, 2008, the weight certificate states that the petroleum cokes actually delivered weighs 26,079.63 tons.

On July 31, 2008, Sinochem applied for a letter of credit in the Singapore Branch of the Bank of Communications of China (Singapore Branch) in which it states that the HGI index of the petroleum cokes is CA. 36-46. On August 27, 2008, the German Co. presented to the Singapore Branch the documents including the inspection certificate issued by A. J. Edmond Co. at the port of loading. The Singapore Branch paid most of the purchase price on September 2, 2008. On September 11, 2008, the German Co. issued the final commercial invoice, determining that the unit price of the petroleum cokes was US $ 301.56 per ton. On September 25, 2008, Sinochem paid the balance of the purchase price through telegraphic transfer. Sinochem had paid to the German Co. US $ 7,756,828.55 in total.

On September 8, 2008, the petroleum cokes arrived at the port of Nanjing. On November 10, 2008, China Inspection Group Jiangsu Co. issued an inspection certificate stating that the HGI index of the petroleum cokes was 32.

From October to December 2008, the price of petroleum cokes in the

Chinese market decreased and the pre-tax price for medium sulfur cokes decreased to 2,048 yuan per ton in October, 1,357 yuan per ton in November, and 1,305 yuan per ton in December.

Sinochem believed that the HGI index of the delivered petroleum cokes was 32, which did not conform to the contract, so that it was very hard to sell them on the Chinese market, and that it constituted a fundamental breach of the contract. For this purpose, it presented a statement made by a research institute.

The German Co. argued that although the HGI index of the petroleum cokes it delivered was 32, from its appearance, it was not in compliance with the contract, but actually it did not constitute a fundamental breach because the HGI index stipulated in the contract was the typical value. The petroleum cokes of HGI 32 could still be sold on the Chinese market. For this purpose, it presented three expert witnesses to testify.

The High People's Court of Jiangsu Province held that the testimony of the three expert witnesses presented by the German Co. could be admitted, and the statement presented by Sinochem was also admissible. However, the part of the testimony involving whether the petroleum cokes with HGI Index 32 were in compliance with the contract should not be admitted since this issue was within the court's province and that the witnesses did not have the right to make the decision on this issue.

The High People's Court considered several issues. The first issue was about the governing law. It reasoned that Sinochem was a Singapore company, the German Co. was a German company, so this case involved a dispute arising from an international contract. Although the parties selected the New York State Law as the governing law in the contract regarding the formation, jurisdiction, and interpretation of the contract, during litigation, the parties both selected the United Nations Convention on Contracts for the International Sale of Goods (CISG) as the basis for their rights and obligations. Since both Singapore and Germany were the signatory states of the CISG, the contract involved in this case should be governed by the CISG.

The second issue is whether the German Co.'s act constituted a fundamental breach of the contract. Since it was stipulated in the contract that the typical value of the petroleum cokes HGI index was 36-46, but the HGI index of the delivered petroleum cokes was only 32, lower than the lowest range of the index stipulated in the contract, thus, the German Co.'s act constituted a fundamental breach.

The High Court also reasoned that Sinochem may declare the contract void and thus the German Co. was liable for compensation.

The German Co. appealed to the SPC. On appeal, the German Co. presents the Uniform Commercial Code of the United States (UCC) and the relevant case law, alleging that the contract is valid according to the US law. Sinochem challenges the statement, arguing that there should be a person specialized in US law to provide an explanation of the US law. Meanwhile, it argues that the CISG should be the basis for determining the validity of the contract.

The SPC reasons that the contract is one with foreign elements, and that the contract was signed before the Law on Application of Laws on the Civil Juristic Relations with Foreign Elements was enacted. According to Article 145 of the GPCL, the parties to such a contract may select the governing law unless otherwise provided by law. In this case, the parties selected the New York State Law as the governing law of the contract, such a choice-of-law is not in violation of any law and therefore is valid. Since Singapore, Germany, and the United States are all signatory states of the CISG, and during the first instance trial, the parties selected the CISG as the legal basis to determine their rights and obligations, and had not excluded the application of the CISG, the lower court correctly applied the CISG to try this case. Regarding the issues not covered by the CISG, the New York State Law should be applied.

Since the CISG does not provide for the validity of the contract or contractual clauses according to its Article 4, the validity of the contract should be governed by the New York State Law selected by the parties in the contract. The German Co. provides the UCC and the relevant cases, arguing that the contract concerned is valid. Sinochem challenges the explanation made by the German Co.'s agent on the US law, but it does not challenge the relevant US law. According to the US law provided by the German Co., the SPC holds that the contract is valid.

Regarding whether the German Co.'s act constituted a fundamental breach of the contract, the SPC reasons that it did breach the contract; however, it was not a fundamental breach because the petroleum cokes involved in this case, although not in compliance with the contract, could still be sold at a discount.

Nevertheless, the SPC reasons that the German Co. delivered nonconforming goods so that the Sinochem could not timely resell the goods, and thus suffered loss owing to the change of the market price. The German Co. is liable for paying the price differences and the interests, as well as the storage fees. Sinochem should assume the expenses such as the taxes or other fees on the ground that some of the losses are part of the market risks that Sinochem should assume.

Finally, the SPC holds that the lower court's decision correctly found the facts, but the application of law was partially incorrect and the liability determined was not appropriate and should be corrected. It thus holds that (1) the German Co. should compensate Sinochem for the loss of purchase price of US $1,610,581.74 plus interests arising from September 25, 2008 to the date of payment determined by this judgment within 30 days after the judgment becomes effective; (2) the German Co. should compensate Sinochem for the storage fee of US $98,442.79 within 30 days after this judgment becomes effective; (3) the other claims of Sinochem are dismissed; and (4) regarding the litigation cost of the first instance trial (306,432 yuan), the German Co. should pay 183,859.2 yuan, and the Sinochem should pay 122,572.8 yuan; regarding the litigation cost for the appeal (306,432 yuan), the German Co. should pay US $183,859.2 yuan, and the Sinochem should pay 122,572.8 yuan.

§ 4:5 Modification of Contract

A duly formed contract is legally binding on both parties to the contract and the parties shall perform their contractual obligations strictly according to the terms and conditions of the contract. Generally, neither party may unilaterally change the terms of the contract or revoke the contract at their own will. This has been recognized as a general principle of the contract law.① However, owing to the complexity of the economic activities, a contract may be affected by the changes made to its economic environment. In order to satisfy the needs for economic development and to reach the goals of the parties to the contract, the civil law allows the parties to modify a duly concluded contract upon agreement through consultation.② Accordingly, the Chinese contract law has established a series of rules to regulate modification of contracts with a view to preventing the parties from abusing their rights and maintaining the social market economic order. The modification of contract may involve changes to the contract terms or changes to the parties to the contract.

§4:5:1 Change of Contract Terms

Before a duly formed contract has been fully performed, any change to the contract terms may change the rights and obligations of the parties. For instance, if the quantity of the subject matter of a contract has been increased after the contract is formed but before it has been fully performed, the seller needs to deliver more of the products than he originally promised to deliver. If the price term is changed — say, increased by 1%, then the buyer will be obligated to pay more than he expected to pay based on the original contract. Therefore, the parties are not allowed to unilaterally change the contract terms at their will.

However, the parties may modify a contract by mutual agreement, and shall obtain approval or file registration if so required by law. To modify a contract, there must be a duly formed contract in the first place. If a contract has been revoked or declared as void, or if an effectiveness-pending contract has not been ratified by the right-holder, then the contract is invalid from its beginning; accordingly, such a "contract" cannot be changed or modified. If a contract is a revocable one, then the party with the right to revocation may, within the specified period, choose to revoke the contract or to rectify the contract.

---

① Article 7 of the Civil Code.
② Article 543 of the Civil Law.

An agreement between the parties to modify the content of a contract must be clear; otherwise it is presumed that the contract is not modified.① After a contract is duly modified, the contract as altered is binding on both parties and they shall perform the contract according to the modified terms and conditions. Any party who fails to fully perform the altered contract commits default and shall bear civil liability. However, the modification made to the contract terms does not affect the right of the parties to claim damages, if any. If, before a contract is modified, a party suffers damage owing to the other party's fault, the aggrieved party may request the party at fault to pay damages even after the contract has been modified, unless the parties agree otherwise.

Sometimes the modification of a contract may require consent from a third person whose interests may be affected by the modification. For example, if there is a surety contract securing the performance of a primary contract, a prior consent of the surety must be obtained before the modification is made to the primary contract; otherwise the modification will not be effective against the surety.

§4:5:2 Change of Parties

The parties to a duly formed contract may assign their contractual rights or delegate their contractual obligations to a third person without changing the terms of the contract. After the assignment or delegation is completed, the obligor and the obligee under the contract have been changed. The change of parties to a contract may affect two kinds of contractual relationships: one is the contractual relationship between the two parties to the original contract, and the other is the contractual relationship between the assignor and assignee, or the delegator and the delegatee. Change to the parties may involve three situations: the assignment of the contractual rights, the delegation of the contractual obligations, and the general succession of both the contractual rights and obligations. The last situation is a combination of the first two and therefore it should conform to the legal requirements for both. The assignment and delegation may not violate law or be against the social public interest.

---

① Article 544 of the Civil Law.

§ 4:5:2:1 Assignment

When an obligee transfers all or part of his rights under a contract to a third person, the contractual rights are said to be assigned. The law allows an obligee to assign his contractual rights to another person as long as the assignment does not violate law or is against social ethics. The underlying rational is that assignment of contracts may encourage transactions and promote the development of the market economy. However, in order to protect the social public interest and maintain the transaction order as well as to balance the rights and interests of both parties to a contract, the civil law also limits the scope of the contractual rights that are assignable. According to Article 545 of the Civil Code, there are three situations where a contractual right may not be assigned.

First, a contractual right may not be assigned to a third person if the nature of the contractual right determines that it is not assignable. For example, if a contract is personal in nature, or is secondary to a primary contract, the contractual rights may not be assigned. Second, if the parties, upon concluding a contract, agree that the obligee may not assign his contractual rights to any third person, then the contractual rights are not assignable as long as such an agreement does not violate law. However, such an anti-assignment agreement is not effective against a *bona fide* third person. Third, if the law prohibits the assignment of the right under a contract, then the contractual right cannot be assigned to a third person. If the law imposes any special requirements for the assignment of a contractual right, these requirements must be satisfied.

When assigning contractual rights, an assignor and an assignee must reach a mutual agreement on the assignment and cannot change the terms of the original contract. The assignor must be the obligee with full capacity to dispose of his rights. An assignment by an obligee with only limited capacity will not be completed unless it is made by the legal representative or a duly authorized agent of the obligee. Article 91 of the GPCL required an assignor or delegator of the contractual rights or obligations to obtain a prior consent from the other party to the contract before assigning contractual rights or delegating contractual obligations. It also prohibited the assignor or delegator from making profits out of the assignment or the delegation. However, Article 80 of the Contract Law waived the consent requirement and no longer required an assignor to obtain a prior consent from the other party, but only required the assignor to notify the other party to the contract about the assignment. It did not mention the profit-making prohibition. Actually, it is unnecessary to prohibit the assignment of a contractual rights or the delegation of a contractual obligations if it neither infringes upon the other party's lawful interests nor increases the other party's burden, as long as the assignment or delegation is done free from fraud, duress, undue influence, serious misunderstanding, or unconscionability. Now the discrepancy of these two laws on this point has been finally resolved by Article 546 of the Civil Code, which adopts the notice approach, and provides that an assignment is not effective against an obligor if the obligee assigns his contractual rights but fails to notify the obligor. In addition, it provides that the notice of assignment once made may not be revoked, unless consented to by the assignee.

After an assignment is completed, it becomes effective both between the assignor and the assignee, as well as among the assignor (obligee), assignee, and the obligor of the original contract. As between the assignor and the assignee, the contractual rights have been assigned by the assignor to the assignee and the assignment becomes effective after the obligor has received notice from the obligee. If an assignor assigns all of his contractual rights to an assignee, the assignee will become a new obligee and have the same right as the original obligee, so that he may request the obligor to perform the contract. If an assignor only assigns part of his contractual rights to an assignee, then the assignee will join the contractual relationship to be a co-obligee of the contract. In this situation, the assignment agreement may clarify whether the assignor and the assignee jointly enjoy the contractual rights or hold the rights by shares. Without clarification in the assignment agreement, they are presumed to jointly hold the contractual rights. Upon the assignment, any accessory right related to the primary right is also assigned to the assignee, unless the accessory right belongs exclusively to the obligee. Even if the assignment of the accessory right is not registered or the possession of the right does not change, the assignee still acquires the accessory right thus assigned.[1] In addition, upon

---

[1] Article 547 of the Civil Code.

assignment, an assignor warrants that the assigned rights are free from defects and that the assignor will be liable for any damage caused by the defects in the assigned rights.

As among the assignor (obligee), assignee, and the obligor, if the contractual rights have been completely assigned to an assignee, then the original obligee is out of the contractual relationship and can no longer request the obligor to perform the contract. If only part of the contractual rights has been assigned and the assignor and assignee have the interests by shares, then the obligor should perform the contractual obligations to both the assignor and the assignee, provided that any expenses for performance increased due to the assignment is to be borne by the original obligee based on the principle of honesty and good faith. ①

After receiving a notice of assignment of a contractual right, the obligor shall perform the contractual obligations to the new obligee to the extent that the contractual rights are assigned hereto. However, the obligor's defenses against the assignor may be asserted against the original obligee, including the defense of concurrent performance, the defense of later performance, and the defense of insecurity. ② Furthermore, if the obligor has a claim against the assignor, the obligor may claim a set-off against the assignee if, when he receives the notice of assignment of a contractual right, the claim becomes due prior to or at the same time of the due date of the assigned claim, or the obligor's claim and the assigned contractual right are generated on the basis of the same contract. ③

§ 4:5:2:2 Delegation

When an obligor transfers, without changing the terms of the contract, his obligations under a contract in whole or in part to a third person, the obligations are said to be delegated and the consent of the obligee must be obtained. The obligor or the third person may demand the obligee to give his consent within a reasonable period of time, and consent is deemed to be given

---

① Article 550 of the Civil Code.
② Article 548 of the Civil Code.
③ Article 549 of the Civil Code.

if the obligee makes no indication.①

If a third person agrees with the obligor to join in the obligation and notifies the obligee thereof, or a third person indicates to the obligee his willingness to join in the obligation, and the obligee has not explicitly made a rejection within a reasonable period of time, then the obligee may request the third person to assume a joint-and-several-obligation with the obligor to the extent of the obligation the third person is willing to assume.②

After a delegation is completed, the delegatee becomes the new obligor. The original obligor is out of the contractual relationship if all of his contractual obligations have been delegated to the delegatee; however, the delegatee may assert a defense of the original obligor against the obligee; where the original obligor has a claim against the obligee, the delegatee may not claim a set-off against the obligee.③ Any accessory obligation related to the principal obligation is also delegated to the delegatee upon delegation, unless the accessory obligation belongs exclusively to the original obligor.④

An obligor may delegate part of his contractual obligations to a delegatee, and in this case, the delegatee and the delegator shall be jointly liable to the obligee or liable in proportion to their shares in the obligation.

A party to a contract may also concomitantly assign his contractual rights and delegate his contractual obligations under a contract to a third person with the consent of the other party.⑤ In this case, the rules on assignment of contractual rights and delegation of obligations should be applied.⑥

§ 4:6 Termination of Contract

A contract is an agreement made by and between the persons of the civil law to establish, modify, or terminate a civil juristic relationship other than a relationship involving a marriage, adoption, guardianship, or the like personal

---

① Article 551 of the Civil Code.
② Article 552 of the Civil Code.
③ Article 553 of the Civil Code.
④ Article 554 of the Civil Code.
⑤ Article 555 of the Civil Code.
⑥ Article 556 of the Civil Code.

relationships that are governed by the other laws. ① The nature of the contract determines that it will not exist forever and its life starts from its formation and ends upon its termination. A contract is terminated when the rights and obligations arising from it are extinguished according to the parties' agreement or by operation of law. After a contract is terminated, the obligee under the contract no longer has any contractual rights and the obligor no longer has any obligation to perform the contract.

§ 4:6:1 Grounds for Termination

A contract may be terminated on various grounds, and once a contract is terminated, any claim or obligation under the contract is also terminated. A contract is terminated if the contract term expires, the contract is rescinded, or the contractual obligation has been performed or offset against another obligation. Other grounds for termination of a contract include that the obligor has placed the subject matter in escrow, the obligee has exempted the obligation, the claim and obligation are merged to be held by a same person, or there exists any other circumstance under which the claim or obligation is terminated as provided by law or agreed by the parties. ② Some of these grounds for termination of a contract are discussed below.

§ 4:6:1:1 Satisfaction

A contract may be terminated upon satisfaction where the party with a contractual obligation to discharge a debt has fully performed his obligation so that the obligee's rights are made whole. The party with an obligation to discharge the debt may be the obligor or his agent, or a third person. When such a third person performs the obligation, generally he may not use his right against the obligee to set off the obligation of the obligor owed to the obligee, but an obligor may. The discharge must be made in full amount, and an obligee may reject the obligor's partial performance of the obligation, unless the partial performance is not detrimental to the interests of the obligee. ③

---

① Article 464 of the Civil Code.
② Article 537 of the Civil Code.
③ Article 531 of the Civil Code.

§ 4:6:1:2 Rescission

A contract may be terminated upon rescission (or cancellation). A duly concluded contract may be rescinded by the parties upon agreement through consultation. The parties may agree to rescind the contract after it is concluded and before it has been fully performed. A party may also reserve a right to rescind the contract and the causes for rescission should be agreed upon by both parties. When such a cause for rescission of contract arises, the party with the right to rescission may rescind the contract. ① A contract may also be rescinded by operation of law. Article 563 of the Civil Code provides the main grounds for such a rescission: *force majeure*, anticipatory repudiation, and delayed performance.

The parties may rescind a contract if its purpose cannot be achieved owing to a *force majeure* event. "*Force majeure*" is defined as an objective condition which is unforeseeable, unavoidable, and insurmountable, and which cannot be overcome by the parties. ② Generally, a person who is unable to perform his obligations due to *force majeure* bears no civil liability unless otherwise provided by law; therefore, it is one of the grounds for rescission of a contract. If the *force majeure* event does not make the whole contract non-performable, whether the parties may rescind the contract depends on whether the purpose of the contract can still be achieved. If the performance of the rest part of the contract does not have any economic benefit to the other party, then the purpose of the contract fails and the contract may be rescinded; otherwise the parties may only request rectification of the contract.

If a party to a contract expressly or impliedly by conduct indicates, prior to the due date of performance, that he will not perform the principal obligation under the contract, then anticipatory repudiation occurs and the other party may rescind the contract. In addition, if a party obligated to perform the obligation before the other party performs decides to suspend his performance based on a defense of insecurity as provided in Article 527 of the Civil Code, if the other party neither restores his ability to perform the obligation nor provides a bond within a reasonable period of time, the party

---

① Article 562 of the Civil Code.
② Article 180 of the Civil Code.

may rescind the contract and request the other party to bear default liability. ①

If a party delays in performing the principal contractual obligation and has not performed it within a reasonable time after being demanded, then the other party may rescind the contract. If the obligation an obligor fails to timely perform is not a principal obligation, whereas the purpose of the contract may not be achieved owing to the non-performance, the other party may also rescind the contract. Based on the nature of a contract and the manifestation of the intention of both parties, if the time of performance is essential to the contract and the delayed performance of one party will make the whole contract meaningless, then the obligee may rescind the contract without firstly sending a demand notice to the other party. However, if the time of performance is not essential to the contract, even if the obligor delays in performance, the purpose of the contract does not completely fail. In this situation, the obligee may send a demand notice to the obligor and give the obligor a grace period to perform. If the obligor fails to perform within the grace period, then the obligee may rescind the contract. If an obligor is required to continuously perform an obligation for an indefinite period of time under a contract, each party to the contract may rescind the contract at any time, as long as the other party is notified reasonably in advance.

In addition, a party may also rescind a contract if the other party's act otherwise constitutes a material breach of the contract so that the purpose of the contract cannot be achieved. For instance, where an obligor is actually not able to perform his obligation so that the purpose of the contract fails, the original obligation will be extinguished and the other party may rescind the contract and request damages based on impossibility of performance. If an obligor is able to perform his obligation but refuses to do so, the obligee may rescind the contract based on refusal of performance. If the goods delivered by an obligor do not comply with the quality requirements stated in the contract, i.e., the performance is defective, the obligee may rescind the contract based on non-conforming or inappropriate performance only if the defective performance is so serious that the purpose of the contract cannot be achieved.

---

① Article 528 of the Civil Code.

Otherwise, the parties may cure the defective performance by repairing, replacing, and returning the goods.

If a party decides to rescind a contract, he must timely notify the other party, and the contract is rescinded at the time the notice reaches the other party, except that when the notice states that the contract is to be automatically rescinded if the obligor fails to preform his obligation within a specified period of time, the contract is rescinded when the obligor fails to perform upon expiration of the specified period of time. Where the other party objects to the rescission, either party may request the court or an arbitration institution to resolve the issue. A party to a contract may also directly go to the court or an arbitration institution requesting a rescission of the contract. Once a judgement or reward is made in favor of the party, the contract is rescinded upon the time a duplicated copy of the complaint or the application letter for arbitration is served on the other party. ①

A right to rescission may need to be exercised within a time limit provided by law or agreed by the parties, otherwise such right will be extinguished. If there is no time limit provided by law or agreed by the parties, the right to rescind a contract will be extinguished after one year from the time the party knows or should have known the causes for rescission, or within a reasonable period of time after being demanded by the other party. ②

§ 4:6:1:3 Set-off

When both parties mutually owe obligations to each other, and the subject matters of the obligations are of the same kind and quality, each party may offset his obligation against the obligation of the other party that becomes due. If the subject matters of the obligations are not of the same kind or quality, the obligations may also be offset upon agreement by the parties through consultation. ③ However, Article 568 of the Civil Code further provides that the obligations cannot be offset if it is prohibited by law or in the contract, or based on the nature of the obligations. A party who decides to claim a set-off

---

① Article 564 of the Civil Code.
② Article 564 of the Civil Code.
③ Article 569 of the Civil Code.

must notify the other party and the notice becomes effective upon reaching the other party. No conditions or time limit may be attached to the set-off.

§ 4:6:1:4   Placing the Subject Matter in Escrow

If an obligee refuses to accept an obligor's performance of a contractual obligation without just cause so that it is difficult for the obligor to discharge his obligation, the obligor may place the subject matter of the performance with a competent department as escrow. Afterwards, the obligor will be deemed to have discharged his obligation and the contract is terminated. ① After a subject matter is placed in escrow, any accrued fruits of the subject matter will belong to the obligee, and any expenses thus incurred and any risk of destruction, damage, or loss of the subject matter will be assumed by the obligee. ②

In addition to the above situation, an obligor may also place the subject matter of a contract in escrow if the obligee cannot be located, or the obligee dies or loses his capacity for performing civil juristic acts but his heirs or estate administrator has not been determined, or his guardian has not been designated. ③ Sometimes the subject matter of a contract is not suitable for being placed in escrow, or the expenses for the escrow are excessively high, then the obligor may sell the subject matter through auction or sale and place the proceeds thus obtained in escrow. ④

Once an obligor has delivered the subject matter or the proceeds obtained from the auction or sale of the subject matter to an escrow agency, the obligor must immediately notify the obligee or his heirs, estate administrator, guardian, or custodian⑤ and then he is deemed to have discharged his contractual obligation. ⑥ After the subject matter of a contract has been placed in escrow, the obligee has both a right and an obligation to take it back within a specified period of time. The escrow agency may only refuse to release the

---

① Article 570 of the Civil Code.
② Article 573 of the Civil Code.
③ Article 570 of the Civil Code.
④ Article 570 of the Civil Code.
⑤ Article 572 of the Civil Code.
⑥ Article 571 of the Civil Code.

subject matter to the obligee upon request of the obligor for the reason that an obligation owed by the obligee to the obligor becomes due. The obligee must perform such obligation or provide a performance bond before collecting the subject matter from the escrow agency. ①

According to the Public Notary's Escrow Rules, an obligee must go to the escrow agency to collect the goods placed in escrow immediately after receiving the notice sent by the obligor, and will lose such right if the obligee fails to take the goods back within five years from the date they are delivered to the escrow agency. In this situation, the goods in escrow will be escheated to the State. This rule now has been integrated into Article 574 of the Civil Code, which also provides that an obligor who delivers the subject matter to the escrow agency may take it back after paying the escrow agency's expenses if the obligee fails to perform his overdue obligation to the obligor, or if the obligee waives his right to collect the goods placed in escrow in writing to the escrow agency.

§ 4:6:1:5 Forgiveness

When an obligee decides to exempt an obligor's obligation, the obligee is said to "forgive" the obligor's debt. Where an obligee forgives part or all of the obligations owed to him by an obligor, the contractual relationship and the contractual rights and obligations are to be terminated in part or in whole, unless the obligor objects within a reasonable period of time. ② An intention to forgive the obligation must be made by the obligee to the obligor, and the forgiveness may not harm the interests of any third person. If an obligee expressed to a third person of his intention to forgive the obligor's obligation, it is not an effective forgiveness. In addition, the obligee who forgives the obligor's obligation must have full capacity for performing civil juristic acts to dispose of his rights; otherwise, the forgiveness must be made by the legal representative or an agent of the obligee. Once made, the forgiveness cannot be revoked.

---

① Article 574 of the Civil Code.
② Article 575 of the Civil Code.

§ 4:6:1:6 Merger

Rights and obligations that are held by different persons may be merged to be held by a same person. Once a merger occurs, the rights and obligations will be changed. For example, an ownership right and a right to usufructs or a security interest may be merged, and as a result, the right to usufructs or a security interest is to be extinguished. The merger of a principal obligation and a security obligation may also extinguish the security obligation. Likewise, when the rights and obligations under a contract are held by a same person, there is a merger and the contractual relationship is terminated unless a third person's interests are harmed. ①

A merger of contractual rights and obligations is mostly resulted from the succession of the said rights and obligations, especially in a context of assignment of contractual rights and/or delegation of contractual obligations. A typical example would be where two companies that have a contractual relationship merge into one company, so that the contractual rights and obligations between the two original companies are extinguished after the merger because they are now both held by the same company.

§ 4:6:2 Consequences of Termination

Once a contract is terminated, the rights and obligations under the contract will be terminated simultaneously so that the obligee does not have any claim against the obligor and the obligor does not have any obligation to perform the contract. Furthermore, any accessory right attached to the principal right, such as a security interest, is also terminated concomitantly, unless otherwise provided by law or agreed by the parties. ② However, under the principle of good faith and honesty, the parties still have a duty to perform such obligations as sending notification, rendering assistance, keeping confidentiality, and recycling the used articles according to the course of dealing between the parties. ③ These obligations are implied in every contract even if they are not expressly set out in the contract. Although termination of a

---

① Article 576 of the Civil Code.
② Article 559 of the Civil Code.
③ Article 558 of the Civil Code.

contract will terminate most of the contract provisions, it does not affect the validity of the winding-up or liquidation clauses. ①

However, if upon rescission of a contract, an obligation has already been performed, the parties may request restoration or compensation for the losses considering the performance status and the nature of the contract. ② If a contract is rescinded owing to a party's default, the other party may request the breaching party to bear default liability, unless otherwise agreed upon by the parties. The rescission of a principal contract may not affect the validity of a security agreement secondary to the principal contract, therefore a security provider is still obligated to secure the obligor's liability unless otherwise provided in the agreement. ③

§ 4:7   Legal Liability

After a contract is formed, both parties to the contract should fully perform it according to the contract and as required by law. If a party fails to perform the contract or if his performance is not in compliance with the contract requirement, the party will bear default liability of specific performance, taking remedial measures, or paying damages. ④ The civil liability is compensatory in nature and may be provided by law or agreed by the parties.

Traditionally, the Chinese civil law focuses more on the breaching party's liability than the non-breaching party's remedies. Therefore, the civil law provides for the liability of the breaching party (or the tortfeasor if in a tort case) but is silent on the remedies that may be granted to the non-breaching party (or the aggrieved party). Actually, the liability of the breaching party and the remedies to the non-breaching party are the two sides of the same coin.

In addition to the liability arising from breach of contract, a party to a contract may also incur liability for conducting other acts, such as engaging in

---

① Article 567 of the Civil Code.
② Article 566 of the Civil Code.
③ Article 566 of the Civil Code.
④ Article 577 of the Civil Code.

consultation with a malicious intention under the guise of concluding a contract, intentionally concealing material facts or providing false information concerning the conclusion of the contract, or conducting any other act contrary to the principle of good faith. ① A party who discloses or improperly uses the trade secrets or other confidential information that are obtained in the course of concluding a contract, and thus causes losses to the other party, shall also bear liability for compensation. This rule applies even if the contract is not ultimately formed. ②

Sometimes a party breaches a contract due to a third person's reason, the party should still bear default liability to the other party and the dispute between the breaching party and the third person should be resolved in accordance with law or the agreement between them. ③

§4:7:1 Default

To impose default liability on a party to a contract, the aggrieved party must prove that there is a breach of contract, which means that the other party fails to perform the contractual obligation or the performance is defective without a valid defense. Default liability may occur either on an anticipatory breach or on an actual breach of a contract.

§4:7:1:1 Anticipatory Breach

An anticipatory breach occurs when one party to a contract without just cause explicitly expresses or indicates by conduct that he will not perform the contractual obligation when it is due. If it happens, the other party may, prior to the due date of performance, request the first party to bear default liability. ④

Since anticipatory breach occurs before the expiration of the period of performance, the interest it infringes upon is an expectation interest instead of an actual interest. An anticipatory breach may be an express one or an implied one. When one party without just cause explicitly and positively states to the

---

① Article 500 of the Civil Code.
② Article 501 of the Civil Code.
③ Article 593 of the Civil Code.
④ Article 578 of the Civil Code.

other party that he will not perform the contract when the time for performance is due, an express anticipatory breach occurs. The non-performance must relate to the principal obligation under the contract so that the other party's reliance interests are harmed. The aggrieved party may choose to wait until the time for performance is due and then bring a lawsuit against the breaching party for damages, or sue the breaching party immediately requesting the latter to specifically perform the contract, pay damages, pay penalties, or rescind the contract. On the other hand, an implied anticipatory breach refers to a situation where one party implies by conduct that he will not perform the contractual obligation when the time for performance is due, and the other party has sufficient evidence to prove that the first party will not perform the contract.

§ 4:7:1:2 Actual Breach

If a party fails to perform or fully perform the contractual obligations when the time for performance is due, an actual breach occurs. Actual breaches may include different situations. First, non-performance constitutes an actual breach of contract. If a party without just cause refuses to perform the contractual obligation when the time for performance is due, there is an actual breach and the non-breaching party may request the breaching party to specifically perform the contract or pay damages. For example, if a party fails to pay the price, remuneration, rent, or interests, or fails to perform another pecuniary obligation, the other party may request such payment. ①

A delayed performance or a defective performance also constitutes an actual breach of contract. A delayed performance may include a delayed payment by the obligor or a delayed acceptance of the goods by the obligee. Sometimes a party performs a contract but the performance is not in compliance with the requirements of the contract. Such a performance is defective. The breaching party will bear default liability as agreed in the contract. If there is no agreement between the parties on the default liability or the relevant agreement is unclear, the parties may make a supplementary

---

① Article 579 of the Civil Code.

agreement according to Article 510 of the Civil Code; if the parties fail to reach a supplementary agreement, the liability is to be determined according to the relevant clauses of the contract or the course of dealing between the parties. If the liability still cannot be determined, the aggrieved party may request the breaching party to bear liability such as repair, redoing, replacement, return of the subject matter, decrease in price or remuneration according to Article 582 of the Civil Code. Such request must be reasonable, considering the nature of the object of the contract and the degree of the losses.

Partial performance or incomplete performance also constitutes an actual breach of a contract. If a party has only partially performed the contract, the other party must firstly request the breaching party to fully perform the obligation according to the contract by making delivery of the rest of the goods or money, and then ask the breaching party to pay default penalties. If the non-breaching party has suffered loss resulting from the partial performance, the breaching party must pay damages. Generally, partial performance does not grant the non-breaching party a right to rescind the contract unless the partial performance constitutes a material breach of the contract. If partial performance ultimately causes the contract rescinded, any performed part should be returned to the obligor.

If a party fails to perform a non-pecuniary obligation or the performance does not conform to the agreement, the other party may request such performance unless the performance is impossible either *de jure* or *de facto*, the object of the obligation is not suitable for specific performance or the expenses for the performance are excessively high, or the obligee fails to request performance within a reasonable period of time.[①] If the obligation may not be enforced owing to its nature, the non-breaching party may request the breaching party to bear the expenses of a substitute performance by a third person.[②]

Where a party fails to perform a contractual obligation or the performance does not conform to the agreement, and afterwards, if the party has performed

---

[①] Article 580 of the Civil Code.
[②] Article 581 of the Civil Code.

the obligation or has taken remedial measures but the other party still suffers losses, the party should compensate for such loss.① The amount of compensation should be equivalent to the losses caused by the breach of contract, including the benefits expected to be obtained should the contract had been performed, except that it may not exceed such losses that the breaching party foresees or should have foreseen at the time of concluding the contract.②

§ 4:7:1:3 Exemptions

A party's obligation to perform a contract may be exempted by law or upon agreement between the parties. *Force majeure* is the main ground on which a party is exempt from liability arising from non-performance or partial performance of a contract. A *force majeure* is an objective condition that the parties cannot predict, avoid, or overcome. It may be one of the natural disasters, such as earthquake, typhoon, flooding, or tsunami. It may also be one of the government actions, such as the making of new policies, laws, or administrative measures by the government after the contract has been made which may cause the contract to be non-performable. Some social abnormalities, like strike or riot, may also constitute *force majeure*. If a party is unable to perform the contract due to *force majeure*, he will be exempted from liability in whole or in part depending on the impact of the event, unless otherwise provided by law. After a *force majeure* event occurs, the affected party should promptly notify the other party about the reasons why it cannot perform the contract, may delay the performance, or can only partially perform the contract, so that the losses that may be caused to the other party may be mitigated. The affected party should also provide proof of the *force majeure* within a reasonable period of time. However, if a party delays his performance in the first place and then the *force majeure* event occurs, the party's obligation or default liability will not be exempted.③

---

① Article 583 of the Civil Code.
② Article 584 of the Civil Code.
③ Article 590 of the Civil Code.

Case 28

Case 28: Chen v. W Co. & Q Co. ①

Chen purchased an apartment developed by W Co. and obtained the title certificate in July 2009. At the same time, W Co. signed a contract for property management with Q Co. under which Q Co. agreed to provide the preliminary property management for the apartment complex and provide maintenance of the common spaces of the complex. In December 2010, Q Co. signed an agreement with Chen assigning parking lot No. 105 to him to park his car. On June 25, 2011, Chen's car was damaged by the enclosing wall of the residential complex, and he had spent 20,654 yuan for the repair and 720 yuan for assessment of the damage.

Chen sued both W Co. and Q Co. in court, and requested them to bear joint and several liability, and also asked the court to assess the decrease in the car's value, which turned out to be 9,770 yuan.

The court reasons that the property management contract signed between W Co. and Q Co. is lawful and valid, and also applicable to Chen, because as a unit owner of the residential buildings within the residential complex, Chen paid the property management fee, and the property management company provides the relevant property services, so that the two parties have formed a contractual relationship under which the property management enterprise has a duty to protect the owners' personal and property safety. The property management enterprise should timely inspect and remove the potential risks in the common space of the complex; otherwise it shall assume default liability to the owners who have suffered loss. In this case, unless the property management company may prove that it has exercised its duty of maintenance regarding the enclosing wall, and that the fall of the wall was caused by a third-party tortfeasor, the company should bear the liability. However, W Co, as the developer, had performed its obligations under the contract for

---

① (2011) Jiang Ning Min Chu Zi No. 04404, reprinted in the SPC Gazette, Issue 5, 2013.

sale of the apartment unit and therefore should not assume the liability.

Finally, the court holds that Q Co. should compensate Chen 31,114 yuan in total, which covers the repair fee, damage assessment fee, and the decrease in the car's value. The money must be paid within 10 days after the judgment becomes effective.

§ 4:7:2 Remedies

As mentioned previously, remedy and liability are the two sides of the same coin and are corresponding to each other. In this sub-section, the default liability will be discussed from the non-breaching party's perspective.

§ 4:7:2:1 Specific Performance

When a party breaches a contract by failing to perform his contractual obligation other than a pecuniary obligation, the other party may request the breaching party to perform the obligation. This remedy is called specific performance. The non-breaching party is granted the right to decide whether or not to request a specific performance. To request a specific performance, the non-breaching party must prove that the breaching party actually breached the contract and that the non-breaching party has requested the breaching party to specifically perform the contract within a reasonable period of time.

Specific performance will be granted only if the performance is possible and commercially reasonable. If an obligor fails to perform a pecuniary obligation under a contract, the obligee has a right to request the obligor to specifically perform the obligation and the latter may not refuse to do so. However, if the obligation under the contract is a non-pecuniary obligation, specific performance may not be granted if performance is impossible in law or in fact, or if the object of the obligation is not suitable for specific performance, the cost a specific performance is excessively high, or if the obligee fails to request a specific performance within a reasonable period of time. ① For instance, if a contractual obligation is to provide personal service, the law will not grant specific performance because such a remedy actually

---

① Article 580 of the Civil Code.

imposes a restriction on the personal freedom of the obligor, which is in violation of the constitution and the other relevant laws. Likewise, if a contract is based on a fiduciary relationship between the parties, such as in the scenario of an entrustment contract, a trust agreement, or a partnership agreement, under which a party relies on the other party's special skills, expertise, or honesty, it is personal in nature. The law will not require the obligor to specifically perform the contract because it will be against the fundamental nature of the contract concerned.

Specific performance may be applied concurrently with some other remedies such as liquidated damages, compensatory damages, or earnest money forfeited, but not rescission of contract.

§ 4:7:2:2 Compensatory Damages

If a party suffers loss owing to the other party's non-performance or defective performance of a contractual obligation, the breaching party must pay compensatory damages according to the law and based on the contract. The nature of compensatory damages is compensatory and the purpose is to make up the loss suffered by the obligee resulting from the obligor's default. An obligee may suffer both actual loss and loss on expected interests. An expected interest is an interest to be realized and received by a party after the contract has been fully performed. Without performance of the contract, such a future interest will not be realized. Therefore, Article 584 of the Civil Code provides that the amount of compensation shall be equivalent to the losses caused by the breach, including the benefits expected to be obtained should the contract had been performed, except that it may not exceed such losses that the breaching party foresees or should have foreseen at the time of concluding the contract. [1]

While the above foreseeability rule limits the liability of the parties to a scope that is foreseeable and predicted, the mitigation rule requires the non-breaching party to take a timely and reasonable measure to mitigate the damage; otherwise the breaching party is not liable for the enhanced damage. [2] However, any reasonable costs and expenses incurred by the party in

---

[1] Article 584 of the Civil Code.
[2] Article 591 of the Civil Code.

preventing the aggravation of the loss are to be borne by the breaching party.

If an obligor who performs the obligation according to the contract suffers loss owing to the obligee's refusal to accept the performance without just cause, the obligor may request the obligee to compensate for the additional expenses thus incurred. Moreover, the obligor does not need to pay interests for the period of delay in acceptance of his performance by the obligee.① If both parties default, each shall bear the corresponding liability. If one party's default causes losses to the other party, and the other party's fault contributes to such losses, the amount of compensation may be mitigated accordingly.②

§ 4:7:2:3 Liquidated Damages

The parties to a contract may agree on a certain amount of liquidated damages in the contract which will be paid by a party to the other party upon default of the first party. This is called default penalties or liquidated damages. When applying the liquidated damages, the circumstances of the breach will be considered and the parties may agree on the method of calculating the amount of compensation for the losses arising from the breach.③

Compared with compensatory damages, the liquidated damages have some special characteristics. Once a party defaults and causes damage to the other party, the latter will receive compensation based on the agreed liquidated damages without proving the scope of damage actually suffered. However, the court or an arbitration institution may intervene in the application of the liquidated damages and order the parties to increase or decrease the amount of compensation upon request of a party if the amount of liquidated damages is lower or excessively higher than the losses caused.④ The liquidated damages will only be granted after default occurs, and the payment of the liquidated damages is independent from the performance of the contract. Thus, if the parties agree on the liquidated damages for delayed performance, the payment of the liquidated damages by the breaching party does not discharge the parties' obligations under the contract, and therefore, the breaching party should

---

① Article 589 of the Civil Code.
② Article 592 of the Civil Code.
③ Article 585 of the Civil Code.
④ Article 585 of the Civil Code.

continue to perform the obligation after paying the liquidated damages. ①

One of the advantages of liquidated damages is that the amount of the damages is agreed by the parties upon concluding the contract, so the parties both understand in advance the scope of liability upon default and do not need to specifically calculate it after default occurs. In this sense, agreeing on the liquidated damages may avoid the difficulties in calculating and proving the amount of damage, so that cost may be saved and litigation may also be avoided. Moreover, since the liquidated damages may co-exist with the compensatory damages, if the amount of liquidated damages is below the actual damage, the aggrieved party may request compensatory damages to the court or arbitration institution.

§ 4:7:2:4 Earnest Money Forfeiture

The parties to a contract may agree that one party provides earnest money with the other party to secure the performance of its contractual obligations. Such an agreement becomes effective only after the earnest money has been actually delivered. ② If the obligor has performed the obligation, the earnest money becomes part of the payment on the contract or be refunded. However, if the party paying the earnest money fails to perform the obligation or fails to perform it in conformity with the agreement so that the purpose of the contract cannot be achieved, the party has no right to take it back. If, instead, the party receiving the earnest money fails to perform the obligation or fails to perform it in conformity with the agreement so that the purpose of the contract cannot be achieved, the party shall refund twice the amount of the earnest money to the other party. ③ It is called earnest money forfeiture rule.

The parties may agree on the amount of the earnest money; however, it may not exceed 20% of the value of the object of the principal contract, and any excessive amount does not have the effect of the earnest money. Since an agreement on the earnest money is not effective until the money is delivered, if the amount of the earnest money actually delivered is more or less than the

---

① Article 585 of the Civil Code.
② Article 586 of the Civil Code.
③ Article 587 of the Civil Code.

agreed amount, the agreed amount of the earnest money is deemed to have been changed. ①

Sometimes the parties may agree on both liquidated damages and earnest money. In this situation, if a party defaults, the other party may choose to request damages either based on the clause of liquidated damages or based on the earnest money forfeiture rule. Where the amount of the earnest money is insufficient to compensate the losses caused by one party's default, the other party may request compensation for the losses in excess of the amount of the earnest money. ②

§ 4:7:2:5 Remedies on Tort Law

Breach of contract by one party may concurrently breach a mandatory duty imposed by law and infringe upon the other party's personal or proprietary rights and interests. Likewise, a tortious act may also directly cause a party to breach a contract. Under these circumstances, the aggrieved party may elect to request the breaching party to bear liability either for breach of contract or for commission of tort. ③

There are various differences between tort law remedies and contract law remedies. The standard for liability is different. Chinese tort law adopts the standard of fault liability, strict liability, and the principle of balance. In a tort case, a tortfeasor's liability will be mitigated only if the aggrieved party acts intentionally or with gross negligence; however, in a contract case, a breaching party's liability may be mitigated if the aggrieved party commits any negligence. The burden of proof is also different. The aggrieved party in a general tort case has a burden to prove that the tortfeasor was at fault, and in a special tort case, the tortfeasor needs to prove that he was not at fault. However, in a contract case, the aggrieved party only needs to prove that the other party breached the contract and do not need to prove whether the other party was at fault or not. The elements to establish liability are different. In a contract case, a party who has breached the contract without any defense will

---

① Article 586 of the Civil Code.
② Article 588 of the Civil Code.
③ Article 186 of the Civil Code.

bear liability. However, in a tort case, damage is the prerequisite for compensation so a plaintiff must prove that he has suffered damage in order to receive remedies. If there is no damage, there is no tort liability. The liability of a third person is also different. In a contract case, if a contract cannot be performed owing to a third person's fault, the obligor is still liable to the obligee but has a right to contribution against the third person. However, in a tort case, a tortfeasor is only liable for the damage caused by his own fault.

Because of the differences, the selection of the legal basis will greatly affect the remedies the aggrieved party may receive.

Case 29

Case 29: Sun v. Auchan Supermarket[①]

Sun discovered in the Auchan Supermarket Jiangning Branch that some of the sausages' shelf life was approaching. On May 1, 2012, he came back and bought 15 packs of sausages, among which 14 packs have passed their shelf life. The value of the 14 packs was 558.6 yuan. He checked out, and then directly went to the service desk to claim compensation and was refused. Sun sued in court, asking the supermarket to compensate him 10 times the purchase price which was 5,586 yuan.

The supermarket defended that Sun knew the sausages had passed their shelf life and still bought them, so his purpose was not for daily life consumption but for gaining inappropriate benefits, therefore he was not a consumer and not entitled to compensation of 10 times the purchase price.

The first issue the court considers is whether Sun is a consumer. The court reasons that Article 2 of the Law on Protection of the Rights and Interests of Consumers (Consumer Protection Law) provides that the rights and interests of consumers who buy and use commodities or accept services for the needs of daily life consumption are protected by this law. Consumer is a concept opposite to seller and manufacturer. The purpose

---

① See (2012) Jiang Ning Kai Min Chu Zi No. 646, reprinted in the SPC's Guiding Cases No. 23.

of a consumer's purchase of a commodity or a service should be for the needs of daily life consumption. In this case, the supermarket has not presented any evidence showing that Sun's purchase of the commodity was for manufacture or sale, and that Sun claimed compensation based on the fact that the food he bought had passed the sell-by date. Sun was exercising his lawful rights and the supermarket's argument that Sun was not a consumer is untenable.

The second issue the court considers is whether the supermarket knowingly sold substandard food. Article 3 of the Food Safety Law provides that the manufacturers and operators of food shall engage in the manufacture and operation in accordance with laws, administrative regulations, and food safety standards, and shall be responsible for the society and public, ensure food safety, accept public supervision, and assume social responsibilities. Article 28 (8) of the same law provides that the food passing the sell-by date is prohibited from manufacturing or selling. The seller of food has a legal duty to guarantee the food safety, and shall timely check the substandard food and take them off the shelf. The supermarket's selling of the sausages passing the sell-by date breached its legal duty, and should be regarded as knowingly selling substandard food.

The third issue the court considers is how the supermarket should assume the liability. Article 96 of the Food Safety Law provides that those who cause personal injury, property damage, or other harms in violation of this law shall assume liability for compensation. For those manufacturing or knowingly selling substandard food, in addition to compensation for the loss, the consumer may also request the manufacturer or the seller to pay compensation 10 times the purchasing price the consumer has paid. In this case, Sun's request for the 10-times compensation, and it should be supported by the court. The supermarket argues that Sun's purchase was for the purpose of gaining inappropriate benefit; however, since the law provides that the plaintiff has the right to obtain the 10-time compensation, the benefit thus obtained by the plaintiff is a benefit protected by law, and the law does not impose any restriction on the subjective motive of the consumer. Therefore, the supermarket's argument has not been supported.

Finally, the court holds that the supermarket must compensate Sun 5,586 within 10 days after the judgment becomes effective.

§ 4:8 Quasi-Contracts

The above sections of this Chapter discuss about the contracts as provided in the Civil Code. This section will analyze two special situations: *negotiorum gestio* and unjust enrichment. They are actually about quasi-contracts since they do not involve any contractual relationship. However, the rules regarding these two situations are included in Part Three of Book Three (Contracts).

§ 4:8:1 Negotiorum Gestio

Negotiorum gestio refers to a situation whereby a person who has neither a statutory nor a contractual obligation voluntarily acts as a custodian to manage another person's affairs in order to prevent the latter person from suffering a loss of interests. The first person who serves as a custodian is an obligee and the latter person is a beneficiary and also an obligor. Article 979 of the Civil Code provides that in this situation, the custodian may request the beneficiary to reimburse the necessary expenses thus incurred. If the custodian suffers losses when managing the beneficiary's affairs, he may request the beneficiary to make appropriate compensation, unless the management of the beneficiary's affairs is contrary to the true will of the beneficiary. However, the true will of the beneficiary must not be in violation of law or against the public order or good morals. ①

A person who voluntarily manages another person's affairs must promptly notify the beneficiary whenever possible. If a matter does not need urgent management, the custodian must wait for the beneficiary's instruction. ② Once a person starts to voluntarily serve as a custodian of another person's affairs, he must act in the best interests of the beneficiary and may not suspend his

---

① Article 979 of the Civil Code.
② Article 982 of the Civil Code.

management without just cause unless the suspension is not detrimental to the beneficiary.① Upon completion of the management, the custodian must report to the beneficiary about the management of the affairs and deliver the property obtained by him during the management of the affairs to the beneficiary.②

It is to be noted that these rules only apply when a person voluntarily manages another's affairs without the latter person's consent. Once the beneficiary ratifies the management by the custodian, the quasi-contract relationship immediately turns to a contractual relationship and the rules regulating entrustment contracts will be applied to it from the beginning of the management, unless the custodian expressly objects to it.③ The purpose of recognition of *negotiorum gestio* is to encourage people to render help and assistance to each other whenever necessary without worrying about the reasonable expenses or costs to be incurred.

§ 4:8:2 Unjust Enrichment

The other quasi-contract relationship provided in the Civil Code arises from unjust enrichment in which a person is unjustly enriched without a legal basis while another person suffers losses. The latter person has a right to request the enriched person to return the benefit. This rule does not apply when the benefit received by the enriched person is actually for performing a moral obligation by the conferor of the benefit, or the payment is made to satisfy an obligation owed by the payor which is not yet due. If a payment is made to discharge an obligation by the person knowing that he does not have any obligation to pay, the unjust enrichment rule is not applicable either.④

While the knowledge of the conferor of the benefit will make the unjust enrichment rule inapplicable, the lack of knowledge of the enriched person may lead to the same result. Article 986 of the Civil Code provides that where a person enriched does not know or should not have known that the enrichment is without a legal basis, and if the enrichment no longer exists, the person has no obligation to return the benefit thus received. In other words, if an enriched

---

① Article 981 of the Civil Code.
② Article 983 of the Civil Code.
③ Article 984 of the Civil Code.
④ Article 985 of the Civil Code.

person has knowledge, no matter actual or constructive, that the enrichment is without a legal basis, the conferor of the benefit may request the enriched person to return the benefit and compensate for any loss thus suffered. ① If the enriched person has gratuitously transferred the benefit to a third person, the conferor of the benefit may request the third person to return the benefit. ②

---

① Article 987 of the Civil Code.
② Article 988 of the Civil Code.

Chapter 5
Tort Law

§ 5:1 General Introduction

Torts are civil wrongs that infringe upon other's civil-law rights and interests, *i.e.*, personal or proprietary rights and interests, through an action or non-action of a person in violation of law.① The person who conducts the wrongful act is called an actor or a tortfeasor and should bear liability of compensation for the damage thus caused. The person whose rights or interests have been infringed upon is sometimes called an aggrieved party, an infringed person, a damaged person, or a victim. In a tort litigation, the plaintiff is the infringed person and the defendant normally is the tortfeasor. In a number of special situations, the defendant may be a person other than the tortfeasor but one having a special relationship with the tortfeasor.

In order to establish tort liability, a plaintiff must prove that the act done by the defendant is in violation of law and the damage thus suffered by the plaintiff is caused by the tortfeasor, except that in some special situations, a tort may be committed even the actor does not have any fault. In other words, an actor who through his fault infringes upon another person's civil-law rights and interests commits a tort and should bear liability. However, sometimes the burden of proving fault is shifted to the defendant if the law presumes that an actor has fault under a certain circumstance. In this situation, the actor who is unable to prove that he is not at fault should bear tort liability to the aggrieved

---

① Article 1164 of the Civil Code.

party.① Sometimes the law provides that whether an actor has fault or not is immaterial. In this situation, an actor will bear tort liability as long as he harms the civil-law rights and interests of another person, disregarding whether or not he is at fault.②

The tortious act must be an objective act which may be done through an action or non-action of the defendant in violation of his duty as provided by law. When a tort is established, the main form of liability to be assumed by the tortfeasor is monetary damages. If a tortious act endangers another person's personal or property safety, the infringed person also has a right to request the tortfeasor to bear tort liability such as cessation of the infringement, removal of the nuisance, or elimination of the danger.③

The provisions of the Chinese Constitution regarding the property ownership system and the provisions on protection of personal and proprietary rights of citizens are the sources of Chinese tort law. Before the Civil Code, the GPCL of 1986 had been the most important source of Chinese tort law even after the Tort Liability Law was enacted in 2009. Now Book Seven of the Civil Code has become the most important source. In addition, some other laws promulgated by the NPC that regulate the various aspects of tort liability, such as the State Compensation Law④ are also part of the legal framework of the Chinese tort law.

§5:1:1 Basis for Finding Tort Liability

The bases for finding tort liability include fault, rebuttable presumption of fault, non-fault, and fairness.

Fault liability is the basic liability recognized by the Chinese tort law. Generally, in order to receive remedies, a plaintiff must prove that (1) the defendant has performed an act that violated the law; (2) the plaintiff has suffered damage owing to the defendant's act; (3) there is a causal link between the defendant's act and the plaintiff's damage; and (4) the defendant

---

① Article 1165 of the Civil Code.
② Article 1166 of the Civil Code.
③ Article 1167 of the Civil Code.
④ The State Compensation Law was promulgated by the NPC on May 12, 1994, amended on April 29, 2010.

must have the required subjective intent, *i.e.*, the fault, when performing the act. Apparently, fault is a necessary element to prove this type of tort liability. ①

Liability of rebuttable presumption of fault is similar to the fault liability except that the fault of the defendant is presumed by law unless rebutted by the defendant. Therefore, the burden of proof of the defendant's fault is shifted from the plaintiff to the defendant. ② For example, if a building, structure, or another type of facility, or any object laid or hanged thereon, comes loose or falls down and thus causes damage to another person, the owner, manager, or user is presumed by law to be at fault unless they can disprove their fault. ③

Non-fault liability is also called strict liability, which does not require the plaintiff to prove any fault of the defendant in order to establish the latter's tort liability. This principle applies only when the law expressly providing that a tortfeasor's liability will be determined solely on the damage caused, and the fault, in this situation, is presumed by law. This liability rule mainly applies to a tort caused by an ultrahazardous activity, an environmental pollution, a defective product, or an animal. The plaintiff only needs to prove three elements: the act of the defendant in violation of law, the damage suffered by the plaintiff, and the causation between the two. The legal basis for this liability is stated in Article 1166 of the Civil Code:

> Where an actor harms the civil-law rights and interests of another person, if the law provides that tort liability shall be borne by such an actor disregarding whether or not the actor is at fault, such provisions shall be followed.

Therefore, a person who infringes upon other's civil-law rights or interests in this situation must bear tort liability regardless of whether the person was at fault or not if the law so provides.

When damage is caused but neither the victim nor the actor was at fault for

---

① Article 1165 of the Civil Code.
② Article 1165 of the Civil Code.
③ Article 1253 of the Civil Code.

the occurrence of the damage, the court sometimes will consider the financial and other situations of the parties to split the liability between them in order to achieve justice.① This is sometimes called the "fair liability" doctrine. Basically, if none of the parties is at fault in causing the damage, they may share the losses according to the actual circumstances. This "fair liability" seems to be more like a liability based on the balance of the parties' situations and has thus invited many discussions and debates among the legal scholars. However, under certain circumstances, the fair liability doctrine indeed reflects equity. For example, where a person suffers damage when he tries to prevent or stop a tortfeasor from infringing upon another person's civil-law rights or interests, if the tortfeasor escapes or is unable to bear liability, the beneficiary, who does not have any fault, should appropriately compensate the infringed person under the fair liability doctrine.② Case 16 (Li & Gong v. May Flowers Co.) reprinted in §2:8:1 of this Book illustrates the applicability of this doctrine in real life, so a re-visit to this case may be helpful to further understand this rule.

§5:1:2 Joint Liability

Sometimes liability may be imposed jointly on two or more persons. The situations include when two or more persons jointly commit a tortious act which causes damage to another person. When it happens, the tort law imposes joint and several liability on all tortfeasors,③ which means that the infringed person may either sue all of the tortfeasors or elect to sue one or more of them for damages.④ This is a scheme to protect the interests of the infringed person and make it much easier for the plaintiff to elect to sue the defendant with the deepest pocket to compensate for his loss. If a person aids or abets an actor in commission of a tortious act, he will also assume joint and several liability with the actor. However, if the actor is a person with no or limited capacity for performing civil juristic acts, the guardian of the actor will only assume

---

① Article 1186 of the Civil Code.
② Article 183 of the Civil Code.
③ Article 1168 of the Civil Code.
④ Article 178 of the Civil Code.

corresponding liability to the extent that he fails to fulfill the duties of guardian.①

The Civil Code has specified other situations when a joint liability may be imposed. Where two or more persons' multiple acts endanger another person's personal or property safety but the damage is caused only by the acts of one or several of them, if the specific tortfeasor or tortfeasors can be identified, the tortfeasor(s) will be liable; if the specific tortfeasor(s) cannot be identified, all of the actors are jointly and severally liable.② On the other hand, where the tortious acts separately committed by two or more persons cause the same damage to another person, the actors are jointly and severally liable if each act is sufficient to independently cause the entire damage.③

When determining the amount of compensation of each joint tortfeasor, the court may consider various factors. For example, the court will determine the amount of compensation owed by each tortfeasor who bears joint and several liability in proportion to their respective share of fault; if such share of fault cannot be determined, they are liable in equal share.④ The joint tortfeasor who has paid more than his share has a right to contribution against the other joint tortfeasors. The liability of a tortfeasor may be mitigated if the infringed person is also at fault for the occurrence or aggravation of the damage to himself,⑤ and if the damage is intentionally caused by the infringed person, the actor may be exempted from any liability.⑥ Sometimes a person may voluntarily participate in a recreational or sports activity with certain inherent risks and thus suffers damage due to another participant's act; in this case, the doctrine of assumption of risks applies and he may not request the other participant to bear tort liability unless the damage is caused by the latter's intentional act or gross negligence.⑦

---

① Article 1169 of the Civil Code.
② Article 1170 of the Civil Code.
③ Article 1171 of the Civil Code.
④ Article 178 of the Civil Code.
⑤ Article 1173 of the Civil Code.
⑥ Article 1175 of the Civil Code.
⑦ Article 1176 of the Civil Code.

§ 5:2 Legal Elements

A plaintiff must prove various elements in order to establish that the defendant has committed a tort. As mentioned above, he must prove that the defendant has performed an illegal act, he has suffered damage, and there is a causal link between the defendant's act and his damage. In addition, the plaintiff may also need to prove that there exists a fault on the part of the defendant unless the law provides otherwise.

An illegal act is an action or non-action done by a natural or legal person in violation of law. It occurs when an actor does something he is legally prohibited from doing, or fails to do something he is legally obligated to do. The action or non-action either violates a legal duty or a law that protects other's rights and interests, or is against the public interest. Damage is an objective fact that the personal rights, proprietary rights, or other rights and interests of the plaintiff have been infringed upon by the defendant's act, and it may include property damage and/or personal injury. ① Property damage may include a conversion of the property and damage to the property while personal injury may include infringement upon the interests of one's personality and identity. The element of causation requires that the illegal act done by the actor is the cause of the damage suffered by the infringed person, and the damage is the result of the illegal act. Without proving the causation, the infringed person cannot establish tort liability against the actor.

The last element for establishing tort liability is that there exists a fault on the part of the actor. Since Chinese tort law recognizes different bases for tort liability, such as fault, rebuttable presumption of fault, non-fault, and fairness, fault is not necessarily one of the required elements for all torts. Some torts require the plaintiff to prove that the defendant acts with fault while the others do not. If fault is required to establish a tort, either the actor's intent or negligence may be sufficient. If an actor could foresee the consequence of an act but still desires it to happen or disregards of its happening, then intent is established. Negligence may include want of care and reckless disregard of the consequence. If an actor could foresee or should have foreseen the adverse

---

① Article 1167 of the Civil Code.

consequence of his act but have not foreseen it, want of care is established; nevertheless, if an actor has foreseen the consequence of the act but believes that it could be avoided, then reckless disregard is established. In either case negligence is established and the duty of care has been breached by the actor.

Case 30

Case 30: Zhao v. W Co. & Z Co.[1]

Zhao and W Co. signed a contract for purchasing Rooms 3407 and 3507 inside W Building B-Wing in December 2009 and Zhao paid the purchase price. On Feb. 3, 2011, W Building had a fire and burned off Zhao's property inside the said apartments. After investigation, the fire was caused by Li, a guest living in W Building A-Wing (which was a hotel). Li was setting off fireworks and the fireworks fell on the platform near Room 1109 of Building B-Wing, which ignited the plastic lawn on the platform. In order to preserve heat, W Building used flammable materials such as plastic extruded boards. The fire burned the insulation materials decorating the external surface of the wall, which in turn made the fire spread rapidly.

After the fire, the relevant institution inspected W Building's materials to conclude that two of the decoration materials were not up to the standard. The Heping District Court of Shenyang City made a criminal judgement holding that the fire was caused by Li's negligence and in turn caused severe damage to public and private property. Li's act constituted a crime of negligently causing a fire, and Li was sentenced to 3 years' imprisonment. The criminal judgment had become effective.

In this litigation, W Co. defended that upon the occurrence of the fire, the disputed apartments had been delivered to Zhao, and thus the risks of damage or destruction of the apartments had also been transferred to Zhao, so that Zhao should assume the liability for property damage by herself. It also defended that its firefighting facilities had passed the inspection and it did not have any fault, therefore, it should not assume

---

[1] See (2018) Zui Gao Fa Min Zai No. 206, reprinted in the SPC Gazette, Issue 5, 2019.

any liability for Zhao's property damage.

The first instance court dismissed Zhao's claims and held that Zhao should pay the litigation cost of 79,400 yuan. Zhao appealed for reversal of the judgment. The second instance court affirmed the judgment, and held that Zhao should pay the cost for appeal of 81,696 yuan.

The case was then re-opened by the SPC. The SPC firstly holds that W Co. was at fault regarding the occurrence of the fire because the evidence showed that the unqualified plastic lawn was one of the causes for the fire. It was the Chinese Lunar New Year's Eve when the fire occurred and W Co. should have foreseen that the residents nearby would fire fireworks during the New Year's Eve, and that based on the general common sense, it is foreseeable that the plastic lawn is flammable which may cause fire. However, W Co. failed to adopt any preventive measure so that the fire occurred. W Co. had subjective false for the occurrence of the fire.

Second, W Co. was at fault for the spreading of the fire. Fire safety is part of the social public interest concerning the citizens' personal and property safety, and ensuring the fire safety of buildings is the legal duty of the construction company. Evidence shows that the insulation materials used in the exterior wall of the disputed building did not conform to the State's mandatory standard. However, W Co. failed to adopt any reasonable or appropriate remedial measures to eliminate the potential danger. W Co. failed to perform its duty of care and apparently was at fault.

In addition, regarding the contract for sale of the apartments between W Co. and Zhao, W Co. as the developer and seller, had a duty to deliver qualified apartments to the buyer. Considering the special nature of the residential apartments, a buyer generally does not have the expertise in inspecting whether the apartments purchased are in compliance with fire safety rules, or which of the construction materials are flammable, whether there is any potential fire safety problem, *etc*. Therefore, the general rules requiring a buyer to timely inspect the quality of delivered goods are not applicable to a contract for sale of real property. Furthermore, based on the contract between Zhao and W Co., the right to use the exterior part of the wall of the building belongs to W Co.. W Co., as the user of the exterior wall of the building, had a duty to manage and maintain the exterior wall of the building. Zhao as a purchaser of the apartments, when using the purchased real estate in a normal way, did not have any fault. However, her property was damaged by the fire caused owing to W Co.'s fault in inappropriately installing flammable materials, and thus there was a causal link between W's fault and Zhao's loss. Accordingly, W Co. is responsible for damages, and its liability should not be exempted by reasons that W Co. had received the certificate of inspection, its fire facilities had been approved, or for other reasons.

Based on the above reasons, the SPC holds that W Co. as the constructor, developer, and user of the exterior wall of the building, should be the holder of liability. However, it delivered the apartments to Zhao before it had performed its duty of care in fire safety, and before it adopted any remedial measure to eliminate the potential danger in fire safety. It apparently was at fault.

The SPC also analyzes that the property management company Z Co. responsible for the building is also liable based on the property management contract signed between it and the unit owners. In this case, Z Co. has failed to perform its duty of care. It knew that the insulation materials in the exterior wall were inflammable but failed to perform its duty. In addition, Z Co. had the ability to control the dangerous activities such as firing fireworks. The location that Li fired the fireworks was within the area that Z Co.'s employees could easily see; however, Z Co. failed to find Li's act and did not adopt any appropriate measure to find the fire or prevent the disaster.

Comparatively, Zhao was at no fault for the occurrence of the fire. The lower courts held that W Co. and Z Co. were not liable for tort, which lead to a decision that the victim without any fault should assume the property damage caused by other's negligence, such a decision is against the fault-based tort law principle and should be corrected.

When analyzing the allocation of the liability, the SPC analyzes that the fire in this case was caused by multiple causes and the main cause of the fire was Li's act which constituted a crime. The tortious act and the causes were successive but not overlapping. Although each party involved had gross negligence, none of them intentionally expected the consequence to happen. W Co.'s fault could not lead to the entire damage suffered by Zhao, and therefore it should not bear primary liability. Although Z Co. failed to perform its duty and had fault, its act did not directly cause the fire either. Therefore, W Co. should assume compensatory liability in the first place, whereas Z Co. should assume the corresponding supplementary liability to the extent that it should have foreseen and that it should have been able to prevented the consequences.

In sum, the SPC holds that the two tortfeasors in this case had neither a common intention nor a common negligence regarding the occurrence of the fire, but the multiple acts of the parties at different periods closely connected with each other and ultimately caused the occurrence of the fire, which caused Zhao's damage. According to Article 12 of the Tort Liability Law, where a same damage is caused by tortious acts independently conducted by two or more persons, if the proportion of each person's liability can be determined, each person shall assume the corresponding liability. The SPC holds that W Co. shall assume 40% of the loss suffered by Zhao, and Z Co. shall be liable for supplementary compensations of no more than 30% of Zhao's loss.

Finally, the SPC calculates the amount of damage suffered by Zhao, and holds that the two defendants should compensate Zhao according to their proportion of their liability. Regarding the first instance litigation fee of 79,400 yuan, W Co. should pay 45,000 yuan, Z Co. should pay 29,000 yuan, and Zhao should assume 5,400 yuan. Regarding the second instance litigation fee of 81,696 yuan, W Co. should pay 45,000 yuan, Z Co. should pay 31,000 yuan, and Zhao should assume 5,696 yuan.

§ 5:3 Categorization of Torts

The rights and interests protected by the Civil Code include the personal rights and proprietary rights. The first group of rights include the right to life, the right to health, the right to name, the right to reputation, the right to honor, the right to likeness, the right to privacy, the right to marital autonomy, the right to guardianship, *etc.* and the second group of rights include the ownership right, the right to usufruct, the secured interests, intellectual property rights, the right to succession, *etc*. Accordingly, torts are categorized into different groups based on the rights and interests that may have been infringed upon by a tortfeasor.

§5:3:1 General Torts

§5:3:1:1 Torts on Other's Person

A natural person's personal liberty is protected by law① and a person who harms other's person with intent or by negligence must bear civil liability. A person's personal liberty is reflected in various rights.

A natural person enjoys the right to life, and his life safety and dignity are protected by law and free from infringement by any organization or individual.② If a person intentionally deprives another person of his life, a crime is constituted and the person will be prosecuted. Meanwhile, the accused person may also be liable for compensation in a civil suit collateral to the criminal proceeding. If a person negligently deprives another person of his life, he should also bear tort liability. If the person who infringes upon another person's right to life is a minor or has mental deficiency, the guardian or legal representative of the tortfeasor shall assume tort liability. The main remedy for tort is monetary compensation, covering both pecuniary and non-pecuniary damage. The close relatives, *i.e.*, the next-of-kin, of the victim have a standing to sue for compensation.

A natural person enjoys the right to corporeal integrity and personal freedom.③ Such right includes both a right to freedom of physical body and a right to freedom of will, which entitles a natural person to act and think according to his own will and interests, and to be free from any confinement, control, or obstruction. When a person, through an intentional act or by negligence, offends another person's physical body, harms the integrity of the latter's body parts, illegally confines or controls another's person or free will,

---

① Article 109 of the Civil Code.
② Article 1002 of the Civil Code.
③ Article 1003 of the Civil Code.

or illegally searched another's body, he commits a tort infringing another's right to corporeal integrity or another's right to personal freedom.① The infringed person may request the tortfeasor to extend apology, stop infringement, and pay compensation. The plaintiff also has a right to request compensation for his mental distress, *i.e.*, pains and suffering. For example, a supermarket infringed upon two girls' right to corporeal integrity and personal freedom when three of its employees searched them without legal cause. The case (Case 7) was reprinted in § 2:3:2:1 of this Book.

A natural person enjoys the right to health, and his physical and mental health are both protected by law and free from infringement by any organization or individual.② When a person, through an intentional act or by negligence, harms another's health, he commits a tort and must bear liability. If the infringed person suffers some special harms like being disabled and thus losing his work ability, compensation should be made accordingly. The personal interests of a fetus are also protected by law and a person who has infringed upon the interests of a fetus must bear tort liability. The personal interests of a fetus may be harmed either directly or indirectly by a tortfeasor. A direct infringement occurs if a person's act directly harms the health of a fetus, whereas an indirect infringement occurs if a person's act harms the health of a pregnant woman so that the health of the fetus is harmed as a result. When such an infringement occurs, once the actor's fault is established, he is liable for compensating the infringed person for both the pecuniary and non-pecuniary loss.

§ 5:3:1:2 Torts on Other's Dignitary Interests

A person's dignity is also protected by law,③ and an actor may commit a tort on another person's dignitary interests if he infringes upon another person's general and dignitary rights to personality and the interests attached hereto. A plaintiff must prove that the defendant is at fault in order to hold the latter liable for infringing upon another person's dignitary interests. The basic

---

① Article 1011 of the Civil Code.
② Article 1004 of the Civil Code.
③ Article 109 of the Civil Code.

remedies include compensation for non-pecuniary damage as well as the other types of remedies such as cessation of infringement, extending apology, removal of adverse effect and restoration of reputation. Property damage, if any, should also be compensated.

A person's dignitary interests are expressed in various forms.

A natural person enjoys the right to name and is entitled to determine, use, change, or allow others to use his name in accordance with law, provided that public order and good morals are not offended. ① Similarly, a legal person or an unincorporated organization enjoys the right to entity name and is entitled to decide, use, change, transfer, or allow others to use its entity name in accordance with law. ② If a person appropriates, impersonates, counterfeits, interferes, or illegally uses another person's name or entity name, the said person commits a tort. ③ A pseudonym, stage name, translated name, trade name, abbreviation of a name or entity name of a social popularity are also protected by law and free from infringement. ④ Case 31 briefed and reprinted below is about a case involving infringement of a person's right to name.

A natural person enjoys the right to likeness and is entitled to make, use, publicize, or authorize others to use his image in accordance with law. ⑤ No organization or individual may infringe upon other's rights to likeness by vilifying or defacing the image of a person, or through other ways such as falsifying other's image by utilizing information technology. Unless otherwise provided by law, no one may make, use, or publicize the image of the right holder without his consent. ⑥ A person who has done any of the above acts commits a tort. If a tortfeasor has received profits out of the using of another's likeness, the profits should be disgorged and the infringed person has a right to receive compensation to the extent of the profit received by the tortfeasor. Case 31 reprinted below also illustrates this situation.

A person of the civil law enjoys the right to reputation, and any

---

① Article 1012 of the Civil Code.
② Article 1013 of the Civil Code.
③ Article 1014 of the Civil Code.
④ Article 1017 of the Civil Code.
⑤ Article 1018 of the Civil Code.
⑥ Article 1019 of the Civil Code.

organization or individual who infringes upon other's right to reputation by insultation or defamation should bear tort liability. ① In order to establish such a tort liability, the infringed person must prove that the defendant has made an untrue statement or performed an act which was defamatory or insulting in nature, the statement or act was publicized to a third person, and the defendant had fault (either with an intent or by negligence). Where a literary or artistic work published by an actor depicts real people and real events or a specific person, with insulting or defamatory content and thus infringes upon another person's right to reputation, the person whose right is infringed upon has a right to request the actor to bear civil liability. If the said work does not depict a specific person, but only some patterns of the story are similar to the situation of such person, the actor has no liability. ② Once liability is established, the infringed person may get remedies including cessation of infringement, restoration of the reputation, removal of the adverse effect, extending apology, and making compensation. For instance, if a person has evidence to prove that the content reported by a media, such as a newspaper, a periodical, or an online website, is inaccurate and thus infringes upon his reputation, he has a right to request the media to take necessary measures including making correction of or deleting the content in a timely manner. ③ Case 33 reprinted below involves a Taobao shop that alleged that its reputation was harmed by a consumer's negative comments but which allegation was not supported by the court.

As a rule of exception, a person whose act adversely affects another person's reputation when reporting news or supervising public opinions for public interest purposes does not bear civil liability unless he has fabricated or distorted the facts, he has failed to fulfill the obligation to reasonably verify the seriously misrepresentative information provided by others, or he has used insulting words, *etc.*, to degrade the other's reputation. ④ When determining whether an actor has failed to fulfill the obligation to reasonably verify the seriously misrepresentative information provided by others, the factors to be considered include the credibility of the source of the information, whether the

---

① Article 1024 of the Civil Code.
② Article 1027 of the Civil Code.
③ Article 1028 of the Civil Code.
④ Article 1025 of the Civil Code.

information that is clearly controversial has been fully investigated, the timeliness of the information, the relevance of the information with public order and good morals, the likelihood that the infringed person's reputation would be degraded, and his ability to verify and the cost for the verification of the information. ①

A person of the civil law has a right to credit standing regarding his financial ability and the reliability evaluated by the society, and may check his own credit report and raise an objection, request that correction, deletion, or other necessary measures be taken where he discovers that the credit report is incorrect. If a person defames, makes a misleading statement on, or imposes undue influence on the financial ability, the ability and attitude to perform a contract, product quality, operational situation, or sales performance, *etc.* of another person, so that the financial ability and situation of the latter person is adversely affected so that proprietary losses have been caused, the person commits a tort and should bear liability.

A person of the civil law enjoys the right to honor and no one may unlawfully deprive him of his honorary titles or defame or degrade his honor. ② If a person illegally deprives of, harms, or stains another person's honor, or detains or trespasses on the property as part of the other person's honor, he commits a tort and should bear tort liability.

A natural person enjoys the right to privacy, and no organization or individual may infringe upon the other's right to privacy by prying into, intruding upon, disclosing, or publicizing other's private matters. ③ Subjective fault of the actor must be found in order to establish such a tort liability against him. A person commits a tort of infringing upon another person's right to privacy if he does any of the following acts:

> (1) intruding upon another person's private life through making phone calls, sending text messages, using instant messaging tools, sending emails and flyers, and the like means;
>
> (2) entering into, taking photographs of, or peeping into other's private

---

① Article 1026 of the Civil Code.
② Article 1031 of the Civil Code.
③ Article 1032 of the Civil Code.

spaces such as the residence or hotel room of another person;

(3) taking photographs of, peeping into, eavesdropping, or disclosing the private activities of another person;

(4) taking photographs of or peeping at the private parts of another person's body;

(5) processing another person's private information; or

(6) infringing upon another person's privacy through other means. ①

Recently, a live-streaming platform broadcasted a gynecological surgery by a physician triggers heated discussions on the internet. The physician was later on arrested for further investigation of criminal liability. It would also be a good civil law exam question to think about whether the patient's right to privacy was infringed upon by the physician's act, and if so, who would bear the liability.

A natural person enjoys the right to decide his own sexual life. If a person forces another person to have sexual activity against the latter's will and causes harm thereto, such as raping, practicing sodomy, molestation, or sexually harassing another person, he commits a crime or a tort. The Civil Code especially provides that a person who has been sexually harassed against his will by another person through oral words, written languages, images, physical acts, or the like has the right to request the actor to bear civil liability. The law also imposes obligations on the State organs, enterprises, schools, and other organizations to take reasonable precautions, accept and hear complaints, investigate and handle cases, and take other like measures to prevent and stop sexual harassment conducted by a person through taking advantage of his position and power or a superior-subordinate relationship. ②

A natural person's personal information is protected by law and any person may retrieve or make copies of his personal information from the information processors in accordance with law. ③ Any organization or individual that needs to access other's personal information may only do so in accordance with law and by guaranteeing the safety of such information, and may not illegally

---

① Article 1033 of the Civil Code.
② Article 1010 of the Civil Code.
③ Article 1034 & 1037 of the Civil Code.

collect, use, process, or transmit other's personal information, or illegally trade, provide, or publicize such information. ① Article 1034 of the Civil Code defines personal information as the information recorded electronically or in other ways that can be used, by itself or in combination with other information, to identify a natural person, including his name, date of birth, identification number, biometric information, residential address, telephone number, email address, health information, or whereabouts. The collection, storage, use, process, transmission, provision, disclosure of another person's personal information must follow the principles of lawfulness, justification, and within a necessary limit, and may not be excessive. Meanwhile, the following conditions must be satisfied:

(1) consent has been obtained from the natural person or his guardian, unless otherwise provided by laws or administrative regulations;
(2) the rules for processing information are publicized;
(3) the purpose, method, and scope of the information processing are clearly indicated; and
(4) it is not in violation of laws or administrative regulations or in breach of the agreement between both parties. ②

A person who discovers that his personal information processed by another person is incorrect, he has a right to raise an objection and request corrections or other necessary measures to be taken in a timely manner. If he finds that an information processor has violated the provisions of law or breached an agreement while processing his personal information, he has a right to request the information processor to delete it in a timely manner and assume civil liability. ③

A person who processes another person's personal information does not bear civil liability if (1) he reasonably performs the act to the extent that the natural person or his guardian consents to, (2) he reasonably processes the

---

① Article 111 of the Civil Code.
② Article 1035 of the Civil Code.
③ Article 1037 of the Civil Code.

information disclosed by the person himself or the other information that has already been legally disclosed, unless the said person explicitly refuses or the processing of the information infringes upon a significant interest of the person, or (3) he reasonably performs the other acts to protect the public interest or the lawful rights and interests of the person. [1]

The Civil Code also protects a deceased person's name, likeness, reputation, honor, privacy, remains, or the like. If a person intentionally or negligently infringes upon the name, likeness, reputation, honor, privacy, remains or bone ashes, or the funeral of a deceased person, he commits a tort. Such a tort infringes upon both the decedent's right in personality and his next-of-kin's right, so the spouse, children, and parents of the deceased person have the right to request the actor to bear civil liability. The other close relatives of the deceased person have a right to request the actor to bear civil liability if the deceased person has no spouse or children, and his parents have also died. [2] If tort liability is established, the remedies may include cessation of infringement, extending apology, and paying compensation. Case 32 reprinted below involves such a case. The defendant wrote several articles trying to allege that the story of the Five Heroes in Langya Mountain was untrue. A descendant of one of the Five Heroes sued on the ground that the articles concerned defamed and infringed upon the Five Heroes' reputation, and requested the defendant to stop infringement, extend apologies, and eliminate the adverse effect.

Case 31

Case 31: Stephen Chow v. Z Co. [3]

Z Co., a company selling construction materials, used the name and picture of Stephen Chow (Chow), a famous movie star, in its commercial advertisement without authorization. The ad was posted in Z Co.'s official website and some other websites with words indicating Chow's identity. Chow sent an attorney's letter to Z Co. in January 2017

---

[1] Article 1036 of the Civil Code.
[2] Article 954 of the Civil Code.
[3] See (2017) Hu 01 Min Chu No. 1211, reprinted in the SPC Gazette, Issue 2, 2020.

requesting it to stop infringement, restore his reputation, eliminate the adverse effect, and extend apology. In September 2017, Chow's friend found a similar ad in a magazine with a more detailed introduction to Chow. Chow sued in court requesting Z Co. to (1) immediately stop using his name and picture in the websites and the magazine, (2) make compensation of 31,125,001 yuan, including, among others, 30,000,000 yuan for proprietary damage and 1 yuan for pains and suffering, and (3) post an apology on the relevant websites, and in the magazine and a national newspaper for its infringement of his right to name and right to likeness continuously for 90 days. When requesting damages, Chow suggested that the amount of compensation be determined based on his remuneration received for advertising the Coco Cola products.

Shanghai No. 1 Intermediate People's Court finds the above facts, and determines that the Law on Application of Laws on Civil Juristic Relations with Foreign Elements should be applied since Chow is a resident of Hong Kong Special Administration Region. Since the parties did not have a disagreement regarding the governing law, the court determines that the parties have agreed that the Law of the PRC should be the governing law. Then the court focuses on two issues: whether Z Co. infringes upon Chow's right to likeness and right to name, and if so, what tort liability should Z Co. assume?

Regarding the first issue, Article 100 of the GPCL provides that citizens enjoy the right to likeness, and no one may use another person's likeness without authorization for purposes of making profits. Article 141 of the SPC's Opinion on Certain issues on Implementation of the GPCL further provides the detailed rules. Based on these provisions, Z Co.'s acts have infringed Chow's right to likeness.

Regarding the second issue, Article 2 of the Tort Liability Law provides that a person who infringes upon other's civil-law rights and interests shall assume tort liability in accordance with the Tort Liability Law, and that civil-law rights and interests include a person's right to name and right to likeness. Article 15 also provides the forms of tort liability that a tortfeasor may be held to assume, including cessation of the infringement, removal of the nuisance, elimination of the danger, restitution, restoration, compensation for losses, extension of apology, and elimination of adverse effects and rehabilitation of reputation. These forms of civil liability may be applied separately or concurrently.① The court specifically analyzes:

(1) Regarding immediate cessation of infringement, Z Co. has already stopped the infringement after receiving a letter sent by Chow's attorney, which fact has been confirmed by Chow, therefore the request for cessation of infringement is not supported by the court.

(2) Regarding the compensation for Chow's loss, Chow is a famous actor who may obtain economic interests through participating in movies or commercial advertisements, therefore his name and likeness have a commercial value. Z Co.'s act of using Chow's name and likeness without authorization has partially damaged the part of Chow's right of personality that has economic interests, therefore Z Co. should compensate for Chow's loss. Regarding the amount of compensation, Article 20 of the Tort Liability Law provides that compensation shall be calculated on the loss suffered by the plaintiff, and where there is a difficulty in assessing the loss, if the parties cannot reach agreement thereon, the court may determine the amount of compensation based on the actual situation. According to Article 18 of the SPC's Rules on Certain Issues on Application of Laws in Adjudicating Civil Disputes involving Infringement of Rights of Personality through Information Network, the reasonable expenses incurred by the plaintiff to stop infringement should be part of the property damage provided in Article 20 of the Tort Liability Law. The reasonable expenses include the reasonable costs incurred by the plaintiff or his attorney to investigate and obtain evidence. The attorney's fee may be calculated within the scope of compensation as long as the fee is in compliance with the rules provided by the relevant departments. The same Article of the Rules also provides that where the loss suffered by the plaintiff or the benefit gained by the tortfeasor cannot be ascertained, the court may determine the amount of compensation within the scope below 500,000 yuan based on the actual situation. The

---

① This article has been integrated into Article 179 of the Civil Code.

court believes that Chow's suggestion of using his remuneration received for advertising Coco Cola products is not acceptable since the evidence provided is not directly relevant to this case and thus cannot prove his loss; neither has the defendant's benefit thus obtained been proved. Therefore, the court determines that the amount of compensation is 580,000 yuan, including the compensation for property damages of 500,000 yuan and the reasonable expenses of 80,000 yuan, considering the litigation costs, the complexity of the case, the workload of the plaintiff's attorneys, and the relevant standard for attorney's fees, *etc*.

(3) Regarding pains and suffering, Article 22 of the Tort Liability Law provides that a person who suffers severe mental distress owing to a tortfeasor's infringement may request the tortfeasor to compensate for pains and suffering. Article 8 of the SPC's Interpretation on Certain Issues on Determination of Compensation for Mental Distress in Tort Cases provides that the court generally shall not support claims for pains and suffering if the infringed person suffers mental distress but no severe consequence has been caused. In this case, Chow's mental distress caused by the infringement is not severe enough, so that the court does not support his claim for the 1-yuan damages for pains and suffering.

(4) Regarding the extension of apology, the purpose of it is to make the relevant recipients know about the truth and eliminate the adverse effect on the infringed person. But the ways to extend the apology should be determined by the actual forms of infringement and the scope of the adverse effect. The court decides to only support the part of the plaintiff's claim which requests the defendant to publicize its apologies on its official website and in the magazine concerned.

Case 32

Case 32: Ge v. Hong[1]

On August 27, 2013, a person named Zhang publicly posted a

---

[1] See (2016) Jing 02 Min Zhong N. 6272, reprinted in the SPC's Guiding Cases No. 99.

statement defaming the Five Heroes in Langya Mountain. After being investigated by police, Zhang admitted that he created false information and dispersed rumors; as a result, he received an administrative detention for 7 days. On September 9, 2013, the then executive chief editor Hong Zhenkuai published an article on caijing. com. cn saying that the story of the Five Heroes in Langya Mountain contained in the elementary school textbook was untrue, and later published another article in a magazine named *Yanhuang Chunqiu* saying that there were many conflicting details in the widely spread story about the five heroes. The article specifically pointed out such "facts" as there were originally six people but one of them betrayed the army, that the five heroes' acts were not for the purpose of trying to protect the people but primarily for catching up with the main army, that the five heroes did not jump off the mountain but that two of them were accidentally rolling out of the mountain, and that the five heroes took other people's property in violation of the disciplines, *etc*. These articles had caused severe adverse effect in the society.

Ge, one of the five heroes' descendants, brought litigation to the court based on Article 38 of the Constitution, the Tort Liability Law, and the other relevant laws and judicial interpretations, requesting the court to order Hong to immediately stop defaming and infringing the five heroes' reputation, post apology to the five heroes in his Sina Weibo and *People's Daily*, *PLA Daily*, *China Daily*, and on several other websites, to eliminate the adverse effect.

Hong defended that the relationship between Ge and one of the five heroes Ge Zhenlin could not be ascertained therefore Ge did not have the standing to sue. He also alleged that his articles were academic, without defamatory language, and his expression of every piece of fact was supported by evidence and did not constitute defamation. He also pointed out that Ge's complaint did not state which part of his article was untrue or was defamatory. He alleged that he was exercising his constitutional right to free thought, free academia, and free speech, for the purpose of exploring the historical truth, and that such right may not be deprived of by anyone.

During the trial, the court finds that in September 1941, the five heroes and the other soldiers in the army, in order to protect more than 40,000 people in Langya Mountain from Japanese army's intrusion, attracted the Japanese army to follow them to the top of the mountain. While there was no way out, finally they decided to jump off the mountain. Three of them died and two of them fell on the trees and survived. One of the survived heroes was Ge Zhenlin. After the war, the five heroes were named as the Five Heroes of Langya Mountain, and the story was also compiled into an elementary school textbook. The five heroes have since been regarded as the national heroes.

The court finds that Ge has a standing to sue. According to article 119 of the Civil Procedure Law, a plaintiff should be a citizen, legal person, or an organization that has an interest in the case. Article 3 of the SPC's Interpretation on Certain Issues on Determination of Compensation for Mental Distress in Civil Disputes provides that, after a natural person dies, if his name, likeness, reputation, or honor is defamed or smeared, his immediate relatives may sue in court. Article 69 of the SPC's Interpretation on Application of the Civil Procedure Law provides that, in a suit for infringement of a deceased person's right to body, remains, name, likeness, honor, reputation, or privacy, an immediate relative of the deceased person has a standing to sue. In this case, based on the evidence provided by the plaintiff, Ge is the son of Ge Zhenlin, one of the Five Heroes who is now deceased. Ge as his immediate relative has a standing to bring litigation on the infringement of Ge Zhenlin's reputation and honor.

Regarding whether the infringed rights and interests involved in this case are protected by law, Article 2 of the Tort Liability Law provides that any person who infringes upon other's civil-law rights or interests shall assume tort liability. Article 3 of the Interpretation on Certain Issues on Determination of the Compensation for Mental Distress in Tort Cases provides that no one may infringe on a deceased person's name, likeness, reputation, or honor by way of insult, defamation, derogation, or uglification; therefore, a person's rights of personality are still protected by law even after he dies.

Furthermore, the Five Heroes have been recognized as the national heroes, and their spirits have become a part of the common memories of the Chinese people and an important part of the core socialist value. These are part of the social public interest. To this extent, the articles involved in this case have infringed upon not only Ge Zhenlin's personal reputation and honor, but also the social public interest into which the heroes' name and reputation have been incorporated.

The articles involved in this case did not mention the basic facts of the Five Heroes, but only commented on where and how they jumped off the mountain, whether the Five Heroes ate people's radishes without permission, and the like. Without solid evidential support, the articles made ambiguous conjecture, challenges, and even evaluation. Although the articles did not include apparently insulting languages, Hong emphasized on something irrelevant to the basic facts leading the readers to doubt about the Five Heroes' story and spirits, and thereby deny the truthfulness of the basic facts, and derogate their image and spiritual value.

Regarding the consequence of the articles, since the articles have been spread through the internet, they have created a greater effect nationwide. They not only harmed Ge Zhenlin's reputation and honor, but also hurt Ge's personal feeling, and in certain extent harmed the feeling of the national social public, and thus harm the social public interest.

Hong raises freedom of speech as his defense; however, free speech is not limitless, and shall not harm other's lawful rights and interests and the other more important social public interest if exceeding a reasonable limit.

Finally, the court orders Hong to immediately stop infringement of Ge Zhenlin's reputation and honor, and extend an apology to Ge in public media within three days after the judgment becomes effective to eliminate the adverse effect. The apology must be published for five days, and the content of the apology as well as the media where the apology is to be published should be approved by the court.

Case 33

Case 33: Shen v. Wang[1]

Shen registered a Taobao shop on Feb. 24, 2009 indicating in its name that it was an agency selling the true quality goods purchased abroad. On November 1, 2014, Wang ordered a pair of Club Monaco leather pants in Shen's shop but was not satisfied with its quality, and she posted a negative comment. Later on, the two parties had a dispute over the comment, so Wang added more comments about her experience. Actually, the shop also received negative comments from the other purchasers before Wang posted the comments.

Shen sued Wang alleging that Wang's comments harmed the goodwill of her shop.

The Huangpu District Court of Shanghai Municipality reasoned that Wang posted negative comments on Taobao based on her own experience and she did not insult or defame Shen, and Shen failed to provide any evidence to prove that the goodwill of her shop suffered loss owing to the negative comments posted by Wang. Therefore, the court dismissed the case on June 6, 2015. Shen appealed.

On appeal, Shanghai No. 2 Intermediate People's Court reasons that the main issue of the case is whether the act of posting negative comments by Wang constituted infringement through the internet to Shen's Taobao shop.

Taobao sets up a platform for the purchasers to make comments, with a purpose of establishing a platform of information symmetry on which the buyers and sellers might receive information based on the buyers' true experience. In this case, Wang as the buyer has the right to decide whether or not to give a negative comment on Shen's Taobao shop. Buyers' comments generally are based on factors such as whether the goods bought are in compliance with the description made by the shop and whether the seller's service is satisfactory. The comments made by a buyer

---

[1] See (2015) Hu Er Zhong Min Yi (Min) Zhong Zi No. 1854, reprinted in the SPC Gazette, Issue 12, 2016.

are subjective, and the seller may not demand all buyers to give a positive comment, as long as the comment is not based on a subjective malice of the buyer.

From the evidence provided by Shen, Wang made the comments not for the purpose of defaming the goodwill of her shop, and therefore, subjectively, her act was not insulting or defamatory and thus did not constitute a tort committed through the internet. The lower court's decision is affirmed.

§ 5:3:1:3 Torts on Other's Relation-based Interests

The relation-based personal rights of a natural person arising from a marital or familial relationship are protected by law.① A person who infringes upon such rights and interests of another person commits a tort and must bear liability if fault is established. The remedies may include cessation of infringement, extending apology, and compensation.

Spousal relationship is protected by law and the spouses owe to each other a duty of loyalty. If a spouse commits adultery, the other spouse's interest in the spousal relationship is infringed upon. In this situation, the spouse at fault breaches the duty of loyalty as a spouse, whereas the third person involved in the adultery breaches the duty not to obstruct other's rights to spousal relationship.

Parent-child relationship is also protected by law and a person who infringes upon such a parent-child relationship should bear liability. The tortfeasor may be a third person, or a person within the parent-child relationship. For instance, a parent may infringe upon the parent-child relationship if he fails to educate, support, or protect the lawful rights and interests of his minor child.

If a person infringes upon another person's right to other kinship, he commits a tort and should bear liability no matter he did it intentionally or by negligence. If the actor is one of the parties to the kinship who infringes upon the right to kinship of the other party by failing to perform his legal duty, he should bear liability only if he has done so intentionally.

---

① Article 112 of the Civil Code.

§ 5:3:1:4   Torts on Other's Real rights

A person of the civil law enjoys real rights in accordance with law which are the rights to directly and exclusively control a specific thing, which rights consisting of the ownership, right to usufruct, and security interests in the property.① A person who infringes upon another person's real rights and thus causes property damage to the latter person must bear civil liability.

When an actor illegally possesses the property owned or possessed by another person without legal cause, he commits a conversion. If an actor intentionally or negligently infringes upon the property owned by another person and causes the property to be damaged or lost so that the value or value in use of the property is depreciated, a tort is committed. Entering onto a lot of land or into a building owned by others without authorization or permission also constitutes a tort infringing upon other's real rights.

When an actor illegally attaches the property owned by another person, hinders him from harvesting crops or fruits, prohibits him from lawfully using, profiting from, or disposing of his own property, *etc.*, so that the latter person, as the right holder, may not exercise his real rights, the actor commits a tort of obstruction of one's exercising of real rights.

An actor may also commit a tort of endangering other's property if he does something that has put another person's real or personal property in danger, although the harm has not yet been caused. In this situation, the tortfeasor will be ordered to remove the danger.

§ 5:3:1:5   Torts on Other's Rights *in Personam*

A right *in personam* is defined as a right of an obligee to request a specific obligor to do or not to do a certain act, as arising from a contract, a tortious act, a *negotiorum gestio*, or unjust enrichment, or otherwise arising by operation of law.② The law protects a person's rights *in personam*.

A contract formed in accordance with law is legally binding on the parties to the contract,③ so the parties are obligated to perform their contractual

---

① Article 115 of the Civil Code.
② Article 118 of the Civil Code.
③ Article 119 of the Civil Code.

obligations. If a party defaults, the other party has a right *in personam* against the defaulting party. Likewise, if a person's civil-law rights and interests are infringed upon due to a tortious act, the person has a right *in personam* against the tortfeasor. ①When a person, without a statutory or contractual obligation, engages in management activities to prevent another person from suffering loss of interests, he has a right *in personam* to request the beneficiary to reimburse the necessary expenses thus incurred. ② Where a person obtains unjust interests at the expense of another person's loss without a legal cause, the person thus harmed also has a right *in personam* to request the enriched person to make restitution. ③

If any of the above rights *in personam* has been intentionally infringed upon by an actor so that the obligee's right cannot be realized, a tort is committed and the actor must bear civil liability. In order to establish liability, the infringed person must prove that there is a lawful right *in personam* exists, the actor must be a person other than the obligor or obligee, the act must be in violation of law, the tortfeasor must have intent as to the occurrence of the result, and that the actor's act must have caused harm to the right *in personam*. The remedy is mainly monetary compensation. The amount of compensation is the loss of the expected profit based on the right *in personam* which cannot be realized.

There are different situations in which such a tort may be committed, such as inducement of breach of contract, impediment of debt performance, or conspiracy of a third person and an obligor to obstruct an obligee's rights.

For example, when a third person induces an obligor not to perform his obligation so that the obligee's rights cannot be realized, the third person is liable; if the obligor knows that the third person intentionally commits the tort and still joins the act, he is jointly and severally liable with the obligor. A third person may also commit a tort if he, through dispersing false information or by the other illegal means with a purpose of harming an obligee's rights, prevents or obstructs an obligor from performing his obligations so that the obligor

---

① Article 120 of the Civil Code.
② Article 121 of the Civil Code.
③ Article 122 of the Civil Code.

cannot perform his debts. Examples include a situation where an obligor decides to deliver the goods to an obligee, a third person intentionally damages or destroys the goods so that the performance cannot be completed, or a situation when a third person imprisons or detains an obligor who is going to perform his obligation so that the obligee of a contract suffers loss.

A tort is also committed if a third person and an obligor maliciously conspire to conceal property or create securities in the property so that an obligee's right cannot be realized. For example, if B owes money to C, B and B's wife A conspire to hide all of their property in A's parents' family so that B does not have sufficient fund to perform his obligation.

§ 5:3:1:6 Torts on Other's Intellectual Property Rights

A person enjoys intellectual property rights in accordance with law and no one may infringe upon such rights. Intellectual property rights are the exclusive rights enjoyed by a right holder over works, inventions, new utility models, or appearance designs, trademarks, geographical indications, trade secrets, layout designs of integrated circuits, new plant varieties, and the other subject matters as provided by law. ① The Civil Code only provides general principles regarding this kind of tort, leaving it to be further regulated by other specific laws on intellectual property rights. Fault must be found to establish liability in this kind of tort, and the remedies include cessation of infringement and payment of compensation.

There are different situations in which a person's intellectual property rights may be infringed upon. First, a tort infringing upon an author's rights to copyright may include an infringement of both the personal rights and the proprietary rights of the author owned in the copyright. If an actor's act violates the relevant provisions of the Copyright Law and causes damage to the author's right to publish, sign his name on, modify, and maintain the completeness of the work, or the author's intangible interests, it is an infringement of the author's personal rights. If an actor uses an author's copyrighted work without paying compensation according to law or agreement and causes damage to the author's right to use and right to compensation or the

---

① Article 123 of the Civil Code.

other proprietary interests of the author, there occurs an infringement of the author's proprietary rights.

Likewise, if an actor violates the Patent Law and infringes upon a right that is exclusively owned by a patent holder through producing, using, selling, counterfeiting the patented product, or by other means, for the purpose of making profits, he commits a tort on other's patent rights. If an actor violates the Trademark Law and infringes upon a right that is exclusively owned by a trademark holder so that the latter's interests in a lawfully registered trademark have been harmed, he commits a tort on rights in trademarks.

§ 5:3:1:7 Torts on Other's Rights to Succession and the Other Rights

A natural person's right to succession, a right of a shareholder, and otherwise a right of an investor are protected by law and anyone who infringes upon such right is liable for committing a tort. ① According to the Civil Code, the private property lawfully owned by a natural person may be transferred through inheritance, and a person may also have the shareholder rights and other investor rights in accordance with law. If an actor illegally obstructs another person's right to succession or right of a shareholder or investor, he commits a tort.

With the development of the digital world, there are new types of rights emerged which need to be protected. For example, the protection of digital data and online virtual assets has become a new issue. The Civil Code does not have any specific rules regulating this area, and leaving the protection of the data and online virtual assets to be regulated by the other laws. ②

§ 5:3:1:8 Commercial Torts

Commercial torts have been developed in recent decades and, because of the garden variety of this type of torts, each such tort may be regulated by a different law. The common feature of them is that either the actor or the infringed person is a person of the civil law engaging in commercial activities.

For example, unfair competition is a tort prohibited by the Law against

---

① Articles 124, 125 and 127 of the Civil Code.
② Article 127 of the Civil Code.

Unfair Competition, which infringes upon an operator's exercise of its right to operation. The specific acts may include monopolized operation, operation by powers, operation through bribes, or false advertisement. Commercial defamation is also a tort under the Law against Unfair Competition, which infringes upon the right to credit standing or reputation of a business operator or its products. Article 14 of this Law provides that an operator may not make up or disperse false information to harm the competitor's commercial reputation or the reputation of the competitor's products. This act not only infringes upon the credit standing and commercial reputation of the infringed operator, but also harms the market order.

Violation of a noncompetition prohibition is a commercial tort. Generally, a person under an employment contract is prohibited, by law or by agreement, from operating by himself or working in another company that engages in a competitive business, against the original employer. This prohibition will continue to be effective for a period of time even after the employment is terminated. If a person violates this prohibition and causes harm to his employer, a tort is committed and the person must bear civil liability.

A person may also commit a tort of appropriation of and profiting from the commercial information that is solely controlled or used by an operator. The commercial information may include the name, account number, passwords, or licenses of an operator which should not be used by any other persons without permission of the operator.

A commercial fraud will be committed if a person harms another person's rights or interests through defrauding the latter in the commercial area. Generally, the adverse consequence of such an act may be cured through granting contractual remedies to the aggrieved party, such as revocation or rectification of the contract. However, if the harm is severe and the remedy granted based on the contract law is not sufficient, tort law should apply.

A tort of obstruction of other's business operation is committed if a person obstructs another person's normal business operation through undue method and causes harm to the latter person. If the harm is only done to the operation, the infringed person may request the actor to stop infringement; if the obstruction is continued on and loss has thus been incurred, the actor is also liable for compensation.

Sometimes, when a person's act violates the Securities law, a tort of infringement on the interests in securities may be committed. This type of torts may include false statement, insider trading, and manipulation.

If a person, in the issuing or buying and selling securities, or when conducting other relevant activities, provides false statement which is untrue, significantly misleading, or which omits significant facts, and thus causes harm to the investors, false statement is committed. A joint and several liability will be imposed on all of the incorporators, issuers and its person in charge, and the securities firm underwriting the sale and its responsible directors, supervisors, managers. Moreover, the registered accountants issuing documents for the issuer and the accounting firm he is associated with, the professional appraisal person and the institution he is associated with, the lawyer and the law firm that he is associated with, the engineer or otherwise professional technician and the institution that he is associated with also assume joint and several liability.

If a person, who obtains confidential information based on his position, employment, or through other means and for the purpose of obtaining benefits or decreasing losses, conducts or suggests others to conduct securities transactions based on the confidential information, or discloses the confidential information to others so that the latter uses this information to conduct securities transactions, he commits insider trading and should bear tort liability if damage is thus caused to the other parties to the transaction or other investors. Sometimes a non-insider may also commit this tort if he, through other undue methods, obtains the confidential information and, based on which, buy or sell or suggests others to buy or sell the relevant securities.

A person may also commit manipulation of the securities market if he intentionally conducts market manipulation to affect the securities price, and thus harms the interests of the investors.

§ 5:3:1:9 Torts of Maliciously Initiating a Litigation or Claim

If a person does not have a real claim but still initiates a litigation with an illegal purpose, he commits a tort. Such a person knows that he will not be able to get anything from the litigation, but initiating the litigation itself will bring an adverse effect on another person.

A person may commit this tort when he maliciously initiates a civil litigation procedure with a view to harming the defendant's proprietary interests through the litigation. The litigation is without factual basis or without just cause, and the purpose of the person is to harm the defendant's rights and interests by taking advantage of the court's proceeding. Similarly, a person may commit this tort if he maliciously causes a criminal proceeding initiated against another person with the purpose of harming the latter's reputation or other personality rights, as well as the proprietary rights. Sometimes a person may also commit this tort if he abuses his right to sue. However, it does not constitute a tort in an administrative litigation because the defendant in an administrative proceeding is the government. Even if such a litigation is not proper, the person who initiates the litigation will not assume liability under Chinese law.

Case 21, reprinted in § 3:2:4:2 of this Book, is a good example illustrating how a legal proceeding may be used to adversely affect another person's rights and interests. This case is worth a re-visit.

§ 5:3:2 Vicarious Liability Torts

Generally, a person whose act causes harm to another person in violation of law will bear tort liability. However, under certain circumstances, when a harm is caused by a person (an actor), another person is required to assume tort liability. For instance, when a minor commits a tort, the parents of the minor will assume the tort liability. This is a vicarious liability which occurs when there exists a special relationship between the actor and the person assuming the vicarious liability. This subsection will introduce the various situations in which vicarious liability may occur. Some special torts, e.g., medical malpractice, may also involve vicarious liability but will be discussed in § 5:3:3.

§ 5:3:2:1 Torts Committed by Persons without Full Capacity

Where a person with no or limited capacity for performing civil juristic acts causes damage to another person, the guardian of the said person will assume tort liability. This vicarious liability may be mitigated if the guardian can prove that he has fulfilled his duties of guardian,① but his liability cannot be completely barred under the fair liability rule. Where an actor who has no or limited capacity for performing civil juristic acts causes damage to another person, compensation should be paid out of his own assets if he has assets, and any deficiency balance should be paid by the guardian. If the actor does not own any assets, the guardian is liable for compensating the damage.② If the guardian of such an actor has delegated the duties of guardian to another person, the guardian should still assume tort liability while the delegated person who is at fault should assume the corresponding liability.③

The above rule does not apply to a person with full capacity for performing civil juristic acts who causes harm to another person due to temporary loss of consciousness or loss of control. Under this circumstance, the person at fault is liable for his own act. If the person is not at fault, he is also liable for appropriately compensating the infringed person based on his financial situation. If the damage is caused by a person with full capacity for performing civil juristic acts due to temporary loss of consciousness or loss of control as a result of intoxication or abuse of narcotic or psychotropic drugs, he should bear full tort liability for the damage.④

§ 5:3:2:2 Torts Committed by Employees

In an employment relationship, an employer controls or enjoys the fruit of an employee's labor, it is therefore vicariously liable for the torts committed by an employee during the course of employment when performing the authorized duty. It may include various situations.

If a legal representative, a person in charge, or another person with similar responsibility of a legal person or an unincorporated organization causes damage to another person while performing his responsibilities in the name of the legal person or the unincorporated organization, the legal person or unincorporated organization should assume tort liability. After assuming the liability, the legal person or unincorporated organization may claim

---

① Article 1188 of the Civil Code.
② Article 1188 of the Civil Code.
③ Article 1189 of the Civil Code.
④ Article 1190 of the Civil Code.

indemnification against the actor who is at fault.① In order to prove liability, the infringed person must prove that the illegal act is done by the legal representative, person in charge, or the person with similar responsibility of the legal person or organization in performing the authorized duty, the illegal act has caused either property damage or personal injury to himself, there is a causal link between the illegal act and the damage, and that the legal person or organization must have fault in selecting, supervising, or managing its legal representative, person in charge, or otherwise a person with similar responsibility.

Where an employee causes damage to another person in connection with the performance of his work, his employer should assume tort liability. After assuming the compensatory liability, the employer may claim indemnification against the employee who acts intentionally or with gross negligence. Where a dispatched employee causes damage to another person in connection with the performance of his work during the period of labor dispatch, the employer receiving the dispatched employee should assume tort liability, and the employer dispatching the employee should also assume the corresponding liability if it is at fault.② When determining the liability, the factors to be considered include whether there is an actual employment relationship between the employer and the employee, whether the employee causing harm to others was performing his duty within authorization, and whether the employer had subjective fault in failing to perform the duty of care in selecting, supervising, or managing the employee. If the employer is held liable, after paying the compensation, the employer has a right to indemnification against the employee who is at fault.

If there is no employment relationship exists, but a labor service relationship has been formed between two individuals, if the party providing labor services causes damage to another person in connection with the labor services, the party receiving labor services should assume tort liability. After assuming the tort liability, the service-receiving party may claim indemnification against the service-providing party who acts intentionally or

---

① Articles 62 and 63 of the Civil Code.
② Article 1191 of the Civil Code.

with gross negligence. Where the service-providing party himself suffers damage in connection with the labor services, both parties should assume corresponding liabilities according to their respective faults. Where an act of a third person causes damage to the service-providing party when such services are provided, the service-providing party has a right to request the third person to bear tort liability, or to request the service-receiving party to make compensation. The service-receiving party may, after making the compensation, claim indemnification against the third person. ①

Where a contractor causes damage to a third person or to himself while completing the contracted work, the ordering party does not assume tort liability, except that the ordering party should assume corresponding liability where he is at fault in placing the order, making the instructions, or selecting the contractor. ② In order to establish such liability, the infringed person must prove that there is a specific contract between the ordering party and the contractor under which the contractor promises to follow instructions given by the ordering party. In addition, the act conducted by the contractor must be done in the course of performing the contract and must not exceed the scope of the contract, and the contractor's act must have infringed upon the civil-law rights of a third person or to the contractor himself. In this case, the contractor, as the actor, causes the harm but the ordering party bears vicarious liability.

§ 5:3:2:3 Torts Committed through a Network

Torts committed through a network are a new type of torts, which seems to be similar to the torts committed by the news media, because the websites may be defined as news media. However, the torts committed through a network are not necessarily caused by the news published on the network, but include various torts such as infringement of other's copyrights on the internet, infringement of other's right to reputation or privacy on the BBS, *etc*. Actually, the network is just a vehicle to provide information to the public so that the public may obtain that information at a selected time and place.

---

① Article 1192 of the Civil Code.
② Article 1193 of the Civil Code.

Network users or network service providers who, through a network, infringe upon the civil-law rights and interests of another person shall bear tort liability unless otherwise provided by law.① Where a network user commits a tortious act through using the network service, the right holder is entitled to notify the network service provider to take such necessary measures as deletion, block, or disconnection of the information concerned. The notice should include the preliminary evidence establishing the tort and the real identity information of the right holder. After receiving the notice, the network service provider must timely forward the notice to the relevant network user and take necessary measures based on the preliminary evidence establishing the tort and the type of service complained about. If it fails to take necessary measures in time, it shall assume joint and several liability for the aggravated part of the damage with the network user. The right holder who causes damage to the network user or network service provider due to erroneous notification will bear tort liability, unless otherwise provided by law.②

After receiving the forwarded notice, the network user may submit a declaration of non-infringement to the network service provider, which should include the preliminary evidence of non-infringement and the real identity information of the network user. After receiving the declaration, the network service provider shall forward it to the right holder who issues the notice, and inform him that he may file a complaint to the relevant department or file a lawsuit with the court. The network service provider should timely terminate the measures taken where, within a reasonable period of time after the forwarded declaration reaches the right holder, it fails to receive notice that the right holder has filed a complaint or a lawsuit.③

A network service provider, who knows or should have known that a network user has infringed upon the civil-law rights and interests of another person by using its network services but fails to take necessary measures, shall assume joint and several liability with the network user.④

---

① Article 1194 of the Civil Code.
② Article 1195 of the Civil Code.
③ Article 1196 of the Civil Code.
④ Article 1197 of the Civil Code.

§ 5:3:2:4 Torts Committed in Public Places or by Organizers of Public Activities

The operators or managers of businesses or public premises such as hotels, shopping malls, banks, bus or train stations, airports, stadiums, and places of entertainment, or the organizers of public activities shall bear tort liability where they fail to fulfill the duty of maintaining safety and thus cause damage to another person. Where the damage to another person is caused by a third person, the third person shall bear tort liability, and the operator, manager, or organizer who fails to fulfill the duty of maintaining safety shall assume the corresponding supplementary liability. After assuming the supplementary liability, the operator, manager, or organizer may claim indemnification against the third person. ①

The legal basis for imposing a duty of providing security and protection is provided in various laws. For example, Article 7 of the Law on Protection of Consumer's Rights and Interests provides that an operator has a duty to provide security and protection to a consumer's person and property. This duty had been included in Article 37 of the Tort Liability Law and now has been integrated into the Civil Code. Actually, this duty may also be inferred from a contract. Based on the principle of honesty and good faith, a party to a contract has a duty to provide security and protection to the other party.

It is to be noted that the law especially protects the minor students' interests by imposing the duty to provide security and protection on the kindergartens, schools, or other educational institutions (hereinafter collectively referred to as "educational institutions"). The liability to be assumed by the educational institutions is based on the capacity of the infringed person.

Where a person with no capacity for performing civil juristic acts suffers personal injury while studying or living in an educational institution, the educational institution shall assume tort liability, except that it will not assume tort liability if it can prove that it has fulfilled its responsibilities in education and management. ② The principle of rebuttable presumption of fault applies

---

① Article 1198 of the Civil Code.
② Article 1199 of the Civil Code.

here.

Where a person with limited capacity for performing civil juristic acts suffers personal injury while studying or living in an educational institution, it shall assume tort liability if it fails to fulfill its responsibilities in education and management.① Since the students have limited capacity, the educational institutions' liability is based on fault.

Where a person with no or limited capacity for performing civil juristic acts, while studying or living in an educational institution, suffers personal injury caused by a third person other than the educational institution, the third person shall bear tort liability, and the educational institution shall assume the corresponding supplementary liability if it fails to fulfill its responsibilities in management. After assuming the supplementary liability, the educational institution may claim indemnification against the third person.② In this situation, the third person tortfeasor bears the primary liability, while the educational institution assumes secondary liability.

Case 34

Case 34: Wu v. Zhu③

Zhu and Wu were first graders at Shuguang School and lived in a same dorm. In December 2004, Zhu threw a tangerine to Wu and injured Wu's right eye. Wu was sent to the school clinic by a teacher. The School notified Wu's parents about Wu's injury in the end of December, and afterwards Wu's parents sent him to hospital. It was diagnosed that Wu's right eye was permanently disabled. Wu sued Zhu for compensation. The main issues in this case include whether a school assumes the duties of guardian over a minor student who lived and studied in the school, who was liable for Wu's injury, and whether the amount of compensation Wu requested was reasonable.

Based on Article 16 of the GPCL and Article 22 of the Tentative

---

① Article 1200 of the Civil Code.
② Article 1201 of the Civil Code.
③ See the SPC Gazette, Issue 12, 2006.

Opinions of the Supreme People's Court on Implementation of the GPCL, where a guardian sends his minor child to school, his duties of guardian has not been delegated to the school, and the school would not naturally assume the duties of guardian over the minor student solely because of admitting the student. If the guardian would like to fully or partially delegate the duties of guardianship to the school, he must reach an express agreement with the school regarding the delegation, without which the school cannot be presumed to have assumed the duties of guardian.

Based on Article 7 of the Interpretation of the Supreme People's Court on Certain Issues on Application of Laws in Adjudication of Cases on Compensation for Personal Injury Cases, although a school does not have the duties of guardian over a minor student studying in the school, the school does have a duty to educate, manage, and protect the student. Where the school fails to perform such duty so that the minor student is harmed by another minor student within the campus of the school, the guardian of the latter student shall be liable, and the school shall assume compensatory liability to the extent of its fault.

After consideration, the court holds that, regarding the damage suffered by Wu, Zhu is liable for 30% and the school liable for 70%.

Case 35

Case 35: Li & Song v. H Middle School[1]

Li is an 11th grade student in H Middle School. On November 8, 2005, when he sat in an exam of political science, he was caught by a proctor for cheating in the exam by secretly carrying a note. Afterwards, the proctor delivered the note to the school authority. In the following morning, the school authority sanctioned him by demerit recording and publicized the result. In the afternoon of the same day, Li did not go to school for the exam, and then committed suicide at his home in the

---

[1] See the SPC's Gazette, Issue 4, 2009.

evening at about 7 pm. The parents of Li sued. The main issue is whether H Middle School is liable for Li's death.

The first instance court found that H School made the decision to discipline Li according to the school rule, and held that the act was not inappropriate. Although the decision was not flawless, there was no causal link between the decision and Li's death. Therefore, H School was not liable for Li's Death so the court dismissed the case. Li's parents appealed to the Intermediate People's Court of Xining City, Qinghai Province.

On appeal, the court considers several issues. First, the court reasons that the school's decision on Li's act of cheating in the exam was not inappropriate. Li as a student of H Middle School secretly carried the note into the exam room knowing that it was in violation of the exam rules of the school. Cheating in an exam is an act in violation of the discipline.

Second, the court reasons that H School's act of posting its decision on campus was not illegal. According to Article 28 of the Education Law, a school has the right to reward or discipline the students.

Third, H Middle School did not deprive Li of his right to petition on the decision of discipline. After Li saw the posted decision, he went to talk to the class advisor, proctor, and the head of the school authority, asking for revocation of the discipline, through which he had exercised his right to petition. Although the school did not approve his request, it did not mean that the school had deprived him of his right to petition, and Li had the right to make a further petition.

Fourth, Li did not attend the exam in the afternoon of the day when the discipline decision was made. The school did not have fault. On the same day, Li went back home at noon as every student did, so it cannot be said that he left school without authorization. After the students returned back home, their parents had a duty to take care of him. For a student who returned home in a normal situation, the school could not foresee any potential risks. Therefore, the school did not fail to perform its duty of care.

Fifth, according to the relevant rules of H Middle School, a discipline decision should be investigated and proved by the dean's office, and then it needs to get approval from the school's council. However, H Middle school did not investigate or verify it with Li before the discipline decision was made, nor reported it to the school council for approval. Although the discipline made by the school was not inappropriate, but the method was over simplified, careless, and not in compliance with the standard, and also violated the requirements of the school. In addition, according to the rules on the middle and elementary school's working procedures, the school should notify the student's parents regarding the discipline. The school also admits that the formal decision has three duplicate copies with the school, the class advisor, and the parents each has one copy. However, the school did not timely notify the parents of Li. The students in elementary and middle schools are minors and are not mature enough, and have limited capacity when facing pressures. As an educational institution, the school must fully consider the psychological endurance of the students, and should try its best to educate the students and provide consultation for them. In this case, however, in order to pursue the timeliness of the punishment, the school failed to fully consider Li's psychological endurance, and did not timely notify Li's parents of the discipline decision, so that the parents did not have a chance to timely guide and educate him, and thus lost the opportunity to prevent the happening of this tragedy. Therefore, there is a certain causal link between the school's violation of the working procedure and Li's death.

According to Article 9 of the Measures on Dealing with the Personal Injury Incurred on Students, where the teachers or other personnel of a school violate the working procedures, operating procedures, professional ethics, or other relevant rules while performing their duties, the school should assume the corresponding liability in accordance with law. Since the main reason of this case was because Li could not properly face the problem, and had limited ability to deal with the pressures, so that the damage was caused, the school should assume 20% of the liability for compensation owing to its fault in working and operating procedures.

Finally, the court reverses the lower court's judgment and ordered that H Middle School compensate Li's parents 31,101.60 yuan, including 20% of the death compensation, funeral fees, and transportation fees, etc.

§ 5:3:2:5 Torts Committed by Civil Servants

Torts committed by the civil servants of the State are a special type of torts regulated by the State Compensation Law. The nature of the liability of this type of torts is also vicarious liability, because the harm is done by one or more civil servants, while the liability is assumed by the State department. In order to establish the liability, the infringed person must prove that the act conducted by the civil servant(s) is illegal.① To determine the illegality, the court will examine whether there was a legal basis for the actor to perform the act, whether the performance of the act violated the legal procedure, and whether the performance violated law. This group of torts may be committed through performing an administrative act or a judicial act.

A tort may be committed when an administrative agency and its staff infringe upon a person's personal or proprietary rights when exercising the administrative authority. The acts that may infringe upon other's personal rights include: (1) illegally detaining, through administrative measures, a person or depriving a person of his personal liberty; (2) causing bodily injury or death to a person by a violent act such as a battery, or through abetting the others to use violent acts against the person; (3) causing bodily harm or death to a person by illegally using weapons or police instruments; and (4) causing bodily harm or death to a person through other illegal acts. On the other hand, the acts that may infringe upon other's proprietary rights include: (1) illegally imposing administrative penalties on a person, such as fines, revocation of a permission or a license, an order to stop operation and production, or forfeiture of the person's property; (2) illegally taking coercive measures such as attaching, seizing, or freezing a person's property; (3) levying unjustified fees on a person in violation of the State regulations; and (4) conducting other illegal acts that cause property damage to a person.

A tort may also be committed during a judicial proceeding when a person's rights and interests are infringed upon. The acts that may constitute this tort include: (1) wrongful detention of a person by an investigative agency, procuratorate, court, or prison administration and their staff without a reasonable doubt or evidence proving that he has committed a crime, so that

---

① Article 2 of the State Compensation Law.

his personal freedom has been infringed upon; (2) wrongful conviction of or unreasonable criminal penalty imposed on a person by a court. If the person is later on found not guilty in the supervisory proceeding of adjudication, the court that made the wrongful conviction should bear tort liability; (3) wrongfully imposing criminal coercive measures on a person by an investigative agency through extortion of confession by torture or other violent acts, or through illegally using police weapons or instruments to cause bodily injury or death to a person; (4) illegally attaching, seizing, freezing, or taking a person's property by an investigation agency, procuratorate, court, or prison administration and their staff, or, if the person is later on found not guilty in a supervisory proceeding of adjudication, but the original judgment imposing fines or forfeiture of property had already been enforced; and (5) the other civil or administrative judicial acts that cause harm to a person, such as in a situation when a court illegally adopts coercive measures or preservation measures against a person, or mistakenly enforces a judgment, ruling, or other effective legal documents and causes harm to the person.

§ 5:3:3 Special Torts

§ 5:3:3:1 Torts Committed in Traffic Accidents

A traffic accident happens when a personal injury or property damage is caused to a person owing to an act or acts done by one or more of the persons, including the driver(s) of motor vehicles, pedestrians, passengers, or other persons engaging in transportation related activities on the road. Where a motor vehicle is involved in a traffic accident causing damage to a person, the liability for compensation is governed by the Law on Road Transportation Safety[①] and the Civil Code.[②] When damage is caused to a person as a result of a traffic accident and the liability is attributed to the motor vehicle driver, compensation generally will be paid firstly by the insurance company that underwrites the compulsory motor vehicle insurance to the extent of its

---

① Promulgated by the Standing Committee of the NPC on Oct. 28, 2003 and effective since May 1, 2004.
② Article 1208 of the Civil Code.

coverage, and any deficiencies should be paid by the insurer that underwrites the commercial motor vehicle insurance in accordance with the stipulations of the insurance contract. Any remaining balance or the part not covered by any commercial motor vehicle insurance shall be paid by the tortfeasor(s). [1] Where an insurer pays the expenses for rescue within the limits of the compulsory insurance liability for motor vehicles, it has a right to indemnification against the person who is liable for the traffic accident. [2]

When determining liabilities, different liability rules are adopted depending on the situation. If an accident occurs between two motor vehicles, the fault liability rule applies and the motor vehicle driver who is at fault shall assume liability. Where both motor vehicle drivers are at fault, they should share the liability in proportion to their fault. However, if an accident occurs between a motor vehicle and a non-motor vehicle or a pedestrian, then the non-fault liability rule applies and the motor vehicle driver shall assume the liability. The motor vehicle driver's liability may be mitigated if it can be proven that the act of the non-motor vehicle driver or pedestrian involved in the accident violated law and contributed to the accident while the motor vehicle driver had already adopted necessary measures to respond. The scope of mitigation is not specified by law, but generally the degree of fault will be considered when determining the scope of the liability to be mitigated. A motor vehicle driver bears no liability only when the accident is intentionally caused by a non-motor vehicle driver or a pedestrian. [3]

The Civil Code has further specified the liabilities that a motor vehicle driver may assume under different circumstances.

Sometimes a motor vehicle is lent or let to another person to drive so that the owner, manager, or user of a motor vehicle are not the same person. If such a motor vehicle is involved in a traffic accident which causes damage to a third person, the user of the motor vehicle shall bear the liability for compensation if the liability is attributed to the motor vehicle driver, and the owner or manager of the vehicle who is also at fault shall each assume

---

[1] Article 76 of the Law on Road Transportation and Security and Article 1213 of the Civil Code.
[2] Article 1215 of the Civil Code.
[3] Article 76 of the Law on Road Transportation and Security.

corresponding liability for compensation. ①

Motor vehicles are required to be registered by law. If a motor vehicle has been transferred and delivered to a person by way of sale or other means but the transferee fails to file for registration of it, the motor vehicle is still registered under the name of the transferor. If such a motor vehicle is involved in a traffic accident causing damage to another person, the transferee of the motor vehicle shall bear the liability for compensation if the liability is attributed to the motor vehicle driver. ②

Sometimes a person uses his motor vehicle in association with an entity to engage in the business of road transportation. If such a motor vehicle is involved in a traffic accident causing damage to another person, and the liability is attributed to the motor vehicle driver, the person and the entity shall assume joint and several liability for compensation. ③

A motor vehicle involved in a traffic accident may be driven by a person other than its owner or manager. If the liability is attributed to the motor vehicle driver, the law provides various rules regarding who should assume the liability. If a person drives another person's motor vehicle without authorization, he shall bear the liability for compensation if the liability is attributed to the motor vehicle driver. The owner or manager of the motor vehicle whose fault contributes to the damage shall also bear the liability for compensation unless otherwise provided by law. ④ If the person driving the motor vehicle is a thief, robber, or snatcher who has stolen, robbed, or snatched the motor vehicle from its owner, manager, or user, he is labile for compensation. However, if the stolen, robbed, or snatched motor vehicle is used by a person other than the thief, robber, or snatcher and causes damage in a traffic accident, if the liability is attributed to the motor vehicle driver, the thief, robber, or snatcher are jointly and severally liable with the user of the motor vehicle. ⑤

The law prohibits a person from transferring or driving on the road an

---

① Article 1209 of the Civil Code.
② Article 1210 of the Civil Code.
③ Article 1211 of the Civil Code.
④ Article 1212 of the Civil Code.
⑤ Article 1215 of the Civil Code.

illegally assembled motor vehicle or a motor vehicle that has reached the end-of-life standard. If such a motor vehicle is transferred by way of sale or by other means, and consequently is involved in a traffic accident causing damage to another person, the transferor and the transferee shall assume joint and several liability for the damage. ①

A person who is involved in a traffic accident while driving a motor vehicle may sometimes escape after the accident occurs. In such a hit-and-run accident, if the motor vehicle is insured by a compulsory insurance, compensation shall be paid by the insurer to the extent of the coverage of the insurance. Where the motor vehicle cannot be identified or located, is not covered by the compulsory insurance, or the rescue expenses exceed the limit of liability of the compulsory motor vehicle insurance, and payment needs to be made against the rescue, funeral, and other expenses incurred as a result of the death or bodily injury of the infringed person, such payment shall be paid from the Social Assistance Fund for Road Traffic Accidents. After the Social Assistance Fund for Road Traffic Accidents makes the payment, its administrative agency has a right to indemnification against the person who is liable for the traffic accident. ②

Where a motor vehicle not engaged in the operation of business causes damage in a traffic accident to a guest passenger who is on the ride for free, if the liability is attributed to the motor vehicle driver, the liability of the user of the motor vehicle for compensation shall be mitigated unless he acts intentionally or with gross negligence. ③

§ 5:3:3:2 **Torts Caused by Medical Malpractice**

Medical malpractice is a type of torts, and the number of disputes between the medical institutions and the patients has greatly increased in recent years in China, so the State Council made the Regulations on Dealing with Medical Accidents to regulate it before the Tort Liability Law was enacted. Now these rules, along with the provisions of the Tort Liability Law, have been integrated

---

① Article 1214 of the Civil Code.
② Article 1216 of the Civil Code.
③ Article 1217 of the Civil Code.

into Book Seven of the Civil Code.

Medical malpractice is constituted when a medical institution and its staff have negligently caused injury to a patient during diagnosis and treatment in violation of laws, regulations, departmental rules, or the medical treatment rules. The medical institution shall assume vicarious liability for compensation for the acts of its staff based on fault. ①

In order to avoid liability, a medical institution and its staff must perform the duties imposed by law. First, they have a duty to explain the medical conditions and treatment measures to a patient when diagnosing and treating him. Where a surgery, a special examination, or a special treatment is needed, the medical staff shall explain to the patient the medical risks, alternative treatment plans, and other information in a timely manner and obtain his express consent. Where it is impossible or inappropriate to do so, the medical staff shall explain it to the patient's close relatives and get their express consent. Where the medical staff fail to fulfill this duty and thus cause damage to the patient, the medical institution shall assume the liability for compensation. ② However, if consent cannot be obtained from the patient or his close relatives in the case of rescuing a terminally ill patient or in any other emergency situation, the medical staff may immediately take corresponding medical measures upon the approval of the person in charge of the medical institution or an authorized person in charge. ③

A medical institution and its staff also have a duty to diagnose and treat a patient up to the then current appropriate medical level. If they fail to do so and thus cause damage to the patient, the medical institution shall assume the liability for compensation. ④ A medical institution and its staff are obligated to properly enter and maintain medical records such as hospitalization logs, medical orders, test reports, surgical and anesthesia records, pathological data, and nursing records in accordance with the regulations. Where a patient make a request for retrieving or making copies of their medical records, they

---

① Article 1218 of the Civil Code.
② Article 1219 of the Civil Code.
③ Article 1220 of the Civil Code.
④ Article 1221 of the Civil Code.

should provide the records in a timely manner. ①

In addition, a medical institution and its medical staff have a duty to keep their patients' private information and personal information confidential. Anyone who divulges the private information or personal information of a patient or discloses his medical records without the patient's consent shall bear tort liability. ② Moreover, a medical institution and its medical staff have a duty not to conduct unnecessary examinations for the patients in violation of the guidelines for diagnosis and treatment. ③

Generally, a fault liability rule applies to a medical malpractice case. However, sometimes a rebuttable presumption of fault will be applied under certain circumstances. The Civil Code provides that a medical institution may be presumed to be at fault if damage is caused to a patient during diagnosis and treatment under any of the following circumstances:

(1) there is a violation of the provisions of laws, administrative regulations, rules, or other relevant guidelines for diagnosis and treatment;

(2) the medical records are concealed or the request for provision thereof is refused; or

(3) the medical records are lost, forged, tempered with, or illegally destroyed. ④

The Civil Code also provides the circumstances under which a medical institution does not assume liability for compensation for any damage caused to a patient during diagnosis and treatment:

(1) the patient or his close relative does not cooperate with the medical institution to go through diagnosis and treatment which is in compliance with the guidelines for diagnosis and treatment;

(2) the medical staff have fulfilled their duty of providing reasonable diagnosis and treatment in an emergent situation, such as rescuing a terminally

---

① Article 1225 of the Civil Code.
② Article 1226 of the Civil Code.
③ Article 1227 of the Civil Code.
④ Article 1222 of the Civil Code.

ill patient; or

(3) it is difficult to diagnose and treat a patient due to the restriction of the then current medical level.

Under the circumstance specified in Subparagraph (1) of the preceding paragraph, the medical institution or its medical staff shall assume corresponding liability for compensation where they are also at fault. ①

If a patient suffers damage owing to a defect in a drug, disinfection product, or medical instrument, or due to the transfusion of substandard blood, the patient may elect to claim compensation against the drug marketing license holder or the manufacturer of the drug, or the blood supply institution, or against the medical institution. If he claims for compensation against the medical institution, the medical institution, after paying compensation, has a right to indemnification against the responsible drug marketing license holder or manufacturer of the drug, or the blood supplier. ②

The law also provides protections to the lawful rights and interests of medical institutions and their medical staff. Anyone, who interferes with the order of a medical institution, obstructs the work or life of the medical staff, or infringes upon the lawful rights and interests of the medical staff, shall bear liability in accordance with law. ③

§ 5:3:3:3 Torts Caused by Buildings and Objects

A building may collapse, a structure may subside, and an object may be thrown out of or fall from a building so as to harm others. There have been some histories regarding the basis for finding tort liability arising from these accidents.

The GPCL applied the rule of rebuttable presumption of fault to the owner or manager of the building, structure, or object, ④ providing that if a building, construction, or facility collapsed and caused harm to others, the owner or manager of the building, construction, or facility is liable, unless they can

---

① Article 1224 of the Civil Code.
② Article 1223 of the Civil Code.
③ Article 1228 of the Civil Code.
④ Article 126 of the GPCL.

disprove their fault. The Tort Liability Law changed the liability rule and adopted a non-fault liability approach to the project owner and the constructor. ① According to Article 86 of the Tort Liability Law, the project owner and the constructor were jointly and severally liable for the damage caused to a person owing to the collapse of a building, construction, or facility, except that if the collapse was caused by a third person's fault, then the third person would bear tort liability. It further provided that after the project owner and constructor had paid compensation, they had a right to indemnification against the responsible person. Apparently, the project owner and the constructor are imposed a stricter liability according to the Tort Liability Law, which reflected a change of attitude of the Chinese legislature to the quality control of constructions. These rules have been integrated into the Civil Code with minor changes so that they are more specific.

Article 1252 of the Civil Code provides that where a building, structure, or otherwise a facility collapses or subsides and causes damage to a person, the project owner and the constructor shall assume joint and several liability unless they can prove that there is no quality defect. Where the damage is due to the fault of another person, the project owner or constructor who has made compensation has a right to indemnification against the responsible person. Where a building, structure, or a facility collapses or subsides, and damage is thus caused to another person due to the fault of the owner, manager, user, or a third person, the owner, manager, user, or the third person shall bear tort liability. ② If a building, structure, facility, or any object laid or hanged thereon comes loose or falls down and causes damage to another person, the owner, manager, or user of the building, structure, facility or the object is presumed to have fault and shall assume tort liability unless it can be proven that he is not at fault. After paying compensation, the owner, manager, or user may claim indemnification against the responsible person who is at fault. ③

Sometimes an object is thrown from within a building or falls off a building

---

① Article 86 of the Tort Liability Law.
② Article 1252 of the Civil Code.
③ Article 1253 of the Civil Code.

and causes harm to a person. Generally, the person who throws it or causes it fallen shall bear tort liability. However, many buildings today have multiple units with each unit owned or used by a different owner or user, therefore, it is not always easy to identify the specific tortfeasor upon investigation. In order to protect the infringed person's interests, the law provides that in this situation, any user of the building who may have caused the damage shall make compensation, unless he can prove that he is not the tortfeasor. A user of the building who has paid compensation has a right to indemnification against the tortfeasor. In order to prevent the occurrence of these accidents, the law imposes a duty of taking necessary security measures on the manager of a building, such as the property management service enterprise. If the manager fails to perform such duty, he should bear tort liability. ①

The Civil Code also provides rules applicable to some similar situations in which a tort liability may arise. For instance, if a person is injured by a stack of objects that collapses, rolls down, or slips down, the principle of rebuttable presumption of fault applies and the person who piles up the stack shall bear tort liability for compensation. ② If damage is caused to a person due to an object stacked, dumped, or left on the public road so that the road is obstructed, the actor shall bear tort liability. The public road manager shall assume the corresponding liability if he cannot prove that he has fulfilled his duties such as the duty of clean-up, protection, and warning. ③

In addition, if a person is injured owing to an excavation of the ground or repair or installation of underground facilities conducted in a public place or on a public road, the constructor is presumed to be at fault and shall bear tort liability if he cannot prove that he has posted an obvious warning sign and taken safety measures. Likewise, if a person is injured by an underground facility, such as a utility access manhole, the manager shall bear tort liability if he cannot prove that he has fulfilled his management responsibilities. ④ If a person is injured by a breaking or falling tree or a falling fruit, the owner or manager of the tree is also presumed to be at fault and shall bear tort liability

---

① Article 1254 of the Civil Code.
② Article 1255 of the Civil Code.
③ Article 1256 of the Civil Code.
④ Article 1258 of the Civil Code.

unless he can prove that he is not at fault. ①

§5:3:4 Non-Fault Liability Torts

Generally, a person who suffers damage may sue the actor for committing a tort if he can prove that the actor acts with fault. However, under some circumstances, the law imposes non-fault liability on some actors in which case the infringed person does not need to prove that the actor was at fault when doing the tortious act which brought damage to him, as long as he can prove that the act was done by the actor, he suffered damage, and that there was a causal link between the actor's act and his damage. Such non-fault liability mainly exists in cases involving product liability, environmental pollution, ultrahazardous activities, and animals.

§5:3:4:1 Torts Arising from Product Liability

The product liability law requires the manufacturer or seller of a defective product that causes harm to other's personal or proprietary interests to bear strict tort liability. ② Generally, the manufacturer of a defective product is liable for the damage caused by the defect, ③ but if the defect is caused by the fault of a seller, the manufacturer who has paid compensation has a right to indemnification against the seller. ④

In order to establish product liability, the plaintiff must prove three elements. First, the product has a defect, including a design defect, a manufacturing defect, or an insufficiency in warning. Second, the infringed person must have suffered personal injury or property damage. Third, there must be a causal link between the defective product and the damage. The manufacturer of the defective product may not be liable if the product has not been put into commerce, the defect causing the damage did not exist when the product was put into commerce, or upon the time the product was put into commerce, the defect could not be reasonably discovered owing to the then development of the scientific technology.

---

① Article 1257 of the Civil Code.
② Articles 1202 and 1203 of the Civil Code.
③ Article 1202 of the Civil Code.
④ Article 1203 of the Civil Code.

If a consumer is injured or damaged by a defective product, he may request either the manufacturer or the seller of the product to compensate for his damage, and the manufacturer or the seller who has paid the compensation may claim indemnification against the other party who is at fault.① Sometimes, a third person, such as a transporter or a warehouser may also be liable if the defect is caused by their fault. In this case, if the manufacturer or seller has paid compensation, they may also claim indemnification against the transporter or warehouser.②

Sometimes a product is found to be defective after it has been put into circulation, then the manufacturer or seller of the product should take remedial measures such as stopping sales, providing warnings, or recalling the product in a timely manner. If damage is aggravated owing to the failure of the manufacturer or seller to timely take remedial measures, or if the remedial measures taken are not effective, the manufacturer or seller should be liable also for the aggravated part of the damage.③ If a defective product is recalled, the manufacturer or seller of the product shall bear the necessary expenses incurred to the infringed person.

If a defect of a product endangers the personal or property safety of a person, the person may request the manufacturer or seller of the product to stop infringement, remove the nuisance, or eliminate the danger.④ If a manufacturer or seller manufactures or sells a product knowing that the product is defective, or failing to take remedial measures in accordance with law, and thus causes death or severe bodily harm to a person, the person has a right to request for the corresponding punitive damages.⑤

§ 5:3:4:2 Torts Arising from Environmental Pollution

China adopts a polluter-pay rule so the non-fault liability rule applies to a polluter. A person who has polluted the environment or harmed the ecosystem

---

① Article 1203 of the Civil Code.
② Article 1204 of the Civil Code.
③ Article 1206 of the Civil Code.
④ Article 1205 of the Civil Code.
⑤ Article 1207 of the Civil Code.

and thus causes damage to others shall bear tort liability. ① Where two or more persons jointly cause pollution to the environment or damage to the ecosystem, the extent of liability of each actor shall be determined according to the factors such as the type, concentration, and quantity of discharge of the pollutants, the way, scope, and degree of damage to the ecological system, and the impact of the act on the consequences of damage. ② In order to establish such liability, the infringed person must prove that the actor's act violates the environment protection law and pollutes the environment, damage has been caused to the infringed person, and that there is a causal link between such act and such damage. If an actor intentionally pollutes the environment or harms the ecosystem in violation of the provisions of law resulting in serious consequences, the infringed person has a right to request for the corresponding punitive damages. ③

An actor may claim that the pollution is caused by *force majeure* and is not avoidable even if he has timely taken reasonable measures. However, the law provides that the actor has a burden to prove that he should not be liable or that his liability could be mitigated as provided by law, and that there is no causation between his act and the damage. ④ An actor may also defend itself by alleging that the pollution to the environment or damage to the ecosystem is caused owing to the fault of a third person, but the infringed person may still elect to sue either the actor or the third person. In case the infringed person elects to sue the actor, after making compensation, the actor may claim indemnification against the third person. ⑤

Where a tortfeasor causes damage to the ecosystem in violation of the State regulations and if restoration is possible, a State authorized agency or an organization authorized by law has the right to request the tortfeasor to bear the responsibility for restoration within a reasonable period of time. Where the tortfeasor fails to restore it within the time limit, the State authorized agency or the organization authorized by law may initiate the restoration on its own or

---

① Article 1229 of the Civil Code.
② Article 1231 of the Civil Code.
③ Article 1232 of the Civil Code.
④ Article 1230 of the Civil Code.
⑤ Article 1233 of the Civil Code.

entrust it with another person, with any expenses thus incurred to be borne by the tortfeasor. ①

Where damage to the ecosystem is caused in violation of the State regulations, the State authorized agency or the organization authorized by law has the right to request the tortfeasor to compensate for the following losses and expenses:

(1) losses caused by loss of service function from the time the ecological environment is damaged to the time the restoration is completed;

(2) losses caused by permanent damage to the function of the ecological environment;

(3) expenses for investigation, appraisal, and assessment of the damage to the ecological environment;

(4) expenses for cleaning-up the pollution and restoring the ecological environment; and

(5) other reasonable expenses incurred to prevent the occurrence or aggravation of the damage. ②

§ 5:3:4:3 Torts Arising from Ultrahazardous Activities or Objects

Ultrahazardous activities or ultrahazardous objects may cause personal injury or property damage to others. In order to minimize the potential damage, the law imposes a non-fault liability on an actor who engages in an ultra-hazardous operation or keeps ultrahazardous objects that have caused damage to others. ③ Meanwhile, in order to encourage the actors to lawfully engage in ultrahazardous operations, the amount of compensation to be paid by such an actor may be limited by law, unless the damage is caused by the actor intentionally or with gross negligence. ④

The Civil Code lists the various situations that may involve this group of torts. For instance, where a civil aircraft causes damage to a person, the operator of the aircraft shall bear tort liability, except that the operator does

---

① Article 1234 of the Civil Code.
② Article 1235 of the Civil Code.
③ Article 1236 of the Civil Code.
④ Article 1244 of the Civil Code.

not assume any liability if it can be proven that the damage is intentionally caused by the victim. ① Another situation involves a nuclear accident. Where a nuclear accident occurs at a civil nuclear facility or when nuclear materials are transported into or out of a civil nuclear facility and damage is thus caused to a person, the operator of the facility shall bear tort liability, except that the operator does not assume such liability if it can be proven that the damage is caused by a war, an armed conflict, a riot, or under other like circumstances, or the damage is intentionally caused by the victim. ②

Where the possession or use of flammable, explosive, highly toxic, highly radioactive, strongly corrosive, highly pathogenic, or other ultrahazardous things causes damage to another person, the possessor or user of these things shall bear tort liability, except that such a possessor or user does not assume any liability if it can be proven that the damage was intentionally caused by the victim or caused by *force majeure*. Where the infringed person is grossly negligent for the occurrence of the damage, the liability of the possessor or user may be mitigated. ③

Sometimes damage is caused to another person by a person engaging in work at a height, high voltage, or underground excavation activities, or by using high-speed rail transport vehicles, the operator shall bear tort liability, except that the operator does not assume any liability if it can be proven that the damage was intentionally caused by the victim or caused by *force majeure*. Likewise, if the infringed person is grossly negligent for the occurrence of the damage, the liability of the operator may be mitigated. ④

Where damage is caused to a person by an ultra-hazardous thing that is lost or abandoned, the owner of the ultra-hazardous thing shall bear tort liability. Where the owner has delivered the ultra-hazardous thing to another person for management, the manager shall bear tort liability, and the owner shall assume joint and several liability with the manager where he is at fault. ⑤ If the ultra-hazardous thing that causes damage is illegally possessed by a person, the illegal

---

① Article 1238 of the Civil Code.
② Article 1237 of the Civil Code.
③ Article 1239 of the Civil Code.
④ Article 1240 of the Civil Code.
⑤ Article 1241 of the Civil Code.

possessor of the ultra-hazardous thing shall bear tort liability. The owner or manager of the thing shall assume joint and several liability with the illegal possessor if he cannot prove that he has fulfilled a high duty of care to prevent the illegal possession. ①

Where a person, without authorization, enters into an area where ultra-hazardous activities are conducted or ultra-hazardous things are stored therein and is thus injured, the liability of the manager of the area may be mitigated or eliminated if it can be proven that he has taken sufficient security measures and fulfilled the duty of sufficient warning. ②

§ 5:3:4:4 Torts Arising from Animals

Since animals may bring about harm to people, anyone who keeps an animal shall abide by laws and regulations, respect social morality, and may not disturb the life of others. ③ Non-fault liability applies to this group of torts.

Where a domesticated animal causes damage to a person, the keeper or custodian of the animal shall bear tort liability, except that his liability may be mitigated or eliminated if it can be proven that the damage is caused by the infringed person intentionally or by gross negligence. ④ If a keeper or custodian of an animal fails to take safety measures on the animal in violation of the rules of management, and thus causes damage to a person, he shall bear tort liability, except that his liability may be mitigated if it can be proven that the damage is intentionally caused by the infringed person. ⑤

If a person breeds or keeps a vicious dog or otherwise a dangerous animal that the law prohibits people from breeding or keeping, he is liable for the damage caused by these animals to others. ⑥ Where an animal of a zoo causes damage to a person, the zoo shall bear tort liability unless it can be proven that it has fulfilled its duties of management. ⑦ If an abandoned or escaped animal causes damage to a person during the period of being abandoned or on the run,

---

① Article 1242 of the Civil Code.
② Article 1243 of the Civil Code.
③ Article 1251 of the Civil Code.
④ Article 1245 of the Civil Code.
⑤ Article 1246 of the Civil Code.
⑥ Article 80 of the Tort Liability Law (Article 1247 of the Civil Code).
⑦ Article 1248 of the Civil Code.

the original keeper or custodian of the animal shall bear tort liability. ① If an animal causes damage to a person due to a third person's fault, the infringed person may claim compensation against either the keeper or custodian of the animal, or against the third person. The keeper or custodian of the animal who has paid compensation may claim indemnification against the third person. ②

§ 5:3:4:5 Workers' Compensation

An employer shall be liable for an employee's injury suffered owing to an occupational disease or by an accident occurred during the time the employee is working for the employer within the working hour and at the working premise. Workers' compensation issue arises from both a work insurance relationship and a tort compensation relationship, and both the law on workers' compensation insurance and the tort law would be applied. Non-fault liability principle applies to these torts. If a worker suffers personal injury owing to or in connection with his work, once the injury has been determined by an administrative department or by a court, the worker has a right to request the employer to compensate for his damage. If the injury is caused by a third person, the worker may request either the third person or the employer to bear liability. After the employer has paid compensation, it has a right to indemnification against the third person. If the accident involves a labor relationship regulated by the Regulations on Workers' Compensation Insurance, then the regulations or insurance policy should be applied. ③

Case 36

Case 36: Xie v. Shanghai Zoo ④

Xie, a 5-year-old boy, went to Shanghai Zoo with his parents on April 10, 2011. At about 3 pm, Xie crossed the protective fence to feed the monkeys, and the middle finger of his right hand was bitten by a

---

① Article 1249 of the Civil Code.
② Article 1250 of the Civil Code.
③ Article 11 of the Interpretations on Compensation for Personal Injuries by the Supreme People's Court.
④ See the SPC Gazette, Issue 8, 2013.

monkey. When it happened, there was no personnel of the Zoo were present. After complaining to the Zoo, Xie's father took him to the hospital and the boy had to have an artificial finger installed. According to the hospital, Xie would need to replace the artificial finger every two years before he reached 18 years old, and then would need to replace it every four years. The annual maintenance fee for the finger would be 5% of the cost of the artificial finger. Xie sued in court.

The Changning District Court of Shanghai Municipality found that the monkey cage was made of metal net, outside which there posted several warnings with both pictures and languages including: No crossing the fence, no knocking, no teasing, *etc*. The distance between each two metal bars of the fences was about 15 cm, and Xie and the other children younger than 10 years old might easily go through the space. The main issues of this case included (1) whether the Zoo had performed its management duty so that its liability would be exempted; (2) whether Xie and his legal representatives were at fault so that the Zoo's liability may be mitigated; and (3) how to determine the amount of compensation.

Regarding the first issue, the court reasoned that the Zoo should assume a higher standard of duty of care. By posting the warnings, the Zoo had performed its duty of warning. The Zoo provided evidence proving that it arranged its personnel to patrol over the Zoo on a regular basis. The incident happened abruptly, and it was impossible to require the personnel of the Zoo to be present at everywhere at any time; therefore, the Zoo had performed its duty of inspection. In addition, the facilities of the monkey cage did not have any safety issue. However, the distance between the fence bars, which was 15 cm, could only prevent adults, but not young kids, from going through. While the Zoo was a public place and it always admitted in thousands of children below the school age, it should have foreseen the potential risks; however, it had not adopted any remedial measure. Therefore, the Zoo was at fault in this regard and had failed to perform its duty of management.

Regarding the negligence of Xie and his legal representative, the direct cause of Xie's injury was that he violated the rules of the Zoo and went through the protective fences to feed the monkeys. Xie was apparently at fault; however, since he was only 4 years old, his fault should be assumed by his legal guardians, i.e., Xie's parents. While Xie's parents saw the warning, they still negligently allowed Xie to cross over the fence bar. Such negligence would mitigate the Zoo's civil liability.

Regarding the amount of compensation, the main and proximate cause of Xie's injury was because Xie's legal representatives failed to take care of Xie. Therefore, they should assume 60% of the liability for compensation. The Zoo was also negligent in that its protective fences had defects and could not effectively prevent Xie from going through it; as a result, the Zoo should assume secondary liability, which was 40%.

Both Xie and Shanghai Zoo appealed to Shanghai No. 1 Intermediate People's Court. The appellate court affirms the lower court's decision, holding that:

(1) The Shanghai Zoo should, within ten days after the judgment becomes effective, compensate Xie for about 30,000 yuan, covering part of his medical expenses, transportation cost, food allowances for hospitalization, nursing fee, nutrition fee, cost for the artificial finger incurred on December 13, 2011, and the disability compensation.

(2) The Zoo should compensate Xie for his pains and suffering of 2,000 yuan, and the attorney's fee of 2,000 yuan.

(3) The appraisal fee of 1,930 yuan should be shared by Xie (1,158 yuan) and the Zoo (772 yuan); the litigation cost of 1,828.42 yuan for the first instance trial (50% off because it was a simplified proceeding) should be shared by Xie (1,428.42 yuan) and the Zoo (400 yuan); the litigation cost for appeal of 3,656.8 yuan should also be shared by Xie (1,828.4 yuan) and the Zoo (1828.4 yuan).

§ 5:4 Remedies and Defenses

§ 5:4:1 Overview of Remedies

The Chinese tort law imposes liabilities on the tortfeasors and grants various remedies to the infringed persons. The most important remedy is monetary compensation. In a tort litigation, the court will grant remedies in accordance with a few principles. The first principle is that a plaintiff's damage must be fully compensated. In other words, the compensation should cover all of the property damage, personal injury, and pains and suffering (also called compensation for mental distress, which is categorized as a kind of non-pecuniary loss in China), no matter the damage is direct, indirect, or consequential. However, the compensation may only be based on the actual and reasonable damage, and may only be made through property compensation by the tortfeasor no matter the tortious act has caused property damage, personal injury, or mental distress of the infringed person, and the tortfeasor's personal freedom may not be restricted. Therefore, a tortfeasor may only need to surrender proprietary interests to compensate for the damage suffered by the infringed person.

In addition, the amount of compensation that the infringed person is entitled to receive may be offset against the benefit that he has received from the tortious act. The contributory negligence of the infringed person may mitigate the tortfeasor's liability. The fairness principle should be applied when determining the scope of damages, and the parties' financial situations must be considered so that equity may be achieved.

The following sub-sections introduces the rules regulating who may initiate a tort litigation and who may be sued.

§ 5:4:1:1 Qualified Plaintiffs

Generally, the person who has a standing to bring a tort litigation against a tortfeasor includes a direct victim and indirect victim of a tortious act, and a fetus and next-of-kin of the person who dies because of a tortious act.

Direct victims are the persons whose rights have been infringed upon by a tortious act and who have therefore suffered direct injuries. Direct victims may include (a) a direct victim with full capacity for performing civil juristic acts; (b) a direct victim with no or limited capacity for performing civil juristic acts represented by his legal representative; (c) multiple direct victims in a collective action or represented action;①and (d) a direct victim whose right to

---

① According to Article 59 of the Opinions on Certain Issues on Application of the Civil Procedure Law of the PRC issued by the Supreme People's Court, if there are more than 10 direct victims, they may initiate a collective action if the number of direct victims has not been determined, or a represented action if the number of the direct victims has been determined.

life has been infringed upon; in this case the persons with a standing to sue include the deceased person who died owing to the tortious act and the next-of-kin of the deceased person who suffers property damage or pains and suffering arising from the death of the decedent.

If a tortious act infringes upon the personal rights of a direct victim, and consequently causes an indirect harm to another person, the latter person is an indirect victim. For example, where an infringed person dies, his close relatives have the right to request the tortfeasor to bear tort liability. In addition, the person who has paid for his medical expenses, funeral expenses, and other reasonable expenses also has the right to request the tortfeasor to compensate the expenses, except for those expenses already paid by the tortfeasor.[①] Indirect victims may include: (a) a person the direct victim had been supporting before he died or lost work ability resulting from the tortious act; (b) the spouse of the direct victim who has lost companion owing to the injury suffered by the direct victim; and (c) a person whose right to health is harmed by being frightened by the tortious act. The fetus left by a direct victim and his next-of-kin also have the standing to sue if the decedent's right to reputation, privacy, likeness, honor, or the deceased' body or remains is infringed upon.

§ 5:4:1:2 Qualified Defendants

The qualified defendants, *i.e.*, the persons who may be sued in a tort litigation are those who infringe upon other's civil-law rights and interests by their acts and thus incur tort liability according to law. A qualified defendant may include a natural person, a legal person, or an unincorporated organization that commits a tort by himself or itself, or by another person's tortious act and is required by law to assume civil liability. Therefore, a qualified defendant may assume direct liability owing to his own act or vicarious liability owing to another person's act as discussed in the previous sub-sections. In addition, a person who bears secondary or supplemental liability according to law is also a qualified defendant in a tort litigation.

---

① Article 1181 of the Civil Code.

§ 5:4:2 Forms of Remedies

The forms of remedies that the tort law grants to an infringed person include proprietary remedies, non-proprietary remedies, and hybrid remedies. ① The proprietary remedies include restitution, restoration, and the various types of damages. The non-proprietary remedies include cessation of the infringement, elimination of adverse effect and rehabilitation of reputation, and extension of apology. The hybrid remedies include removal of the nuisance and elimination of the danger.

Among the proprietary remedies, damages may include compensatory damages and punitive damages, with the compensatory damages as the most important and fundamental remedies under the tort law, covering damages for property damage, personal injury, and pains and suffering. After damage has been caused, the parties may negotiate the method of payment of the compensation. Where they fail to reach an agreement, compensation shall be paid in a lump sum, or may be paid in installments where it is truly difficult for the tortfeasor to make a lump-sum payment, except that the infringed person may request the tortfeasor to provide a corresponding security. ② The court may allow such a request after considering the financial ability of the defendant and the security provided therefor. However, the expenses incurred before the ending of the argument phase of the first instance trial, the compensation for wrongful death, and the compensation for pains and suffering must be paid in a lump sum. ③

If the act of a tortfeasor violates the administrative law or criminal law in addition to the tort law so that he has to concurrently bear civil, administrative, and criminal liabilities, the assumption of administrative or criminal liabilities by the person may not affect the civil liability he should bear. If his assets are insufficient to pay for all the liabilities, the civil liability shall be paid first. ④

§ 5:4:2:1 Remedies for Personal Injury

Personal injury under the Chinese law includes physical injury, wrongful

---

① Article 179 of the Civil Code.
② Article 1187 of the Civil Code.
③ Article 20 of the Interpretations on Compensation for Personal Injuries.
④ Article 187 of the Civil Code.

death, and the infringement to a person's right to corporeal integrity. Where a person suffers personal injury as a result of an infringement by another person, compensation shall be made for his medical expenses, nursing expenses, transportation expenses, nutrition expenses, food allowances for hospitalization, and the other reasonable expenses for treatment and rehabilitation, as well as the lost earnings due to missed work. Where a person is disabled as a result of an infringement by another person, compensation shall also include the costs of auxiliary equipment and disability compensation. Where a person dies as a result of an infringement by another person, compensation shall also include his funeral expenses and death compensation. ① The main types of damages for personal injury include the following:

(1) General compensation for personal injury. It includes the reasonable expenses incurred for treatment and recovery, such as medical expenses, lost wages, nursing fees, transportation costs, the fees for nutrition, and the lost income due to the missed working hours resulting from the injury.

(2) Compensation for loss of work ability. If a person is disabled owing to a tortious act, he loses his work ability. The SPC's Interpretations on Compensation for Personal Injuries provided that in this situation, the amount of compensation should be determined on the degree of the plaintiff's loss of work ability or the degree of the plaintiff's disability. The damages may cover the compensation for disability, life-support facilities, the necessary fees for recovery, nursing fees, and the subsequent treatment expenses.

(3) Compensation for wrongful death. If the victim dies, the compensation should also cover the wrongful death compensation, the funeral fees, the living expenses of the person supported by the deceased, and the other reasonable fees. Since there are huge differences in the living standards of urban cities and rural areas, and among different provinces and cities, the amounts of compensation granted by different courts vary, which creates some adverse effect when the plaintiffs died in a same accident received different amount of compensations. The Civil Code now has unified the rule by providing that if a same tortious act causes multiple deaths, the same amount of death

---

① Article 1179 of the Civil Code.

compensation may be applied to all of the victims. ①

(4) Compensation for support fees. If the victim has lost his work ability or has lost his life owing to a tortious act, a person who had been supported by the victim is entitled to receive compensation from the tortfeasor.

(5) Other remedies. If the tortious act endangers the personal or property safety of any other person, the infringed person may request such other remedies as cessation of the infringement, removal of the obstruction, or elimination of the danger. ②

§ 5:4:2:2 Remedies for Property Damage

Property damage is the loss that an infringed person has suffered owing to a tortious act done by a tortfeasor which infringes upon his personal rights and interests or proprietary interests and may be a direct or indirect property damage. In other words, property damage may be caused by two kinds of torts, one is a tort infringing upon the infringed person's personal rights and interests, and the other is a tort infringing upon the infringed person's proprietary rights and interests. Under the first circumstance, compensation for the indirect property damage shall be made according to the damage suffered by the infringed person or the interests gained by the tortfeasor. Where it is difficult to determine the damage suffered by the infringed person and the interests gained by the tortfeasor, and where the infringed person cannot agree with the tortfeasor on the amount of compensation and thus files a lawsuit with the court, the court shall determine the amount of compensation according to the actual situation. ③

Under the second circumstance, the direct property damage includes conversion and trespass on the property. Conversion occurs when a tortfeasor illegally possesses the property owned by another person so that the original owner loses possession or even the ownership right over the property. Typical examples include illegal seizure or illegal detention of other's property. Trespass occurs when a tortfeasor brings harm to the property owned by

---

① Article 1180 of the Civil Code.
② Article 1167 of the Civil Code.
③ Article 1182 of the Civil Code.

another person so that the value or value in use of the property has been damaged or totally destructed, and the original owner's real rights in the property are lost or decreased in value. In addition to the ownership right, other proprietary rights such as a right to usufruct, a secured interest, a right to possession, a right *in personam*, and intellectual property rights may also be harmed.

Both direct and indirect damage on the proprietary rights must be fully and reasonably compensated according to law. The compensation for direct property damage shall be calculated according to the market price at the time the damage occurs or by other reasonable methods.① Such compensation may be based on appraisal or sale, including compensation in kind, such as restitution and restoration of the property to its original condition. The compensation for indirect property damage may only be made through appraisal and sale. If the property that has been damaged cannot be restored to its original condition or the original property cannot be physically returned, the loss that the property has suffered should be appraised and compensated by monetary damages.

The plaintiff who suffers property damage may also request other remedies, such as cessation of the infringement, removal of the obstruction, or elimination of the danger.②

§ 5:4:2:3 Remedies for Pains and Suffering

The tort law also allows remedies for non-pecuniary damage including compensation for loss of intangible interests and for the pains and suffering.

Where, owing to an actor's intentional or grossly negligent act, a specific thing of personal significance of a natural person is infringed upon, which causes serious mental distress to the person, the infringed person has a right to request compensation for the loss of the non-pecuniary intangible interests. Generally, compensations for the loss of non-pecuniary intangible interests arise from the infringement of a real right and the interests harmed include the loss of the various personality rights or relation-based rights. The "specific

---

① Article 1184 of the Civil Code.
② Article 1167 of the Civil Code.

thing" may have less material value but may have symbolic significance. This rule must be implemented strictly on the basis of necessity, and the property must not be a normal property, but a specific property with special symbolic significance which involves interests in personality. The purpose of the compensation is to comfort the victim's pains and suffering, punish the tortfeasor's wrong doing, and warn the public.

Where an infringement upon the personal rights and interests of a natural person causes serious mental distress, the infringed person has a right to request compensation for pains and suffering.① Compensation for pains and suffering is also called compensation for mental distress or consolation, and covers the pains and suffering arising from infringement of a person's right to life, right to corporeal integrity, and right to health. Infringement of a person's right to corporeal integrity or right to health may bring about pains and suffering to the person, and infringement upon a person's right to life may bring about pains and suffering to the next-of-kin of the person. The purposes of remedies for pains and suffering are also to comfort the plaintiff, punish the tortfeasor, and warn the public.

The scope of compensation for pains and suffering has been a heated topic in China. When a tortfeasor deprives a person of his right to life, the next-of-kin of the victim may ask for compensation for wrongful death. If a tortfeasor's act makes the victim disabled with the working ability lost, the victim is entitled to compensation for disability. Therefore, for quite some time, the compensation for wrongful death and the compensation for disability were regarded as compensation for pains and suffering in China, and the Chinese law on compensation for pains and suffering has experienced a long history. The GPCL did not provide for compensation for pains and suffering at all. The Measures on Dealing with Traffic Accidents tried to cure the insufficiency of the GPCL by providing wrongful death compensation to remedy pains and suffering, but it was defined as the compensation for infringement upon the right to life. Then the Law on Protection of the Rights and Interests of Consumers and the State Compensation Law both provide the compensation for wrongful death and for disability in tort cases. These

---

① Article 1183 of the Civil Code.

compensations were generally regarded as compensation for pains and suffering, which was confirmed by the Interpretations on Compensation for Pains and Suffering issued by the SPC.

However, the SPC's Interpretations on Compensation for Personal Injuries decided that the compensations for wrongful death and disability were actually compensations for property damage caused by personal injury, which was not for pains and suffering. Article 18 of the Interpretations provided that if a victim or the next-of-kin of the victim who died because of a tortious act had suffered pains and suffering, he might ask the court to grant compensation for pains and suffering according to the Interpretations on Certain Issues on Determination of the Compensation for Pains and Suffering in Tort Cases. It further provided that the right to compensation for pains and suffering generally could not be transferred or inherited. The amount of compensation for pains and suffering should be determined after considering the degree of fault of the tortfeasor, the method, circumstance, and the way of the tortious act, the consequence caused by the tortious act, the benefit received by the tortfeasor, the financial ability of the tortfeasor to assume liability, and the average living standard of the people living in the place where the court is located.① The compensation must be paid for the reasonable losses, and the principle of fairness and honesty and the principle of good faith must be observed.

Finally, the Civil Code has integrated the rules developed in the judicial practice and provides a unified rule in Article 1183 providing that an infringed person may request compensation for pains and suffering if a tortfeasor's act infringes upon his personal rights and interests which causes serious mental distress to him. It is quite clear that the compensation for death or disability is not regarded as the compensation for pains and suffering any more.

The other ways of remedies for pains and suffering include cessation of infringement, removal of adverse effect, restoration of one's reputation, and extending apology.

§ 5:4:2:4 Punitive Damages

Punitive damages had not been recognized in China for a long time until

---

① Article 5 of the Interpretations on Compensation for Pains and Suffering.

1993 when the Law on Protection of the Rights and Interests of the Consumers was enacted. This is the first law in China that plaintiffs are allowed to request punitive remedies in a civil suit. It provides in its Article 49 that if a provider of commodity or service commits fraud, the consumer may request an enhanced amount of compensation which may be up to twice the amount of the purchase price or the service fee that the consumer has paid for it. Since the amount of compensation allowed exceeds the amount of actual loss suffered by the consumer, it is regarded as punitive damages, and this Article is regarded as having established the punitive damage system in China.

Upon endeavor of many scholars, the legislature finally adopted the punitive damages rule into Article 47 of the Tort Liability Law, which likewise has been integrated into Article 179 of the Civil Code. Although punitive damages are not listed as one form of civil law remedies, it does provide that punitive damages may be applied if so required by law. Currently, the Civil Code provides three situations where punitive damages may be imposed. The first situation is where a person's intellectual property rights have been intentionally infringed upon by another person and the circumstances are serious, whereby the infringed person may request for punitive damages. ① The second situation is when a manufacturer or seller manufactures or sells a product knowing that the product is defective, or failing to take remedial measures in accordance with law, so that death or serious physical harm is caused to a person, whereby the infringed person may request punitive damages. ② The third situation is when a tortfeasor intentionally pollutes the environment or damages the ecosystem in violation of the provisions of law resulting in serious consequences, and then the infringed person may request punitive damages. ③ In addition, other laws, such as the Law on Protection of the Rights and Interests of Consumers and the Food Safety Law, *etc.*, also provides for punitive damages. However, the standard and amount of the punitive damages have yet been clarified. It is expected that the Supreme People's Court will soon make Interpretations on this issue based on judicial practices.

---

① Article 1185 of the Civil Code.
② Article 1207 of the Civil Code.
③ Article 1232 of the Civil Code.

§ 5:4:3 Defenses

Defenses are the facts that defendants may raise to prove that the cause of action alleged by the plaintiff is not valid or not completely valid. They may use general defenses and special defenses.

§ 5:4:3:1 General Defenses

The following are the general defenses available to a defendant in a tort litigation.

(1) Authorized acts. If a person, during the course of performing his duty according to law, infringes upon the personal or proprietary rights of another person for the purpose of protecting social public interest and the lawful rights and interests of the other citizens, the person is not liable for the harm thus caused if his act is within the scope of authority. However, the person is liable for compensation if his act is not lawful. In order to defend oneself on the ground of an authorized act, the defendant must prove that the act at issue is lawfully authorized for the purpose of protecting social public interest and the lawful rights and interests of the other persons, the act of performing the duty is lawful and has not exceeded the authority, the procedure and method used are also lawful, and the act is necessary under the circumstance.

Sometimes even if an act is not authorized, an actor may also be exempted from liability according to law. For example, a person who is sued for committing a tort against another person's right to likeness may be exempted from liability if he can prove that he uses the image of a person for personal study or scientific research purposes, or for news reporting, *etc.*, as provided by law. ①

(2) Justifiable defenses. If a person, in order to protect his own interests, public interest, the interests of another person from being harmed, infringes upon another person's rights or interests, he is not liable on the ground of justifiable defense if he can prove that his purpose is justified, the harm is going on and illegal, his act is against the person who is inflicting the harm, and his act has not exceeded a necessary limit. If his act exceeds the necessary

---

① Article 1020 of the Civil Code.

limit and thus causes harm to another person, he should bear appropriate civil liability.①

(3) Necessities. When a person causes harm to another person when seeking to avoid a risk in response to an emergency for the social public interest or for protecting himself or another person to avoid a greater harm, he is not liable if he can prove that his act is a "had to" act, the act has not exceeded the necessary limit, and the damage inflicted is less serious than the risks. The person who creates the risk is liable for damages.

However, if the risk is caused by a natural force, the person who causes harm to others when seeking to avoid the risk bears no civil liability, but may be required to make appropriate compensation. If the measures adopted by him are improper or exceed the necessary limit and thus cause undue harm to others, he shall bear appropriate civil liability.②

(4) Assumption of risk. If it was the plaintiff who invited the defendant to perform an act which infringed upon his rights, the plaintiff is said to have voluntarily assumed the harmful result as long as the act was not in violation of law or against public ethics. The plaintiff may make a commitment in advance to exempt all or part of the liability that may be imposed on the defendant, except that such an exemption clause in advance is not valid if it involves the personal injury or property damage to be done to the other party. Where a person voluntarily participates in a recreational or sports activity with certain inherent risks and thus suffers damage due to another participant's act, he may not request the other participant to bear tort liability unless the damage is caused by the latter's intentional act or gross negligence.③

(5) Self-help. Under certain circumstances, a right-holder may adopt other self-help measures in an emergent situation to protect his own rights. Specifically, where a person's lawful rights and interests are infringed upon and he may suffer irreparable harm if actions are not immediately taken because the situation is urgent and no protection from the State organ is immediately available, he may take reasonable measures such as seizing the property of the

---

① Article 181 of the Civil Code.
② Article 182 of the Civil Code.
③ Article 1176 of the Civil Code.

tortfeasor to the extent necessary for protecting his lawful rights and interests, provided that he shall immediately thereafter request the relevant State organ to handle it.① In order to defend himself on this ground, the person must prove that there is a valid debtor-creditor relationship existing before he uses the self-help measure to protect himself. A person who has taken an improper measure so that damage is caused to another person shall bear tort liability.

§ 5:4:3:2 Special Defenses

Special defenses are also called mitigating factors because they may mitigate liability or sometimes completely relieve the defendant from liability. Special defenses include the following:

(1) The plaintiff was at fault (contributory or comparative negligence). If the damage is caused or enhanced only by the plaintiff's intentional act, the defendant is not liable. However, the defendant's liability will only be mitigated if the plaintiff's fault simply contributed to the damage.②

(2) A third person was at fault.③ If a third person, other than the plaintiff or the defendant, intentionally harms the plaintiff or enhances the harm, the third person is liable and the defendant's liability will be completely barred or mitigated to the extent of the aggravated harm.④ A tortfeasor's liability may also be completely barred if the damage is caused solely by the third person's fault; otherwise, the tortfeasor and the third person will be jointly and severally liable, and each of them shall bear the liability in proportion to their respective share of fault if the share of fault can be determined or in equal share if it cannot be determined.⑤

(3) *Force Majeure*. *Force majeure* refers to the objective conditions which are unforeseeable, unavoidable, and insurmountable.⑥ It is independent from human act, and is not controlled by human will. *Force majeure* events include natural causes, such as earthquake, typhoon, flood, *etc*. and social events such

---

① Article 1177 of the Civil Code.
② Article 1173 of the Civil Code.
③ Article 1175 of the Civil Code.
④ Article 1174 of the Civil Code.
⑤ Article 1172 of the Civil Code.
⑥ Article 180 of the Civil Code.

as wars. When *force majeure* happens and harm is caused, the parties generally will not assume any civil liability if the *force majeure* is the only cause of the damage. This rule is subject to exceptions. For example, Article 34 of the Postal Law provides that the post offices will not be relieved of compensation liability even if the loss of the money remittance or value-insured packages was caused by *force majeure*.

Case 37

Case 37: Jiang & Zeng v. Qin & Su[①]

Qin and Zeng are both vegetable farmers in a village of Nanhai District, Foshan City, Guangdong Province and live in the work sheds in a vegetable farm. In the morning of January 15, 2015, Su came to their farm to pick up vegetables. When Su saw Qin's grandson, he gave the boy a few plantains. Qin and his wife saw that their grandson was eating plantains, and asked Su, who confirmed that the plantains were given by Su. Qins did not say anything, and then Su left. In the morning at about 11 am, Zeng's granddaughter came to the farm to play with Qin's grandson, each of them ate a plantain. At about 2 pm, the two children were playing along the farm, and Qin suddenly heard his grandson yelling. Qin and his wife went up to find that Zeng's granddaughter fell on the ground without consciousness, and a half-eaten plantain was found there. Qin called out for Zeng who was working nearby. Zeng and his wife came up knowing that their granddaughter ate a plantain, they thought the girl was poisoned and called 110 and 120. Afterwards, Zeng, Qin, and another villager sent the girl to the local clinic. The clinic doctor and the doctors from No. 8 People's Hospital of Nanhai District, Foshan City who subsequently arrived extended rescue, and took out from the girl's body a piece of plantain of 5 centimeters in diameter with blood on it. Zeng's granddaughter died at 3:20 pm and the cause of her death was asphyxia through inhalation of foreign bodies.

[①] See (2015) Fo Zhong Fa Min Yi Zhong Zi No. 1211, reprinted in the SPC Gazette, Issue 11, 2016.

The girl's parents went to work in the morning of the day when the incident happened, and the girl was left with her grandparents. They sued on January 26, 2015 requesting Qin and Su to compensate 737,646.5 yuan in total for their loss.

The first instance court examined the fact, and found the following:

(1) the plantain was not poisonous and complied with the food safety standard. Su only gave some plantains to Qin's grandson and obtained consent of Qin and his wife. Su did not give any plantain to Zeng's granddaughter, and Su was not present when it happened, so Su could not have foreseen that the plantain would finally be given to Zeng's granddaughter, let alone that Zeng's granddaughter would be choked. Therefore, Su was not at fault for the result, and there was no causal link between Su's delivery of the plantain and the death of Zeng's granddaughter.

(2) Su gave the plantain to Qin's grandson after obtaining consent from Qin and his wife, and afterwards, the plantains were under the control of Qin. There was no evidence proving that the plantain was taken by Zeng's granddaughter herself or given by Qin or Qin's grandson. No matter what, Qin or Qin's grandson would not have the intent to harm Zeng's granddaughter. Zeng was five years old and had already gone to the kindergarten. Based on the common sense, a child at her age would be able to independently take food by herself. Although Qin was present when the girl was eating the plantain, Qin was not her legal guardian, when she was eating the plantain by herself. After finding the girl falling on the ground, Qin timely notified Zeng's family and assisted them in sending the girl to the hospital. Qin had performed a reasonable rescue and did not have any subjective intent or negligence regarding the girl's death. Therefore, Qin was not at fault.

(3) Su's giving the plantains to Qin's grandson, or Qin's giving the plantains to Zeng's granddaughter was a good sharing act among neighbors and friends. The act of sharing food itself would not cause the death. The cause for the death of Zeng's granddaughter was that she bit too much of the plantain, and swallowed too quickly so that she was choked. This was an unexpected tragedy caused by incidental factors. The acts of Qin and Su were only the factual cause but were not the legal

cause of the girl's death. Neither Qin nor Su sought the damaging consequence or let it go unchecked, and neither of them were at fault legally or morally. It was unfortunate that the plaintiffs were sad about their daughter's death, but only with the factual cause, no liability could be imposed on Qin or Su who were not at fault.

Finally, the court dismissed the case in a summary proceeding, and requested the plaintiffs to pay the litigation cost reduced by half which was 2,094.12 yuan.

Zeng and Jiang appealed.

On appeal, the Intermediate People's Court of Foshan City reasons that Article 6 of the Tort Liability Law provides that an actor who infringes upon other's civil-law rights or interests owing to his fault shall assume tort liability. This article provides the principle of liability based on fault, which means that a person may not necessarily assume liability for compensation solely because damage is caused, but it is more important to see whether the actor is at fault. There will be liability only if there is fault. Generally, fault includes intentional fault and negligent fault. Intentional fault refers to a situation whereby an actor conducts an infringing act for the purpose of harming others, or knowing that his act would cause damage to others. Negligent fault refers to a situation whereby an actor fails to perform his duty of care owing to his negligence or indolence. Based on the facts found in this case, the appellate court agrees with the lower court's finding of the facts that Qin had neither intentional fault nor negligent fault for the death of Zeng's granddaughter. Therefore, the lower court's decision is affirmed. The cost of 4,188.23 yuan for the second instance proceeding should be paid by Jiang and Zeng.

Chapter 6
Family Law

§ 6:1 General Introduction

The core members of a typical family in China include a husband, a wife, and one or more children. Sometimes the other next-of-kin of the core members, such as the parents and siblings of the husband and wife, as well as the children of their children are also part of the family. Each family member has rights against and obligations to the other members, and their rights and obligations are regulated by, among others, the family law. Family law, as part of the civil law, regulates the proprietary and personal relationship within a marriage, between the husband and wife, and among the family members. It also applies to an adoptive relationship and the other intra-family matters. Therefore, Chinese family law in its broader sense includes the marriage law, adoption law, and succession law. This Chapter mainly introduces Chinese marriage law and adoption law.

§ 6:1:1 Historical Development of Chinese Marriage Law

Marriage is the unity of a man and a woman for the purpose of permanently living together. The development of the Chinese marriage and family law has experienced a long history.

The first Marriage Law was enacted and became effective in 1950 with only eight chapters and 27 articles. It was one of the important laws enacted right after the founding of the new China. The basic principles of this law were to abolish the feudal system of marriage and family which featured arranged and forced marriages, the superiority of men to women, and ignorance of the children's interests, and to adopt a new democratic marriage system which was to feature marital autonomy, monogamy, equality of rights of both women and men, and protection of the lawful interests of women and children. Article 2 of this law clearly prohibited bigamy, taking concubines or child brides, interference with a widow's right to re-marriage, or demanding property in the name of marriage. The 1950 Marriage Law had been effective for 30 years, during which period it had served an important purpose of destroying the feudal system and establishing a socialist system of marriage and family. It had granted to Chinese people, especially Chinese women the right to marital autonomy, and had improved the family and marriage relationships in China. In order to further remove the obstacles and disturbances and strongly implement the Marriage Law, the State Council set the March of 1953 as the Movement Month for Implementing the Marriage Law.

The second Marriage Law was enacted on September 10, 1980 and took effect since January 1, 1981 to repeal the first Marriage Law. The Civil Affairs Department, upon approval of the State Council, issued the Measures for Marriage Registration on November 11, 1980 to guide marriage registration, which was later on replaced by the new Measures in 1986. The enactment of the second Marriage Law symbolized that the legislation on marriage and family in China had entered into a new era. While many provisions of the 1950 Marriage Law had been integrated into the 1980 Marriage Law and almost remained unchanged, the new law had also made the necessary modifications and supplements on various important issues arising from the new situations based on the judicial practices. It had five chapters and 37 articles. The first chapter, the General Principles, was about the purposes and principles of the marriage law. Chapter two was about entering into marriage, including the conditions and procedure for establishing a marriage. Chapter three was about family relationships, providing the rights and obligations of the spouses, parents and children, and their immediate relatives. Chapter four was about divorce, including the principles in dealing with the dissolution of marriages, and the issues on custody of children and disposition of property upon divorce. Chapter five was supplementary provisions, which was about the punishment for non-compliance and implementation and enforcement of the law.

The 1980 Marriage Law maintained the principles of marital autonomy, monogamy, and equality of men and women stated in the old marriage law, and expanded the principle of protecting the lawful interests of women and children, so that the lawful rights and interests of the elderly and the principle of family planning are added. In addition, it had new provisions prohibiting arranged marriage and mercenary marriage, and prohibited abuses and abandonments by family members. The law also changed the conditions for entering into marriage. The legal age for marriage provided by the old law was 20 for males and 18 for females, but the new legal age had been changed to 22 for males and 20 for females. The old law prohibited marriages between relatives based on the local custom, but the new law clearly prohibited a person from marrying a collateral relative by blood up to the third degree of kinship.

Regarding the parent-child relationship, the 1980 Law had added the rights and obligations of the parents to discipline and protect their minor children. It had also expanded the scope of the immediate relatives, added the rights and obligations between grandparents and grandchildren, between and among the grandchildren, and between and among the siblings. In order to further reflect the principle of equality of men and women, the 1980 Law added a provision that children might follow their father's family name or their mother's family name, and regarded family planning as a mutual obligation of both spouses. It also modified the divorce procedure. If one spouse requested a divorce, he might go to the relevant department for mediation first, or directly go to the people's court to petition for divorce. It allowed the court to rule for divorce if mutual affection no longer existed between the spouses, and if the mediation did not work.

The 1980 Marriage Law had been effective from January 1, 1981 to April 28, 2001, for over twenty years. With the economic development, Chinese people's living conditions and life styles have been changed, and there have been emerged new issues in the marriage and family law area. Chinese legislature had put the re-discussion of the Marriage Law on the agenda of the NPC in 1995. After five years, the amended Marriage Law was enacted on April 28, 2001. The draft of this Law was publicized for public comments on January 11, 2001 before it was finally made. Until February 28, 2001, the legislature had received 3,829 comments, covering almost all issues that the legislature had encountered during the deliberation of the draft. Therefore, the third Marriage law of the PRC was enacted after fully considering the public opinions. In the General Provisions of the amended Marriage Law, there had been provisions directly regulating the new issues existing in the marriage and family areas. For example, since there had been concerns about illegal cohabitations and domestic violence in the society, the new Law provided that "bigamy or cohabiting with another person while being married" and "practicing domestic violence, or abusing or abandoning family members" are the legal causes of divorce, if mediation fails. In order to implement the amended Marriage Law, the Supreme People's Court made four judicial interpretations① in 2001, 2004, 2011, and 2018 respectively. Now the Marriage Law and its judicial interpretations have all been integrated into Book Six of the Civil Code which has become the most important source of Chinese family law.

§6:1:2 Principles of Chinese Family Law

The Civil Code has integrated the various principles established in the previous versions of family law upon considering the new development in this area.

§6:1:2:1 Principle of Marital Autonomy

Marital autonomy is the most fundamental principle of Chinese marriage law under which the parties to a marriage have the right to form and dissolve the marriage relationship by their own will and according to the legal procedure, and are free from other's illegal intervention. The Constitution prohibits anyone from restricting others' marital autonomy.② The Civil Code also expressly provides that a marriage system is based on marital autonomy.③ The Criminal Law provides that any violent interference with other's marital autonomy could constitute a crime, and those who commits this crime will be

---

① The first is Interpretations I on Certain Issues Arising from Application of the Marriage Law of the PRC; the second is Interpretations II on Certain Issues Arising from Application of the Marriage Law of the PRC.
② Article 49 of the Constitution.
③ Articles 1041 – 1042 of the Civil Code.

sentenced up to two years imprisonment or detention. If the victim died because of such interference, the accused person may be sentenced to imprisonment for 2 - 7 years.[1]

Marital autonomy infers both freedom of entering into a marriage and freedom of divorce. Under this principle, when getting married, the two parties must be completely voluntary and any coercion by the other party or by any third person is not allowed. The parties intending to enter into a marriage must comply with the legal conditions and procedures. The marital autonomy is a civil-law right of the citizens in the marital relationship, and it equally applies to unmarried people intending to get married and divorced people intending to get remarried. On the other hand, the spouses have the right to divorce by agreement, or go to court requesting a divorce if the spouses' mutual affection no longer exists and the spousal relationship cannot be maintained. Divorce must also comply with legal conditions and procedures.

To implement the marital autonomy, the Civil Code expressly prohibits arranged marriages, mercenary marriages, and the other acts interfering with the right to marital autonomy. An arranged marriage is normally defined as a marriage arranged by a third person, including a parent, against the will of the parties. A mercenary marriage refers to the situation in which a third person, including a parent, for the purpose of gaining a large amount of money or property, arranges and forces other people to get married. The other activities that interfere with the marital autonomy may include interference of a child's marriage by parents, interference of a parent's re-marriage by a child, and interference with others' freedom of divorce.

§ 6:1:2:2 **Principle of Monogamy**

The Chinese marriage system is based on monogamy, which means that only one man and one woman may form a marriage and become spouses. Neither of them may have two or more spouses either publicly or secretly. Article 1042 of the Civil Code expressly prohibits bigamy, and provides that no one who has a spouse may cohabit with another person. Among the situations provided in Article 1051 in which a marriage is void, bigamy is listed as one of

---

[1] Article 257 of the Criminal Law.

them. If a spouse has committed bigamy or cohabited with another person, which causes divorce, the other spouse has a right to claim compensation.[①] All of these provisions reflect the spirit of the principle of monogamy, which means that no one may have two or more spouses at the same time, no one may re-marry before his spouse dies or they divorce, and any public or secret marriage of one husband with more wives or one wife with more husbands are illegal and subject to punishment.

Bigamy is committed when a person with a spouse re-marries another person or cohabits with another person in the name of spouses, or if a person who marries or lives with another person in the name of spouses while he knows that the other person has a spouse. Bigamy may be in one of three forms: legal bigamy, factual bigamy, and long-term cohabitation. Legal bigamy occurs when a person registers a new marriage with someone else before the first marriage is dissolved. Factual bigamy occurs when a person cohabits with someone else in the name of spouses but has not registered the marriage before the first marriage is dissolved. The third form, which was provided by the amended Marriage Law, occurs when a person with a spouse had been cohabiting with someone else continuously and stably but not in the name of spouses. All these constitute bigamy. The circumstance would be more serious if a person cohabits with someone who is the spouse of a military personnel on active duty, and if a crime of disrupting the marriage of an army man would be constituted. The general principle for dealing with bigamy is to maintain the first marriage and dissolve the subsequent marriage. Even if the spouse of the first marriage requests a divorce, the divorce disputes will be dealt with after the subsequent marriage is determined to be invalid and dissolved. In addition to bigamy, there are other situations where the monogamy may be destroyed, such as adultery and cohabitation.

§ 6:1:2:3   Principle of Equality of Men and Women

The status of men and women in a marriage or family represents their social status. Historically, women did not have an equal right with men. However, this situation has been changed after the PRC has been founded.

---

① Article 1091 of the Civil Code.

Article 48 of the Chinese Constitution clearly provides that both men and women are equal in political, economic, cultural, social, and marital life, which is called "five equality" of men and women. Article 1055 of the Civil Code also recognizes the equality of men and women as the basic principle of the family law, specifying the "five equality" provided by the Constitution. It mainly emphasizes the equality of men and women in marital relationship and family relationship.

The equality of men and women in marital relationship means that both men and women have an equal right to entering into a marriage and dissolve a marriage, i.e., divorce. The conditions for both men and women to get married or divorce in law are equal. In addition, the status and the rights and obligations of the wife and husband are equal. The Civil Code has a provision requiring the spouses to be loyal to each other, respect each other, and care for each other, emphasizing the mutual obligations between the spouses. ①

The equality of men and women in family relationship also means that the spouses have equal status in a family. Specifically, both spouses have an equal right to retain their own surname and given name, ② both spouses are free to engage in production and other work, and to study and to participate in social activities. Neither party may restrain or interfere with such freedom of the other party. ③ They also have an equal right to enjoy personal freedom, to inherit each other's estate, to own the community property of the spouses, to support their children, to implement family planning, and to support each other. Furthermore, the relationship between parents and children is also equal. Both the father and the mother have equal rights and joint duties to raise, educate, and protect their minor children, ④ and also have the equal right to be supported by their children. At the same time, both the son and daughter have the equal right to receive their parents' support and education, and they have the equal duty to support their parents as well. Between and among the parents and children, they have the equal right to inheritance. After divorce, both the parents have an equal right to guardianship and

---

① Article 1043 of the Civil Code.
② Article 1056 of the Civil Code.
③ Article 1057 of the Civil Code.
④ Article 1058 of the Civil Code.

visitation of their children under the same conditions. In addition, the other family members, such as grandparents, grandchildren, and brothers and sisters, *etc.*, also have an equal relationship in the family.

§ 6:1:2:4 Principle of Protecting the Lawful Rights and Interests of Women, Children, and the Elderly

Article 49 of the Constitution provides that marriages, families, mothers, and children are protected by the State and it is prohibited to disrupt the marital autonomy, or abuse the elderly, women, or children. This fundamental principle grants protections to three groups of persons: women, children, and the elderly.

Historically, women's rights in the marital and familial relationship had not been well protected. In order to correct the situation, better protect the women's lawful rights and interests, and fully implement the equality of men and women, the NPC passed the Law on Protection of Women's Rights and Interests on April 3, 1992. Article 142 of the Civil Code (and its predecessor, Article 3 of the Marriage Law) provides that domestic violence and maltreatment or desertion of family members are prohibited. The law also prohibits a husband from filing for divorce during his wife's pregnancy, within one year after his wife delivers, or within six months after termination of her pregnancy, unless it is the wife who applies for a divorce, or the court deems it necessary to hear the divorce request made by the husband. ① Upon divorce, the community property of the spouses shall be partitioned by them upon agreement, or, where no such an agreement is reached, adjudicated by the court in light of the actual state of the property and in compliance with the principle of favoring the rights and interests of their children, the wife, and the no-fault party. It may be inferred that under the same condition, women may get more property upon divorce in order to satisfy their needs for living. The law also protects the rights and interests of both the husband and wife arising from the contractual management of land based on the household. ②

Traditionally, most of the time it is a married woman who raises children,

---

① Article 1082 of the Civil Code.
② Article 1087 of the Civil Code.

takes care of the elderly, and assists the other party in his work while having her own work, and some women even choose to stay home taking care of the family so that she loses the opportunity to work outside the home. Upon divorce, they may lose everything including the earning ability. The law provides that where one spouse is burdened with additional duties for raising children, looking after the elderly, or assisting the other spouse in his work, the said spouse has a right to request for compensation upon divorce against the other party, and the other party shall make due compensation. The specific arrangements for making such compensation shall be determined by the spouses upon agreement, or adjudicated by the court where no such an agreement is reached.① Although this article equally applies to both the husband and the wife, has actually granted special protection to the women since most of the time it is the wife who takes these responsibilities. The law also provides that where one party is in financial hardship upon divorce, the other party, if financially capable, shall render appropriate assistance. Likewise, the specific arrangements shall be determined by the spouses upon agreement, or adjudicated by the court where no such an agreement is reached. This provision also provides special protection to women because in reality, most women may face difficulties after divorce and need financial help.

Protection of the lawful rights and interests of children is also one of the tasks of the marriage law. Children born out of wedlock have equal rights as children born in wedlock, and no organization or individual may harm or discriminate against them. A natural parent who does not have physical custody of his out-of-wedlock child shall pay child support for such child who is a minor or who is an adult but incapable of supporting himself.② The same protection has been also extended to a stepchild who has been raised and educated by his stepfather or stepmother, and the stepparent may not maltreat or discriminate against a stepchild.③ An adopted child is also equally protected once an adoptive relationship is established in accordance with law. The provisions of the Civil Code governing the parent-child relationship also apply to the rights

---

① Article 1088 of the Civil Code.
② Article 1071 of the Civil Code.
③ Article 1072 of the Civil Code.

and duties between the adoptive parents and the adopted children. The provisions governing the relationship between children and the close relatives of their parents also apply to the rights and duties between the adopted children and the close relatives of their adoptive parents, except that the rights and duties arising between the adoptee and his natural parents as well as the latter's other close relatives shall be terminated. ①

Parents have the right and duty to educate and protect their minor children. Where a minor causes damage to others, his parents shall bear civil liability in accordance with law. ② The parent-child relationship is not dissolved upon divorce of the parents. Whether a child is under the physical custody of the father or the mother, he remains to be the child of both parents. After divorce, parents continue to have the rights and duties to raise, educate, and protect their children. As a matter of principle, a mother shall, upon divorce, have physical custody of her child under the age of two. Where parents fail to reach an agreement on the physical custody of their child over the age of two, the court shall adjudicate it in compliance with the principle of acting in the best interest of the minor child and in light of the actual situations of both parents. ③ After divorce, no matter a child lives with the father or mother, he is still the child of both parents, and the parents still have the rights and obligations to support and educate their children. Where a parent has the physical custody of his child, the other parent shall pay for the child support in part or in whole. The amount and duration of such payment shall be determined by both parents upon agreement, or, where no such an agreement is reached, adjudicated by the court through making a judgment. Such agreement or judgment may not preclude the child from making reasonable demand, when necessary, of payment on either parent in excess of the amount specified in the agreement or judgment. ④ Paternal or maternal grandparents, if financially capable, also have the duty to raise their minor grandchildren whose parents are deceased or are incapable of such raising. ⑤ Elder brothers or

---

① Article 1111 of the Civil Code.
② Article 1068 of the Civil Code.
③ Article 1084 of the Civil Code.
④ Article 1085 of the Civil Code.
⑤ Article 1074 of the Civil Code.

sisters, if financially capable, have the duty to raise their minor siblings whose parents are deceased or are incapable of such raising. ① In addition, parents and children have the right to inherit each other's estate. ②

Respecting the elderly has been the tradition of China. Article 45 of the Constitution provides that the citizens of the PRC, when getting older, having contracted diseases, or having lost work ability, have the right to receive financial and proprietary help from the State and the society. The State develops the social insurance, social welfare, and medical institutions to guarantee the citizens' such rights. The lawful rights of the elderly include both proprietary rights and personal rights. The elderly parents have the right to be supported by their children. If an adult child fails to fulfill the duty to support his parents, his parents who lack the capacity to work or are in financial hardship have the right to claim support payments against the adult child. ③ grandchildren, if financially capable, have the duty to support their paternal or material grandparents whose children are deceased or are incapable of providing such support. ④ It is prohibited to maltreat or desert the elderly. ⑤ Criminal liability may also be imposed on those who have maltreated the elderly or refused to perform their obligations to support the elderly when the circumstance is serious.

§ 6:1:2:5 Principle of Maintaining an Equal, Harmonious, and Civilized Marriage and Family Relationship

This principle has been integrated into Article 1043 of the Civil Code which provides that families shall establish good family values, promote family virtues, and enhance family civility. Husband and wife shall be loyal to each other, respect each other, and care for each other. Family members shall respect the elderly, take care of the young, help each other, and maintain a marital and familial relationship with equality, harmony, and civility.

---

① Article 1075 of the Civil Code.
② Article 1070 of the Civil Code.
③ Article 1067 of the Civil Code.
④ Article 1074 of the Civil Code.
⑤ Article 1042 of the Civil Code.

§ 6:1:3 Kinship

Kinship is one of the closest social relationships of human beings recognized by law and created by marriage, by blood, or by operation of law. People within kinship have rights against and obligations to each other. Affinal kinship is a social relationship created by marriage and exists between spouses and among the other relatives of the spouses. Blood kinship (consanguinity) is formed by birth of a person where blood is the nexus of the relationship, such as one between parents and children, brothers and sisters, grandparents and grandchildren, *etc*. Kinship may also be created by operation of law when people who do not have any blood relationship become kins and have rights against and obligations to each other through a juristic act or a juridically significant fact. For example, a child of one person may become another person's child through adoption, and a kinship may also be created between stepparents and stepchildren through the establishment of an actual support relationship. This type of kinship is a legally created blood relationship.

China recognizes three types of kin: spouses, blood kin (consanguinity), and affinal kin. Among them, blood kin include natural blood kin and blood kin created by law, such as the one created through adoption or an actual support relationship.

§ 6:1:3:1 Degree of Kinship

The concept of kinship, especially the blood kinship, is very important in China and many provisions of family law are based on the kinship. For example, persons who are lineal relatives by blood, or collateral relatives by blood up to the third degree of kinship are prohibited from being married. ① The degree of kinship is counted by generations of the blood kinship. For lineal kinship by blood, oneself is counted as the first degree, going up to one's parents as the second, then one's grandparents the third, and so on. Similarly, going down the line, one's children are in the second degree and one's grandchildren are the third.

To determine the degree of collateral kinship by blood between two persons, the nearest common ancestor of both persons should be determined

---

① Article 1048 of the Civil Code.

first, and then counting down to each person respectively, the higher degree should be the degree of kinship between the two. For example, in order to determine the degree of kinship between A and his cousin B, the common ancestor of A and B should be determined first, say in this case, the grandparents of A. Counting up, the degree of kinship between A and the common ancestor is the third. Then counting down from the common ancestor to B, the degree between the common ancestor and B is also the third. So, the degree of kinship between A and his cousin B is the third degree. Suppose we now need to determine the degree of kinship between A and B's daughter C. Again, the degree between A and his common ancestor with B is still the third; however, the degree between their common ancestor and C is the fourth. Therefore, the degree between A and C is the fourth.

§ 6:1:3:2 Legal Effect of Kinship

As aforementioned, the degree of kinship may affect whether two persons may marry each other under the marriage law. Kinship may also affect a support relationship, inheritance, and a person's right in the common property. The marriage law imposes a duty on the spouses, parents and children, and sometimes even the grandparents and grandchildren and siblings, to support and help each other.① A person's statutory heirs are also to be determined by the kinship. For example, only the deceased person's spouse, parents, children, brothers and sisters, grandparents, and grandchildren would have the right to inherit the estate of the deceased.② For another example, during the period when a marital relationship exists, all property earned by any spouse would become part of the community property and the spouses each has an equal right to dispose of them, unless otherwise provided by law or agreed upon by the parties.③

Kinship may help determine the legal representation and guardianship, and may also determine who is eligible to initiate a proceeding relating to a person's missing, death, or insanity. A person with no or limited capacity for

---

① See Articles 1058-1059, 1067-1068, 1074-1075, and 1084 of the Civil Code.
② See Article 1027 and 1061 of the Civil Code.
③ See Article 1062 of the Civil Code.

performing civil juristic acts may be represented by his next of kin. For example, parents are the guardians and legal representatives of their minor child (ward), and may conduct civil activities on behalf of the child. ① The next of kin of an insane person may be his guardian, and should protect the personal and proprietary rights and interests of the person. ② When the personal, proprietary, or other civil-law rights or interests of the ward are infringed upon, the guardian has a right to ask the infringer to stop infringement, make apology, compensate losses, restore the property to its original status, and also may sue or be sued in the name of the ward. Where a ward causes damage to another person, the guardian of him shall assume tort liability. The guardian's tort liability may be mitigated if the guardian has fulfilled his duties of guardian. When a ward causes damage to another person, compensation shall be paid out of his own assets if he has assets, and any deficiency shall be paid by the guardian. ③ In addition, a person's next of kin may go to the court requesting the court to declare that the said person is missing, is dead, or lack of capacity for performing civil juristic acts owing to insanity, or may request the court to revoke the declaration thereof.

Under Chinese Criminal Law, some crimes require the existence of a certain kinship between the defendant and the victim as one of the elements for constituting the crime, such as the crime of maltreating or deserting a family member. Some criminal charges may only be made by the victim or the victim's next of kin; otherwise the court will not entertain the case. Such crimes include violent interference with other's marital autonomy while no severe personal injury or death is caused.

Kinship may also be relevant on recusal, appeal, retrial, and application for enforcement according to the procedure law. In a civil, criminal, or administrative litigation, if any of the judges, prosecutors, investigators, clerks (court reporters), or authenticators is one of the parties or a next of kin of a party in the case, he should recuse himself; otherwise, the parties to the litigation may request him to recuse. Any objection to the recusal petition

---

① Article 27 of the Civil Code.
② Article 28 of the Civil Code.
③ Article 1188 of the Civil Code.

should be decided by the judicial committee, procuratorate committee, or the president or presiding judge of the court by a ruling. In addition, the party's next of kin, upon consent of the party, may petition for an appeal against the judgment or ruling made by the first instance court. If the judgment or ruling has become legally effective, the next of kin may petition for a review. The judgment made in a civil case or a civil suit collateral to a criminal proceeding, or a ruling or mediation agreement that involves proprietary interests may be enforced by the next of kin of the judgment creditor or obligee if the obligor fails to perform his duty.

Kinship is also relevant to the obtainment, loss, or restoration of a person's citizenship under the Law on Citizenship. ① A person who was born in China or in a foreign country will obtain the Chinese citizenship as long as one or both of his parents are Chinese citizens. ② However, where one or both of a person's parents are Chinese citizens, if they reside in a foreign country so that the person has received a foreign citizenship upon birth, the said person does not have Chinese citizenship. ③ If a person's parents live in China but do not have a citizenship of any country, or if it is not clear about their citizenship, the person who was born in China has Chinese citizenship. ④ If a foreign citizen or a person without any citizenship is next of kin of a Chinese person, upon approval, he may apply to join the Chinese citizenship. ⑤ Similarly, if a Chinese citizen is next of kin of a foreign citizen, upon approval, he may withdraw from the Chinese citizenship. ⑥

A person's kindred may also enjoy some other benefits under Chinese Law. For example, if an employee dies in the course of employment or dies after he retired owing to disability suffered at work, the employer should pay support fee to the lineal blood kin of the employee on a regular basis. ⑦ For another

---

① The Law on Citizenship was promulgated by the Fifth NPC on September 10, 1980 and effective from the same day.
② Articles 4 & 5 of the Law on Citizenship.
③ Article 5 of the Law on Citizenship.
④ Article 6 of the Law on Citizenship.
⑤ Article 7 of the Law on Citizenship.
⑥ Article 10 of the Law on Citizenship.
⑦ Article 73 of the Labor Law (promulgated by Standing Committee of the Eighth NPC in July 1994, effective since Jan. 1, 1995).

example, a person is entitled to a paid leave to visit his next of kin for a certain amount of days each year, to visit them once every certain years, and the travel cost will be reimbursed by the employer.① If the spouses are not living in the same place, they have the right to visit each other once a year for thirty days and the employer of the spouse who travels for such purpose should pay salary and the travel costs for the employee.② Likewise, an unmarried child who is living in a different place from his parents may visit them once a year for twenty days; if the child is married, he has a right to visit his parents every four years for twenty days. In this situation, the employer should also pay salary and part of such travel costs to the employee.③

§ 6:1:3:3 Scope of Kinship

The scope of kinship provided by different laws varies. For example, the next of kin provided by the Criminal Procedure Law include spouse, parents, children, and siblings born from the same parents of the person.④ The next of kin in a civil litigation include spouse, parents, children, siblings, grandparents, and grandchildren of a person,⑤ and the next-of-kin in an administrative litigation include spouse, parents, children, siblings, grandparents, grandchildren, and other relatives who support or are supported by the person.⑥ Among others, "children" include children born in or out of wedlock, adopted children, and stepchildren who has been raised and educated by the stepparent. "Parents" include natural parents, adoptive parents, and a stepparent who raised and educated the child. Under certain conditions, a daughter-in-law or a son-in-law may also have the equal rights with a child of the deceased in succession.⑦

---

① See Rules of the State Council on Employees' Visit of Kindred (国务院关于职工探亲待遇的规定), hereinafter referred to as "Rules on Kindred Visit," approved by the Standing Committee of the Fifth NPC on March 6, 1981, and issued by the State Council on March 14, 1981.
② Article 3 of the Rules on Kindred Visit.
③ Article 3 of the Rules on Kindred Visit.
④ Article 82 of the Criminal Procedure Law.
⑤ Article 12 of the Supreme Peoples' Court's Interim Opinion on Certain Issues Arising from Implementing the General Provisions of Chinese GPCL.
⑥ Article 11 of the Supreme Peoples' Court's Interpretation on Certain Issues Arising from Implementation of the Administrative Procedure Law of the PRC.
⑦ Article 1129 of the Civil Code.

§ 6:2 Entering into Marriage

§ 6:2:1 Marriage in General

Entering into marriage is a civil juristic act by which a man and a woman establish a spousal relationship. The subjects of a marriage must be a man and a woman under the current Chinese law. Although some countries have granted certain rights and obligations to the same-sex couples, and in China people are also more and more tolerant of the same-sex relationship, the law does not recognize the same-sex marriage at the moment. The purpose of getting married must be to establish a spousal relationship between the two persons who plan to permanently live together. A married person should not remarry during the period the marital relationship exists, and adultery and illegal cohabitation are also prohibited.

The parties entering into a marriage must go through a certain legal procedure and must satisfy the legal requirements. The Civil Code provides the conditions and procedures of entering into marriage.①

§ 6:2:2 Legal Requirements for Entering into Marriage

A man and a woman must voluntarily marry each other. The principle of marital autonomy requires that a marriage must be formed upon both parties' free will, and no party may force the other party to marry, neither may a third person interfere with the other's marriage.②

Both the two parties getting married must have reached the legal age for entering into marriage, which is 22 for the man and 20 for the woman.③ The marriage registration authority will not register a marriage if the applicants have not reached the legal age.④ If a person gets married before he reaches the legal age, the marriage is null and void.⑤ In the early years, the State encouraged people to get married at an older age and give birth to a child at a later time because late marriage and late childbirth may help implement the

---

① Articles 1046-1054 of the Civil Code.
② Article 1046 of the Civil Code.
③ Article 1047 of the Civil Code.
④ Article 6 of the Regulations on Registration of Marriages.
⑤ Article 1051 of the Civil Code.

family planning policy by extending the birth circle. However, this policy has been removed in recent years.

The parties entering into marriage must observe the principle of monogamy which requires that one person may only have one spouse at one time. If a person is married, before his spouse dies or the marriage relationship is dissolved, he may not remarry; otherwise bigamy is constituted and criminal liability may be imposed on him.

In addition to the above three conditions for entering into marriage, the law has also imposed certain prohibitions on the parties who plan to enter into a marriage. For example, two persons who are lineal relatives by blood, or collateral relatives by blood up to the third degree of kinship are prohibited from being married. ① The prohibition on the persons who are lineal relatives by blood from marrying each other is based on the eugenics as well as morals and ethics. It also applies to the lineal blood kinship created by law, including adoptive parents and adopted children, adoptive grandparents and adopted grandchildren, and stepparents and their stepchildren who are raised and educated by them. Although there is no blood relationship between these people, marriage between them is forbidden because the law has recognized that they have the equal rights and obligations as the natural blood kinship. Collateral relatives by blood up to the third degree of kinship include brothers and sisters (both full and half), uncles and aunts, and nephews and nieces. The prohibition on such collateral relatives by blood from marrying each other is based on the fact that they all have the same grandparents; however, this prohibition may not be expanded for any purpose.

The old marriage law also prohibited a person who suffered from a disease that was regarded as medically inappropriate to marry from marrying anyone. These diseases included hereditary diseases and infectious diseases. If a person suffering from such a disease had been married, the marriage would be held void. However, in reality, these prohibitions had never been strictly implemented, and ultimately this prohibition had been removed by the Civil Code. ② Now Article 1053 of the Civil Code provides that if one of the parties

---

① Article 1048 of the Civil Code.
② Article 1053 of the Civil Code.

suffers from a serious disease, he shall truthfully inform the other party of such disease prior to marriage registration; where such information is not truthfully provided, the other party may apply to the court to annul the marriage. The application to annul a marriage shall be made within one year from the date when the party knows or should have known of the cause of the annulment.

§ 6:2:3   Marriage Agreement

A marriage agreement is an agreement made by a man and a woman for the purpose of getting married in the future. The parties may have a marriage agreement, but having a marriage agreement is not a necessary condition for a marriage. There are no provisions on marriage agreement in the marriage laws, neither in any regulations on marriage registration. Therefore, a marriage agreement does not have any legal effect in China and may not be enforced by law. However, the parties may have a dispute arising out of the proprietary relationship formed between the parties before they get married. The SPC issued the Second Judicial Interpretation of the Marriage Law specifically dealing with the proprietary disputes arising out of a marriage agreement. According to this Interpretation, if the parties had actually pursued a mercenary marriage in the name of making a marriage agreement, the property received by one party would be regarded as illegal gains and should be escheated to the State's treasury. If a person, in the name of dating or making a marriage agreement, actually practiced fraud, criminal liability would be imposed under the Criminal Law; if any party requested a termination of the marriage agreement, all the property thus received by a party through fraud must be returned to the other party.

The gifts exchanged between the two parties before they got married may be regarded as unconditional gifts or conditional gifts. If, during the period the two persons were dating and making a marriage agreement, one party voluntarily paid for the expenses incurred for both parties' traveling or hanging out together, or for some inexpensive clothes, the payment would be regarded as an unconditional gift and does not need to be returned upon dissolution of their relationship. If, however, one party gave the other party an expensive gift or a large amount of money, the court may determine that the person actually gave out the gift in anticipation of getting married, so the gift would be regarded as a conditional one; upon rescission of the marriage agreement, the gift should be properly returned.

The Interpretation also considered the traditional "gift for marriage" that a man needed to give to a woman's family in order to marry the daughter of the family according to the local customs. If the parties decided not to register their marriage, the court would allow the man to request a return of the gift for marriage. If they had registered their marriage but not lived together, or if the property was given prior to the marriage and caused financial difficulties to the man's family, the court would allow the man to request a return of the property upon divorce. These rules have been integrated into the Interpretation I of the Marriage and Family Book of the Civil Code.

§ 6:2:4 Procedure for Entering into Marriage

In order to establish a marriage and marital relationship, the parties to a marriage must register their marriage and receive a marriage certificate, and registration is the necessary and only legal procedure for establishing a marital relationship in China. The marriage registration authorities for the residents of Chinese mainland are the civil affairs departments of the people's government at or above the county level, or the township government. The people's government at the provincial level may designate a specific agency or institution as the marriage registration authority for the residents living in the countryside. If a Chinese citizen decides to marry a foreign citizen, or if a resident of the mainland decides to marry a resident of Hong Kong, Macao, or Taiwan, or if a Chinese citizen permanently residing in a foreign country applies for a marriage registration, they should go to the registration authority that is determined by the civil affairs department of the people's government at the provincial level. The jurisdiction of the marriage registration authority is principally based on the location where the party's household is registered. If the households of the two applicants are registered in the same district, they should register their marriage with the local marriage registration authority in that district. If the households of the two applicants are not registered in the same district, they may go to the marriage registration authority of either place where one of the applicants registers his household.

The specific procedure for marriage registration includes the application, examination, and registration.

An application for marriage registration must comply with both the form requirements and the substantive requirements. The form requirements are provided in Article 5 of the Regulations on Marriage Registration which provides that the parties to a marriage should present the following certificates or proof upon application: each party's household registration certificate, ID card, and a signed affidavit that the applicant does not have a spouse, and that he is not the other applicant's lineal relative by blood or collateral relative by blood up to the third degree of kinship. With these documents, they may go to the civil affairs department of the place where their households are registered, co-sign the statement of the marriage registration application, and apply for registration of their marriage. The substantive requirements are provided in Article 22 of the Interim Rules on Marriage Registration issued by the Ministry of Civil Affairs. First, the parties must go to a marriage registration authority that has jurisdiction over the application. Second, the two applicants must come to the registration authority in person and both must have reached the minimum legal age for marriage as required by law. In addition, each applicant must have no spouse and the two applicants are not lineal relatives by blood or collateral kinship by blood up to the third degree of kinship. The two applicants must voluntarily decide to marry each other, and they need to provide three 2-inch recent photos with both of them on it, and submit the other documents as required by law.

After receiving the application, the registration authority must examine the application to determine whether the application complies with the conditions for registering the marriage, and will consult with the parties if there is any doubt. When necessary, they may ask the parties to provide relevant proof. After examination, the marriage registration authority will register the marriage right away and issue the marriage certificate to the applicants. If the application is not in compliance with legal requirements, the authority will not register it and will explain the reasons to the parties. The registration authority will not register a marriage if any of the substantive requirements mentioned above is not satisfied.① The applicants may petition

---

① Article 6 of the Regulations on Marriages Registration.

for a review according to the Regulations on Administrative Review if they believe that the rejection to their application is ungrounded. If the parties are not satisfied with the review decision, they may initiate an administrative litigation according to the Administrative Procedure Law.

A marital relationship is formally established once the marriage is registered and the parties receive the marriage certificates. A marriage certificate is a legal document issued by the marriage registration authority proving the establishment of a marital relationship between the applicants. If the certificate is lost or destroyed, the parties may request a replacement by presenting their household registration certificate and their ID cards to the original registration authority or the authority in the place where one party's household is registered.

§ 6:2:5 Invalid Marriages①

If, owing to an illegal act done by one or both parties to a proposed marriage or by a third person, a relationship which is otherwise similar to a marital relationship is established but the legal requirements for entering into a marriage are not met, then the marriage is null and void. In this situation, the act of intending to enter into a marriage is illegal and the establishment of the relationship does not comply with the legal elements of a marriage, either in form or in substance. From its appearance, such a relationship is a quasi-marital relationship because the parties normally would call each other husband and wife, and there may actually exist a sort of marital relationship involving rights and obligations. The parties live together in the name of spouses and the public may also regard them as spouses. The person at fault may be one or both parties of the relationship, or a third person.

A null or void marriage may occur in different situations. For example, such a marriage may have been registered but the legal requirements are not fully met, i.e., the marriage may lack one or more substantive elements. For instance, a marriage is null and void if one or both parties are under the legal age, are involuntary regarding entering into the marriage, commit bigamy by entering into such marriage, or the parties are next of kin in violation of the

---

① See Articles 1051-1054 of the Civil Code.

marriage requirements. If a marriage is registered through fraud or deception, it is also null and void. Another typical example of an illegal marriage is one that has not been registered at all. For example, a factual marriage is unregistered and short of form requirement, although it does have the substantive elements of a marriage.

Article 1051 has integrated these requirements and provides that a marriage is void if either party to the marriage commits bigamy, the parties to the marriage fall within the relative relations prohibited by law from marrying each other, or either party to the marriage is under the statutory marriageable age. If a marriage is formed owing to coercion, the coerced party may apply to the court to annul the marriage within one year from the date the coercive act ceases. If the coerced party whose personal freedom is illegally restricted wishes to annul the marriage, the application to annul the marriage shall be made within one year from the date when the party's personal freedom is restored.① In addition, if one party suffers from a serious disease but fails to truthfully inform the other party of such disease prior to marriage registration, the other party may request the annulment of the marriage within one year from the date when he knows or should have known of the cause of the annulment. ②

There are legal consequences if a marriage is annulled or held void. Once a marriage is declared as void or annulled, it does not have any legal effect from the beginning so that the parties do not have any marital rights against or obligations to each other. Any property acquired during the cohabitation period will be disposed of by mutual agreement. If the parties cannot reach an agreement through consultation, the court should adjudicate the case in compliance with the principle of favoring the no-fault party. If the marriage is voided due to bigamy, the disposal of the property acquired during the marriage may not infringe upon the proprietary rights and interests of the parties to the lawful marriage concerned. However, the children born by the parties to a void or annulled marriage are equally protected by law. ③ Article 22 of the SPC's Interpretation I of the Marriage and Family Book of the Civil

---

① Article 1052 of the Civil Code.
② Article 1053 of the Civil Code.
③ Article 1054 of the Civil Code.

Code provides that once a marriage is voided or annulled, the property acquired by the parties during the period of their cohabitation shall be deemed as jointly owned by the parties, unless it can be proven that it is separately owned by one of the parties. In addition, where a marriage is void or annulled, the no-fault party has a right to request for damages. ①

The Civil Code does not clearly provide a procedure for invalidating a marriage, but according to the SPC's judicial interpretation, a marriage may not be automatically voided or dissolved, but may only be annulled or voided by the court upon request of the parties to a marriage or an interested person. If the cause of action for invalidating a marriage is that one party commits bigamy, an interested person may be the other party's next of kin or the local organization. If the cause of action for invalidating a marriage is that one or both parties are below the legally marriageable age, an interested person may be the next of kin of the party who has not reached the legal age. If the cause of action is that the parties have a relative relationship in violation of law, then the interested person is the next of kin of the parties. ②

§ 6:3 Spousal Relationship

A spousal relationship is created by law between a man and a woman during the period that a marital relationship exists between them, and is a relationship which is lawful, exclusive, and permanent, with equality as its core principle. Article 48 of the Constitution provides that women in China have equal rights with men in political, economic, cultural, social, and family life. Article 1055 of the Civil Code also provides that the husband and wife are equal in marriage and family. A spousal relationship may be reflected in both personal relationship and proprietary relationship.

§ 6:3:1 The Personal Relationship between Spouses

The personal relationship between spouses refers to a relationship of rights and obligations between the wife and the husband which closely relates to the

---

① Article 1054 of the Civil Code.
② Article 9 of the Interpretation I of the Marriage and Family Book of the Civil Code.

spouses' person and has no direct pecuniary interest. The most important rights of spouses include the right to their own names, the right to personal freedom, and the other relevant rights.

A right to name is an important civil-law right of personality based on personal relationship, which means that both the wife and husband may retain their own surname and given name after being married. ① The children of the spouses may take the surname of either his father or mother, and may also take a surname other than his father's or mother's in certain situations, such as taking the surname of a senior lineal relative by blood, taking the surname of a foster parent, other than the legal care provider, who provides care to him, or taking a surname with other legitimate reasons that do not offend public order or good morals. ②

A right to personal freedom is one of the fundamental rights of each citizen and reflects the equality of the husband and wife in a familial relationship. Both the husband and wife are free to engage in production and other work, and to study or participate in other social activities. Neither party may restrain or interfere with the other party's such right. ③ The Law on the Protection of Women's Rights and Interests has a separate chapter entitled "the Personal Rights" especially protecting women's personal freedom from being infringed upon.

Other personal rights of spouses include a right to live together, a right to decide where to live, and a right to represent each other.

A person with a spouse is prohibited from cohabiting with anyone other than his spouse. ④ If the spouses have been separated for no less than two years due to marital discord, divorce may be allowed. ⑤ If a person with a spouse cohabits with another person and thus causes divorce, the party without fault has the right to request compensation. ⑥

In old China, a woman after marriage would become a member of her

---

① Article 1056 of the Civil Code.
② Article 1015 of the Civil Code.
③ Article 1057 of the Civil Code.
④ Article 1042 of the Civil Code.
⑤ Article 1079 of the Civil Code.
⑥ Article 1091 of the Civil Code.

husband's family. This tradition has long been changed by the marriage law. Article 1050 of the Civil Code provides that after a marriage is registered, by mutual consent, a woman may become a member of the man's family, a man may also become a member of the woman's family. ① In other words, both the husband and wife have equal rights to decide where to live, which is an important reform of the traditional practice under which a woman must live in the residence of her husband's family.

Each spouse has a right to representation, which means that a civil juristic act performed by one of the spouses to meet the daily needs of the family is binding on both spouses unless otherwise agreed between the third person and the spouse performing the act. Even if the spouses impose a restriction on the scope of civil juristic acts performed by each other, such restriction is not effective against a *bona fide* counterparty. ②

§ 6:3:2 The Proprietary Relationship between Spouses

A proprietary relationship between spouses is derived from the relation-based relationship between the husband and the wife and is fundamental to a family. It is about or relates to the rights to own, manage, utilize, profit from, or dispose of the property received by the spouses before and after the marriage, repayment of debts, and settlement upon dissolution of the marriage. Articles 1062 – 1066 of the Civil Code specify the rules on these issues.

Generally, the following property acquired by one or both spouses during their marriage are community property and jointly owned by the spouses: (1) salaries and wages as well as bonuses and other remunerations received from services rendered; (2) proceeds obtained from production, business operation, and investment; (3) proceeds arising from intellectual property rights; (4) property inherited or received as a gift unless it belongs to only one spouse as specified in a will or gift contract; and (5) the other property that shall be jointly owned by the spouses. The wife and husband have equal rights

---

① Article 1050 of the Civil Code.
② Article 1060 of the Civil Code.

when disposing of the community property.①

On the other hand, the following property are regarded as separate property of one of the spouses: (1) premarital property of one spouse; (2) compensation or indemnification received by one spouse for injury inflicted upon him; (3) property that belongs to only one spouse as specified in a will or gift contract; (4) articles exclusively used by one spouse for his daily life; and (5) the other property that shall be owned by one spouse.②

Despite of the above provisions, the spouses or a man and a woman in anticipation of a marriage may agree that their premarital property or the property to be acquired by them during their marriage may be owned by them separately or jointly, or partially owned separately and partially owned jointly. Such an agreement must be in writing and is binding on both spouses.③ In summary, the marital property includes community property, separate property of each spouse, and the property that the spouses may agree on their ownership.

Debts can also be community debts or separate debts. If a debt is jointly signed by both spouses, or signed by one spouse and subsequently ratified by the other spouse, the debt is said to be incurred according to the common expression of intent of both spouses. In addition, if a debt is incurred by one spouse in his own name during the marriage to meet the daily needs of the family, it also constitutes a community debt. On the other hand, a debt incurred by one spouse in his own name during the marriage in excess of the daily needs of the family is not a community debt, unless the creditor can prove that such debt is incurred for the purpose of providing for both spouses' daily life or for the production and operation jointly conducted by both spouses, or such debt is incurred according to the common expression of intent of both spouses.④ However, where the spouses agree that the property acquired during the marriage is to be owned by them separately, a debt incurred by one of the spouses shall be paid off with his separate property to the extent that the third

---

① Article 1062 of the Civil Code.
② Article 1063 of the Civil Code.
③ Article 1065 of the Civil Code.
④ Article 1064 of the Civil Code.

person concerned is aware of such an agreement. ①

Either spouse may apply to the court for partition of their community property during their marriage, but the court may only allow the partition under limited circumstances. For example, the court may allow such an application only when the other spouse has concealed, transferred, sold, destructed or damaged, or squandered the community property, created a false community debt, or committed other acts that seriously infringe upon the interests of the community property. The court may also allow the partition if a person, whom one of the spouses has a statutory obligation to support, is suffering from a serious disease and needs medical treatment, but the other spouse does not agree to pay the relevant medical expenses. ②

A proprietary relationship may also arise from a marital relationship based on spousal support. Both spouses have the duty to support each other. If one spouse fails to perform this duty, the other spouse that needs spousal support has the right to ask the first spouse to pay the matrimony support. ③ This duty is mandatory and the spouses may not exclude it through making an agreement.

In addition, the husband and wife have the right to inherit the estate of each other. ④ In order to exercise such right, the person must establish that he is the lawful spouse of the deceased person. If a marriage is not registered, the parties to the "marriage" will not have the right to succession. Before succession opens, the community property jointly owned by the spouses and the common property jointly owned by the family members should be set aside and partitioned first to avoid infringing upon the lawful rights and interests of the surviving spouse and the other family members. ⑤ Each spouse may dispose of his property through a will; however, when writing a will, a spouse should reserve necessary shares of the estate for his spouse and the other heirs who has special financial difficulties and is unable to work. ⑥ If the spouse fails to do so, upon distributing the estate, due consideration will be given to the surviving

---

① Article 1065 of the Civil Code.
② Article 1066 of the Civil Code.
③ Article 1059 of the Civil Code.
④ Article 1061 of the Civil Code.
⑤ Article 1153 of the Civil Code.
⑥ Article 1130 of the Civil Code.

spouse or other heirs before the rest of the estate is disposed of according to the will.① The surviving spouse who remarries may dispose of the property he has inherited from the deceased spouse free from interference by any organization or individual.②

Case 38

Case 38: Tang 1 v. Li & Tang 2③

Tang died intestate of a sudden illness on September 16, 2011 during a business trip, survived by his wife Li, his son Tang 2, and his daughter Tang 1 from a prior marriage. Tang 1 has been living with Tang's ex-wife after they divorced. Tang's parents both died.

On October 2, 2010, Tang and Li signed a separation agreement, in which it stated that since the mutual affection between the two no longer existed, they decided to separate in order to avoid hurting their son's feeling. They agreed that the houses located in the Wealth Center and Huigugen Garden belonged to Li, who may dispose of them freely from Tang's obstruction or objection, and Tang should assist her in handling the relevant matters. The houses on Huguangzhong Street and Huajiadi belonged to Tang, who may dispose of them freely from Li's obstruction or objections, and Li should assist him in handling the relevant matters. The agreement also stated that their Son Tang 2 would live with Li, and Tang would assume the obligations of guardianship, support, and education of him, and would pay 5,000 yuan each month as the support fee. The parties also agreed that in order to resolve their problem, they would divorce, but they would still live under the same roof. In order to achieve a better result, neither party might interfere the other party's private life or affairs. They both signed the agreement.

Regarding the house in Wealth Center, Tang as the purchaser signed

---

① Article 25 of the SPC's Interpretation I of the Succession Book of the Civil Code.
② Article 1157 of the Civil Code.
③ See (2014) San Zhong Min Zhong Zi No. 09467, reprinted in the SPC Gazette, Issue 12, 2014.

the purchase contract under which the purchase price was 1,579,796 yuan. The house was still under the name of Tang at the time of his death, and he still owed a bank loan of 877,125.88 yuan. In addition, there were two more houses as well as cars and bank savings under Li and Tang's names.

The main issue of the trial was how to determine the scope of Tang's estate.

Chaoyang District Court of Beijing reasoned that Tang 1 and Tang 2 were Tang's children, Li was Tang's spouse, so that they were Tang's heirs first in order, and each should receive an equal share of Tang's estate.

When determining the scope of Tang's estate, the court found that the house located in the Wealth Center was still registered under Tang's name. Although in the separation agreement they agreed that it belonged to Li, this agreement had not been actually performed. According to the principle that a real right must be registered in order to be effective, the court held that this house was still part of the community property of Tang and Li, and its value should be the amount of the appraised value after deducting the outstanding loans. Half of it belonged to Li, and the other half would be Tang's estate, for which Li, Tang 1, and Tang 2 each would receive an equal share of the other half. Since Tang 2 was still a minor, and Tang 1 asked for cash, the court held that the house belonged to Li, and Li should pay cash to Tang 1 based on the appraised price and Tang 1's share. Li is responsible for repaying the outstanding loan. The other estate should be divided and distributed according to the succession law.

Li and Tang 2 appealed to Beijing No. 3 Intermediate People's Court. Li alleged that the house in Wealth Center should belong to herself because the separation agreement was an agreement of partition of property within their marriage, no matter in whose name it was registered.

On appeal, the main issue is the disposition of the house in Wealth Center. In order to resolve this issue, there are three sub-issues to be resolved.

The first issue is the nature of the separation agreement signed by Tang and Li on October 2, 2010. The court reasons that this agreement is an agreement partitioning property between the spouses within their marriage, and not an agreement of partitioning property upon divorce. From the content of the agreement, Tang and Li admitted that their mutual affection no longer existed, but stated clearly that they did not want to harm their son's feeling, so that they decided to resolve their problems by separation but not leaving home. This is not an agreement based on divorce. In addition, nowhere in the agreement mentioned "divorce" and the similar words. Instead, there were words like "separation" and "not leaving home" that showing that the two tried to avoid divorce by reaching this agreement. Furthermore, Article 19 of the Marriage Law clearly provides that the spouses may agree that the property acquired by them during their marriage and their premarital property may belong to them separately or jointly, or partially owned separately and partially owned jointly. Such an agreement must be in writing. In this case, under the separation agreement concerned, Tang and Li expressly stated that they agreed to partition their property in this way, it is a partition not based on their anticipation of divorce, but an agreement regarding which form of spousal property is to be adopted by them.

The second issue is which law should be applied, the real rights law or the marriage law.

Li and Tang 2 alleges that according to Article 19 of the Marriage Law, as long as the spouses make an agreement in writing regarding how to partition their property, the agreement becomes effective and there is no need to register the alteration of the real right over the property; however, Tang 1 argues that this case should be governed by Article 9 of the real rights law, which provides that the alteration of a real right on immovables does not have any legal effect without being registered.

After consideration, the court holds that the relevant rules of Marriage Law shall be applied in priority, because the real rights law mainly focuses on the relationship between the persons of the civil law and the property, the purpose of the legislation is to ensure the security of transactions to promote the effective utilization of the resources. However, the marriage law is a law on relation-based status, the purpose of which is to regulate the personal and proprietary relationships between the husband and wife, and the proprietary relationship is subordinated to the personal relationship, which only represents a relationship of rights and obligations between the spouses or among the family members. Such a personal relationship does not feature a direct economic purpose. Therefore, the provisions of the marriage law regarding the special relationship between and among the spouses and children are not created for a utilitarian purpose, but with a nature of "public law" or social security. Therefore, in the field of regulating the proprietary relationship between spouses, the real rights law should be restrained and the rules of marriage law should be respected, especially regarding an agreement between the spouses on the selection of a specific property system within their marriage.

Therefore, an agreement between the spouses on a specific property partition should not be over-regulated by the real rights law. In this case, the partition of the house in Wealth Center by Tang and Li is an internal agreement on the property, not involving any external relationship out of the family, so the marriage law should be applied in priority, with the real rights law applied as a supplement.

The third issue is whether the registration requirement in real right law is mandatorily applicable to the partition of spousal property. The court says no. Since the separation agreement stated that the said house belonged to Li, the fact that it is still registered under the name of Tang does not affect the validity of the disposition made by the two parties. Although registration as provided by the real rights law is one of the required elements for alteration of a real right, in practice, however, a real right is not always be duly registered owing to such reasons that the registration is exempted by law, there is an error occurred in the registration, the law has been changed, etc. However, such a real right is recognized and protected by law. Articles 28 through 30 of the real right law illustrate some of these situations whereby a real right is altered. These illustrations do not exhaust all possible situations, and the relevant situations provided in the marriage law or its judicial interpretations should also be included therein.

The court further reasons that in the field of spousal property, there are many situations where by one spouse signs a contract for purchase of a house and registers the title of the house under his own name. Under this circumstance, both spouses enjoy joint ownership over the property, unless otherwise agreed by them. This practice is based on the statutory property system provided by the marriage law and not based on the juristic acts between the two spouses. On the other hand, if the spouses mutually decide to adopt a specific form of spousal property in writing regarding the attribution of the jointly-owned property, such a decision is based on the principles of equality, voluntariness, and truthfulness of expression of intent. It is the result of autonomy of will and should be respected and protected by law. Therefore, in the family law area, a real right may be altered without a juristic act.

In summary, when a dispute arises over the ownership of immovable property acquired by the spouses during their marriage, the court should comprehensively consider whether the causative act of altering a real right is effective and whether any interest of a third person is involved, but should not consider the registration of the real right as the sole legal basis. Only when disposition of a real right to a third person outside the family is involved, should the provisions of the real rights law be applied.

In this case, the spouses agreed that the house concerned belonged to Li, and the said house had not entered the market, so the determination of its attribution does not involve an order of priority or security of transactions. Although Tang 1 challenged the validity of the separation agreement, she is not the third person in the sense of the real rights law. Therefore, the said house should belong to Li, disregarding the fact that it is not registered under Li's name.

Finally, the court holds that the said house belongs to Li, and Li would be responsible for repaying the outstanding loan on it. The lower court's decision on the other matters are affirmed.

§ 6:4 Relationship between Parents and Children

§ 6:4:1 Parent-Child Relationship in General

According to the Chinese law, parents and children have rights against and owe obligations to each other. Specifically, both parents have equal rights and joint duties to raise, educate, and protect their minor child① and adult child who is incapable of supporting himself. Where a parent fails to fulfill such duty, a minor child or an adult child who is incapable of supporting himself has a right to claim child support payment against such parent. ② If a minor child causes damage to others, his parents shall bear civil liability in accordance with law. ③ Likewise, an adult child has a duty to support his parents. If he fails to perform such duty, his parents who lack the capacity to work or are in financial hardship may claim support payment against him. ④ Children should respect their parents' right to re-marriage and may not interfere with their parents' right to divorce or remarriage, or interfere with their marital life thereafter. A child's duty to support his parents does not end with the change of his parents' marital relationship. ⑤

Parents and children are the closest lineal blood kinship, and have close personal and proprietary relationship. According to the succession law, children and parents are both heirs of each other in the first order. ⑥ Parents have the right to inherit their children's estates, and *vice versa*. ⑦ This right to succession is equal, which means that the right of a child to inherit his parents' estate is not affected by the gender or age of the child. Similarly, the right of a parent to inherit his or her child's estate is not affected by the gender or age of the parent. Especially, the right to succession of a mother or a married daughter should not be interfered with or deprived of. It is to be noted that a child born out of wedlock has the right to inherit his blood parents' estate; an adopted child has the right to inherit his adoptive parents' estate, but have no right to inherit his blood parents' estate. If a support and education relationship has been formed between a stepparent and a stepchild, they have the right to inherit each other's estate, and also have the right to individually inherit the estate of their blood children or blood parents.

---

① Article 1058 of the Civil Code.
② Article 1067 of the Civil Code.
③ Article 1068 of the Civil Code.
④ Articles 26 and 1067 of the Civil Code.
⑤ Article 1069 of the Civil Code.
⑥ Article 1127 of the Civil Code.
⑦ Article 1070 of the Civil Code.

When exercising parental rights or performing parental duties, if there is a disagreement between the parents, they should resolve the disagreement based on the principle of protection of the child's interests. If they cannot reach an agreement, the relatives or a mediation committee may mediate the dispute, and the child should also be consulted with if he has reached a certain age. If consultation does not lead to an agreement, the court will make a ruling considering the specific situation of the parents and the interests of the child. If one parent dies or loses capacity for performing civil juristic acts during the period that the marital relationship exists, the other parent has the right and duty to raise, educate, and protect their child.

Parental rights may involve both personal and proprietary rights. The personal rights include (1) a right to support and educate the child, (2) a right to discipline, punish, and protect the child, (3) a right to have their minor child back if he has been illegally sold, hidden, or detained, (4) a right to decide the domicile for the child, (5) a right to permit the child to work in compliance with the Labor Law and the Law on Protection of Minor Children, (6) a right to be the legal representative of the minor child, and (7) with regard to a minor child with limited capacity for performing civil juristic acts who has done an act that are appropriate with his age or intelligence, a right to give consent thereto. The proprietary rights include (1) a right to represent and give consent to the child in disposing of property, accepting gifts, or inheriting shares of estate, (2) a right to manage the minor child's property, (3) a right to use the minor child's property, provided that the property's value should not be harmed, the attributes of the property should not be changed, and the income may only be used for supporting and educating the minor child, and (4) a right to dispose of the minor child's property for his own interests and benefits.

The parental rights may be extinguished for the following causes: (1) the parent is declared as a person with no or limited capacity for performing civil juristic acts, (2) the parent fails to perform his duty and the situation is so severe that the minor child has suffered serious harm, (3) the parent has committed a crime against the minor child or abetted the minor child to commit a crime, (4) the parent has been sentenced to imprisonment, or (5) the parent loses such right for other significant reasons, such as the establishment of an adoption relationship. The persons with a standing to challenge a parent's parental rights to a child include the other parent, the next of kin of the minor child, the employer(s) of the minor child's parent (s), or the residents' committee or villagers' committee of the place where the minor child is resides.

Nevertheless, the loss of the parental rights to his child does not relieve a parent from his duty to support and educate the child, thus such a parent still needs to pay part or all of the support and education fee for the child. The parent's right to visit the child is not affected either, as long as the visit will not harm the child. If one parent loses the parental rights to the child, the other parent still has such rights. If both parents lose the rights, a guardian will be nominated for the minor. The parent who has lost the parental rights to a child may regain such rights when legal requirements are satisfied. For example, if the cause that makes the parental rights to a child lost has been removed, upon application of an interested person, the court will revoke the declaration of depriving a parent or parents of the parental rights to the child.

If a child was conceived and delivered during the period that a marital relationship exists between his parents, the child is one born in wedlock. Many countries adopt a presumption that a child is presumed to be born in wedlock unless there is evidence to the contrary. Chinese law does not expressly adopt such a presumption, but it has been actually recognized in practice. Where a parent challenges maternity or paternity with just cause, either parent may file a lawsuit with the court for affirmation or denial of such maternity or paternity. Where an adult child challenges maternity or paternity with just cause, he may file a lawsuit with the court for affirmation of such maternity or paternity. ①

Chinese law has extended the parental rights to cover the grandparent-grandchild relationship, and the relationship between or among brothers and sisters. Article 1074 of the Civil Code provides that paternal or maternal grandparents, if financially capable, have a duty to raise their minor grandchildren whose parents are deceased or are incapable of such raising. Likewise, paternal or maternal grandchildren, if financially capable, have a

---

① Article 1073 of the Civil Code.

duty to support their grandparents whose children are deceased or are incapable of providing such support. Article 1075 provides that elder brothers or sisters, if financially capable, have a duty to raise their minor siblings whose parents are deceased or are incapable of such raising. Younger brothers or sisters who have been brought up by their elder siblings and who are financially capable have a duty to support such elder siblings who lack both the capacity to work and the means to support themselves.

In a parent-child relationship, a child born out of wedlock, a stepchild, or an adopted child, has the same rights as a child born in wedlock.

§6:4:2 Children Born out of Wedlock

A child born out of wedlock may be born to the parents who are not married or born to a married person with a third person. Historically, a child born out of wedlock had been deserted or discriminated, and some of them were even killed upon birth. Their status in the family and their status in the society were both very low. Now the attitude of the society toward a child born out of wedlock has changed to be more tolerant. For a child born out of wedlock, if his natural father does not recognize him and he is living with his mother, the parent-child relationship is established between the child and his mother. If the natural father has recognized the child, such a relationship is established between the child and both parents.

Under the Chinese law, a child born out of wedlock has equal rights as a child born in wedlock, and no organization or individual may harm or discriminate against him. ① The law applying to parent-child relationship also applies to the parents and their child born out of wedlock. A natural parent who does not have physical custody of his out-of-wedlock child shall pay child support for such child who is a minor or who is an adult but incapable of supporting himself. ② The amount of support fee and the method of such payment should be agreed upon by the parents, or, if no such agreement is reached through consultation, the court will make a ruling according to the income of the natural father and mother, and the actual needs of the child

---

① Article 1071 of the Civil Code.
② Article 1071 of the Civil Code.

born out of wedlock. If a natural parent fails to perform the duty of support and education, the minor child or adult child who has no ability to live independently has a right to request the natural parent to pay the support fee.

§6:4:3 Stepchildren

A stepchild is a child born to a person and his ex-spouse. A parental relationship between a stepparent and a stepchild may be established when one of the child's parents died and the surviving parent remarried, or when the child's parents divorced and one or both of them remarried. Under Chinese law, it is very important to determine whether a support and education relationship has been established between a stepparent and the stepchild, which may bring about different legal consequences. If the stepparent has raised and educated the stepchild, then a parental relationship between the stepparent and the stepchild is established which is actually a legally created kinship by blood, and the law governing parental relationship applies to the relationship between the stepparent and the stepchild; otherwise it is only a relationship created by marriage.

For a stepchild, a parent-child relationship is established between the stepchild and the stepparent if the stepchild has been raised and educated by the stepparent. In this case, although the stepparent and the child's natural parents have equal rights to raise and educate the child, the stepparent and the natural parent who is living with the child should have the parental rights based on the principle of convenience.

A stepchild may be in one of the four different situations: (1) when one of his parents remarries, the stepchild is already an adult and lives independently; (2) when one of his parents remarries, the stepchild, who is still a minor or an adult who cannot live independently, has not been supported or educated by the stepparent; (3) when one of his parents remarries, the stepchild is still a minor or an adult who cannot live independently, and the support and education fee of the stepchild has been provided by the other natural parent of the child, but the stepchild has been living with the stepparent for a long time and the latter has provided care and education to the child; and (4) when one parent remarries, the stepchild, who is a minor or an adult who cannot live independently, has been living with the stepparent for a long time and the latter has provided part or all of the support and education fee for the child. Among the above situations, a support and education relationship has been formed in the latter two situations but not in the first two situations. Actually, Chinese law does not specify under what circumstances a support and education relationship is established between a stepparent and a stepchild; but in any event, a stepparent may not maltreat or discriminate against a stepchild, and *vice-versa*. ①

It is to be noted that even after a support and education relationship is established between a child and a stepparent, the relationship between the child and his natural parent or parents still exists because such relationship will not extinguish owing to divorce of the parents according to Chinese law. Therefore, a stepchild is in double relationships, one is with his natural parents, and the other is with his stepparent.

A stepparent may also adopt the stepchild upon consent of his natural parents of the stepchild. ② Through adoption, the relationship between a stepparent and a stepchild turns to a relationship between an adoptive parent and an adopted child, and the adoption law applies. For an adopted child, a parent-child relationship is established between the adoptive parent and the child, meanwhile such a relationship between the child and the other natural parent of his is extinguished upon establishment of the adoptive relationship. ③ Adoption law is further discussed in the next sub-section.

* * *

In recent years, there is an increasing number of couples who decide to have tube babies. Generally, if both spouses have been consulted with and consented to the way of childbirth, a parent-child relationship between the parents and the tube baby is established and both parents may co-exercise their parental rights in accordance with law. If one of the spouses has independently implemented the plan and given birth to a tube child, a parent-child relationship has only been established between this parent and the child.

---

① Article 1072 of the Civil Code.
② Article 1103 of the Civil Code.
③ Article 1111 of the Civil Code.

Case 39

Case 39: In Re Support of a Child Born from Artificial Insemination[①]

W and H married in July 1978 and had no children for several years. In early 1985, they went to a hospital to do artificial insemination. After having tried three times, W was pregnant and gave birth to a son in January 1986. Afterwards, the spouses frequently had quarrels for daily chaos, and then separated for a long time; as a result, their affection broken. H said that if W insisted on divorce, he would agree, except that the child was born without his consent, and that the child did not have any blood relationship with him. Therefore, he said that, if the child was to be raised up by him, he would like to support him; otherwise, he would not pay the support fee.

The SPC issued a reply on July 8, 1991 regarding the legal status of a child born from artificial insemination, stating that during the existence of spousal relationship, a child born from artificial insemination upon consent of both spouses would be deemed as the child born in wedlock and the relationship between the parents and the child would be governed by the relevant provisions of the Marriage Law. Therefore, such a child would enjoy the same equal legal status as other children born in wedlock.

Since the parties did not have a disagreement regarding the property division, the court made a judgment in 1996, allowing the parties to divorce and ruling that the child would live with W, but held that H should pay the child support fee of 130 yuan per month since July 1996 until the child could live independently.

There are many cases involving artificial insemination. For a case involving a succession dispute arising from an agreed artificial insemination, see Case 41 reprinted in § 7:2:2 of this Book.

---

① See the SPC Gazette, Issue 1, 1997.

Case 40

Case 40: He v. He[①]

He and Wang (deceased) have five children. Now He has lost work capacity and has no economic income except for the basic living allowances of 320 yuan, and he needs his children to support him in daily life. He has lived with each of his children, other than his son Hua, by rotation. Since the other children's economic situation and housing conditions were not good, He requested Hua to pay support fee and help resolve his housing issue. Hua was not happy, and frequently spoke strong languages to him and threatened and cursed him so that He suffered emotional fear and depression. He sued in court requesting Hua to pay support fee and help resolve his living issue.

The court notified Hua for several times but Hua did not respond, and continued to threaten He. During the litigation, He applied for a protective order for his personal safety, requesting the court to adopt measures to prevent Hua from threatening or cursing him. The court considered the situation and held that such request was in compliance with the law, and issued a ruling prohibiting Hua from threatening, cursing, insulting He or conducting any other act that may cause He to be feared, worried, or frightened. Meanwhile, the court admonished Hua, informing him that detention, fines or other like coercive measures would be adopted against him if he continued to perform the above acts. The court also ordered Hua to pay 600 yuan each month to He as support fee.

§6:4:4 Adoption

Adoption is a civil juristic act to create a parent-child relationship between the people who are not originally related as such. It is an important and a necessary supplement of the kinship by natural blood. The adoption system also provides important protections to the minors for them to grow up healthily. The parties to an adoption include an adoptive party (adoptive parent or

---

[①] See the SPC Gazette, Issue 2, 2015.

parents), a child to be adopted, and a party placing the child for adoption. The latter party includes the parents or other guardians of the child to be adopted or a social welfare institution.

Historically, the adoption system had feudal significance in China for the purpose of securing that the father's name and wealth would be carried on so that the family ruled by fatherhood would last forever. Therefore, the conditions for adoption were very strict. After the founding of the new China, the feudal system of adoption had been abolished. The 1980 Marriage Law recognized a new adoption system, but only in a general and broad way. In December 1991, the Adoption Law was enacted by the NPC and effective since April 1, 1992. On the effective date of the Adoption Law, the Ministry of Civil Affairs issued Certain Regulations on Registration for Adoptions by Chinese Citizens; and nine days later, it issued a Notice on Certain Issues Arising from the Registration for Adoptions by Foreigners in the PRC. Subsequently on November 3, 1993, the Ministry of Civil Affairs and the Ministry of Justice co-issued the Implementation Measures on Adoption of Children by Foreigners in the PRC. The enactment of these laws and regulations has established a new adoption system. The Adoption Law was revised on November 4, 1998, and finally is integrated into Chapter V of Book Five of the Civil Code.

The fundamental principles of the new adoption system include the principle of benefiting the growth of the adopted minors, the principle of protecting the lawful rights and interests of the adoptive parents and the adopted children, the principle of equality and voluntariness, and the principle of compliance with public order and ethics. The most important purpose of implementing the adoption system is to ensure the minor children to grow up healthily under the support and education of the adoptive parents.

§ 6:4:4:1 Substantive Requirements for Adoption

There are three parties to an adoption, *i.e.*, the adopted child, the party placing the child for adoption, and the adoptive parent(s). Under Chinese law, all of these three parties must meet qualification requirements in order to establish an adoptive relationship. Both adoption and placing for adoption must be based on mutual consent, and where a minor adoptee is aged eight or above, his consent must be obtained. ①

A qualified minor for adoption may be an orphan bereaved of parents, a minor whose natural parents cannot be traced, or a minor whose natural parents are incapable of raising him due to unusual difficulties. ② The "unusual difficulties" may include the situations in which a parent has a severe disease, has lost the ability to work, or loses the capacity for performing civil juristic acts, or cannot appropriately support the child. ③

A qualified individual or organization who may place a minor for adoption may be the guardian of an orphan, a children's welfare institution, or a minor's natural parents who are incapable of raising him due to unusual difficulties. ④ Where neither of the parents of a minor has full capacity for performing civil juristic acts, generally the child may not be placed for adoption by another person unless the parents may seriously harm the minor, in which case, the guardian of the minor may place such minor for adoption. ⑤ This limitation is imposed to protect the rights and interests of the incapacitated parents because alteration of the parent-child relationship is adverse to their interests. Once their child is adopted by others, they will lose the expected rights and interests of being supported by the child. However, if the natural parents of a minor may cause serious harm to him, the guardian may place the minor for adoption in order to protect the rights and interests of the minor child. However, where a guardian intends to place an orphan under his guardianship for adoption, he shall obtain the consent of the person who has a duty to raise the orphan. Where the person with a duty to raise the orphan does not consent to the adoption and the guardian is unwilling to continue exercising the duties of guardian, a successive guardian shall be appointed in accordance with law. ⑥ The natural parents may also place their child for adoption if they act in concert. Where one of the natural parents is unknown or cannot be traced, the other parent may place the child for adoption by himself. ⑦ However, if one

---

① Article 1104 of the Civil Code.
② Article 1093 of the Civil Code.
③ Article 1094 of the Civil Code.
④ Article 27 of the Civil Code.
⑤ Article 1095 of the Civil Code.
⑥ Article 1096 of the Civil Code.
⑦ Article 1097 of the Civil Code.

spouse dies and the surviving spouse intends to place their minor child for adoption, the parents of the deceased spouse (grandparents of the minor) have priority in raising the child. ① The legal basis is that paternal or maternal grandparents, if financially capable, have the duty to raise their minor grandchildren whose parents are deceased or are incapable of such raising. ② Likewise, elder brothers or sisters, if financially capable, have the duty to raise their minor siblings whose parents are deceased or are incapable of such raising. ③

A person who is qualified to adopt a minor child must meet all the following conditions:

(1) having no children or having only one child;
(2) being capable of raising, educating, and protecting the adoptee;
(3) not suffering from any disease that is deemed medically unfit to be an adopter;
(4) having no criminal record unfavorable to the healthy growth of the adoptee; and
(5) having reached the age of thirty. ④

In addition, a childless adopter may adopt two children, and an adopter with one child may adopt only one more child. ⑤ If a person with a spouse intends to adopt a child, both the person and his spouse must jointly adopt the child. ⑥ Where a person without a spouse intends to adopt a child of a different gender, the prospective adopter must be at least 40 years older than the adoptee.. ⑦ These restrictions are imposed based on the considerations of both social ethics and the needs for protection of the adopted minors.

The Civil Code also considers some special situations in which the restrictions may be lifted. Adoption of a child from one's collateral relative by

---

① Article 1108 of the Civil Code.
② Article 1074 of the Civil Code.
③ Article 1075 of the Civil Code.
④ Article 1098 of the Civil Code.
⑤ Article 1100 of the Civil Code.
⑥ Article 1101 of the Civil Code.
⑦ Article 1102 of the Civil Code.

blood of the same generation and up to the third degree of kinship may be exempted from some of these restrictions; likewise, adoption of a child by an overseas Chinese from his collateral relative by blood of the same generation and up to the third degree of kinship may also be exempted from some of the restrictions.① Adoption of an orphan, a minor with disabilities, or a minor in a children's welfare institution whose natural parents cannot be located may be exempted from the restrictions on the number of children that the adoptive party may adopt. ② An orphan or a child whose natural parents are incapable of raising him may be raised by the relatives or friends of his natural parents. The restrictions do not apply to such a relationship between two persons one of whom is raised by the other. ③ Certain restrictions do not apply to adoption by stepparents, because the relationship between a stepchild and a stepparent is one created by the remarriage of the natural parent of a child and a third person, so a stepparent may, with the consent of the natural parents of the stepchild, adopt the stepchild. ④

§ 6:4:4:2 Procedural Requirements for Adoption

Adoption is a civil juristic act that alters a parent-child relationship which involves both personal and proprietary relationships. In order to establish an adoptive relationship, the parties must personally go to the civil affairs department of the local people's government at or above the county level to register the adoption, and the spouses who plan to co-adopt the child must be present at the same time. The party who cannot go there in person for a cause should present an authenticated or notarized power of attorney. The adoptive relationship is established only upon registration. In the case of adopting a minor whose parents cannot be traced, the civil affairs department for adoption registration shall make public notice prior to the registration. The parties to an adoptive relationship may enter into an adoption agreement on a voluntary basis. Upon request of both parties or one of the parties to an adoptive relationship, an adoption shall be notarized. The civil affairs

---

① Article 1099 of the Civil Code.
② Article 1100 of the Civil Code.
③ Article 1107 of the Civil Code.
④ Article 1103 of the Civil Code.

department of the people's government at or above the county level shall evaluate the adoption in accordance with law. ①

Upon application, the adoptive party needs to submit an application statement, the identification and household registration certificate of him, the proof document prepared by the applicant's employer or residents' or villagers' committee regarding the applicant's marital status, whether he has any child, his ability to support and educate the child to be adopted, and the physical examination report prepared by a medical institution above the county level proving that the applicant does not have the disease which is recognized as medically inappropriate for adopting a child. An applicant for adopting a stepchild may only present the identification and household registration certificate and the proof of marriage of the adoptive person with the adopted child's natural parent.

The person placing a child for adoption should submit his identification and household registration certificate and a written opinion of the person who has a legal duty to support the child. If a child is placed for adoption by a social welfare institution, the institution should submit the original records of the child upon admitted into the institution, the proof prepared by the police proving how the child was found, or the proof that the natural parents of the child are deceased or have been declared as dead. If the person placing a child for adoption is the guardian of the child, he should present a proof that he has actually assumed the obligation of a guardian, a proof that the child's parents are deceased or have been declared to be dead, or a proof that the natural parents of the child have no capacity for performing civil juristic acts and may cause severe injury to the child. If the person placing a child for adoption is the natural parent of the child who has special difficulties and has no ability to support the child, he should submit a proof of the special difficulty, which should be prepared by his employer or the residents' or villagers' committee. If the child to be adopted is handicapped, the person placing the child for adoption must provide a proof of disability prepared by a medical institution above the county level.

Upon receiving an application for registration of adoption and the relevant

---

① Article 1105 of the Civil Code.

materials, the registration authority will examine the application and register the adoption within 30 days, or refuse to register it with an explanation. Once the adoption is registered, an adoptive relationship is established on the date of registration.

§ 6:4:4:3 Effect of Adoption

The establishment of an adoptive relationship creates a new type of kinship and extinguishes the original family relationship and the rights and duties attached thereto. Once adoption is completed, the adopted child joins the adoptive parents' family, and the rights and obligations between the adoptive parents and the adopted child is regulated by the law on parent-child relationship. ① The adopted child may follow the adoptive father's family name or the adoptive mother's family name, or may keep his original family name upon consultation among all parties. If an adopted child predeceases his adoptive parent, the natural or adopted child of him may inherit the estate of his adoptive parent by representation. Meanwhile, the rights and duties arising from the relationship between the adopted child and his natural parents as well as the latter's other next of kin are terminated. However, the blood relationship still objectively exists and cannot be terminated by law; thus, the provisions prohibiting marriage between the persons related by blood still apply to them.

Since adoption is a juristic act, it must comply with the legal requirements for a valid juristic act as provided in Article 143 of the Civil Code. In order to be valid, the parties to an adoption must have the capacity for performing civil juristic acts, the intent expressed by the persons involved must be true, and the adoption must not violate law or offend public order or good morals. Therefore, an adoption may be invalid if the adoptive party or the party placing the child for adoption does not have the required capacity for performing civil juristic acts, if the adoption is achieved by fraud, duress, or taking advantage of one party's emergent or desperate situation in violation of one's true will, or, if the adoption violates any law or administrative regulation, or offend the social public interest through deceiving the registration authority or maliciously collaborating to buy and sell the child in the name of

---

① Article 1111 of the Civil Code.

adoption.

There are two ways to invalidate an adoption if any of the above-mentioned situation occurs. First, a party to an adoption or an interested person may, through litigation, request the court to declare that the adoption is invalid. Alternatively, a court may also take an initiative to declare that the adoption is invalid if it, when trying a related case, discovers some irregularities in the adoption. Second, a party may request the adoption registration authority to declare the adoption is invalid based on the Measures on Registration of Adoption of Children by Chinese Citizens. If an adoption is registered through fraud or deceit, the registration authority will revoke the registration and forfeit the registration certificate.[①] If an adoption is declared as invalid by court or by the registration authority, it is ineffective from the beginning.

§ 6:4:4:4 Termination of Adoptive Relationship

Since the purpose of an adoption is to protect the rights and interests of the parties and especially guarantee the support, education, and healthy growth of the adopted minor child, an adoptive relationship generally may not be terminated before the adopted child has reached the majority age. However, since an adoptive relationship is a legally created relationship, sometimes it can not continue for some significant causes.

Article 1114 of the Civil Code provides that no adopter may dissolve an adoptive relationship before the adoptee has reached the majority age unless there is an agreement between the adopter and the party who places the child for adoption to dissolve such relationship. Where an adoptee is aged eight or above, his own consent should also be obtained. Where an adopter fails to perform the duty to raise the adoptee or commits maltreatment, desertion, or other acts infringing upon the lawful rights and interests of the minor adoptee, the person who has placed the child for adoption has a right to request that the adoptive relationship be dissolved. Where an adopter and a party who has placed a child for adoption fail to reach an agreement for dissolution of the adoptive relationship, either party may file a lawsuit with the court.[②] When an

---

① Article 12 of the Measures on Registration of Adoption of Children by Chinese Citizens.
② Article 1114 of the Civil Code.

adopted child has grown up and the relationship between the child and the adoptive parents has deteriorated so that they are unable to live together any longer, the adoption may be terminated. ① If they cannot reach an agreement, they may request the court to dissolve the adoptive relationship.

Generally, an adoptive relationship may be terminated in two ways: upon agreement or through litigation. If the parties decide to terminate the adoptive relationship upon agreement, they should go to the civil affairs department to de-register the adoption. ② The parties should go to the registration authority in person and present their identification and household registration certificates, the adoption registration certificate, and a written agreement on terminating the adoptive relationship. The authority will examine the application materials within thirty days upon receipt of the application, deregister the adoption if the application is in compliance with law, take back the adoption registration certificate, and issue a certificate terminating the adoptive relationship. If the parties cannot reach an agreement on termination of adoption, they may go to the court. The court should firstly mediate such a case, trying to urge the parties to voluntarily reach an agreement of either maintaining or terminating the adoption. Upon mediation, if the parties have reached an agreement to terminate the adoptive relationship, the court should make a letter of mediation, and the adoption is lawfully terminated from the day the letter of mediation is signed. If no agreement is reached through mediation, the court will make a judgment of either granting or denying the request for terminating the adoption. The court is required to comply with the principle of protection of the lawful adoptive relationship and maintaining the lawful rights and interests of the parties, especially the adopted minor child's rights and interests. The adoptive relationship will be lawfully terminated on the day the judgment terminating the adoption becomes effective.

Upon dissolution of an adoptive relationship, the rights and duties between the adoptee and his adoptive parents as well as the latter's other close relatives shall be terminated, and the rights and duties between the adoptee and his natural parents as well as the latter's other close relatives shall be automatically

---

① Article 1115 of the Civil Code.
② Article 1116 of the Civil Code.

restored. However, if, upon dissolution of the adoption, the adopted child has become an adult, whether the rights and duties between the adoptee and his natural parents as well as the latter's other close relatives are to be restored may be decided through consultation between or among the parties. ①

Nonetheless, even after an adoptive relationship is dissolved, an adoptee who has been raised up by the adoptive parents and now become an adult should still provide living expenses to his adoptive parents who lack both the capacity to work and the means to support themselves. The amount of the living expenses will be determined on the actual needs of the adoptive parents and the situation of the adopted child. Where an adoptive relationship is dissolved because the adopted child maltreats or deserts his adoptive parents after the adopted child has become an adult, the adoptive parents may request the adoptee to compensate for the expenses incurred to raise the adoptee during the adoption period. Where dissolution of an adoptive relationship is required by the natural parents of the adoptee, the adoptive parents may request the natural parents of the adoptee to appropriately compensate for the expenses incurred to raise the adoptee during the adoption period, unless the adoptive relationship is dissolved because the adoptive parents maltreat or desert the adoptee. ②

§ 6:4:4:5 Adoption by Foreigners

In recent decades, there have been many foreigners who adopt minor children from China. The Ministry of Civil Affairs issued the Measures for Registration on Adoption of Children by Foreigners in the PRC on May 25, 1999, and issued a Notice on Further Strengthening Adoption by Foreigners on December 31, 2000, which established various principles. One of the principles is that Chinese citizens had priority to adopt Chinese children and the adoption of Chinese children by foreigners is only a substitute or alternative way, so the number of adoptions by foreigners should be limited to a reasonable extent.

Article 1109 of the Civil Code provides the general rules for foreign adoptions:

---

① Article 1117 of the Civil Code.
② Article 1118 of the Civil Code.

Foreign nationals may adopt children in the People's Republic of China in accordance with law.

The adoption of a child by a foreign national in the People's Republic of China shall be subject to the review and approval of the competent authorities of the foreign national's country of residence in accordance with the law of that country. The foreign adopter shall submit documents issued by the competent authorities of his country of residence certifying such personal information as his age, marital status, occupation, financial situation, physical condition, and whether he has criminal record. The foreign adopter shall conclude a written agreement with the person who places the child for adoption and register the adoption in person with the civil affairs department of the people's government at the level of provinces, autonomous regions, or municipalities directly under the State Council.

The certifying documents provided in the preceding paragraph shall be authenticated by the diplomatic authorities of the country in which the foreign national resides or by an agency authorized by the said diplomatic authorities, and then authenticated by the embassy or consulate of the People's Republic of China in the said country unless otherwise provided by the State. ①

Basically, foreigners who decide to adopt Chinese children in China should comply with the regulations of China regarding adoptions, and should also comply with the laws and regulations of the adoptive person's country. If disputes arise out of any discrepancy between the law of the adoptive person's own country and the Chinese law, the competent departments of both countries' governments should consult with each other. ②

§ 6:5 Divorce

§ 6:5:1 Termination of Marriage in General

A marital relationship may be dissolved owing to the occurrence of a certain judicially significant fact, such as the death of one spouse, or divorce.

---

① Article 1109 of the Civil Code.
② Article 3 of the Measures on Registration of Adoption of Children in the PRC by Foreigners.

A spouse may die naturally or be declared to be dead according to law. If one spouse is declared by court as dead, the marital relationship between the spouse declared to be dead and the other spouse is terminated since the date of death determined by the declaration, or since the date of the occurrence of an accident which results in the declaration of death.① A marital relationship with a spouse declared dead ceases to exist from the date the declaration of his death is made. However, where the declaration of death is revoked by court, the marital relationship will be automatically resumed from the date the declaration of death is revoked if the person's spouse is not remarried, or if the person's spouse states in writing to the marriage registration authority the unwillingness to resume the marriage. If the spouse has remarried, even if he later on divorces or the new spouse is deceased, the original marital relationship would not be automatically resumed.②

Divorce is a juristic act by which a marital relationship between spouses is terminated during the life of both spouses. Freedom of divorce is part of the principle of marital autonomy and has been protected by Chinese law. The divorce system had been reflected in both the 1950 and 1980 Marriage Law. Article 17 of the 1950 Marriage Law provided that if both spouses voluntarily applied for divorce, the court should allow the divorce. If one of the spouses insisted on divorce, the court might allow the divorce after firstly mediating the case. In addition to the procedure for a divorce, the law had also provided the principles for dealing with divorce cases, including the principles that the lawful rights and interests of women and children must be protected when considering support and education issues upon divorce, and that disposition of property and arrangement of living, especially in the repayment of debts upon divorce, the female spouse should be treated more favorably. Under these principles, the community debts of the spouses should be repaid from the community property; if there is no community property, or if the community property is not sufficient to repay the debts, the male spouse was responsible for the repayment. These provisions were very positive and helpful to improve the situation of women and their social status in the beginning of the 1950s.

---

① Article 48 of the Civil Code.
② Article 51 of the Civil Code.

The 1980 Marriage Law had reserved most of the effective provisions of the old Marriage Law, and further clarified the two ways of divorce, *i.e.*, uncontested divorce upon agreement and divorce through litigation. These rules now have been integrated into the Civil Code. ①

§6:5:2 Legal Requirements and Procedure for Divorce

§6:5:2:1 Divorce upon agreement

Divorce upon agreement is a voluntary divorce under which the parties to a marital relationship both agree to terminate their relationship through an administrative procedure. ② Where husband and wife both agree to divorce, they shall enter into a divorce agreement in writing and file divorce registration in person with the marriage registration authority. A divorce agreement must include the expression of the intent of both parties to voluntarily divorce and their mutual agreement on such matters as child support, property division, and allocation of debts. ③ The Civil Code has added a "cooling period" for the spouses intending to dissolve their marital relationship. Specifically, after the parties have submitted their application for divorce, if either party later on changes his mind and is unwilling to divorce, he may withdraw the divorce registration application within thirty days after the application is received by the marriage registration authority. These "thirty days" are the "cooling period." Then, within thirty days after expiration of the cooling period, both parties must personally visit the marriage registration authority again to apply for issuance of a divorce certificate. If the parties fail to do so, the divorce registration application is deemed to be withdrawn. ④ The new rule of the Civil Code has actually made the uncontested divorce a bit more difficult.

The registration authority will allow the divorce, de-register the marriage, and issue a divorce certificate to each person if, through investigation, it ascertains that the divorce is voluntarily intended and that the two parties have actually reached an agreement on child support, property division, and

---

① Articles 1076 and 1079 of the Civil Code.
② Article 1076 of the Civil Code.
③ Article 1076 of the Civil Code.
④ Article 1077 of the Civil Code.

allocation of debts. ①

§ 6:5:2:2 Divorce through litigation

The previous sub-section discusses the situation where both spouses agree to divorce and have reached an agreement regarding the child custody and property division. However, sometimes only one spouse requests a divorce, and the other spouse does not agree. In this situation, the case may be mediated by a relevant organization, or directly resolved by the court. ②

The pre-litigation mediation is outside the litigation proceeding, and the parties may decide whether or not to have their case mediated based on their own will. If they agree to have their case mediated, the employer of either party, the residents' or villagers' committee, or the marriage registration authority may conduct the pre-litigation mediation for them. The mediation must comply with the legal requirements and must be based on the principle of voluntariness. If any party is not willing to have their case mediated, or if the mediation fails, the parties may directly go to the court to petition for a divorce.

If the case goes to the court, the court should also offer a mediation first, but this mediation is different from the pre-litigation mediation. The pre-litigation mediation is not part of the judicial proceeding and the parties may voluntarily decide whether or not to do it, whereas the judicial mediation is conducted during the litigation proceeding and is required by law. In other words, the mediation conducted during a divorce trial is a necessary phase of a divorce litigation in China. ③

There may be three possible results of the court mediation. The first result is that after mediation, the parties may reach an agreement to reconcile, so the plaintiff withdraws the petition for divorce. The court does not need to make a letter of mediation in this case, but should record the content of the mediation agreement for records, and the parties, judges, and clerks should sign or seal on the records, then the case is closed. The second result would be that the

---

① Article 1078 of the Civil Code.
② Article 1079 of the Civil Code.
③ Article 1079 of the Civil Code.

parties may reach an agreement for divorce, and the case turns from a case of contested divorce to a case of consented divorce. The court should, based on the divorce agreement, issue a letter of mediation to both parties. The letter of mediation becomes effective after being signed by both parties, and the marital relationship is terminated accordingly. The third possible result is that the mediation for reconciliation fails, and the court finds that the parties' mutual affection no longer exists. In this case, the court will allow the divorce.[1] Article 1079 of the Civil Code further provides the circumstances under which a court may grant divorce:

> A divorce shall be granted where any of the following circumstances exists and the mediation fails:
> (1) one spouse commits bigamy or cohabits with another person;
> (2) one spouse commits domestic violence or maltreats or deserts a family member;
> (3) one spouse habitually commits acts such as gambling, drug abuse, or the like, and refuses to correct such behavior despite of repeated warnings;
> (4) the spouses have been separated for no less than two years due to marital discord; or
> (5) there exists any other circumstance under which mutual affection no longer exists between the spouses.
> Where one spouse is declared to be missing and the other spouse files for divorce, such divorce shall be granted.
> Where, after a judgment has been made against divorce and the spouses have been separated for one more year, such divorce shall be granted where one of the spouses files again for divorce with the people's court.

When declaring the judgment of divorce, the court must notify the parties that each of them may not marry with a third person before the judgment becomes legally effective. If the party or parties are not satisfied with the first instance court's judgment, they have the right to appeal to the court at a higher level within fifteen days from the date the judgment is served. The second

---

[1] Article 1079 of the Civil Code.

instant court will make the final judgment. If the final judgment is one not permitting divorce, the plaintiff may not bring a divorce litigation again within six months unless there are new situations or new causes arise.

A marital relationship is dissolved upon completion of the registration of divorce when a judgment of divorce or mediation letter of divorce comes into effect. ①

§ 6:5:2:3 Special Regulations on Divorce

The Civil Code also provides for some special regulations on divorce. For example, where the spouse of a military personnel on active service make a request for divorce, the consent of the spouse who is a military personnel on active service must be obtained unless he is at serious fault. ② A military person on active service refers to a person who is currently serving in the people's liberation army or the people's armed police, and registered as a military person. The spouse of a military person on active service is limited to the person with a marital relationship with the military person on active service, excluding a person who has a marriage agreement or cohabitation relationship with the military person. This restriction only applies to the situation where only one spouse is a military person on active service and the spouse who requests the divorce is not. The serious fault of a military person may include bigamy, illegal cohabitation with someone else, domestic violence, abuses, or desertion.

The Civil Code also provides that a husband may not file for divorce during his wife's pregnancy, within one year after his wife delivers, or within six months after termination of her pregnancy, unless the wife applies for divorce, or the court deems it necessary to hear the divorce request made by the husband. ③ This provision is aimed to protecting the health of both the women and the babies. It does not completely bar a husband from filing for divorce, but only postpones the time that he may make such a request. The situations in which the court may think it necessary to entertain a husband's divorce request during these periods may include the following: (1) where there occurs a

---

① Article 1080 of the Civil Law.
② Article 1081 of the Civil Code.
③ Article 1082 of the Civil Code.

significant and emergent event and the parties can no longer continuously live together; for instance, one party may impose a threat of bodily harm on the other party; (2) where the wife committed adultery during the marriage and is pregnant, which fact is undisputed or can be proven by evidence. Article 45 of the Law on Protection of Women's Rights and Interests provides the identical restrictions.

§6:5:3 Legal Consequences of Divorce

Divorce terminates a marital relationship between spouses and may have a significant effect on the children born to the spouses and the property acquired by the spouses during their marriage. After divorce, the spouses' duty to live together and the duty to be loyal to each other have been removed and each party is free to remarry anyone else. If the divorced parties later on intend to resume their marital relationship, they must personally go to the marriage registration authority where one party's household is registered to file for re-registration of their marriage. ①

§6:5:3:1 Effect on Children

Divorce has a huge impact on children, especially minor children. Although it does not affect the parent-child relationship established during the marriage, it may have a certain effect on a parent's right to guardianship, the right to support, and the right to visitation.

Since the parents are the legal guardians of their minor children, ② upon divorce, both parents have equal rights to be the guardian of their children, and continue to have the rights and duties to raise, educate, and protect their children. No matter a child is under the physical custody of the father or the mother, he remains to be the child of both parents. As a matter of principle, a mother shall, upon divorce, have physical custody of her child under the age of two. Otherwise any parent may have the custody of the child based on an agreement between the parents. The rationale is that for a baby under two years old, it would be beneficial for him to live with his mother who is feeding

---

① Article 1083 of the Civil Code.
② Article 27 of the Civil Code.

him. This is regarded as both a right and duty of the mother. If the mother is not appropriate to raise the baby or has no ability to support the baby, then the father has the responsibility and duty to do so.① The SPC issued the Opinions on Certain Child Support Issues for Courts to Deal with Divorce Cases on November 3, 1993, providing that a child below two years of age should generally live with his mother, unless (1) the mother is suffering a serious disease and it is not appropriate for the baby to live with the mother; (2) if the mother has the ability to support but fails to perform this duty, and the father may request the child to live with him; or (3) owing to other reasons, the child cannot live with the mother. The court may allow the child below two years of age to live with his father if both parents agree and if it is not adverse to the healthy growth of the child.

For a child over two years of age, the court will first look at whether the parents have reached an agreement regarding who will have the physical custody of the child. If the parents fail to reach such an agreement, the court will make a judgment in compliance with the principle of acting in the best interests of the minor child and in light of the actual situations of both parents.② Nevertheless, in any event, the parent living with the child has no right to reject the other parent's right to guardianship, unless the parent who is not living with the child has committed a crime against the child, abused the child, or is obviously in a position that is adverse to the child. If the child is an adult with no or limited capacity for performing civil juristic acts and without a spouse, the parents, after divorce, are still the guardians of the child, and no one may shirk responsibility in the name of the divorce.③

After divorce, where a parent has the physical custody of his child, the other parent shall pay for the child support in part or in whole. The amount and duration of such payment shall be determined by both parents upon agreement, or, where no such an agreement is reached, adjudicated by the court through making a judgment. Such agreement or judgment may not preclude the child, when necessary, from making reasonable demands of

---

① Article 1084 of the Civil Code.
② Article 1084 of the Civil Code.
③ Article 28 of the Civil Code.

payment on either parent in excess of the amount specified in the agreement or judgment. ①

Divorce will not affect either parent's right to visit their children. After divorce, a parent who does not have the physical custody of his child has the right to visit the child, and the other parent is obligated to facilitate the visit. The manner and schedule for exercising the right to visitation shall be determined by both parents upon agreement, or, where no such agreement is reached, adjudicated by the court. However, if a parent's visit to the child is detrimental to the child's physical or mental health, the visit shall be suspended by the court in accordance with law, and the visit shall be resumed when the cause for such suspension no longer exists. ②

§ 6:5:3:2 Effect on Property

Divorce also terminates the proprietary relationship between the spouses. After divorce, the duty of the spouses to support each other and the right of the spouses to inherit each other's estate are terminated, and the community property co-owned by the spouses should be partitioned upon divorce. However, the property separately owned by each spouse, the property of the children or other family members, and the common property co-owned by the other family members should not be affected.

The partition of the community property should be in accordance with the agreement between the spouses; if there is no agreement, the court will make a judgment based on the actual state of the property and in compliance with the principle of favoring the rights and interests of their children, the wife, and the no-fault party. The rights and interests of the husband or wife arising from the contractual management of land based on the household shall be protected in accordance with law. ③ Other principles in partitioning the community property upon divorce include the principle of equality of the husband and wife and the principle of beneficial to production and convenience for living. The partition of property should not damage the function, utility, or economic

---

① Article 1085 of the Civil Code.
② Article 1086 of the Civil Code.
③ Article 1087 of the Civil Code.

value of the property. Any spouse who conceals, transfers, sells off, destructs or damages, or squanders the community property, or fabricates a false community debt in an attempt to unlawfully seize the property of the other spouse may be awarded a smaller percentage of or no property upon partition of the community property during the divorce proceedings. Where one of the aforementioned acts committed by one spouse is found after divorce, the other party may file a lawsuit with the people's court for re-partition of the community property. ①

Upon divorce, the spouses may also ask for compensation for their contribution to the family. Where one spouse is burdened with additional duties for raising children, looking after the elderly, or assisting the other spouse in his work, the said spouse has the right to request for compensation upon divorce against the other party, and the other party shall make due compensation. The specific arrangements for making such compensation shall be determined by the spouses upon agreement, or adjudicated by the court where no such an agreement is reached. ②

The community debts should be jointly paid off by both spouses upon divorce. Where the community property is insufficient to pay off the debts, or the property is owned by each spouse separately, such debts shall be paid off by the spouses upon agreement, or adjudicated by the court where no such an agreement is reached. ③

If one party is in financial hardship upon divorce, the other party, if financially capable, should provide appropriate financial help which may range from providing a dwelling to helping the other spouse with other financial support. The specific arrangements shall be determined by the spouses upon agreement, or adjudicated by the court if there is no such agreement reached. ④ This economic help is conditional, however. The spouse requesting financial assistance must have actual difficulties in living, and the other spouse must have the financial ability to render help. In addition, the assistance generally is temporary and not for a long term, except that the needy spouse is old or

---

① Article 1092 of the Civil Code.
② Article 1088 of the Civil Code.
③ Article 1089 of the Civil Code.
④ Article 1090 of the Civil Code.

weak, and has not remarried.

Partition of the residence of the spouses is an important issue in China. The court will follow the principle of protecting the lawful rights and interests of women and children, the principle of protecting the ownership rights over the house, the principle of prioritizing the protection of the children, the party who is disabled, or the party who is in a financial hardship, and the principle of protecting the no-fault party. Article 48 of the Law on Protection of Women's Rights and Interests provides the guidelines for partitioning a house separately owned or co-owned by the spouses, and the houses co-leased by the spouses.

§ 6:5:3:3 Damages Arising from Divorce

If a marital relationship is terminated owing to one spouse's significant fault, the no-fault party who has suffered damage owing to the divorce may ask the other party to compensate his loss. The scope of the damages covers both pecuniary damages and pains and suffering. According to Article 1091 of the Civil Code, a no-fault party may claim compensation where divorce is caused by one of the following acts of the other spouse:

(1) having committed bigamy;
(2) having cohabited with another person;
(3) having committed domestic violence;
(4) having maltreated or deserted a family member; or
(5) having acted with any other serious fault. ①

Articles 86 – 88 of the SPC's Interpretation I on the Marriage and Family Book of the Civil Code further provide specific rules on the damages arising from divorce. In order to claim damages arising from divorce, firstly, the parties must be lawful spouses, *i.e.*, their marriage must have been lawfully registered. Second, the party entitled to request for such damages must be the no-fault party to a litigation for divorce. If the court denies the request for divorce, the request for damages should also be denied. If a spouse only

---

① Article 1091 of the Civil Code.

requests the court to grant damages during their marriage, but does not request a divorce, the court will not entertain the case. However, where the parties have already registered divorce with the marriage registration authority, if one party requests the court to grant damages arising from the divorce, the court should try the case unless the parties have expressly agreed to waive such right upon divorce, or if the claim is raised after one year since the divorce has been registered.

When adjudicating a divorce case, the court should notify the parties about their relevant rights and duties under Article 1091 of the Civil Code. When applying Article 1091, the court should distinguish different situations. On the one hand, if the no-fault party is the plaintiff in a divorce litigation, his request for damages must be raised in the divorce proceeding. On the other hand, if the no-fault party is the defendant in a divorce litigation, he may initiate a separate litigation requesting such damages if he neither agrees to divorce nor requests damages in the litigation. There is also a third possible situation in which the no-fault party, as a defendant in a divorce litigation, fails to request damages during the first instance trial, but requests damages during the appeal. In this situation, the court should mediate the matter first, and then instruct the no-fault party to initiate a separate litigation if the mediation fails. However, if both parties agree that this matter may be adjudicated by the court on appeal, the court may rule on this matter when making a judgment.

§ 6:6 Foreign-Related Marriages

In order to regulate the issues arising from foreign-related marital and family relationship and to resolve the conflicts of family and marriage laws of various countries, the Ministry of Civil Affairs once issued Certain Regulations on Marriage Registration by Chinese Citizens with Foreigners on August 26, 1983, which was later repealed. The GPCL of 1986 had a special chapter entitled "Application of Laws in Civil Juristic Relations with Foreign Elements," which covered both the general principles and specific rules on the application of law, but the NPC later on expanded this chapter into a separate statute by promulgating the Law on Application of Laws in Civil Juristic

Relations with Foreign Elements (hereinafter "Law on Application of Laws")① in 2010. This law provides the fundamental legal basis for dealing with the foreign related marriage and family relationship.

§6:6:1 Entering into Marriage

Generally, the substantial elements for a Chinese citizen entering into a marriage with a foreign citizen, or two foreign citizens entering into a marriage in China are governed by the law of the place where both applicants are residing in, or the law of the country where both applicants are citizens thereof. If their citizenships are different and they intend to enter into marriage in one person's habitual residence or country of citizenship, then the law of the place where they are going to marry shall apply.② Thus, when a foreign citizen marries a Chinese citizen in China, the Chinese Civil Code shall be applied.

The registration authority is the civil affairs department of the people's government of the province, autonomous region, or municipality directly under the State Council, or an authority designated thereby. The Chinese applicant must present the required proof documents such as the identification and household registration certificate, and a signed statement that the applicant does not have a spouse and is not related to the foreign applicant by lineal blood relationship or collateral blood relationship up to the third degree of kinship. The foreign citizen should also present his valid passport or other valid international travel certificate, and a proof that he does not have a spouse. Such a proof should be prepared by the notary public or an authoritative authority of the foreign country and must be authenticated by Chinese embassy or consulate. Both applicants must go to the registration authority in person to apply for the registration. After examination, the authority will register the marriage according to Chinese law, and issue a marriage certificate to each of the applicants. The marital relationship is established thereafter.

If a Chinese citizen who has been residing in a foreign country marries a

---

① This Law was promulgated by the Standing Committee of the 11th NPC on October 28, 2012, and has become effective since April 1, 2011.
② Article 21 of the Law on Application of Laws.

Chinese citizen living in the mainland, the applicable laws are the Civil Code and the relevant regulations on marriage registration issued by the Ministry of Civil Affairs. If both applicants are Chinese citizens who are residents of a foreign country, the Chinese law encourages them to register their marriage according to the law of the country where they are residing in. If the local authority asks the Chinese embassy or consulate to provide authentication, the embassy or consulate may provide oral or written statement for this purpose if the marriage complies or basically complies with the Chinese Marriage Law. If the marriage violates the Chinese Civil Code, the embassy and consulate may neither recognize the validity of the marriage, nor provide any statement to this effect.

§6:6:2 Divorce

§6:6:2:1 Uncontested Divorce

If a foreign element is involved, where the spouses voluntarily decide to divorce through making an agreement, the spouses may select the applicable law upon agreement from the laws of one spouse's habitual residence or country of citizenship. Without such a selection, the applicable law will be the law of both spouses' habitual residence, or the law of both spouses' country of citizenship, or the law of the place where the spouses decide to register their divorce.①

An uncontested divorce filed in China between a Chinese citizen and a foreign citizen is regulated by the Regulations on Marriage Registration, which requires both spouses to go to the marriage registration authority where the Chinese citizen's household is registered. Divorce will be allowed as long as they have reached an agreement regarding child custody, child support, and the division of property. Both parties must go to the registration authority in person to register their divorce.

The applicants should present the documents and proof of their identity, as well as the divorce agreement co-signed by them. The foreign citizen should also present his valid passport or other international travel documents. The

---

① Article 26 of the Law on Application of Laws.

authority should examine the documents and verify the relevant information. If the authority is satisfied with the fact that the parties have voluntarily decided to divorce and have reached an agreement on child custody, child support, division of marital property, and debts payment, the authority should register the divorce and issue a divorce certificate.

If both spouses are foreign citizens, or if one party is a Chinese citizen residing in a foreign country and the other party is a foreign citizen, upon divorce, both applicants should apply to the authority in their country of residence. If the spouses originally registered their marriage in China or through the Chinese embassy or consulate, and if the relevant authority of the country of their residence does not accept their divorce application, they may come to China and file with an intermediate court petitioning for divorce.

§ 6:6:2:2 Contested Divorce

If one spouse cannot go to the registration authority in person, or if the spouses have a dispute regarding the divorce, they must divorce through litigation. The law of the place where the court is located is to be applicable.[①] If the spouses decide to sue for divorce in a Chinese court, then they should go to the court where the Chinese resident-spouse registers his household. If the spouse living in a foreign country has already initiated litigation with a foreign court, the party living in China may adopt necessary legal steps and the embassy or consulate of China in the foreign country should grant necessary assistance.

If the parties decide to divorce through litigation in China, they must go to an intermediate court with jurisdiction. One of the parties must be present within the territory of China and have registered his household in China, or has a residence in China and has continuously lived in China for over one year. If the defendant is living in a foreign country, a qualified plaintiff may go to the intermediate court located in the place where he registers his household; if the plaintiff is living in a foreign country, he may go to the intermediate court where the defendant registers his household.

When dealing with a foreign related divorce, the court will apply the

---

[①] Article 27 of the Law on Applicable Laws.

provisions of Chinese law and the relevant regulations. Where the divorce involves child support, partition of the community property, or the financial assistance issues, and the foreign party is a judgment debtor, the court generally should ask the foreign party to pay the judgment amount in a lump sum in order to protect the lawful rights and interests of the Chinese citizen and their children. The reason is that the judgment may not be easily enforced in a foreign country since China has not signed judicial assistance agreement with many countries. If the foreign spouse has an actual difficulty in paying the relevant support fees, *etc.*, in a lump sum, he may provide a guarantor who is a Chinese or foreign citizen residing in China and who has property located in China. If the foreign applicant fails to perform his payment obligations, the guarantor will perform instead.

Chapter 7
Succession Law

§ 7:1 General Introduction

Succession of wealth is a legal system under which a person's property and real rights will be transferred to someone else according to law when the property owner biologically dies or is declared to be dead by law. The property and real rights left by a deceased person is called his estate, and the persons who have the legal right to inherit the estate are called his heirs. The succession system is also called inheritance system. A natural person's right to inheritance is protected in China. [1]

A natural person's estate covers the property lawfully owned by such person upon death and all estate would be inheritable unless it is not inheritable according to the provisions of law or based on the nature of the estate. [2] For instance, a right to habitation is a new system recognized by the Civil Code under which a person may acquire a right to live in an apartment for life; however, upon his death, such right will cease to exist and cannot be inherited by anyone. The estate may include the person's income, houses, savings, living facilities; poultry and livestock; culture relics, books and materials; the production materials that law permits the citizens to own; the intellectual property rights, and the other lawful property owned by the person, such as the securities with a value, and a right *in personam* the subject matter of which is property.

---

[1] Articles 124 and 1120 of the Civil Code.
[2] Article 1122 of the Civil Code.

§7:1:1 Basic Principles of Chinese Succession Law

The Chinese succession law has established various principles of inheritance, including the principle of protecting citizens' right to inherit private property, the principle that both men and women have equal right in inheritance, and the principle that rights and duties are corresponding to each other. The other principles include the principle of mutual understanding and mutual accommodation, amity and unity, and taking care of the elderly, the young, the sick, and the disabled family members.

§7:1:1:1 Principle of Protecting the Right to Inherit Private Property

The fundamental principle of the Chinese succession law is the principle that the succession of private property lawfully owned by a natural person is protected.① Generally, a person's right to inheritance and the ability to inherit other's private property are equally protected and may not be restricted even if the person has no or limited capacity for performing civil juristic acts. An heir's right to inheritance may not be deprived of without legal cause; however, the heir may disclaim an inheritance by manifesting his decision in writing before the estate is distributed. In the absence of such a manifestation, the heir is presumed to have accepted the inheritance.②

Under Chinese law, succession may be processed as an intestate succession or as a testate succession if there is a will. Both intestate and testate succession should respect the intent of the deceased person in dealing with his property, and the order of the heirs by law is based on the degree of closeness between the heir and the deceased person.③ A person may make a will according to law to give his estate to one or more of his statutory heirs and may designate an executor in the will. A person may also write a will to donate his estate to the State or a collective, or an organization or individual other than his statutory heirs. In addition, a person may sign an agreement of testamentary gift for *inter vivos* support to give all his estate to a person who agrees to take care of him during his life and take care of his funerals after he dies. A person may

---

① Article 124 of the Civil Code.
② Article 1124 of the Civil Code.
③ Article 1127 of the Civil Code.

also establish a testamentary trust through writing a will. ①

A person whose right to inheritance is infringed upon by anyone may ask for legal remedy. The statute of limitations for such a dispute is three years, since the date when the heir knows or should have known that his rights have been infringed upon. However, if twenty years have passed since the starting date of the inheritance, no litigation may be brought. ②

§ 7:1:1:2 Principle of Equality of Men and Women in Succession

The second important principle of the Chinese succession law is the equality of men and women in the rights of inheritance. ③ Basically, men and women are equal in their right to inheritance, and within the same grade of statutory heirs, women heirs may not be discriminated. ④ In addition, a surviving spouse, no matter a man or a woman, who remarries has the right to dispose of the property inherited from the deceased spouse, free from any interference. ⑤ After succession opens, if an heir who had not disclaimed his right to inheritance died before the estate is partitioned, his right to inheritance will be transferred to this statutory heirs and no gender restriction would be imposed.

§ 7:1:1:3 Principle of Co-existence of Rights and Duties

The third principle of the Chinese succession system is that a person's rights and duties should be corresponding to each other. This is actually one of the fundamental principles stated in Article 33 of the Constitution and reflected in the Civil Code. Under this principle, the scope and order of inheritance of a statutory heir are determined on whether he has performed the corresponding duties.

For example, the Civil Code provides that the estate of a deceased person shall be succeeded in an order of priority. Among the statutory heirs of a

---

① Article 1133 of the Civil Code.
② Article 188 of the Civil Code.
③ This principle is reflected in Article 48 of the Constitution, Articles 4 and 1126 of the Civil Code, and Article 34 of the Law on Protection of the Rights and Interests of Women.
④ Article 1130 of the Civil Code.
⑤ Article 1157 of the Civil Code.

deceased person, the spouse, children, and parents of the deceased person are the heirs first in order, while his siblings and grandparents are only second in order. When the succession proceeding starts, the heirs first in order shall inherit the estate to the exclusion of the heirs second in order, and the heirs second in order may only inherit the estate in default of any heir first in order.① The rationale behind this rule is that a minor's grandparents, brothers, or sisters only have the duty to support the minor when his parents have both died or are unable to support him. Since the minor's grandparents and siblings only have a secondary duty to support the minor, their right to inherit the estate of the minor is also second in order.

For another example, a widowed daughter-in law or son-in-law who has made predominant contributions in supporting his or her parents-in-law shall be regarded as successors of the parents-in-law first in order.② Article 1130 of the Civil Code also provides that upon distributing an estate, an heir who has made predominant contributions in supporting the now decedent, or who has been living with the now decedent may be given a larger share. On the other hand, an heir who had the ability and was in a position to support the now decedent but failed to fulfill the duty of support shall be given no or a smaller share. Even a person other than an heir who has made considerable contributions in supporting the now decedent may get an appropriate share of the estate.③

Article 1161 also provides that a successor should pay the taxes and debts legally payable or owed by the decedent to the extent of the actual value of the portion of the estate he inherits, and assumes no such payment responsibility if he disclaims the inheritance. These provisions fully reflect the principle that rights and duties must be corresponding to each other. The bigger the duty, the greater the right.

§7:1:2 Heirs v. Donees-by-Will

There are two types of successors under the Chinese succession law: the heirs and the donees-by-will. Heirs, also called "statutory heirs," are the

---

① Article 1127 of the Civil Code.
② Article 1129 of the Succession Law.
③ Article 1131 of the Civil Code.

natural persons with the right to inherit a person's estate upon death of the person. The scope of the heirs is determined by law based on a relationship by blood or by marriage, and their order in the inheritance is based on the closeness of the relationship. According to the Civil Code, a decedent's heirs include his spouse, children, parents, siblings, and grandparents.① If a decedent is predeceased by a child or a sibling of his, the lineal descendants of the predeceased child or sibling will inherit in subrogation. However, the successors who inherit in subrogation themselves are not heirs so they may only take the share of the estate per stirpes.② A heir's right to inheritance is not affected by the fact that he does not have full capacity for performing civil juristic acts.

An heir must be the deceased person's kin, and the persons outside this kinship who may receive a gift according to a will or based on other considerations is not an heir but a done-by-will.

§7:1:3 Rights to Inheritance

A right to inheritance includes a right to confirm or disclaim inheritance. After succession opens, an heir has a right to manifest his willingness to accept a share of the estate of the deceased person and a right to actually receive the share of the estate according to law or the decedent's will. An heir may also disclaim inheritance and waive his right to the estate after succession opens but before the estate is disposed of. These rights can be exercised unilaterally and once made, the confirmation or disclaimant will become effective right away and no one's consent is needed. However, the confirmation by an heir of his right to inheritance will be assumed if no express confirmation is made, whereas the waiver of the right to inheritance must be made expressly; otherwise, the heir is presumed to have confirmed his right to inheritance.③

When an heir's right to inheritance is infringed upon, he has a right to request the court to confirm his right to inheritance and receive the share of the estate. The statute of limitations for a case involving an inheritance dispute is

---

① Article 1127 of the Civil Code.
② Article 1128 of the Civil Code.
③ Article 1124 of the Civil Code.

three years, since the date when the heir knows or should have known that his right has been infringed upon. However, no litigation will be entertained by the court if twenty years have passed after the cause occurred.

The right to inheritance may not be lost based on the heir's will but may be lost according to law. The loss of the right to inheritance may be permanent or temporary. If an heir intentionally killed the now decedent or killed any other heirs in fighting over the estate, the heir's right to inheritance will be permanently lost which will never be resumed even if the forgiveness had been received from the now decedent. ① Thus, if the deceased person had designated in his will that part or all of his estate would be distributed to this heir, the will is to be declared as invalid in part or in whole. ② The permanent loss of the right to inheritance does not affect the gift made by the deceased person to the heir during his lifetime; however, if a donee-by-will intentionally killed the now decedent, he will lose his right to receive the testamentary gift.

On the other hand, if an heir deserted the now decedent or maltreated him, forged, tampered with, concealed, or destroyed the will, or through fraud or duress, compelled the testator to write, alter, or revoke a will or interfered with such acts, and the circumstance is serious, the heir will be disinherited. Nevertheless, his right to inheritance will be resumed if he later on truly repents and mends his ways, and is later on forgiven by the now decedent or is thereafter appointed as one of the successors in the decedent's will. ③

§ 7:2 Intestate Succession

§ 7:2:1 In General

After succession opens, if the deceased person had signed a valid agreement on testamentary gift for *inter vivos* support during his life, the estate will be distributed according to such agreement; if the deceased person had otherwise written a valid will, the estate will be distributed according to

---

① Article 1125 of the Civil Code.
② Article 1125 of the Civil Code.
③ Article 1125 of the Civil Code.

the will.① Only when a person dies without a will or an agreement on testamentary gift for *inter vivos* support, will his estate be inherited by his heirs according to law. Such an inheritance is called intestate succession, statutory inheritance, or inheritance by operation of law.

In an intestate succession, the estate of the deceased person will be transferred to his heirs in accordance with law. The scope of the heirs, each heir's priority order in the inheritance proceeding, and the share of the estate that each heir may receive, are all directly provided by law. Specifically, a person's estate will only be disposed of through intestate succession if: (1) all successors designated in a will and/or all donees-by-will disclaim the inheritance or gift, (2) all testamentary successors are disinherited or all donees-by-will are disqualified as such, (3) a testamentary successor predeceases the testator, or a donee-by-will predeceases the testator or is terminated prior to the decedent's death, and there is no other successors or donees-by-will designated in the will, (4) if a will or a part of a will affecting the estate is invalidated, or (5) a portion of the estate is not disposed of by the will.②

The scope and the heirs' priority order in intestate succession are provided in Article 1127 of the Civil Code:

> The estate of a decedent shall be succeeded in the following order:
> (1) first in order: spouse, children, and parents;
> (2) second in order: siblings, paternal grandparents, and maternal grandparents.
>
> When succession opens, the successor(s) first in order shall inherit to the exclusion of the successor(s) second in order. The successor(s) second in order shall inherit the estate in default of any successor first in order.
>
> "Children" referred to in this Book include children born in or out of wedlock, and adopted children, as well as stepchildren who were raised up by the decedent.
>
> "Parents" referred to in this Book include natural parents and adoptive parents, as well as stepparents who raised up the decedent.
>
> "Siblings" referred to in this Book include siblings of whole blood and

---

① Article 1123 of the Civil Code.
② Article 1154 of the Civil Code.

half blood, and adopted siblings, as well as stepsiblings who supported or were supported by the decedent.

The spouse of the decedent is the heir first in order in the inheritance, therefore, identifying the spouse is very important in a succession proceeding. If the decedent and the person had registered their marriage, even if they had never lived together, the person who survives the decedent has the right to inherit the latter's estate as his spouse. If the decedent and the person had not registered their marriage but had lived together in the name of spouses, generally the surviving person does not have the right to inheritance as a spouse; however, he may get some shares of the estate if the requirements of Article 1131 of the Civil Code is satisfied. Article 1131 provides that an appropriate share of the estate may be given to a person, other than an heir, who has been a dependent of the now decedent, or to a person, other than an heir, who has made considerable contributions in supporting the now decedent. If a spouse dies during the period that a divorce litigation is pending or before a divorce judgment becomes effective, the surviving spouse has the right to inherit the decedent's estate as the spouse.

Children are also heirs first in order in the inheritance. Children here include the children born in or out of wedlock, adopted children, and the stepchildren who were raised up by the decedent. Sometimes a daughter-in-law or a son-in-law who survives their spouse is also treated as one of the "children" of the deceased parent-in-law, and is regarded as an heir first in order if he has made predominant contributions in supporting the deceased parent-in-law. ①

Parents also are heirs first in order in succession. Parents include natural parents, adoptive parents, and stepparents who raised up the deceased child. Generally, parents have the right to inherit the estate of their biological child, no matter he was born in or out of wedlock, unless the child had been adopted by someone else.

As the heirs second in order, brothers and sisters include siblings of whole blood and half blood, adopted siblings, and step siblings who supported or were supported by the decedent. Grandparents are also heirs second in order,

---

① Article 1129 of the Civil Code.

including natural grandparents, adoptive grandparents, and step grandparents who raised up the deceased grandchild.

As a general rule, the heirs in the same order may inherit an equal share of the estate. However, it is to be noted that a fetus is deemed as having the capacity for enjoying civil-law rights in estate succession, acceptance of gift, and other situations where protection of a fetus' interests is involved.① Thus, when partitioning an estate, a share shall be reserved for a fetus. If the fetus is stillborn, the reserved share shall be disposed of as in an intestate succession.②

§7:2:2 Inheritance by Representation and Re-Inheritance

Sometimes, a child may have predeceased the decedent. In order to secure that the descendants of such a predeceased child will get a share of the estate, Article 1128 of the Civil Code allows the lineal descendants of the predeceased child to inherit the estate in subrogation. This may be called inheritance by representation, and the grandchildren or their lineal blood kinship downward are the heirs by representation. They are not heirs first in order because they only have the right to inherit the share that their father or mother (the child of the decedent) would have inherited were they still alive. Similarly, where a deceased person does not have any heirs first in order, and one sibling predeceased the decedent, the children of the predeceased sibling will inherit the estate in subrogation.

There are two things to be noted here. First, if the person represented is a child of the decedent, who would have been an heir first in order if he were still alive, then this child's lineal descendants may inherit the estate in subrogation; however, if the person represented is a sibling of the decedent, who would have been an heir second in order if he were still alive, then only the sibling's children may inherit the estate in subrogation. Where the predeceased sibling was predeceased by all of his children, even if he is survived by a grandchild, the grandchild does not have the right to inherit the estate in subrogation.

Second, a person who inherits the estate in subrogation generally may only

---

① Article 16 of the Civil Code.
② Article 1155 of the Civil Code.

take the share of the estate *per stirpes*, which means that an heir by representation may only inherit the share of the estate that his parent or lineal ascendant would have had inherited if his parent or lineal ascendant were still alive.

Re-inheritance is different from inheritance by representation, and it happens when an heir of the decedent survived the decedent but died before the decedent's estate is disposed of. In other words, after succession opens, an heir who has not disclaimed the inheritance dies before the estate is partitioned. In this case, the share of the estate that he would have inherited were he still alive will be inherited by his heirs, unless otherwise provided in the will.① It involves two types of heirs: (1) an heir of the decedent (the first heir), no matter he is an heir first in order or second in order, and regardless whether he is a statutory heir or an heir by will; and (2) an heir of the first heir (the second heir). The share of the estate that the second heir(s) may inherit is limited to the share that the first heir had the right to inherit. The re-inheritance may be involved in both intestate succession and testate succession.

There are significant differences between re-inheritance and inheritance by representation. First, the scope of the first heir in re-inheritance and the person being represented in inheritance by representation is different. In an inheritance by representation, the person who is represented is limited to the children or siblings of the decedent; while in a re-inheritance, the first heir is not limited to the children of the decedent, but may be any statutory heirs or heirs by will. Second, the scope of the second heir(s) in re-inheritance and the scope of heir(s) representing the predeceased heirs are different. The latter is only limited to the person or persons who are lineal descendants by blood of the person being represented, but the former may be any heir of the first heir, including the spouse, children, parents, siblings, and grandparents of the first heir. When the first heir has no heirs first in order, his heirs second in order may inherit the estate in the re-inheritance proceeding. In addition, the subject of inheritance by representation is the estate of the decedent; while in a re-inheritance, the subject of inheritance is the estate of the first heir. In an inheritance by representation, all the heirs by representation may only co-

---

① Article 1152 of the Civil Code.

inherit the share of the estate that the person being represented had the right to inherit, and may not receive equal shares with the other heirs. Lastly, inheritance by representation only exists in intestate succession, but re-inheritance may exist in either intestate or testate succession.

Case 41

Case 41: Li & Fan v. Fan 1 & Teng[①]

Li and Fan 2 married in March 1998. Fan 2 was the son of Fan 1 & Teng. In August 2002, Fan 2 bought an apartment in the Qinhuai District by paying 14,582.16 yuan, among which 10,000 yuan were borrowed from his parents. In September 2002, Fan 2 registered the apartment in his own name. In March and October 2005, Li repaid 10,000 yuan in total to Fan 1 and Teng. At the time of litigation, the current value of the apartment in March 2006 was 193,000 yuan.

On January 30, 2004, Li and Fan 2 signed an agreement in a local hospital on artificial insemination, and then Li was pregnant.

In April, Fan 2 was sick and admitted to hospital. On May 20, 2004, Fan 2 wrote a holographic will and then died on May 23, 2004. Li gave birth to a son, Fan, on October 22, 2004.

Li claimed that she, Fan, and Fan 2's parents were heirs of Fan 2 and should equally inherit the apartment concerned. However, Fan 2's parents claimed that the apartment concerned was not community property of Fan 2 and Li, because they paid 10,000 yuan which accounted for 2/3 of the purchase price, therefore, they owned at least 2/3 of the apartment. In Fan 2's will, he devised the apartment to his parents; therefore, the statutory inheritance rules should not be applied to the apartment. They also claimed that Li's son did not have blood relationship with Fan 2, and before Fan 2 died, he tried to persuade Li to perform abortion but Li did not agree. They alleged that Fan 2 wrote in his will that he did not want to support this child, which should be respected; and therefore, Li should

---

① See the SPC Gazette, Issue 117, 2006.

be responsible for supporting Fan, and Fan should not be listed as Fan 2's heir.

The Qinhuai District People's Court of Nanjing City reasons that according to the SPC's reply on how to determine the legal status of the children born from artificial semination after the spouses divorce, where the spouses both agree to have artificial semination during the marriage, the child thus born should be regarded as the child born in wedlock and the relationship between the child and the parents should be governed by the relevant rules of the Marriage Law. Based on the fact, Fan 2, who was infertile, signed an agreement consenting to do the artificial semination. It is sufficient to show that he intended to have a child with Li, and the child thus born should be regarded as the child of both spouses during marriage, no matter whether the child has a blood relationship with one or both parties. Article 57 of the GPCL provides that a juristic act, since its formation, is legally binding and may not be changed or rescinded unless done in accordance with law or obtained the other parties' consent. Fan 2 changed his mind after he got sick; however, his wife was already pregnant. If he wanted to stop it, he must obtain the consent from Li; otherwise his signature on the agreement had legal force and could not be changed or revoked unilaterally. Therefore, Fan 2's denial of the paternal relationship in his will was an invalid juristic act. Fan was the statutory heir of Fan 2.

Article 5 of the Succession Law provides that after succession opens, it shall be processed as an intestate succession, or as a testate succession by the successor(s) or donee(s)-by-will where there is a will; or be processed in accordance with the agreement on testamentary gift for *inter vivos* support, where there is such an agreement. Article 26 of the Succession Law provides that when partitioning an estate, where community property of husband and wife is involved, unless otherwise agreed upon, half of the community property shall be allocated first to the surviving spouse as separate property, while the remaining property shall be part of the decedent's estate. Article 38 of the SPC's opinion on certain issues on the implementation of the Succession Law provides that if a testator intends to dispose by will of the property belonging to the State, collective, or other persons, this part of the will should be held invalid.

Accordingly, the court reasons that the apartment concerned in this case was community property acquired by the parties during their marriage. After Fan 2 died, half of the apartment should belong to Li, and the other half should be part of Fan 2's estate. In Fan 2's will, he tried to dispose of the whole apartment to his parents, which disposition would infringe upon Li's right and therefore this part of the will is invalid.

Article 19 of the Succession Law provides that a necessary portion of the estate must be reserved in a will for a successor who has neither the ability to work nor the source of income. Article 28 provides that when partitioning an estate, a share shall be reserved for a fetus. If the fetus is stillborn, the reserved share shall be disposed of as in an intestate succession. Fan 2 knew that Li was pregnant through artificial semination after consented by himself, but he wrote in his will disposing all of his property to his parents on the ground that he did not want to keep this child. Although Fan was born after Fan 2 died, Fan is the son and a legal heir of Fan 2. As a minor, Fan did not have work ability or source of income. If Fan 2 did not leave any necessary share for Fan, it is against Article 19 of the Succession law. The court holds that when dealing with Fan 2's estate, necessary share must be firstly reserved for Fan, and the rest may be disposed of according to his will.

Since the appraised value of the apartment concerned is 190,000 yuan, half of it should belong to Li, the other half, 96,500 yuan is Fan 2's estate, among which 1/3 must be preserved to Fan, and the rest is to be inherited by Fan 1 and Teng. According to the actual situation, the apartment should be owned by Li, and Li should give Fan, Fan 1, and Teng each 32,166.7 yuan.

§ 7:3   Testate Succession

§ 7:3:1   In General

Testate succession is also called inheritance by will or designated inheritance, which is one of the two ways that a decedent's estate may be succeeded. A person may make a will during his lifetime. Through writing a will, a person may make an arrangement which will become effective only upon his death to deal with his estate or other matters. The person who writes a will is the testator, and the persons designated to receive the testator's estate are the heirs by will or donees-by-will, depending on whether they are the statutory heirs of the testator or not. Making a will is a unilateral juristic act of the testator which does not need to be consented to by anyone, and it must be done by the testator in person. A testator also may unilaterally alter or revoke the will he has made. If a testator acts inconsistently with the content of his will, the pertinent part of the will is deemed to be revoked. If a testator has made several wills and their contents are inconsistent with each other, the will made last in time shall prevail. ①

In order for a will to be valid, a testator must have the ability to make a will. He must be a person with full capacity for performing civil juristic acts, so a will made by a person with no or limited capacity is void. A will must manifest the genuine intention of the testator; thus, a will made under fraud or duress or a forged will is void. If a will is illegally tampered with, the affected part of the will is also void. ② The content of a will must be in compliance with law, and a will may not dispose of a property that is not owned by the testator. A will must observe the provisions of law which provide for preservation of shares for some special groups of people, including a fetus and an heir who lacks work ability and living resources. In addition, a will must strictly comply with the form requirements provided by law; otherwise the will may be held void.

Whenever there is a will, the succession of the estate affected by the will must be proceeded as a testate succession. The heirs in an intestate succession must follow a priority order provided by law, but there is no such a restriction in a testate succession. The heirs by will are the persons who will directly receive all or part of the estate of the testator according to a legally effective will upon the death of the testator; they are also called the designated heirs. The designated heirs must be selected from the scope of the statutory heirs

---

① Article 1142 of the Civil Code.
② Article 1143 of the Civil Code.

provided by law, and anyone other than the statutory heirs may not be an heir by will.① After an heir by will has received the estate in accordance with the will, he also has a right to inherit the rest part of the estate that the will does not dispose of according to the provisions of intestate succession.②

A person may also, by making a will, donate his estate to the State or a collective, or an organization or individual other than his statutory heirs.③ The State, collective, or the designated persons other than the statutory heirs are only regarded as donees-by-will, but not heirs. Where intestate succession, testate succession, and testamentary gift concurrently exist, the taxes and debts legally payable or owed by the decedent shall be paid by the intestate heirs, except that the taxes or debts in excess of the actual value of the portion of the estate inherited by the intestate heirs should be paid by the testamentary heirs and donees-by-will in proportion to the shares of the estate each of them has received.④ The execution of a testamentary gift may not affect the payment of taxes and debts legally payable or owed by the testator,⑤ which means that a donee-by-will will receive the testamentary gift only after taxes or debts owed by the decedent have been fully paid off from the estate.

§7:3:2 Ways of Making a Will

A person may make a will in different ways allowed by the Civil Code.⑥ First, a person may write a holographic will, which is a will written by the testator's hand and signed by him, specifying the year, month, and day of its making. The making of a holographic will is very easy, as long as it is written by the testator's hand, it neither needs any witness to be present and sign it, nor needs to go through any procedure. The legal requirements for such a will are that the testator must personally write it by hand, sign it, and indicate the year, month, and day of the will.⑦ A person may also request another person to write a will on behalf of him if he cannot or for some other reasons cannot

---

① Article 1133 of the Civil Code.
② Article 6 of Interpretation I of the Succession Book of the Civil Code.
③ Article 1133 of the Civil Code.
④ Article 1163 of the Civil Code.
⑤ Article 1162 of the Civil Code.
⑥ Articles 1134-1139 of the Civil Code.
⑦ Article 1134 of the Civil Code.

personally write the will. In order for such a will to be effective, there must be two or more witnesses attesting the will, one of whom writes the will, specifying the year, month, and day of its making, and signs it along with the other witness or witnesses and with the testator. ①

A person may type and print a will, but such a will must be attested by two or more witnesses, and both the testator and the witnesses must sign and specify the year, month, and day on each page of the will. ② A person may make a will in the form of an audio or video recording. Such a will must also be attested by two or more witnesses. The testator and the witnesses must record their name or likeness in the recording and specify the year, month, and day of its making. ③ A person may make a nuncupative will when facing imminent danger. Such a will must also be attested by two or more witnesses. When the imminent danger is removed and where the testator is able to make a will in writing or in the form of an audio or video recording to replace the nuncupative will, the nuncupative will thus made becomes invalid. ④

A person may make a will before a notary public officer. A notarized will has a stronger effect because of its stronger evidential value, so that many people feel more secure to execute a notarized will. ⑤ A notarized will had been regarded as the most authoritative form of will which may prevail over all of the other forms of will no matter the latter will is made prior to or after the notarized will is made. However, the situation has been changed by the Civil Code. Now a notarized will has the same effect with the other forms of will. It makes the making of a will much easier, but people still could have their will notarized if they hope to do so.

The witness of a will must be a person with full capacity for performing civil juristic acts. A person with no or limited capacity for performing civil juristic acts, or a person otherwise incompetent to attest a will is not eligible to act as a witness to a will. In addition, a witness to a will should not be a successor or a donee-by-will or a person having any interest with a successor or

---

① Article 1135 of the Civil Code.
② Article 1136 of the Civil Code.
③ Article 1137 of the Civil Code.
④ Article 1138 of the Civil Code.
⑤ Article 1139 of the Civil Code.

donee-by-will. ①

Case 15 reprinted in the end of §2:5:5 of this Book involves a will witnessed by a lawyer. The will was held invalid so that the law firm had to compensate for the loss suffered by the designated heir.

§7:3:3 Content of a Will

A will should firstly designate the testate heirs or donees-by-will, and then specify the way of distributing the estate, including the specific items or the share of the estate that each heir or donee will receive. If the items or the share of the estate are not specified, the law presumes that all of the decedent's estate will be disposed of by the will, and the heirs and donees each will get an equal share. A will should also indicate the purpose of use of a certain property and explain the requirements for the heirs or donees. If a testator writes in a will requiring an heir or donee to perform a certain duty, the heir or donee must perform the duty; otherwise, the court may, upon request of the relevant organization or individual, terminate his right to receive the estate. A will should also appoint an executor to execute the will. ②

A testator may freely designate the heirs or donees-by-will in his will, and may also designate successor heirs or donees and the takers in default in case the designated heirs or donees predeceases the testator. Since a will is not effective until the testator dies, the testator may change part of the will or revoke the will during his life. ③ A testator must have the capacity for performing civil juristic acts when altering or revoking his will, and the alteration or revocation must truly reflect the intent of the testator. Both the content and form of the alteration must be in compliance with the legal requirements. A will may be revoked by the testator through making a declaration of revocation or through making a new will to replace it. If a testator has made several wills the content of which are conflicting with each other, the will made on the most recent date is regarded as valid, while all of the other wills are deemed as revoked. ④ If, after a testator makes a will in

---

① Article 1140 of the Civil Code.
② Article 1133 of the Civil Code.
③ Article 1142 of the Civil Code.
④ Article 1142 of the Civil Code.

which he decides to give some property to a certain heir or donee, the testator changes his mind and decides to give it to someone else, the will is deemed to be revoked.

§7:3:4 Administrator and Executor

An administrator is a person provided by law or appointed by the court to administer the estate of a deceased person. An executor is a person appointed by the testator or provided by law to execute the will. Upon opening of a succession, the executor of the will is the administrator of the estate. If no executor is designated in the will, the successors shall elect an administrator in a timely manner. Where the successors fail to do so, all of the successors are co-administrators. Where there is no successor or where all of the successors disclaim the inheritance, the civil affairs department or the villagers' committee in the place where the decedent was domiciled at the time of his death shall serve as the administrator.① Where a dispute arises over the determination of an administrator of the estate, any interested person may request the court to appoint an administrator.②

A testator may appoint one of his statutory heirs or someone else to be the executor of his will. The executor may be a natural person or a social organization. An executor of a will must have full capacity for performing civil juristic acts. The functions and responsibilities of an executor include the following:

(1) verifying and making an inventory of the estate;

(2) reporting to the successors about the inventory of the estate;

(3) taking necessary measures to prevent the estate from being destructed, damaged, or lost;

(4) clearing the decedent's claims and debts;

(5) partitioning the estate in accordance with the will, or in accordance with law; and

---

① Article 1145 of the Civil Code.
② Article 1146 of the Civil Code.

(6) performing any other act necessary for managing the estate.①

Where there are two or more executors, they should perform their duties through consultation. If they cannot reach an agreement, they may execute the will based on the majority executors' opinion on the condition that the testator's will is not breached and that the beneficiaries of the will have been fully consulted with. An administrator shall perform his duties in accordance with law, and shall bear civil liability if any heir, donee-by-will, or creditor of the decedent suffers damage caused by his intentional act or gross negligence.② An administrator may receive remuneration in accordance with law.③

The administrator and executor system is a new system in China, and there will be more specific rules to be made in the future.

§7:3:5 Testamentary Gift and Agreement on Testamentary Gift for *Inter Vivos* Support

When a person writes a will under which he gives all or part of his estate to the State, collective, or someone other than his statutory heirs, he is making a testamentary gift. The testator is the donor, and the person who is going to receive the gift is the donee-by-will. The testamentary gift will only be effective upon the death of the testator. A donee-by-will must manifest his decision to accept or disclaim the testamentary gift within sixty days after he learns of the gift. In the absence of such a manifestation within the specified period, he is deemed to have disclaimed the gift.④ Apparently, the protection granted to a donee-by-will is less than the protection granted to a testamentary heir, because an heir is presumed to have accepted the inheritance unless he manifests his decision in writing to disclaim an inheritance. The Chinese law requires that the execution of a testamentary gift should not affect the payment of taxes or debts legally payable or owed by the testator.⑤ A testamentary gift may become invalid if the donee has lost the right to receive the gift or

---

① Article 1147 of the Civil Code.
② Article 1148 of the Civil Code.
③ Article 1149 of the Civil Code.
④ Article 1124 of the Civil Code.
⑤ Article 1162 of the Civil Code.

predeceases the donor, or if the gift falls outside the scope of the estate.

The Chinese law recognizes a special system which allows a person to enter into an agreement on testamentary gift for *inter vivos* support with an organization or individual other than an heir. Such organization or individual assumes, in accordance with the agreement, a duty to support the said person during his lifetime, and attends to his interment after death, in return for the right to receive the testamentary gift under the agreement.① Such an agreement must be in writing, and may be notarized if necessary. Different from a will, such an agreement is effective once it is formed; therefore, the legal effect of such an agreement is superior to that of testate or intestate succession.

Case 3 briefed and reprinted in the end of § 1:5:1 of this Book involves an agreement on testamentary gift for *inter vivos* support. The person who agreed to take care of the elderly failed to perform her duties. A review of the case is suggested.

§ 7:4　Disposal of Estate

§ 7:4:1　General Principles

Succession starts when a person biologically dies or is declared to be dead by the court through a special legal proceeding. When disposing of a decedent's estate, several principles must be observed.②

First, successors same in order generally shall inherit share and share alike. This is the core principle in the succession law. Based on this principle, all the heirs under the same condition will get an equal share of the estate. When determining whether the heirs are under the same condition, the court will consider whether the heirs are in the same order of inheritance, whether their financial conditions are basically the same, and whether the heirs have similarly performed their duty to support the deceased.

As a rule of exception, however, when distributing an estate, due consideration must be given to a successor who has special financial difficulties

---

① Article 1158 of the Civil Code.
② Article 1130 of the Civil Code.

and is unable to work. For example, an heir who lacks work ability and has special difficulties in life, and an heir who lacks work ability and does not have living resources will get more shares. In addition, a person other than an heir who has been relying on the support provided by the decedent, lacks work ability, and does not have living resources may also receive more shares. Likewise, when distributing an estate, a successor who has made predominant contributions in supporting the now decedent, or who has been living with the now decedent may be given a larger share; whereas a successor who had the ability and was in a position to support the now decedent but failed to fulfill the duty of support shall be given no or a smaller share. In addition, a person other than a successor who has made considerable contributions in supporting the now decedent is also entitled to receive an appropriate share of the estate.

In addition, successors may take unequal shares upon agreement among them. The agreement made by the successors is given high respect. ① As long as all of the heirs agree unanimously, the share of estate that each heir will get may be unequal under the same condition, whereas the share of estate that each heir will get may be equal when the conditions are not the same, provided that the shares necessary for those who lack work ability and have no living resources have been preserved. Any issue arising from succession shall be dealt with through consultation with and among the successors in the spirit of amity, unity, mutual understanding, and accommodation. The time and mode for partitioning the estate and the shares of the estate to be distributed shall be determined by the successors through consultation. If they cannot reach an agreement through consultation, they may apply to a mediation committee for mediation or directly file a lawsuit with the court.

Upon opening of a succession, a successor who has knowledge of the death of the decedent shall notify the other successors and the executor of the will in a timely manner. Where none of the successors knows about the death of the decedent or is able to make the notification upon learning of the death of the decedent, the organization to which the decedent was employed at the time of his death, or the urban residents' committee or the villagers' committee in the place where the decedent was domiciled at the time of his death shall make the

---

① Article 1132 of the Civil Code.

notification.① If one or more heirs cannot be notified, the court should preserve the share of estate for the said heir or heirs and designate a custodian to keep the estate.② Anyone who has in his possession the property of a decedent must properly keep such property, and no organization or individual may misappropriate or contend for it.③

Since succession proceeding may also start upon the declaration of death of a person by the court, which is an assumption of death by law, the person may or may not have actually died. If a person declared to be dead reappears, upon request of the said person or any interested person, the court should revoke the declaration of death, and the person has the right to request those who have obtained his property under the succession law to return the property, or make appropriate compensation if the property cannot be returned.④ If the property has been lawfully received by a *bona fide* third person, the third person generally has no duty to return the property.

§7:4:2 Distribution of Estate

An estate is the property lawfully owned by a natural person upon death and to be transferred to his successors and/or other donees according to the succession law. The scope of the estate is provided by law. An estate not inheritable according to the provisions of law or based on the nature of the estate may not be inherited.⑤

The succession proceeding will ultimately lead to the partition of the estate and distribution of the share of the estate to the successors or donees. Partition of the estate will follow the principle that testate succession preempts intestate succession, which means that if the decedent had made a lawful and effective will, the estate should be firstly distributed according to the will, and will only be distributed according to law if there is no will or for some reasons the will is not valid. However, part of the estate may still be inherited according to law if one or more testate successors waive or have lost their right to inheritance,

---

① Article 1150 of the Civil Code.
② Article 30 of the Interpretation on the Succession Book of the Civil Code.
③ Article 1151 of the Civil Code.
④ Article 53 of the Civil Code.
⑤ Article 1122 of the Civil Code.

predeceased the decedent, or if the will only disposes of part of the estate owing to partial invalidity of the will or for other reasons, then the rest of the estate should be distributed as intestate succession. ①

When partitioning an estate, where community property of husband and wife is involved, unless otherwise agreed upon by the spouses, half of the community property shall be allocated first to the surviving spouse as separate property, while the remaining property shall be part of the decedent's estate. When partitioning an estate, where the decedent's estate is a portion of the common property of the family, the portion of the property belonging to the other family members shall firstly be separated from the decedent's estate. ②

When partitioning an estate, a share shall be reserved for a fetus. If the fetus is stillborn, the preserved share should then be disposed of as in an intestate succession. ③ The partitioning of a decedent's estate shall be conducted in a way beneficial to production and people's livelihood, and without diminishing its efficacy. If partition of an estate is inappropriate, it may be disposed of by such means as appraisal, appropriate compensation, or co-ownership. ④

Regarding the specific ways of partitioning an estate, if a testator has determined a specific method of partition in a will, the method should be adopted. If the testator has not determined the way of partition of the estate, the heirs may decide through consultation the time, method, and shares of the partition. If consultation fails, they may apply for mediation, or directly sue in court. ⑤ Where an estate is divisible and the quality of the estate will not be changed and the value of the estate will not be harmed through physical partition, the estate may be directly partitioned, i.e., the heirs will each receive an equal share of the property. Where an estate is not suitable for physical partition, i.e., the physical partition of the property may change the quality of the property or decrease the value of the estate, the estate may be partitioned through appraisal, appropriate compensation, or co-ownership. A

---

① Article 1154 of the Civil Code.
② Article 1153 of the Civil Code.
③ Article 1155 of the Civil Code.
④ Article 1156 of the Civil Code.
⑤ Article 1132 of the Civil Code.

property may be appraised and sold, and the heirs will share the proceeds. If the property is not suitable for appraisal and sale, it may be distributed to one heir who will in turn compensate the other heirs through money payment according to their shares of inheritance. Alternatively, the property that is not suitable for appraisal and sale may be co-owned by part or all of the heirs, and each heir may exercise the ownership rights and assume corresponding duties.

§7:4:3 Disposal of Estate without an Heir or Donee

After succession opens, if there is no heir to inherit the estate or no one to accept the testamentary gift within a specified period, the estate is regarded as one without an heir or donee. It happens when a deceased person has no statutory heir and (1) has not written a will to designate a donee, (2) has not signed any agreement on testamentary gift for *inter vivos* support with any person, (3) all of his heirs have waived or lost the right to inheritance, and (4) all of the donees-by-will have also waived the right to receive the testamentary gift. It may also happen when the deceased person has no statutory heir but has written a will; however, the will only disposes of part of his estate, then the rest of his estate becomes the estate without an heir or a donee. In this situation, upon request of any person, the court may post a public notice so that the heirs or donees may come to claim on the estate. If there is no heir or donee claiming on the estate within one year after the public notice is posted, the court may determine that the estate is one without any heir or donee. If after such a decision is made, an heir or a donee of the estate appears, he may claim against the estate within the limitation period, and the court may revoke the original ruling if it finds the situation is true.

An estate without any heir or donee will be escheated to the State or collective organization for public interest purposes according to Chinese law.[①] The debts that the deceased owed to others should be repaid from the estate before it is escheated to the State or collective, but the payment of debts is limited to the actual value of the estate. A person other than an heir who has been a dependent of the decedent or who has made considerable contributions

---

[①] Article 1160 of Civil Code.

in supporting the decedent may receive an appropriate share of the estate. ① If the estate has already been escheated to the State or collective because there is no heir or donee, the above person may make a request for their share of the estate. ②

Case 38 reprinted in the end of § 6:3:2 of the book involves an internal agreement between the spouses regarding the partition of their community property. A dispute arises upon succession regarding whether such a disposition is valid. A review of the case is suggested.

§ 7:5 Foreign-Related Succession

Succession may be complicated when foreign factors are involved. For example, a deceased person or an heir of him may be a foreign citizen, the estate may be located in a foreign country, or the deceased person may have died or written a will in a foreign country. In these situations, the inheritance of movable property is to be regulated by the law of the place where the deceased resided upon his death, while the inheritance of immovable property is to be regulated by the law of the place where the real property is located. If there is a convention or treaty that China has joined in or become a party, or if China has signed an agreement with a foreign country, then the convention, treaty, or agreement should be applied. The service of the judicial documents and other documents by the final court of China or another country or region is regulated by the Hague Convention on the Service Abroad of Judicial and Extra-Judicial Documents in Civil or Commercial Matters. This Convention has been approved and become effective to China since January 1, 1992.

For policy reasons, if succession involves a person from Hong Kong or Macau, the provisions of the succession law or other relevant laws on foreign related inheritance may be applied *mutatis mutandis*. If there is any dispute, the court will have exclusive jurisdiction over the case as long as the deceased person dies in the mainland or the main estate is located in the mainland. Generally, the right to inheritance of a person residing in Taiwan is equal with

---

① Article 1131 of the Civil Code.
② Article 41 of the Interpretation on the Succession Book of the Civil Code.

that of a person residing in the mainland. If any resident of Taiwan claims against an estate located in the mainland, the court will grant protection. However, if twenty years have passed, a dispute on inheritance will not be tried by the court. Nevertheless, many inheritance disputes brought about by the Taiwan residents have actually exceeded 20 years, and the court may still consider the case as a special situation by extending the period of limitations according to Article 188 of the Civil Code.

Conclusive Remarks

China has established a comprehensive civil law system which is based on the development of law through the past decades. The promulgation of the General Provisions of Chinese Civil Law had been playing an important role in China since 1986, and the enactment of the Marriage Law, the Succession Law, the Contract Law, the Real Rights Law, and the Tort Liability Law had further strengthened the Chinese civil law system and made the codification of the Chinese civil law realistic. The finalization of the Civil Code in 2020 is quite a milestone in Chinese legislative history. This book is aimed at introducing the Chinese civil law system to the international students who are interested in learning the Chinese law.

The previous chapters introduce a general legal framework of the Chinese civil law, covering the General Part and the other Books of the Civil Code. The first Chapter gives an overview of the Chinese civil law system, which reviewed the history of the codification of the Civil Code, the general legal framework, and the general principles adopted through the Chinese civil law. Some important civil procedures are also briefly discussed in order to help the readers understand how the civil-law rights and interests are protected in China. Chapter 2 concentrates on the general part of the Civil Code, with a view to introducing some important concepts and systems covered by the Civil Code, especially including the civil juristic relationship which involves the persons of the civil law, the civil law rights and obligations, and the juristic acts. Other contents such as the agency relationship, civil liability and defenses, and the limitation periods are also briefly discussed. Starting from Chapter 3, each chapter focuses on one Book of the Civil Code, specifically covering the real rights law, contract law, tort law, family law, and succession law, with the exception that the Book on Personality Rights is not discussed in a separate chapter. Instead, the content of the persoality rights has been scattered and discussed in several chapters such as Chapter 2 and Chapter 5.

The discussions through this Book include discussions on the statutes as well as the cases. Some of the provisions of the Civil Code and other laws have been quoted in the text, but others are only cited in the footnotes. As mentioned earlier, China is not a case law country, so that the cases are not binding on the Chinese court; however, the Supreme People's Court has selected and published a series of cases as guiding cases or typical cases for the lower courts to follow. These cases have high persuasive value in judicial practice. Most of the cases discussed in this Book come from these guiding cases or typical cases, not reprinted in its original but only briefed and translated for discussion purpose.

We have a hypothetical case in the beginning of this Book, and now it is time for us to review it to see whether the questions may be well answered, and, this would conclude the whole Book.

> West Co., a company registered in New York, U. S., plans to sell a special kind of electronic dictionary — E-Books to East Co., a company registered in Shanghai, China. West Co. and East Co. are negotiating a contract for sale of the E-Books. Who will be the qualified representative of each company responsible for negotiating the contract? Will the contract signed by such individual persons bind the two companies? If a Chinese consumer is somehow injured by an E-Book owing to explosion of its battery, who will be liable, which law is to be applied, and what will be the remedies? Suppose West Co. has decided to establish a joint venture (JV) in China and Mr. White is to be one of the JV's directors who will be relocated to China, may Mr. White purchase an apartment in Shanghai? May he invest his income in the Chinese stock market or remit the money back home? May he marry a Chinese girl? May he adopt a Chinese baby? If he later on divorces his Chinese wife, what will be his support obligations? May he inherit his Chinese mother-in-law's estate?

Index of Cases

Case 1: Liu v. China Mobile [(2011) Quan Shang Chu Zi No. 240 (Quanshan District Court, Xuzhou City, Jiangsu Province), reprinted in the SPC's Guiding Cases No. 64]

Case 2: Wang v. Lu [(2017) Zui Gao Fa Min Shen No. 2483 (the SPC), reprinted in the SPC Gazette, Issue 7, 2018]

Case 3: Mao & Long v. Mei [(1998) Qian Min Zai Zi No. 25 (the High People's Court of Guizhou Province), reprinted in the SPC Gazette, Issue 5, 2000]

Case 4: Ran v. Xie [(2021) Yu 0101 Min Chu No. 2425 (Wanzhou District People's Court, Chongqing Municipality, April 20, 2021)]

Case 5: Jiang & Meng v. Uncle Qiao [(2017) Hu 0105 Min Te No. 19 (Changning District People's Court of Shanghai Municipality), reprinted in the Case Study Institute of the SPC in Typical Cases Involving Protection of Rights and Interests of Minors and Innovation of Juvenile Judicial System]

Case 6: Contractual Disputes on Transfer of Land-Use Rights [(2005) Min 1 Zhong Zi No. 104 (the SPC)]

Case 7: Ni & Wang v. China International Trade Center [(Chaoyang District People's Court of Beijing Municipality) reprinted in the SPC Gazette, Issue 1, 1993]

Case 8: Liu & Guos v. Sun and L Co. [(2019) Yu 1503 Min Chu No. 8878 (Pingqiao District People's Court, Xinyang City, Henan Province), reprinted in the SPC's Guiding Cases No. 142]

Case 9: Ye v. Anzhen Hospital, *et al* [(Beijing No. 2 Intermediate People's Court) reprinted in the SPC Gazette, Issue 6, 2003]

Case 10: L Co. & Huang v. Zhao [(2018) Jing 03 Min Zhong No. 725 (Beijing No. 3 Intermediate People's Court), reprinted in the SPC's Guiding Cases No. 143]

Case 11: Peng v. *China Story* Magazine [(the High People's Court of Sichuan Province) reprinted in the SPC Gazette, Issue 6, 2002]

Case 12: Lin & Chen v. Cai [(2016) Yue 0512 Min Chu No. 217 (Haojiang District People's Court of Shantou City, Fujian Province), reprinted in the SPC Gazette, Issue 11, 2020]

Case 13: Zhangs v. Zhang [(Tangu District People's Court of Tianjin Municipality) reprinted in the SPC Gazette, Issue 1 (1989)]

Case 14: Disputes Regarding Transfer of a Land Use Right [(2004) Min Yi Zhong Zi No. 106 (the SPC), reprinted in the SPC Gazette, Issue 3 (2007)]

Case 15: Wang Baofu v. Law Firm [(Beijing No. 2 Intermediate People's Court) reprinted in the SPC Gazette, Issue 10, 2005]

Case 16: Li & Gong v. May Flower Co. [(the High People's Court of Guangdong Province) reprinted in the SPC Gazette, Issue 2, 2002]

Case 17: Yu's Case [the announcement published by the Public Security Bureau of Kunshan City, Jiangsu Province on September 1, 2018]

Case 18: Wangs v. Huai An Museum [(2011) Huai Zhong Min Zhong Zi No. 1287 (the Intermediate People's Court of Huanan City, Jiangsu Province), reprinted in the SPC Gazette, Issue 5, 2013]

Case 19: Great Wall Broadband Network v. China Tietong [(2014) Jiangning Min Chu Zi No. 3935 (Jiangning District People's Court of Nanjing City, Jiangsu Province), reprinted in the SPC Gazette, Issue 12, 2019]

Case 20: Xinhua Daily Press v. H Co. [(the SPC) reprinted in the SPC Gazette, Issue 3, 1996]

Case 21: Yu v. Tian & Liu [(2015) Hu Er Zhong Min Er (Min) Che Zhong Zi No. 1 (Shanghai No. 2 Intermediate People's Court), reprinted in the SPC Gazette, Issue 7, 2018]

Case 22: CCB v. Zhongyi Co. & China Export Co. [(2001) Min Er Zhong Zi No. 155 (the SPC), reprinted in the SPC Gazette, Issue 7, 2004]

Case 23: Yangtze River Delta Commodity Exchange Co., Ltd v. Lu [(2014) Xi Min Zhong Zi No. 1724 (the Intermediate People's Court of Wuxi City, Jiangsu Province), reprinted in the SPC Gazette, Issue 1, 2017]

Case 24: Time Group v. Land Bureau of Yuhuan County, Zhejiang Province [(2003) Min Yi Zhong Zi No. 82 (the SPC), reprinted in the SPC's Gazette, Issue 5, 2005)]

Case 25: Xu v. Z Co. [(Beijing No. 1 Intermediate People's Court) printed in the SPC Gazette, Issue 9, 2005]

Case 26: Zhang v. H Co. [(2008) Er Zhong Min Zhong Zi No. 00453 (Beijing No. 2 Intermediate People's Court), reprinted in the SPC's Guiding Cases No. 17]

Case 27: Sinochem International (Overseas) Pte Ltd v. Thyssen Krupp Metallurgical Products GmbH [(2013) Min Si Zhong Zi No. 35 (the SPC), reprinted in the SPC's Guiding Cases No. 107]

Case 28: Chen v. W Co. & Q Co. [(2011) Jiang Ning Min Chu Zi No. 04404 (Jiangning District People's Court of Nanjing City, Jiangsu Province), reprinted in the SPC Gazette, Issue 5, 2013]

Case 29: Sun v. Auchan Supermarket [(2012) Jiang Ning Kai Min Chu Zi No. 646 (Jiangning District People's Court of Nanjing City, Jiangsu Province), reprinted in the SPC's Guiding Cases No. 23]

Case 30: Zhao v. W Co. & Z Co. [(2018) Zui Gao Fa Min Zai No. 206 (the SPC), reprinted in the SPC Gazette, Issue 5, 2019]

Case 31: Stephen Chow v. Z Co. [(2017) Hu 01 Min Chu No. 1211 (Shanghai No. 1 Intermediate People's Court), reprinted in the SPC Gazette, Issue 2, 2020]

Case 32: Ge v. Hong [(2016) Jing 02 Min Zhong N. 6272 (Beijing No. 2 Intermediate People's Court), reprinted in the SPC's Guiding Cases No. 99]

Case 33: Shen v. Wang [(2015) Hu Er Zhong Min Yi (Min) Zhong Zi No. 1854 (Shanghai No. 2 Intermediate People's Court), reprinted in the SPC Gazette, Issue 12, 2016]

Case 34: Wu v. Zhu [(Chuzhou District People's Court of Huaian City, Jiangsu Province) reprinted in the SPC Gazette, Issue 12, 2006]

Case 35: Li & Song v. H Middle School [(the Intermediate People's Court of Xining City, Qinghai Province) reprinted in the SPC Gazette, Issue 4, 2009]

Case 36: Xie v. Shanghai Zoo [(Shanghai No. 1 Intermediate People's Court) reprinted in the SPC Gazette, Issue 8, 2013]

Case 37: Jiang & Zeng v. Qin & Su [(2015) Fo Zhong Fa Min Yi Zhong Zi No. 1211 (the Intermediate People's Court of Foshan City, Guangdong Province), reprinted in the SPC Gazette, Issue 11, 2016]

Case 38: Tang 1 v. Li & Tang 2 [(2014) San Zhong Min Zhong Zi No. 09467 (Beijing No. 3 Intermediate People's Court), reprinted in the SPC Gazette, Issue 12, 2014]

Case 39: In Re Support of the Child Born from Artificial Insemination [reprinted in the SPC Gazette, Issue 1, 1997]

Case 40: He v. He [reprinted in the SPC Gazette, Issue 2, 2015]

Case 41: Li & Fan v. Fan 1 & Teng [(Qinhuai District People's Court of Nanjing City, Jiangsu Province) reprinted in the SPC Gazette, Issue 7, 2006]

图书在版编目(CIP)数据

中国民法：法律、案例与材料＝Chinese Civil Law：Statutes，Cases，and Materials：英文/高凌云编著.—上海：复旦大学出版社，2023.9
中国商法系列教材
ISBN 978-7-309-16852-5

Ⅰ.①中… Ⅱ.①高… Ⅲ.①民法-中国-教材-英文 Ⅳ.①D923

中国国家版本馆 CIP 数据核字(2023)第 085574 号

Chinese Civil Law：Statutes，Cases，and Materials
Gao Lingyun 编著
责任编辑/张 炼

复旦大学出版社有限公司出版发行
上海市国权路 579 号 邮编：200433
网址：fupnet@fudanpress.com http://www.fudanpress.com
门市零售：86-21-65102580 团体订购：86-21-65104505
出版部电话：86-21-65642845
上海盛通时代印刷有限公司

开本 787×960 1/16 印张 32.25 字数 614 千
2023 年 9 月第 1 版
2023 年 9 月第 1 版第 1 次印刷

ISBN 978-7-309-16852-5/D·1161
定价：158.00 元

如有印装质量问题，请向复旦大学出版社有限公司出版部调换。
版权所有 侵权必究